La Causa Politica

A CHICANO POLITICS READER

F. CHRIS GARCIA
Editor

UNIVERSITY OF NOTRE DAME PRESS
NOTRE DAME
LONDON

Library of Congress Cataloging in Publication Data

Garcia, F Chris, comp.
La causa política: a chicano politics reader.

Includes bibliographical references.
1. Mexican Americans–Politics and suffrage–
Addresses, essays, lectures. I. Title.
E184.M5G358 323.1'16'872073 73-22582
ISBN 0-268-00542-7
ISBN 0-268-00543-5 (pbk.)

Manufactured in the United States of America

This anthology of readings is published in connection with the Mexican American Studies Program of the University of Notre Dame, which is under the direction of Julian Samora and is sponsored by a grant from the Ford Foundation.

PREFACE

THE LAST FEW YEARS HAVE WITNESSED A MAJOR CHANGE IN THE RELAtionship of Chicanos to the American political system. This at one time "invisible minority" has become a significant political and social force in the country's affairs.

Unfortunately, the current impact of the Chicano movement has not yet been proportionately reflected in the writings of scholars and social observers. Thus, even though the movement has been gathering momentum for the past several years and the American of Mexican descent has been involved in American Politics for over a century, anyone wishing to examine this situation more closely immediately confronts the problem of inadequate reading materials. As of this writing, for example, there is no textbook on the subject of Chicano politics, nor even another collection of readings on the topic. While in the past few years there has been a great outpouring of material directly and indirectly dealing with the subject, much of it is difficult to obtain for use in the classroom. Many of the best writings appear only in mimeographed form or in magazines, newspapers, and other periodicals of very limited distribution.

This collection, therefore, is intended to bring together many of the best writings on the subject of Chicano politics and make them available for use in the classroom, as well as for the perusal of any interested person. The collection does not intend to point a direction that Chicano politics should take but to present some variety of viewpoints on the state of things, the reasons behind it, and the present currents of *La Causa Política.*

I would like to express my sincere appreciation to the authors and publishers who permitted their articles to be included in this volume and to the University of Notre Dame Press, its Acting Director, Mr. John Ehmann, and fine editor, Ann Rice.

F. Chris Garcia
The University of New Mexico

CONTENTS

INTRODUCTION

OVER THE LAST DECADE THERE HAS BEEN AN UPSWING OF INTEREST IN the study of the politics of minority groups. Social scientists are currently engaged in numerous research projects which will soon yield much information about the politics of this nation's minorities, particularly the colored minorities—the black, the Indian, and the Chicano. The growing interest in this subject is reflected in the political science departments of the nation's colleges and universities. Many universities have instituted courses on the politics of ethnic groups and several now offer more particularized studies of black politics and Chicano politics. By and large this increased awareness of the role that ethnicity has played in American politics has been the result of the dramatic and sometimes forceful moves of the minorities to bring themselves to the attention of politicians and political scientists.

Heretofore ethnicity as a factor in politics has been very little researched, even neglected. The first sixty years of the century saw only a handful of articles on the subject and these mainly dealt with so-called "white ethnics."[1] Not until demands from blacks, Chicanos, Indians, and Orientals became vociferous and these same groups developed scholars, researchers, social scientists of their own was much heed paid to their participation in the American political system. One measure of the attention they have generated is seen in a recent listing of political scientists which includes 274 who consider ethnic politics as one of their major fields.[2]

But even at the time of this writing only one general survey of ethnic politics is available as a text. This book, entitled *Ethnic Politics in America* by Edgar Litt (1970),[3] has consequently had a great effect on the study of ethnic minorities. For this reason our collection of readings on Chicano ethnic politics in America will generally follow the pattern of the Litt volume. The basic organization of topics corresponds to the progression of subjects in the Litt book. The articles, therefore, have not been placed in chronological order, but the date of their original publication can be seen in the source note provided with each article.

Our first section, dealing with the foundations of Chicano politics, will explore their socio-historical as well as their psychological or individual base; the organizational or institutional base will then be surveyed. Litt has divided ethnic political styles into two major groupings. The first is termed "accommodation politics" or "old politics," and this will be the subject of the second major grouping of articles. These politics of accommodation, which are conventional in nature and which work within established political norms of the current system, are further divided into three major types: 1) the politics of recognition, 2) collective welfare benefits politics, and 3) preferments and secondary benefits. After examining Chicano participation in these three kinds of accommodation politics, we turn our attention to what can be termed nonconventional or "new-style" politics. Included are some selections on the politics of separatism as well as articles on two types of radical strategies—the politics of ideology and the politics of passion. The next section deals with perhaps the most extreme form of passionate politics, where violence is employed as a political tactic. In conclusion, we review the status of Chicano politics and venture some glances into the future political situation of the American of Mexican-Spanish ancestry.

In our introductory selection, the current status of the Chicano is eloquently recounted by Senator Joseph M. Montoya in his remarks to the United States Senate on May 6, 1971.

NOTES

1. The most well-known examples include Michael Parenti, "Ethnic Politics and the Persistence of Ethnic Identification," *American Political Science Review* 61 (September 1967), 717-726 and Raymond R. Wolfinger, "The Development and Persistence of Ethnic Voting," *American Political Science Review* 59 (December 1965) 896-908.

2. American Political Science Association, *Biographical Directory, 1973* (6th ed.), p. 610.

3. Edgar Litt, *Ethnic Politics in America* (Glenview, Ill.: Scott, Foresman and Co., 1970).

1: WOE UNTO THOSE WHO HAVE EARS BUT DO NOT HEAR

Joseph M. Montoya

Mr. MONTOYA. Mr. President, America numbers among her citizens today more than 9.2 million Spanish-speaking people, according to the U.S. Bureau of the Census. Most live below the poverty line. Most are confronted, as their forebears were, by staggering obstacles to social and economic progress. Today such barriers have been compounded by recession, social upheaval, and an ever-increasing pace of change.

The Census Bureau report shows the total includes 5.1 million persons who told census officials they were of Mexican origin, 1.5 million Puerto Ricans, and 600,000 each of Cuban and Central or South American origin. Another 1.6 million people are included in a general category entitled "Other Spanish-Speaking People." I believe there are 10 million such people.

The new report also shows that more Spanish is spoken in American homes than any language except English. Five Southwestern States hold 61 percent of this population, but colonies of these citizens are to be found almost everywhere. Several hundred thousand now reside in the Chicago area. New Jersey and lower New England contain significant groupings.

All the Rocky Mountain and Great Plains States contain growing communities of these people. That census count also shows that their jobless rate is nearly twice that of any other group.

America continues to pay loud lip-service to the aspirations of these people. Such superficial concern is surpassed only by the paucity of what our society is doing to aid them escape conditions of life afflicting so many of them. It is one of our worst national disgraces, staining our national conscience indelibly.

From *The Congressional Record,* Vol. 117, Part II (May 6, 1971), pp. 13811-13814. By permission of Senator Joseph M. Montoya.

One other element has changed in this disgraceful equation—the attitude of Spanish-speaking people themselves. Today there is a burning awareness of heritage, pride, and history among them that has hitherto been subdued. They know conquistadores were here carving out a new world before any others arrived to lay claim to it. They know blood has been spilled by exploiters—that young Spanish Americans have so often perished for causes our country has espoused. This is especially true today.

Many call themselves "Chicanos."

In their mouths it becomes a title of pride. Great numbers are returning veterans who have given of health and years to the Nation. They seek justice, economic opportunity, and social recognition. America denies it to them at her peril.

Such people look at our world through new eyes. They have seen what can be attained: through education, through equal opportunity, through hard work. All they seek is a chance. Yet, it is just that which America continues to deny them. Today's society can no longer afford the shameful luxury of barring any road to advancement to such a significant group of Americans.

Our Spanish-speaking people are now well aware of their guaranteed rights as citizens. They understand our State and Federal constitutions and wonder why so many double standards exist.

They ask how it can be that Spanish-speaking Americans are subjected to brutality by certain elements in selected areas of our Nation. They ask why some judges and prosecuting officers of more than a few courts can make examples of Spanish-speaking people who violate laws, while Anglos are seemingly judged by different standards entirely. It is proper that they should wonder aloud at such injustices, for it is a sad truth they are widespread.

They are aware disproportionate numbers of them are drafted into our Armed Forces. This imbalance is reflected in casualty figures in Vietnam. One statistic bearing on my own State of New Mexico is indicative of this situation. Defense Department figures shows 44.6 percent of all New Mexico fighting men killed in Vietnam between 1961 and 1967 were Spanish surnamed. Yet, about 30 percent of the population of New Mexico is Hispano-surnamed.

The same Pentagon figures are revealing across-the-board: 25 percent of all Texans killed there in that same period are Spanish surnamed; 24 percent of those from Colorado; 17 percent of Arizonans; 15 percent of all Californians. Death in combat of Spanish-American boys crosses our domestic/political boundaries with ease. I am also informed that there are combat units close to 90 percent Chicano.

Hundreds of thousands of young Spanish-speaking people have been taken into military service. Up to now they have gone with scarcely a murmur to do battle for their country, exhibiting fervent patriotism. This is their kind. This is their quality. America seems to have taken little notice of this cumulative sacrifice.

In fact, precious little has been done voluntarily or even under pressure to roll back barriers of bigotry, prejudice, and discrimination confronting our Spanish-speaking citizens.

Consider the image scores of millions of Americans presently entertain regarding Spanish-speaking Americans. That mental picture is a totally degrading stereotype. Let me remind you of what it consists of. A sleepy, lazy, dirty Mexican in a sombrero dozing under a cactus. A greasy-looking, overweight, bandit type with bandoleers slung across his body, galloping off to stir a tinpot revolution. An image of a person lacking ambition, honesty, elementary habits of hygiene and self-respect.

It is disgusting. But it is prevalent. It is being fostered by mass media and advertising agencies running campaigns to sell, among other things, Frito-Lay products. It fosters bigotry in the name of humorous selling of a product. Hurrah for bigotry, as long as it is profitable.

Some people think the Frito bandito is cute, as he dances across our publicly licensed airwaves.* The Americans he caricatures do not think so. and have said so publicly again and again. Why do not the Frito-Lay people and their advertising agency personnel journey to Vietnam and play their "cute" commercials to Spanish boys risking their lives over there daily–I would enjoy such a presentation–or journey to our barrios and give special showings? It should prove enlightening.

I would appreciate seeing the executives of Young & Rubicam and Foote, Cone & Belding, who are responsible for these Frito bandito advertisements, putting across to young Chicano soldiers their concept of charm in commercials.

It is time to expose the hitherto faceless agencies behind such commercials. For too long they have been getting away with anonymous perpetration of these media atrocities.

And while such disgusting parodies persist, realities of Spanish life in America grow uglier daily. It is worth taking careful note of such Americans for time is running out. There has been violence in recent months in several Spanish-speaking barrios. Such disturbances are indications of what is coming. We should heed them immediately.

Our Spanish-speaking citizens have never before participated in or initiated massive urban violence. The Los Angeles "zoot suit" disturbances were begun by outsiders invading barrio areas. This time matters have taken a different ugly turn. Usually peaceful people have taken to the streets in violent protests. But only after a serious situation has shown no signs of alleviation or improvement. The leadership of periodic protest rallies has called for nonviolent demonstrations. Yet Ruben Salazar is dead. And during the last upheaval another young Spanish boy was killed.

*[The Frito bandito commercials have since been discontinued.–Ed.]

I see ominous portents of things to come. A small but growing group in our Spanish-speaking community is beginning to despair of making real progress. It feels only deliberately fostered turbulence will awaken our power structure and Nation to their needs. I reject such an approach entirely, yet certainly understand both the motivation, frustration behind it. America must seek a deeper, swifter comprehension of it as well.

The most notable success achieved by Spanish-speaking Americans has been through the religious-oriented nonviolent Union of Farmworkers of Caesar Chavez. His bitter drawn-out struggle inches along in the face of staggering obstacles. Younger Chicanos admire him but also note the barriers consistently thrown in his path. Most do not feel they should have to battle so long for elementary progress on a road traveled successfully long ago by so many others.

They see prejudice against Mexican Americans enduring 122 years after the Mexican War. They observe their culture under incessant attack as that belonging to a conquered people. It is constantly disparaged in a thousand ways as bad or worse than the media stereotype I mentioned earlier. A recent report from the Census Bureau put an official stamp upon America's shame. Americans of Spanish origin stand on one of the lowest rungs of America's ladder. I ask unanimous consent to have printed in the RECORD, a recent article from the Washington Post summarizing the findings of the report.

There being no objection, the article was ordered to be printed in the RECORD, as follows:

LATINS IN UNITED STATES TRAIL IN INCOME

(By William Chapman)

Americans of Spanish origin earn only about 70 per cent of the average American family's income, are more likely to be out of work and have limited access to white-collar jobs.

They also are persons with strong family ties, as likely to speak Spanish as English at home, and they are less educated than other Americans—though this gap is closing.

That profile of Spanish-origin Americans emerges from a Census Bureau analysis regarded as the most extensive social and economic study yet of this group.

It provides support for the contention of Spanish-surname lobbying groups that their people are disadvantaged, somewhat isolated from American life, and deserving of more public aid.

An official of the Cabinet Committee for the Spanish Speaking asserted that the study should pave the way for a greater share of federal education and urban development funds for his people.

At the same time, the official, Executive Director John Bareno, claimed that the study grossly underestimated the number of Spanish-origin residents in the U.S.

The survey identified 9.2 million Spanish-origin residents in November, 1969. Bareno claimed that local and state reports he has examined indicate the total is closer to 12 million, including perhaps one million working here illegally on temporary visitation permits.

The census study identified 55 per cent of the people as Mexican, 16 per cent as Puerto Rican, 6 per cent as Cuban, 6 per cent as Central or South American and 17 per cent as "other Spanish." Three-fifths live in five Southwestern states.

Within those classifications were found substantial differences. Reflecting the flight from Castro's Cuba of middle-class emigres, the Cuban population now in this country is older, better educated and more prosperous than, for example, Mexicans and South Americans.

Specific Points

Among the study's specific findings were the following:

Spanish-origin workers are more concentrated in lower-paying occupations than other Americans. Only 25 per cent of the men were in white-collar jobs, compared with 41 per cent of men of all other origins. But the percentage of Cuban males in those jobs was nearly twice as high as the Mexican-born.

In November, 1969, the seasonally adjusted unemployment rate for the Spanish-origin worker was 6 per cent, compared with 3.5 per cent for the remainder of the civilian population. Bareno claimed that even that 6 per cent figure understates unemployment because it does not include the thousands of Mexican-Americans employed seasonally as migrant farm workers.

Although Spanish-origin citizens lag significantly in formal education—as measured by years of school attended—there are signs of a closing of the gap. For example, half of the Mexican-Americans over 35 years old had completed only 7.3 years of school. In a younger group, 25 to 34, the Mexican-Americans had averaged 10.8 years. The younger Cubans and other immigrants, however, averaged 12.4 years.

The average family income of Spanish-origin families was $5,600 in November, 1969, about 70 percent of that earned by families of other origins.

Spanish is currently spoken in the homes of half of the Spanish-origin population and, with the exception of English, is spoken by more persons than any other language in the U.S. The Census Bureau interpreted that as indicating unusually strong family bonds.

English was more apt to be spoken in Mexican-American homes than in those occupied by Puerto Ricans, Cubans and Central and South Americans.

Mr. MONTOYA. Mr. President, it is possible to add further figures to those revealed in this article. More than one-third of the Mexican American population in our five Southwestern States is illiterate or functionally so, compared to 5 percent of the Anglo population so rated.

In East Los Angeles, 75 percent of Mexican American real income dropped between 1960 and 1965. Homeownership declined. Housing deteriorated. Ninety percent of Mexican Americans there noticed no results whatsoever from civil rights efforts on their behalf.

A Mexican American is seven times more likely to live in substandard housing than an Anglo. The chance that his baby will be born dead, or will die before his first birthday, is roughly twice as great.

When touching on jobless statistics among the Spanish-speaking it is well to remember that 80 percent of those employed work at unskilled or semiskilled jobs.

Numerous vocational education projects are one of the keys to changing this, as I have maintained through the years. Unfortunately, adequate funds for such endeavors have not been forthcoming.

Numerous academic and social practices are such, so as to impose upon Mexican American children a sense of social and cultural inferiority. Only in the past several years have we managed to undertake bilingual education programs and appropriate minimal funds for their extension. As matters stand now, we have had to battle bitterly just to keep this concept barely alive.

The U.S. Government has done more to help citizens of other lands learn English than it has for non-English-speaking American citizens in this country.

Meanwhile, selective service boards across the Southwest contain slightly less than 6 percent Spanish-speaking American membership. Yet, Chicanos account for nearly 20 percent of all southwesterners killed in Vietnam.

The United States-Mexico Border Development and Friendship Commission ceased to exist on November 5, 1969, because of funding.

In a report published by the U.S. Civil Rights Commission, entitled "Mexican Justice in the Southwest" we find the following quote:

> Belief in law enforcement prejudice is widespread and indicative of a serious problem of Police-Community relations between Police and Mexican-Americans in the southwest.

Mr. President, I believe the statement to be not only true but the politest possible way of stating the case. A recent event in New Mexico illustrates in the most devastating manner the double standard too often found in criminal cases involving Mexican Americans.

Two Mexican American boys in Roswell, N. Mex., were caught stealing several kegs of beer. They were placed in jail and kept there for 11 days. Bond was set for them at $3,000 each. Their parents are humble people who could no more afford a $3,000 bond than they could $3,000,000 worth. The victimized distributor actively sought to drop all charges. The district attorney, Mr. Hanagan, insisted upon pressing charges. Numerous prominent citizens sought alleviation of the boys' situation. A presentencing report recommended leniency in sentencing. The judge, George Reese, saw fit to sentence these two young people to 60 days in the State penitentiary, less the 11 days they had spent in county jail. These 49 days were to begin January 16, 1971. Both boys are presently seniors in high school. Total sentence each received was 5 years, with all suspended except for the actual 49 days.

Gov. Bruce King of New Mexico, showing true compassion and understanding, pardoned both boys. After I spoke out against this abuse of authority in a speech before a joint session of the New Mexico State Legislature, one member got up to excuse the judge's prejudice by saying he had a right to do what he did. I find no fault nor have any dispute with the right of any district attorney to prosecute offenders or any judge to pronounce sentence. I do roundly condemn as evil, backward, and barbarous such practices as I have described. They were out of place by the turn of this century.

There are thousands of district attorneys and judges similar to the two I have just mentioned. They are scattered across the land, filled with apprehension and indignation because those who have heretofore remained silent have found new voices. They deem as upstarts and presumptuous those among Spanish speaking Americans who will no longer accept a double standard in the administration of justice. They feel the full weight of authority must be used in an attempt to intimidate those who have the temerity to speak out.

Let such prosecuting officers and judges beware of the indignation of an aroused people, who will persist in seeking the full protection of our system of justice in a most energetic fashion. Such realities as I have described, however, are what millions of Spanish-speaking Americans must live with on a daily basis across this country. It is unendurable for them any longer.

There are too many law enforcement people who are heavy-handed rather than judicious in enforcing laws as they affect these people. They prefer to yearn for yesterday's status quo instead of heeding today's realities. A new state of mind is germinating in Spanish-America's consciousness. It will not accept that status quo or the backwardness, persecution, discrimination and double standards that are part of it. America must realize this and take immediate, constructive action to anticipate their desires–to correct these wrongs. It must be done.

Yet, it is our Federal Government itself which has been setting the worst possible example in one instance after another. Its non-record in opening up doors to Spanish-speaking Americans is shameful. Thirty-four agencies did not have a single hispano in any capacity under the GS pay system. The least it could do is provide the same proportion of opportunities for them to advance at home in government as it does for them to die abroad in military service. We are first in janitors, first in infantry units, last in equal opportunity. Although we are at least 5 percent of the population, we possess less than 3 percent of the Federal jobs.

A few weeks ago, the FBI released figures on its employees. This agency has slightly more than 100 non-Anglo agents among its force of nearly 8,000. Of these, 41 are Spanish-speaking Americans. Of 18,592 employees, including several agents, it possesses 257 Spanish-speaking Americans.

What kind of chance do such citizens find in other areas of our Government structure? What doors have opened for them? In 1968, there were three ambassadors of Spanish descent. Now there are none. Granted that Messrs. Raymond Tellez, Ben Hernandez, and Raul Castro were of a different political persuasion than is the present administration. Yet, could they not have been replaced with other competent Spanish Americans? Such appointments would reflect credit and prestige upon our entire Spanish-speaking community. To deny such elementary recognition is a blatant insult to them. No such appointments have been made.

Dr. Hector Garcia was an American representative to the U.N. He has been replaced. No prominent Spanish-speaking American has been named by this administration in his stead. This in spite of the vast number of dealings we consistently engage in with the sprawling Spanish-speaking world.

The only high-ranking Spanish Americans appointed by the administration have been callously let go. One was Hilario Sandoval, former head of the Small Business Administration. Next to leave was Martin Castillo, former Chairman of the Cabinet Committee on Opportunities for the Spanish speaking. The Equal Employment Opportunity Commission in Washington has few Spanish-surnamed employees on its staff, particularly in higher positions. Its legal counsel in Washington headquarters does not have a single Mexican-American or Spanish-surnamed individual on its staff. There is not a single such person in charge of any EEOC divisions in Washington.

At the National Institutes of Health, there are 59 Spanish-surnamed employees out of a total work force of 11,167. This comes to a staggering total of 0.5 percent of all workers there.

There are no Spanish-surnamed employees in grades 16 through 18 in the Department of State, Aid, and Peace Corps. Our dealings in each of these vital areas with Spanish-speaking nations are numerous and on the upswing. Yet, when such countries deal with us, they have few encounters at upper levels with people they can relate to directly. This is short-sighted and injurious to America as well as direct evidence of discrimination.

The same is true of these same Government grades at the Department of the Treasury as well as at the Army, Navy, and Air Force. I cannot help but call to mind scores of thousands of young Chicanos who have volunteered to fight for America in each of our modern conflicts. How freely they have sacrificed for her. How bravely they have fought. Their blood has stained a thousand battlefields. Yet they are not represented in the upper echelons of those very services they serve in and die for. And many wonder why there is anger in some young hearts and violence in the barrios of several American cities. Let us probe a bit deeper. There are no Spanish-surnamed employees in GS grades 16 through 18 in the Departments of Agriculture and Commerce. The last two are particularly strange situations, in light of the fact so many Spanish-speaking Americans live close to the land, and that Commerce deals so extensively with Spanish-Americans who would be instant assets to our Government in dealing with essential areas of responsibility.

At the rate of progress these agencies have been making, an award of some kind should go to the Departments of Justice, Interior, and Labor. Let us call it the order of tokenism, first class, because each of these vast organizations has one Spanish surnamed employee operating in this high area of employee responsibility.

HEW has two such people at these levels. Perhaps their order of tokenism should come with an oak leaf cluster. HUD, GSA, NASA, VA, and AEC each emerge with a blank in these categories as far as Spanish-speaking employees are concerned. Such an accomplishment, Mr. President, speaks for itself. It is a national disgrace, inexcusable by nature, and degrading in fact. My list is as long as it is sad. One difference, however, can be shown between this situation and the past. Now millions of Spanish-speaking people are fully aware of what is going on. This is especially true of younger people and returning Vietnam veterans–scores of thousands of them.

Yesterday's shame burns in their hearts and minds. Today's discrimination and bigotry is a lump in their collective throats they absolutely refuse to swallow. America ignores their indignation and turns her back on their outrage at her peril.

Today it is the norm to pay lipservice to equality while denying it in reality. America's Hispanos are fully aware of this as well. Their faith in broken promises and paper programs is waning rapidly.

Here lies the nub of our tragedy. Anglo America actually believes in the reality of the image of the Hispano it has itself created. Most Americans even peripherally aware of such problems do not consider it in any kind of serious light. It will go away, they feel. They are not really serious, they think. They will go back to their chili and siestas, many actually believe. And our media does nothing to disabuse the mass of Americans of either such false images or false sense of security. Rather, they make matters worse. So the explosion, growing increasingly more severe, actually comes as a shocking surprise to most Anglo Americans.

Further, certain elements in American national life are exacerbating the situation by their actions and comments.

The formerly revered and once respected Director of the FBI makes derogatory comments about Mexican-Americans in a national magazine interview. Height qualifications for law enforcement personnel effectively bar most Hispano citizens from entering such vital work. This in spite of excellent qualifications possessed by so many returning veterans. They are seemingly good enough to make excellent marines and airborne troops, but not qualified to make policemen or State troopers.

Cesar Chavez goes to jail because his poor exploited farmworkers seek to gain in 1971 what most American labor realized and has been enjoying since the New Deal. And the Pentagon repeats an atrocious policy by escalating lettuce buying just as it suddenly discovered a need in past years to support nonunion grape growers through increased purchase of grapes. I am just selecting some of the worst random samples. There are many, many more in addition to local atrocities taking place everyday in America. They range from coldblooded shooting of Hispanos in rural Texas towns to the incident I referred to in the city of Roswell in my own State.

Wounds bleed daily. How, then, can people wonder at young Chicano rage at a society they seek a share of, but which bars them at each turn? There are, although exact figures are unavailable, probably more Hispanos in penitentiaries and in jails than there are in our institutions of higher learning.

Now is the time to lay out these facts, and I have sought to do just that. More data is available and I shall offer it. Yet I cannot help but wonder aloud as to whether any tangible advances will be made.

Will anyone lift a finger to make their dreams move forward even slightly? What is going to be done on behalf of the thousands upon thousands of young Chicanos returning monthly to their homes from military service?

These young men are leavening the lump. They are pushing into the realm of activism. Many vigorous protests are going to be forthcoming in times to come in what most Americans will consider the most unlikely places. Chicano communities demand political power and equal opportunity. If it is not forthcoming, there will be terrible violence, like it or not.

Mr. President, I have spoken in this manner not because of any desire to posture or aggravate an already severe situation. It is well known that I have raised my voice again and again on behalf of moderation and working within the system. It is because of my love of our ideals and my people that I speak out now.

It is imperative that America listen closely, intently, and sincerely. Above all, it is vital that we act. Promises are not enough.

At a very minimum, demeaning characterizations of Hispanos must be removed from publicly licensed facilities and airwaves. If Frito Lay will not act, then Government and the communications industry must.

Outrageous discrimination existing in higher levels of Government employment must be removed instantly. The Civil Service Commission and administration have the power to act and should immediately do so.

Appointments of capable Spanish Americans to an entire series of high-visibility, high-responsibility positions should come high on our agenda of reform. Such signs of recognition and accomplishment regardless of politics, are vital as a sign of the Nation's Hispano community.

Relaxation of ridiculous restrictions which insult more than they protect the public should come next. The Federal Government can and should set an example. If willing young men are refused work on minor technical grounds, they will shortly strike at society in angered frustration from the outside.

Above all, however, let the administration recognize that these people are outraged, frustrated, and increasingly impatient. Let our society open its eyes as to what is going on in the minds and hearts of these millions of good people. We shall have no excuse of ignorance to plead this time.

I. Foundations of Chicano Politics

A. The Socio-Historical Base

WE BEGIN OUR EXAMINATION OF CHICANO POLITICS BY LOOKING AT SOME of the social and historical experiences that underlie the current relationship of the Mexican American people to the social system of the United States. The selections make it quite evident that the Mexican American has historically been oppressed by the dominant Anglo American culture.[1] He certainly has not been included in any purported melting pot of American ethnic groups. From the Chicano viewpoint, U.S. society is not culturally pluralistic, for his own culture has often been the object of derogation. For the most part he has been excluded from participation in the social, economic, and political activities of the Anglo American core culture. A few individuals have sacrificed or surrendered their native Mexican American culture and have been totally acculturated and assimilated. These have "made it" into the Anglo system. But, by and large, the Mexican American remains a stranger in his own land.

Ralph Guzmán's article demonstrates how the racial ideology of the majority group has greatly hindered the political development or politicization of the Chicano. One of the major reasons the Chicano has not participated fully in the politics of the larger society has been the discouragement and fear instilled in him by actions of the majority group. Yet in spite of these obstacles, the Chicano has always participated in U.S. politics to some extent—that is, he has continually attempted to exert influence on the public decision-makers of the United States. Alfredo Cuéllar reviews the stages of the Chicano's conventional and nonconventional political participation from the era of conquest and conflict, through the more accommodative stages, and up to the current Chicano *movimiento.*

NOTES

1. Some of the better histories of the Mexican American are: Rodolfo Acuña, *Occupied America: The Chicano's Struggle toward Liberation* (San

Francisco: Canfield Press, 1972); Carey McWilliams, *North from Mexico: The Spanish-Speaking People of the United States* (New York: J. P. Lippincott Co., 1961); and Matt Meier and Feliciano Rivera, *The Chicano: A History of Mexican Americans* (New York: Hill and Wang, 1972).

Perhaps the most succinct and insightful short analysis of the Mexican American experience is by Rodolfo Alvarez, "The Psycho-Historical and Socioeconomic Development of the Chicano Community in the United States," *Social Science Quarterly* 53 (March 1973), pp. 920–942.

2: THE FUNCTION OF ANGLO-AMERICAN RACISM IN THE POLITICAL DEVELOPMENT OF CHICANOS

Ralph Guzmán

THE SOUTHWEST IS A REGION THAT DIFFERS FROM THE EASTERN SEABOARD geographically and sociologically. The conditions of social contact between those who held political power and those who did not were not the same. Thus the political socialization of minority groups like the *Chicanos*[1] followed paths that were only vaguely reminiscent of the Irish experience and that of other European immigrants who came to the East Coast.

Why the *Chicano* experience should differ so drastically from that of the European immigrants is explored in this essay. My thesis is that historical conditions of social contact between a group-in-power and a group-out-of-power, generate a number of attitudes, assumptions, judgments, and stereotypes—one of the other, that have a *major* influence upon both. These, I argue, are part of the political socialization of a people. To understand the political development of *Chicanos* in the Southwest, one must analyze two kinds of ideologies. One is the aggregation of articulated views, judgments, and presuppositions about ethnic groups that have been held by the dominant society—the Anglo view. For convenience, these are labeled *Anglo group ideologies.* The other is the aggregation of perceptions of the larger society by the minority and its internal self-appraisal, labeled *Chicano group ideologies*—the *Chicano* view. My focus here is on Anglo group ideologies.

Contrary to an assumption popular in the East, the Southwest and Far West do not have a tradition of racial tolerance. The historical conditions of social contact between *Chicanos* and the larger Southwest society bear ample testimony to the opposite. A relevant contrast between this region and the rest of the United States is the different origin of the "foreigners.". Histori-

From the *California Historical Quarterly,* 50, No. 1 (September 1971), pp. 34-42. Reprinted by permission of the California Historical Society.

cally, the Southwestern "foreigners" were mainly American Indians and *Chicanos.* There were few blacks. After some time, people of recent European origin penetrated the Southwest. Many had already become "Americanized" elsewhere in the United States and they embraced the Anglo-Saxon notion of the subordinate position of Orientals, *Chicanos,* and Indians with great zeal. Thus, racial ideologies prevailing elsewhere in the nation found ready acceptance in the Southwest–only the targets were different.

The American obsession with race has indeed had a powerful influence on the *Chicano* people. This influence has differed in intensity from place to place as well as over time. In Texas, prevailing views of race have a Southern tinge, with blacks, as the reference population. In California racial views reflect the North, the South, and other regions of the country.

One of the effects of the majority's racial ideologies has been the social, political and economic suppression of *Chicanos.* Politics has been one of the main arenas of competition in which *Chicanos* have long been unable to act with maximum effectiveness. This failure, often attributed to political apathy, in fact seems to reflect clear knowledge of Anglo institutional repression. Apathy implies a choice not to act while knowing that action is possible. In the past much of the reluctance of *Chicanos* to compete in politics reflected their belief that such action was not possible. *Chicanos* did not vote, not because voting was an Anglo thing, but because Anglos forbade *Chicano* involvement at the polls. American society imposed clear restrictions based on law and custom. These were enforced with violence and terror.

The political socialization of a minority group is retarded when the host society is perceived to be, or is indeed, hostile. By comparison, cultural factors, such as the often cited *individualism* of *Chicanos,* language deficiencies, and the apathy usually associated with poverty, have probably been of secondary importance. Fear has been a strong inhibiting factor in the world of the exploited: fear of the society that controls him, fear of his ethnic brothers, and often fear of himself. Fear stunts the political growth of any group and it also damages its educational and economic development. In the case of the *Chicanos,* some of their political development was, in fact, effectively reduced through self-stereotypes which often duplicated the majority's perjorative views of the *Chicano* minority. The Anglo judgment that *Chicanos* are emotional can provide a convenient excuse for political and social failure. Similarly, transference of the opinion that *Chicanos* do not work hard from the economic sector to the political arena severely limits the *Chicano* community's opportunities to acquire meaningful political power. Both majority views establish the parameters for self-fulfilling prophecies.

The discussion of majority ideologies in the Southwest is divided in the following pages into decades so as to allow judgments on the varying degrees to which they inhibited *Chicano* political growth. Decades have been selected for this purpose without any claim that the society's articulated views really changed with the passage of each 10-year period. Evidently, majority views of the *Chicanos* were formed throughout the entire period of social contact that began in the early years of the nineteenth century.[2] In large measure, the stereotypes formed during this period conformed to nativistic themes, emphasizing foreign-ness, hinting at radicalism, and at the unacceptability of Catholicism. Almost always *Chicanos* were assumed to represent a different religion and a different race. These themes sometimes led to sympathetic concern, but increasingly, with the wave of immigration that accompanied the Mexican revolution, they led to expressions of alarm.

In 1912 a sociology student from the University of Southern California conducted a study of *Chicanos* living in Los Angeles that was published in a Methodist mission magazine. Although his orientation was sympathetic, the student faithfully reproduced the view of *Chicanos* held in the dominant society of that time. His writings appeared at a time when border raids by Francisco (Pancho) Villa were common topics of conversation.

> It is generally estimated that there are from 20,000 to 40,000 Mexicans within the city boundaries. . . . Economic reasons [are] of great influence in causing them to come to the United States. . . . Very few of the Mexicans are naturalized, due in the main to their ignorance of the possibility and somewhat to their prejudice against Americans and American customs. . . . The Mexican laborer is generally regarded as *less efficient* than other labor. . . . The chief fault found with the Mexican laborer is his *irregularity and uncertainty.* Much of this is caused by drunkenness. . . .
>
> The Mexican *plane of living is probably the lowest* of any race in the City. . . . There is general antipathy for the Mexicans, and they are looked down upon by all races. The Mexicans meet this attitude with one of haughty indifference. . . . The social life of the Mexicans is meager in the extreme.
>
> The Mexicans furnish more than their proportion of *criminals.* . . . These people are non-moral rather than immoral, but their conditions are immoral from the viewpoint of Christian civilization and are a perpetual challenge to us to improve them. . . . The small children attend public school. . . . but as soon as it is possible for them to do so, they *quit school and go to work.* The small children are very bright, quick, attentive and responsive, but, after reaching the fifth grade, they become slow and dull. A general cause of this mental condition is more or less irregular attendance, due to home conditions. The problems presented by this *race of ignorant, illiterate and non-moral people, complicated by their low plane of living, their tendency to crime, and their bad housing conditions,* are serious in the extreme and urgently demand the attention of all Christian reformers and social workers. . . . [Emphases added][3]

The document focuses attention on the reality component in the stereotyped view of *Chicanos.* Though admittedly using primitive research techniques, the above generalizations represent the student's attempt at systematic exploration of reality; official statistics are cited, interviews conducted, and some direct observations are made. In the political arena, on the other hand, ethnic stereotypes are based on a process of abstraction which—unlike the attempt at objectivity even in this primitive empirical research—often selects, exaggerates, and preserves observations without continuous check on "reality." (Congressional hearings and similar investigations may be exceptions.) Once established as conventional categories, ethnic stereotypes, at least latently, incorporate a plan of action toward the ethnic group. As already indicated, the minority often inadvertently "cooperates" with the majority in perpetuating the stereotype. For example, accommodative minority leaders may find it convenient to relate to the dominant system in conventional terms, and "special concessions" may be made to the ethnic group based on its stereotyped characteristics. In this regard, the stereotype may become in part a self-fulfilling prophecy, insofar as its preservation establishes a universe of discourse within which *both* majority and minority can interact.

Thus, the statements made in this document were like—and yet unlike—statements made about *Chicanos* in the ensuing years. I turn to a detailed account of the period of the twenties.

Nativist feeling was at a high pitch in the 1920's. Concern over the preservation of the "American stock" was the subject of extensive public debate. In the Southwest, the debate took the form of fears that the region might be mongrelized by "Mexicans." Samuel J. Holmes, a professor of zoology at the University of California, argued that *Chicanos* like the African slaves of an earlier era, represented a problem that might not end for centuries.[4] Similar warnings about the "danger of building up in this state a large mongrel population" were issued in Texas.[5] Apprehension that the American stock would be diluted by *Chicanos* was expressed by Robert F. Foerster, a Princeton professor of economics, in these words:

> It is a deplorable fact that numerous, intelligent and enterprising one hundred per cent Americans, to say nothing of other brands, are busy helping along this insidious elimination of their own breed in favor of the progeny of Mexican peons who will continue to afflict us with an embarrassing race problem.[6]

The relative racial qualifications of the *Chicano* people were a subject of extensive discussion, often centering on the concept of the *mestizo* or the mixed race. Hybrids produced by the union of distant stocks might tend to be "superior to the poorer strain and inferior to the better strain."[7] On this basis, the exemption of Western Hemisphere immigrants from the national quota system of 1924 was debated on the floor of both the U.S. Senate and the House of Representatives, but an amendment to include them in the system was soundly defeated. The issue was reopened in the years 1926 to 1930 when public debate focused for the first time directly on immigration from Mexico. Again, however, no action was taken. In the main, the insistence of Southwest agricultural employers that they needed Mexican labor, combined with foreign policy considerations, was sufficient to ward off attempts to legislate a curtailment of Mexican immigration. But the Congressional debate revealed again the then current preoccupation with race. Congressman John Box of Texas, who sponsored a bill in 1926 to include the Western Hemisphere countries under the quota law, stated that Mexican immigrants were "illiterate, unclean, peonized masses" who stemmed from "a mixture of Mediterranean-blooded Spanish peasants with low grade Indians who did not fight to extinction but submitted and multiplied as serfs."[8] Likewise, Senator John B. Kendrick observed "that of all the alien races they [the *Chicanos*] amalgamate the least with the white man; they live entirely in a separate way." But he added that they were really an orderly people in our country.[9]

In Texas, the dominant society tended to equate *Chicanos* with blacks, and notions of racial inferiority were easily transferred from one group to the other. The African strains that some *Chicano* people reflected were attributed to 19th century runaway slaves from Texas and Louisiana who settled in the state of Veracruz. It was reported that the Indian women of Veracruz like the "liveliness and good humor" of the persecuted blacks "better than the quieter ways of their own countrymen."[10] The fact that a few *Chicanos* were, indeed, descendants of black slaves from the South helped to validate the tendency to equate all *Chicanos* or at least the darker ones with black Americans.

Interestingly, the hopeful notion of the melting pot, so commonly applied to European immigrants in the 1920's was seldom invoked with respect to *Chicanos*. It was generally assumed that the latter represented a separate race with such foreign ideas and habits, social standards, and historical traditions that they were disqualified from membership in American society. To one writer *Chicanos* were an underprivileged and unassimilable group of people that threatened to "lessen the racial homogeneity of our population."[11]

Not all articulated views were so negative. For example, one writer stressed the *Chicano* population did produce good citizens when they were paid a living and a stable wage.[12] Another believed that the *Chicano* was a *peon* (a peasant) who was not such a bad fellow even though he was "hopelessly more alien to the United States than any European."[13] Still another observer concluded that the *Chicanos* were confused in their own minds as to whether they were or were not Americans.[14]

Because the *Chicano* was not seen as being assimilable and because he was not a black, it was suggested that he might represent a third separate group. The notion of a "third race" was also upheld by some Mexican intellectuals during this period. For example, Enrique Santibañez, the Mexican Consul General in San Antonio, Texas, said:

> Judging the bronze race by its color and remembering that the Anglo-Saxon was not mixed with the colored races one must conclude that future generations of Mexicans, living in the United States, will live apart from the larger society, which is basically white and nordic, for as long as we can see. In other words, Mexicans will never be an integral part of the spiritual life of the American people. . . .
>
> Consequently, the United States will never be a harmonious social unit as it was when it was founded. Instead the United States will be a society divided into three parts: white, bronze, and black.[15]

Pressure from the white people to keep *Chicanos* on the same level as the black was resisted by the *Chicano* people, according to Handman. Pressure of this type, Handman predicted, would someday cause bitterness, animosity, and conflict. Interestingly, he intimated that *Chicanos* would revolt against the larger society before the blacks did. In this respect Handman's comment is noteworthy.

> The Negro-white situation is difficult enough, but it is simple. The Negro has his place in the scheme of things. He is disfranchised and he accepts it—for how long I do not know—but he accepts it. He is limited in his educational opportunities and in his occupational field, and he accepts that also. But the Mexican is theoretically limited neither in his educational opportunities nor in his occupational field. Neither is he disfranchised.[16]

Enough has been said to suggest that, reflecting a general trend in American Society, the core of the Southwest ideology between 1920 and 1930 in regard to *Chicanos* was clearly racial. However, the thrust of this concern was not *how Chicanos* could be brought into the larger community. It was instead focused on differentiation, on characteristics that served to rationalize the social exclusion of the group. Differentiation was made using social referents familiar to the majority; namely black people and American Indians. Majority group ideologies in the 1920's, of course, greatly deterred the political socialization of *Chicanos*. With the possible exception of the League of United Latin American Citizens (LULAC), a middle class group with important links in the larger society, *Chicanos* appeared to offer no significant resistance to this condition. Yet they were not silent and they did not accept the ideological judgments of the larger society. Reaction came on the *barrio* level in neighborhood *platicas* (conversations) and only sporadically from organized *Chicano* groups. The attempted formation of a Federation of Mexican Laborers' Unions and the strike of cantaloupe pickers in California's Imperial Valley in the late 1930's is one example of organized *Chicano* reaction. However, both of these episodes tended to confirm the Anglo view that *Chicano* organizations were susceptible to foreign ideologies that threatened the American social order. The violent Imperial Valley strike, a precursor of labor strife, served notice that *Chicanos* could be effective revolutionaries, proving themselves to be considerably less docile than was commonly believed.[17]

Anglo preoccupation with race in the 1930's centered on the masses of Mexicans who had poured into the United States in the previous decade and who continued to cross the border without formal immigration. These illegals were called "wet" Mexicans because they often waded or swam across the Rio Grande. They entered the United States, it was charged, to "become the fathers of born-on-the-soil offspring, whose right to American citizenship cannot be denied."[18] The prolific birth rate of these people was seen as a threat to American society. *Chicano* children were considered a hybrid race of inferior quality. "Their white strain," one observer said, "may be 1/16, 1/32, or 1/64. The rest may be Amerind (American Indian), Negro, or a mixture of the two."[19]

With the growth of the feminist movement in the United States, attention turned to the plight of the *Chicano* woman who was believed to be completely submissive to the whims and wishes of the male. According to this notion, the freedom that American women enjoyed was incomprehensible and bewildering to *Chicanas.* To the militant feminists, *Chicanas* were stark reminders of an archaic social system where the males possessed absolute authority. Unfamiliar with the English language and long conditioned to a life of personal sacrifice, *Chicanas* apparently were not recruited by the feminist movement of this era. However, a few middle class *Chicanas* became involved in prototypical protest movements.[20]

The empathy and chagrin of the American woman was expressed by Ruth Allen who wrote:

> Uncomplainingly, she labors in the field for months at a time and receives as a reward from the head of the family, some gew-gaw from the five and ten cent store, or at best, a new dress. The supremacy of the male is seldom disputed. First her father, then her husband, or, if she becomes a widow, her son, receive her unquestioning service.[21]

As the *Chicano* people became more evident in or near large urban centers, the majority's attention turned to the problem of crime. *Chicanos* were considered a people with substantial and perhaps irradicable criminal proclivities. There was an assumption of criminality particularly in confrontations between school, police, and social welfare officials. The young with their stylishly long hair, bizarre dress habits, and reputed drug habits were the special targets of an irate majority group. The belief that all *Chicanos* had deeply imbedded criminal tendencies was not easily disproved when the jails were almost always crowded with *Chicano* inmates.

The judgment of criminality and the numbers who were actually in prison combined to cement the view that *Chicanos* were, in fact, dangerous to the social order. In California, for example, a state prison report claimed that sixty per cent of the violations of prison laws and rules were caused by *Chicano* prisoners who refused to conform. One writer noted that California has "as many Mexican prisoners as the entire prison population of two American states."[22]

Another significant ideology during the 1930's was the view that *Chicanos* were a docile, unintelligent people who were susceptible to communism. This view was stressed as the Anglo fear of communism increased. Bogardus, a sociologist, warned that "A Christmas basket for one day in the year and poverty for 365 days . . . [was] poor philanthropy . . . to keep the Mexican from becoming a bolshevist."[23] Communist recruitment in *Chicano barrios* during the 1930's remains as another unwritten chapter in the history of these people. For example, the International Workers of the World and other radical groups entered *Chicano* neighborhoods in massive efforts to recruit members. Their limited success in recruiting bore strange fruit in the 1950's when the federal government arrested and deported scores of *Chicanos* who had joined the IWW during this earlier period.

As the Southwest became engulfed in the Great Depression, protection of native labor and the reduction of welfare expenses were Anglo concerns. In an attempt to resolve both needs, *Chicanos,* whatever the legality of their presence in the United States, were rounded up and forcibly removed from the United States. This episode of extreme Anglo hostility represents still another little known chapter in the history of the *Chicanos.*

During the 1930's interactions between *Chicanos* and the larger society became varied, and so did mutual perceptions. The conditions of social contact which were previously rural and caste-like in quality altered slightly. A few (very few) obtained membership in traditional labor unions. Others attended meetings of organizations like the IWW. The era of the New Deal, with its stress on social reforms, helped to change a few majority group attitudes toward *Chicanos* but not in a substantial manner. Still, on the whole, the caste-like relationship that typified life in the rural areas was modified. An unsteady foundation, the beginning of the urban phase of the *Chicano* people's political socialization had been established.

World War II increased the urbanization of *Chicano* population; but urban institutions were ill prepared to cope with the *Chicano* people. Both public and private agencies saw *Chicanos* as problems, and rarely as potential contributors to society. School systems established special schools and police agencies made special efforts to discover the inner workings of the *Chicano* mind. An example of law enforcement research in this area can be seen in a 1942 report to the Los Angeles County Grand Jury by a member of the Sheriff's Department from the same county. In the early 1940's juvenile disorders involving *Chicanos* had increased. The Los Angeles County Sheriff's Department assigned Ed Duran Ayres to make a study. His analysis included the conclusion that all *Chicanos* were biologically inferior and disposed to violence. Officer Ayres said that *Chicanos* were unlikely to respect the American tradition of a fair fight because of their peculiar genetic make-up. The Ayres report states in part:

> The caucasian, especially the Anglo-Saxon, when engaged in fighting, particularly among youths, resorts to fisticuffs and may at times kick each other, which is considered unsportive, but this Mexican element considers all that to be a sign of weakness, and all he knows and feels is a desire to use a knife or some lethal weapon. In other words, his desire is to kill, or at least let blood. That is why it is difficult for the Anglo-Saxon to understand the psychology of the Indian or even the Latin, and it is just as difficult for the Indian or the Latin to understand the psychology of the Anglo-Saxon or those from Northern Europe.[24]

The Chief of the Los Angeles Police Department wrote a letter to the foreman of the Grand Jury endorsing the Ayres findings:

> Lieutenant Ayres of the Sheriff's Department, gave an intelligent statement of the psychology of the Mexican people, particularly the youths. He stated many of the contributing factors that caused the gang activities.[25]

A year later, in June, 1943, the Los Angeles zoot-suit riots began. The riots were widely reported, and they brought *Chicanos* before the nation much more forcefully than had the meager ethnic writings of the past. The riots were violent upheavals. The participants were, on the one hand, young *Chicanos*—teenagers and young adults—called *pachucos* by the *Chicano* bourgeoisie. Armed forces personnel and white civilians of all ages represented the other side.[26] Sporadic fighting in bars, theatres, streetcars, and the public streets continued for five days.

Newspaper accounts were, in large part, unfavorable to the *Chicanos*. There were racial overtones in the reporting and much of what officer Ayres had written provided a basis for hasty journalism. The good guys were Anglos and members of the armed forces and the bad guys were *Chicanos*. On a purely impressionistic level, there was something quite natural about these confrontations; *Chicanos* and Anglo-Americans squared off against each other as they had for generations, only this time the battleground was the city of Los Angeles instead of the agricultural fields and the mining camps of the past. *Chicanos* objected to the role of the newspapers but there was little that they could do. Daily newspapers published stories in which armed forces personnel were always cleared of wrongdoing.

A number of well-known public figures addressed themselves to the issue of race. Eleanor Roosevelt suggested that the riots could be traced to longstanding discrimination against *Chicanos*. She expressed concern for the welfare of *Chicanos* living in California and in states along the border. In Los Angeles, authorities denied Mrs. Roosevelt's allegations, and so did the California State Chamber of Commerce.[27] Earl Warren, then Governor of the

State, argued that "this isn't a Mexican problem, this is an American problem. It is one of juvenile delinquency . . ."[28] There is no question that the riots had serious social consequences. On the one hand, they added one more bitter experience to the history of the *Chicano* people; on the other, they convinced many members of the larger society that *Chicanos* were not assimilable.

Significantly, sources for this period are generally letters, official documents, and newspaper accounts. Serious scholarly analysis of these events is scarce. In an article for the *American Journal of Sociology* Turner and Surace did a content analysis of newspaper articles that appeared during this period.[29] Yet newspapers and other literature remain as principal sources.

The *Christian Century* magazine noted that news pictures supported the conclusion that these were race riots. Overt hostility was clearly directed at *Chicanos* because "no white wearers of these bizarre clothes [zoot-suits] were disturbed" and because "hundreds of Mexicans and Negroes who were not wearing zoot-suits were attacked."[30]

It is, of course, difficult to link the overt behavior of Anglo mobs to Anglo ideology. It is similarly quite a task to show empirically that *Chicano* street corner societies based their actions on a minority ideology. Nevertheless, substantive assumptions of social roles were involved on both sides of the conflict. On one side, second generation *Chicano* youths refused the subservient social roles that American institutions demanded for them. They fought the larger society without strategies, without internal communications, and almost, it seemed, with suicidal recklessness. For young *Chicanos* the zoot-suit riots were not unlike a pogrom; the street battles involved "us" and "them" explicitly and without gentle protocol. On the other side, equally young Anglos from many parts of the United States, a terribly frightened mass of confused, uprooted draftees with over-blown notions of Americanism found ideal conditions for the displacement of pressured frustrations in the foreign-looking *Chicano* neighborhoods. With only a slight mental adjustment, the *Chicano* could even look Japanese. For *Chicanos,* the sounds of hate and the acts of violence were not unfamiliar—they were deeply rooted in the folklore, the ballads and the legends of *la raza.* Uniformed or not, the Anglos were, as always, the enemy.

Turner and Surace saw a conflict of ideologies within the majority group. Some *Chicanos* were associated with romantic Olvera Street (an important tourist attraction), and other romantic images. Others were linked with a rising tide of juvenile vandalism and deviant social behavior. In order to resolve this contradiction, and to provide a more explicit moral justification for racial discrimination, an unambiguous, unfavorable symbol was needed. The two sociologists suggested that the zoot-suit label had connotations of sex crimes, draft-dodging, gang warfare, and other unsavory images. The zoot-suit label which technically applied across ethnic and class lines to all wearers of the garb, was simply equated to *Chicanos.* Thus *Chicanos,* whatever their clothing preferences, were beaten, arrested and otherwise humiliated by non-discriminating members of the larger society.[31]

The conditions of social contact between *Chicanos* and the larger society were altered by the demographic change from rural to urban but they were not improved. Greater social mobility–meaning freedom to live where they chose, eat at restaurants they could afford, visit public facilities that offered comfort and rest–was not forthcoming for all *Chicanos.*

The ground rules of American society in the cities were often even more explicit than they were in the agrarian areas. Signs on house porches and in employment agencies advised *Chicanos* in Spanish and in English that they were not welcome. When written signs were missing the silent language of the doorman, the foreman, the school principal, and others, made it apparent that social ingress was not possible.

The state of Texas to this day provides the best examples of social exclusion. For example, in 1945 a U.S. Senate Subcommittee on Education learned that *Chicanos* from McCarney, Texas, traveled forty-five miles to Fort Stockton for a haircut because Anglo barbers would not cut *Chicano* hair and *Chicanos* could not legally become barbers in McCarney.[32] Other witnesses reported that they could not use a public street to celebrate a Fourth of July because the holiday was "for white people only."[33] In a Texas restaurant a *Chicano* customer, asked to identify his race, answered "Misanthrope" and was promptly served.

The war years forced *Chicanos* to interact widely and intensely with the larger society. Change had to take place because *Chicanos* and other disadvantaged groups were needed in the defense factories and in the battlefields. The competence of *Chicanos* as semi-skilled workers modified some stereotype attitudes. At one Los Angeles area aircraft company an enterprising *Chicano* rose from the position of custodian to a high administrative post "mostly on nerve and need."[34]

On the battle front, the fighting qualities of *Chicano* servicemen serving in integrated units similarly influenced majority group reservations about their loyalty. While the war years did not completely reverse majority views of the past, they did bring about increased social interaction between *Chicanos* and non-*Chicanos.* For *Chicanos,* the war years became another important stage in their urban political socialization. The war experience and post-war developments, such as the educational opportunities offered to *Chicanos* through the G.I. Bill of Rights, helped *Chicanos* to see American society more clearly.

The majority's views of *Chicano* political behavior have, of course, a very direct bearing on the political participation of *Chicanos.* These views have been a part of the Anglo ideologies as far back as the early years of this century. Among the most important are (1) that *Chicanos* in general are submissive and, therefore not capable of effective political activity; (2) that

Chicanos are deeply imbued with foreign values and, therefore, cannot understand the American political system; and (3) that *Chicanos* cannot achieve ethnic unity. These views have more or less persisted to the present day.

It was often said that *Chicanos* had values that were not consonant with the American value system. In politics, for example, *Chicanos* were not expected to understand cherished beliefs about the rights of man, freedom of religion, and other constitutional guarantees. *Chicanos* were considered products of a semi-feudal, colonial social system where the poor obeyed the dictates of benevolent employers. *Chicano* women, Anglo ideologues argued, were shamefully mistreated by their husbands. Finally, it was argued that Roman Catholics, particularly primitive Roman Catholics, could not possibly practice religious freedom.

The assumption of submissiveness carried with it the belief that *Chicanos* were not interested in the acquisition of political power. It was held that members of this minority were accustomed to the commands of priests and labor *patrones.* Consequently, personal initiative was not a well developed trait. People without personal initiative, it was rationalized, could not aspire to the control of political institutions.

The conclusion that *Chicanos* were irrevocably Catholic and eternally foreign was a powerful and pervasive conclusion. The Roman Catholic Church was, indeed, foreign and totally overwhelming. Fear existed that *Chicanos* would react according to the direction of the Church once they acquired political power. Traditional Anglo mistrust of the Roman Catholic Church found a new target in the *Chicano* group. In Los Angeles, civic meetings held in parish halls reinforced the belief that priests and nuns guarded the political life of their impressionable but devout parishioners. The truth is that the Roman Catholic Church, operated by Anglo nuns and priests, did exercise substantial political control over devout *Chicanos.*

Well-meaning individuals who were willing to help the *Chicano* people during the early post-war years were openly skeptical about the ability of these people to organize effectively. Liberal democrats in particular were doubtful. In Los Angeles they greeted the first mass registration of *Chicano* voters in the country with aplomb. While viewing the figures that reported great success, a liberal Democrat said, "So they're registered, will they vote?"

Ideologies are often inconsistent. For example, in the 1930's a view diametrically opposed to the assumption of an incurable ethnic disunity existed. *Chicanos* were considered to be group-minded, and thus there was apprehension that they might develop a Tammany Hall type of organization. Evidence for this fear of *Chicano* bloc voting and machine politics came from experience in the state of New Mexico. Ethnic politics in that state proved to some observers that *Chicanos* practiced a religious-ethnic solidarity even within the political system. Only one party, the Democrats or the Republicans, received the votes of the *Chicanos* according to one Anglo scholar. He indicated that New Mexico's *Chicano* population would accept whatever political party their leaders designated. As a consequence, recruitment of *Chicano* voters by *non-Chicano* outsiders was considered difficult. "This is something our Anglos . . . find extremely irritating," a writer commented.[35] New Mexico, then, where the political involvement of the *Chicanos* was extremely high (when one compares that state with the rest of the Southwest), justified an ideological conclusion that was out of phase with judgments about disunity made in other regions.

Why the Anglo majority would appear to emphasize ethnic unity in New Mexico while underscoring disunity elsewhere is not difficult to understand when region and time are considered. The *Chicano* population was deeply rooted in New Mexico when American political institutions were imposed. The state's institutions were already in *Chicano* hands, and group mindedness and religious-ethnic solidarity was indeed a reality. New Mexicans reacted negatively to outsiders–the conquering Anglos who seized their land with the force of arms. Nevertheless, in terms of time, New Mexico *Chicanos* had a head start of a few generations over *Chicanos* from other states, particularly those who came later in the 20th century. *Chicanos* in New Mexico represented an original population as opposed to the immigrant population from Mexico that followed. New Mexicans appeared to interact with American society *as a group* with a solidarity that distinguished them sharply from *Chicanos* living elsewhere.

Still another image of *Chicanos* was that as a group they were easily controlled. While this notion appealed to many members of the dominant Anglo society, it tended to repel others. In the 1920's and 1930's, fear was expressed that *Chicanos* would not vote for the "vested interests" in agriculture and industry on which they depended and that rural landlords, in particular, would be able to herd them to the polls with "banners flying."[36] On the other hand, it was said that the group was also easy prey for demagogues. "Socialism, the I.W.W. and Communism find a ready soil for their seed among the Mexicans in our country," said one writer who deplored *Chicano "gullibility."*[37]

Thus, the apprehensions of Anglo society militated against political activity by *Chicanos*. Adding to the Anglo majority's fears was a feeling of uncertainty, ambivalence, and frustration with regard to *Chicano* leadership. Until World War II it was commonly believed that the group was devoid of responsible leaders who could stimulate a sense of collective commitment–part of an Anglo ideology that *Chicanos* were quiescent and satisfied with life as it was. Typical of this view was an Anglo businessman's statement that *Chicanos* were a contented and leaderless people "who did not, in the last analysis, know what they wanted. They are like children."[38] Finally, *Chicanos* were considered to be even more handicapped because socially mobile *Chicanos*, the economic achievers, tended to forsake life in the *barrio*, thus depriving lower class *Chicanos* of an articulate middle class.[39]

Anglo expectations concerning *Chicano* leadership have always had a significant impact on the political participation of this minority. This impact became even greater after World War II when growing urbanization and the return of *Chicano* veterans who did maintain their contact with people living in the *barrio* increased the political potential of the group. The importance of Anglo ideologies stems partly from the fact that the validation of *Chicano* leaders has often come not from the minority itself but from Anglo society—a condition that parallels the political history of other ethnic or racial groups in this country and has only recently been modified in the case of blacks who prefer self-determination. Thus, Anglos would urge *Chicanos* to find and develop leaders, with the implicit understanding that these would be "acceptable"; or they would express distrust of individuals who represented themselves as *Chicano* spokesmen. It was the political power structure of the dominant Anglo society that ultimately decided who were legitimate *Chicano* leaders. The problem of the validation of *Chicano* leadership has continued to this day.

The aggregated views, judgments, and presuppositions about the *Chicano* minority held by the larger Anglo society have been described. To recapitulate, they constitute constellations of ideologies that differ from one place to another and from one historical period to the next. In order to clarify what is meant by majority ideologies, the notion of conditions of social contact between the minority and the majority was re-examined in terms of other American ethnic groups. In each instance it was shown that social contact between the minority and the majority generated mutual views that usually hampered and only occassionally assisted the minority group to grow politically. Conditions of social contact on the eastern seaboard were different from those that existed in the Southwest; the ethnic actors were different and so were their reasons for being in this social order. *Chicanos* initially bypassed the well-known process of urban political socialization. While there were few political machines in the Southwest, fear that they might become common in *Chicano* areas was expressed. This fear, and other social expressions concerning *Chicanos*, impinged upon their political experience. They grew politically within an oppressive, racist environment that clearly restricted social opportunity. Within this context of explicit and implicit social discrimination and economic exploration, *Chicanos* created counter-ideologies that contained judgments of the Anglo social order. The contents of those counter-ideologies and their function in the increased political consciousness of *Chicanos* remains to be examined.

NOTES

1. The term *Chicano,* once used almost exclusively by poor, lower class Mexicans who struggled for economic survival in the crowded *barrios* of the Southwest, was also avoided by the Mexican bourgeoisie who lived in more comfortable surroundings. Today, the term has been re-enforced, particularly by the young descendants of both economic classes. It reflects the central thesis of this paper: that American racism in the Southwest limited and attempted to destroy the political development of a people whose major crime was grinding poverty. The term Mexican is used here only to refer to citizens of Mexico or in order to make clear a particular point requiring the use of that term. Otherwise *Chicano* is used throughout the essay.

2. See Cecil Robinson, *With the Ears of Strangers* (Tucson, 1965).

3. *El Mexicano* (November-December, 1913), I; (January, 1914), I; and (April, 1914), 2.

4. Kenneth Roberts, "The Docile Mexican," *Saturday Evening Post,* CC (February 18, 1928), 165.

5. William E. Garnett, "Immediate and Pressing Race Problems of Texas," *Proceedings of the Southwestern Political and Social Science Association* (Austin, 1925), 35-36.

6. Samuel J. Holmes, "Perils of Mexican Invasion," *North American Review,* CCXXVII (1929), 622.

7. Robert F. Forester, *The Racial Problems Involved in Immigration from Latin America and the West Indies to the United States* (Washington, D.C., 1925), 330-331.

8. For details and documentation see Ronald Wyse, "The Position of Mexicans in the Immigration and Nationality Laws," in Leo Grebler, *Mexican Immigration to the United States: The Record and its Implications* ("Mexican American Study Project," Advance Report 2, University of California, Los Angeles, 1966), D-9 to D-11.

9. See U.S. Congress, Senate, *Restriction of Western Hemisphere Immigration,* 1928, Hearings, 71.

10. Kenneth Roberts, "Wet and Other Mexicans," *Saturday Evening Post,* (February 4, 1928), 11.

11. Frederick Simpich, "The Little Brown Brother Treks North," *Independent,* CXVI (February 27, 1926), 239.

12. "Let it be said that there is no doubt as to the ultimate ability of the Mexicans to become a good citizen. Pay him a living and stable wage which will enable him to raise his family to the American standard, and put him in an American community which opens its schools and other friendly agencies to him, and he soon surprises and silences his detractors." Charles A. Tomson, "What of the Bracero?" *Survey,* LIV (June 1, 1925), 292.

13. Richard Lee Strout, "A Fence for the Rio Grande," *Independent,* CXX (June 2, 1928), 520.

14. Helen W. Walker, "Mexican Immigrants and American Citizenship," *Sociology and Social Research, 1928-1929,* XIII (1929), 470.

15. Translated from Enrique Santibañez, *Ensayo acerca de la imigracion Mexicana en los Estados Unidos* (San Antonio, 1930), 95.

16. Max Sylvanus Handman, "The Mexican Immigrant in Texas," *Proceedings National Conference of Social Work,* LIII (1926), 338.

17. See *Mexicans in California,* Report of Governor C.C. Young's Mexican Fact-Finding Committee (San Francisco, 1930), 171. Discussion of this point can also be found in Leo Grebler, *Mexican Immigration,* 24.

18. C. M. Goethe, "Peons Need Not Apply," *World's Work,* LIX (November, 1930), 47.

19. *Ibid.*

20. Middle class *Chicanas,* or at least women who could read and write the English language and who had an economic base, led some of the protests of the *barrio* in the 1930's. They would storm the court house, the offices of the social workers, or would bar the path of investigating officials while shouting and gesturing in a most "un-Mexican" manner. Their little known role suggests still another area deserving intensive historical analysis.

21. Ruth Allen, "Mexican Peon Women in Texas," *Sociology and Social Research,* XVI (November-December 1931), 131.

22. Goethe, "Peons Need Not Apply," 48.

23. Emory Bogardus, *The Mexican in the United States* (Los Angeles, 1934), 48.

24. Letter written by Ed Duran Ayres to E. W. Oliver, Foreman, Los Angeles County Grand Jury, 1942, 2. Copy on file with the UCLA Mexican American Study Project.

25. C. B. Horrall, Letter to Foreman Oliver, on file with the UCLA Mexican American Study Project.

26. The garments that these young people wore were called "drapes," "zoots," and were synonymous with *Chicanos.* A newspaper explanation of the history and use of zoot suits includes the observation that "many a young Mexican in a zoot suit works hard and takes his money home to mamacita for frijoles refritos, . . ." Timothy Turner, "Zuit Suits Still Parade Here Despite OPA Ban," *Los Angeles Times,* March 22, 1943, sec. II, 8.

27. Fletcher Bowron, then Mayor of Los Angeles, told newspaper reporters that, "Nothing that has occurred can be construed as due to prejudice against Mexicans or discrimination against young men of any race. Neither is there a foundation for anyone to say that attacks or arrests have been directed toward members of minority groups." *Los Angeles Daily News,* June 10, 1943, 3.

28. *Los Angeles Examiner,* June 17, 1943, Sec. I, I.

29. The use of the term *Mexican* in newspapers is carefully traced by these two scholars over a ten and one-half year period. The use of the symbol, they say, led to overt hostility on the part of members of the majority group who were, inadvertently, goaded to act against the *Chicanos.* For further details about this hypothesis see Ralph H. Turner and Samuel J. Surace, "Zoot Suiters and Mexicans: Symbols in Crowd Behavior," *The American Journal of Sociology,* LXII (July 1956), 14-20. See also comments by Neil J. Smelser, *Theory of Collective Behavior* (London, 1962), 105-106.

30. "Portent of Storm," *Christian Century,* LX (June, 1943), 735.

31. This discussion rests heavily on the article by Ralph H. Turner and Samuel J. Surace.

32. Statement of Alonzo S. Perales, Chairman, Committee of One Hundred, Director General, League of Loyal Americans, San Antonio, Texas, U.S. Congress Senate, Subcommittee of the Committee on Education and Labor, Hearings, Fair Employment Practice Act on S.101, S.459, 79th Congress, 1945, 150.

33. *Ibid.*

34. Mr. Paul Zamudio (pseudonym) was first a janitor, then an interpreter, and eventually a high ranking officer in the company.

35. The ideological conclusion that *Chicanos* represented a threat is well documented by Mary H. Austin, "Mexicans and New Mexico," *Survey Graphic,* LXVI (May, 1931), 143.

36. See Kenneth L. Roberts, "Wet and Other Mexicans," 12.

37. Thomas Brown, "The Challenge of Mexican Immigration," *The Missionary Review of the World,* L (September, 1927), 193.

38. Frances Jerome Woods, *Mexican Ethnic Leadership in San Antonio, Texas* (Washington, D.C., 1949), 23-24, 49.

39. Leonard Broom and Eshref Shevky, "Mexicans in the United States," *Sociology and Social Research,* XXXVI (1951-1952), 54.

3: PERSPECTIVE ON POLITICS: Part I

Alfredo Cuéllar

THE POLITICAL DEVELOPMENT OF MEXICAN AMERICANS CAN BE TRACED through roughly four periods of political activity that begin with the American conquest of the Southwest.

Such a survey must begin with conflict. Though the first three generations of American rule (from the late 1840s until about 1920, the first phase of political development for Mexican Americans) can be termed "apolitical," it is a period that covers widely disparate activities. Through the first generation (until perhaps the mid-1870s) there was widespread violence and disorder accompanying the consolidation of the conquest. In the following 50 years throughout most of the Southwest Mexican Americans were politically submerged. Neither the violence of the first generation nor the quiescence of the second and third can be considered "normal" American political participation. Force and its aftermath of suppression were the rule.

There were two exceptions to the dominant apolitical pattern. Organized political activity was very much present in New Mexico. Here the political system, even during the long period of territorial government, reflected the demographic and social weight of a large Spanish-speaking population. In southern California, moreover, a wealthy land-owning group of Mexicans retained substantial, although declining, political power until the late 1880s and the coming of the railroads.

In the second period, what may be considered conventional political activity began, born in a context of violence and suppression. This period (beginning roughly in the 1920s) was a time of adaptation and accommodation, reflecting the changing position of Mexican Americans in the social structure of communities in the Southwest. A small Mexican American middle class began to gain some strength and tried to come to terms politically with a still hostile and still threatening social environment.

This period of accommodation was typified by the efforts of the new Mexican American groups to prepare and to "guide" the lower-class and newly arrived immigrant Mexican Americans to "become Americans." Notably, they did *not* press for full political participation. As we shall see, it was also during this period that at least some of the negative ideological assumptions about Mexicans held by the majority were reflected in their political activity.

The third period, beginning in the 1940s, saw increased political activity. Although the results fell far short of full participation in American political life, this period was characterized by a more aggressive style and more organization. During this time, so to speak, the Mexican Americans began to "play the game" according to Anglo political rules. The new idea of progress became associated with exercising the franchise and attempting to gain both elective and appointive office. The political achievements of Mexican Americans in New Mexico exemplified political progress. There, they had kept a political voice through the change from Mexican to U.S. rule: there were Mexicans in the state legislature and in Congress. Most areas, however, fell short of the accomplishment in New Mexico, especially south Texas, where political exclusion and manipulation were the heritage of violence and suppression. This exclusion and manipulation continued in many communities to be enforced by the local Anglo power structure.

The new aggressiveness that appeared after World War II was largely a phenomenon of urban life and reflected again the changing situation of Mexican Americans. They were becoming more urbanized, and more were middle class; they were increasingly American-born. World War II itself was one of the most important forces for change: hundreds of thousands of Mexican Americans served in the armed forces and gained radically new experiences, being sent outside their five-state "*barrio*" and given opportunities to develop a drastically changed view of American society.

In recent years a fourth type of political activity is becoming important. For convenience, it may be called the radicalization of Mexican American political activity. This new style is exemplified in the growth of the *Chicano* movement. Although this movement assumes different forms in various parts of the Southwest and although its acceptance is far from uniform, it is a very different concept of political activity. It questions and challenges not only the assumptions of other generations of Mexican American political leaders but some of the most basic assumptions of American politics as well.

These four phases are roughly sequential, as noted in this outline, but they also overlap a good deal. Violence continues to suppress Mexican American political activity in many communities and to foster an apolitical attitude. In other areas there is a tentative and fearful kind of accommodation politics. Conventional political activity is slowly bringing a quite new political visibility to the Mexican Americans, which is particularly evident in Washington with the recent creation of the Interagency Committee on Mexican American Affairs. Radical politics is also becoming institutionalized in some parts of the Southwest. Despite this confusing and complex overlapping and coexistence, we will discuss each type of political activity separately.

CONFLICT AND POLITICS

Conflict between Mexicans and Anglo Americans characterized the American Southwest for the better part of the nineteenth century.[1] Let us recall some of the history of the region with specific reference to its political consequences. . . . The first sizeable number of Anglos who entered this region settled in Texas in 1821 under the leadership of Stephen Austin. Alarmed by their rapid increase in numbers and their failure to accept Mexican law and custom, the Mexican government shut off further Anglo immigration in 1830. The end result was the Texas Revolution of 1835-1836, just 15 years after the first legal immigration began. In spite of the Texas declaration of independence from Mexico, there were then 10 years of sporadic warfare, culminating in open warfare between the United States and Mexico in 1846 after the annexation of Texas by the United States.

The Treaty of Guadalupe Hidalgo ended the declared war, but it did not end the fighting between Mexicans and Anglos. Even in New Mexico, acquired "bloodlessly," an abortive rebellion followed the American occupation. In Texas, the next generation lived through an almost endless series of clashes, which reached the status of international warfare again in the late 1850s. Mexico's defeat and the humiliating invasion she suffered cost her nearly a third of her territory. For years afterward elements in Mexico dreamed of reconquest. On the American side the new territories were vast and remote from the central forces of government. The feeble hold that the United States had on the Southwest, the recurrent fears of Indian rebellion, and the divisive forces unleashed by the Civil War were all reflected in American fears of reconquest. Today, with the United States stretching from sea to sea, we rarely question the inevitability of this pattern. But a hundred-odd years ago, this "Manifest Destiny" had something of the character of a crusade, a national mission to be accomplished despite the acknowledged existence of great obstacles. In this climate of opinion, defeating Mexico was a very special victory, and holding these territories a special cause.

Anglos used force to gain control, and Mexicans retaliated with force. Texas, the scene of virtually all of this activity and the home of most Mexicans resident in the United States, saw hostilities between substantial armies and a nearly constant state of guerilla warfare. Many Mexicans, perhaps, the most dissident, chose to return to Mexico. From the Texas point of view, many of those who remained were ready as always to join any successful marauder from across the border.

Of these, the most successful was Juan Cortina, who first invaded Texas in 1859 in a series of skirmishes known now as the Cortina Wars. These long "wars" illustrate many of the important themes in Texas-Mexican-American history, showing the comparative lack of distinction between "Mexican" and "Mexican American." They illustrate the racial nature of the conflicts, and they also show that these early decades of conflict were inextricably linked with some larger American problems, most notably the Civil War.

. . . It should be reiterated that the shift in land use [in Texas] entailed a shift in ownership. Often, political promises were made and broken; legal contracts were made and broken; legal protection for Mexicans–landowners and others–was promised and withheld. As Webb concludes in his history of the Texas Rangers, "The humble Mexicans doubted a government that would not protect their person and the higher classes distrusted one that would not safeguard their property. Here, indeed, was the rich soil in which to plant the seed of revolution and race war."[2]

Juan Cortina's expeditions began as a personal vendetta in Brownsville, Texas against an Anglo sheriff who used unnecessary force in arresting one of Cortina's former ranchhands. Cortina soon extended his campaign to a call for the general emancipation of Mexicans from American rule. He exhorted Mexicans to rise against their oppressors, to claim their lands and to drive out the *gringos.* Mexicans on both sides of the Rio Grande flocked to his camp. His army engaged troops in Texas in numerous battles, although eventually he and his army were forced to retreat into Mexico.

A few years later, after the Civil War, Cortina "helped" U.S. federal troops in the skirmishes and military occupation that preceded Reconstruction, an act that confirmed his unpopularity among Texas Anglos. Cortina went on to become brigadier general in the Mexican army and later, governor of the border state of Tamaulipas in northern Mexico. But as late as the middle of the 1870s he was still leading raids into Texas.

Hundreds of other leaders led groups ranging from the pseudo-military to the simple bandit (though Mexicans often viewed such bandits as *guerilleros* fighting for their people). In California, "outlaws" such as Tiburcio Vásquez and Joaquín Murieta (the latter so romanticized that it is difficult to separate fact from fantasy) and in Texas, Juan Flores Salinas, were variously remembered by Anglos anxious for law and order and by Mexicans unwilling to recognize the legitimacy of the American regime. A monument to Salinas was erected in 1875 and carries the inscription: *que combatiendo murió por su patria* ("who died fighting for his country").

The end of the Civil War, however, released troops for the "pacification" of the southwestern Indians, and the railroads could bring in hordes of Easterners looking for land and a new frontier. The era of overt violence between Anglo and Mexican American came to an end and was followed by a long period of quiet. With the beginning of revolution in Mexico in 1910 came the beginning of large-scale immigration. This process rekindled the historical distrust of Mexican Americans, especially now that their numbers were being rapidly increased by refugees from Mexico. It was therefore not surprising that this process would have a depressive effect on political participation among Mexican Americans at this time.

There seemed always to be incidents to keep the Americans fearful. In 1915, for example, a Mexican agent was arrested in a Texas border city with a detailed "Plan de San Diego, Texas," for an insurrection in the Southwest in which "all Anglos over the age of 16 would be put to death." Bandit activities in Texas were being carried out to finance the revolutionary plans of the Flores Magon brothers, who were then operating out of Los Angeles in an effort to begin yet another revolution in Mexico. I.W.W. and anarchist activities among the Mexicans added to the anxiety. Then, in 1916 General Pancho Villa climaxed a number of border raids with an attack on Columbus, New Mexico. The United States retaliated with the Punitive Expedition of General John Pershing into northern Mexico. This comic-opera rerun of the tragic war with Mexico 70 years earlier increased distrust and resentment toward the Mexican American population. Then came the famous Zimmerman Note of 1917, which appeared to confirm all suspicions: the Germans offered to unite Mexico and Japan with Germany for a war against the United States to restore the Southwest to Mexico and give the Far West to Japan. Mexico showed no interest in the scheme, but it touched a sensitive nerve in the United States. As usual, the Mexican Americans in the Southwest were caught in the middle.

Given the background of distrust and violent suppression it is not surprising that the style of the first important Mexican American political groups should have been very circumspect. They could not have been anything but accommodationist.

THE POLITICS OF ADAPTATION

The politics of accommodation can be traced from the 1920s with the appearance of several new political organizations. A good example was the *Orden Hijos de America* (Order of the Sons of America), founded in San Antonio in 1921.[3] The founding members came almost entirely from the newly emerging middle class. Apparently, though, a few refugees from the Mexican Revolution were also involved. More important, both the social and the economic position of these founding members were precarious, and one can note in their announced objectives important concessions to the Anglo definition of the proper role for Mexicans in politics. For example, the goals of the OSA did *not* include demands for equality, either between Mexican

Americans themselves or in terms of the dominant majority. Thus, only "citizens of the U.S. of Mexican or Spanish extraction, either native or naturalized" were eligible to join.[4] This exclusion by citizenship was meant—and acted—as an exclusionary mechanism. The implication was that Mexican Americans were more trustworthy to Anglos than Mexican nationals, and also more deserving of the benefits of American life.

This can be understood partly as a reaction to the Anglo conception of Mexicans as an undifferentiated group of low status, regardless of social achievement or citizenship. Hence, all were equally to be distrusted. As an organization of upwardly mobile individuals (albeit of modest achievements) OSA was concerned to show the dominant Anglo majority that they were different from other, "trouble-making" Mexicans. Of course citizenship would have been functionally useful if the *Orden* had been a truly political group, but the symbolic meaning of the requirement is indicated by another regulation. The organization declared itself "to assume no partisan stand, but rather to confine itself to training members for citizenship."

Obviously, "training members for citizenship" is not a strong political position, although presumably this included some activities aimed at increasing political participation, such as by voting. In general, though, this adaptive position could be interpreted as a reflection of the great social and economic vulnerability of Mexican Americans during the 1920s. Validation and recognition meant being as noncontroversial as possible—and preferably with declarations of loyalty to the United States of America.

OSA functioned for nearly ten years. By that time some splintering had begun to occur in the group and its chapters, and on February 17, 1929, several Mexican American groups, among them the OSA itself, the Order of Knights of America, and the League of Latin American Citizens, met in Corpus Christi, Texas. Out of this meeting a new organization emerged to meet the need for harmony and to present a unified front to the Anglo American community. The theme of unity was embodied in the name of the new organization: the League of United Latin-American Citizens, or LULAC. Once again, membership was restricted to citizens of Mexican or Spanish extraction, one of the group's aims being "to develop within the members of our race the best, purest and most perfect type of a true and loyal citizen of the United States of America."[5]

This obvious sensitivity to Anglo opinion was intensified by the debate in Congress and in the press at the time concerning the rising tide of Mexican immigration. This affirmation of loyalty and citizenship may therefore be interpreted as one further example of a protective device used by middle-class Mexican Americans vis-à-vis the Anglo society.

Thus in 1929, to protect themselves from social and economic sanctions, the willingness of Mexican Americans to assert even minimum political demands was tempered at all times and in all expressions by a desire to reaffirm citizenship and loyalty to the United States. It is not surprising that there was at this time no pressure for Mexican civil rights, particularly if it might have involved any kind of open demonstrations. (As a matter of fact, Article 1 of the LULAC's by-laws contains one item that states, "We shall oppose any radical and violent demonstration which may tend to create conflicts and disturb the peace and tranquility of our country.") Once again, a statement designed to appease, to reassure those Anglos who feared the worst. And it also served as a warning to Mexicans who might conceivably entertain such radical notions.

Notable by its omission among 25 articles is any demand for any form of cultural pluralism, despite the willingness of some members to preserve a semblance of their ethnic identity.

Throughout, the aims and purposes of the new organization reflected its middle-class orientation, a conformity to the standards of Texas Anglo society, and above all, an emphasis on adapting to American society, instead of emphasis on aggressive political participation, and much less on any kind of political participation based on a separate ethnic identity.

Such circumspection must, as we have noted earlier, be judged in the context of the political milieu of Texas in the 1920s. Both Mexicans and Negroes "knew their place." Although Mexicans did vote in Texas, in some counties the votes were under the control of an Anglo political boss.[6] In other counties Mexicans seldom voted because of the poll tax and other such limitations. The influence of the Anglo *patrón* may be seen in the following letter written by one such boss, who felt it necessary to scold his "Mexican-Texas friends" for forming such a group as LULAC:

> I have been and still consider myself as your Leader or Superior Chief . . . I have always sheltered in my soul the most pure tenderness for the Mexican-Texas race and have watched over your interests to the best of my ability and knowledge. . . . Therefore I disapprove the political activity of groups which have no other object than to organize Mexican-Texas voters into political groups for guidance by other leaders. . . . I have been able to maintain the Democratic Party in power with the aid of my Mexican-Texas friends, and in all the time that has passed we have had no need for clubs or political organizations.[7]

Between hostility and economic vulnerability Mexican Americans were making the best of a difficult situation, which was very slow to change. LULAC gained power among the middle class and ultimately became a spokesman for those Mexican Americans who had achieved a measure of economic and social advancement. In Texas it is still an important political group. Other organizations (as well as branch chapters of LULAC) appeared throughout the Southwest, and many were modeled after LULAC. All of them skirted the question of aggressive political action with considerable skill. Accommodation was the style in the 1920s and 1930s; it may very well have been the only possible style. Since World War II LULAC has taken a much more aggressive stance, a change preceded by a number of changes in the structure of the Mexican American population.

THE POLITICIZATION OF MEXICAN AMERICANS

The politicization of Mexican American communities in the Southwest dates only from the years following World War II. For the most part politicization was prefaced by deep social changes among the Mexican American population, discussed elsewhere in this book. In sum, they brought Mexicans into new and partly unforeseen contact with American society, particularly in urban areas. The word "urbanization" hardly conveys their impact. A demand for labor brought hundreds of thousands of Mexicans into cities from rural areas, and at the same time many hundreds of thousands of young Mexican American men found themselves in uniform–and racially invisible to Anglos from other areas of the United States and to other peoples in foreign lands. At the same time, however, their families began to find that the urban areas of the Southwest, like rural ones, were highly discriminatory (this was the time of the "zoot suit riots" in Los Angeles and San Diego, California[8]). (In the rural areas, however, the social fabric that supported and justified discrimination was hardly changed.)

In the cities the urban migrants could find only poor housing, the lowest unskilled employment, and restricted access to schools and other public facilities. As before, few Mexican Americans took part in political activity, although the tradition of political accommodation now seemed outmoded. So did the political organizations built to formalize this relationship to the larger community. A middle class had begun to increase rather rapidly as a result of wartime prosperity, and it was increasingly dissatisfied. Against this background a group of articulate former servicemen (helped substantially by the educational and training benefits of the G.I. Bill of Rights) began to press for changes in the community. In Los Angeles a more open environment facilitated a new alliance with labor elements, Anglo civil leaders, and religious leaders.

One outcome of this alliance was the California-based Community Service Organization (CSO). In Los Angeles the CSO tried to develop indigenous leaders to organize community activity around local issues, using the techniques of larger-scale grassroots community organization. In this manner the Community Service Organization mobilized large segments of the Mexican American community into activities directed against restricted housing, police brutality, segregated schools, inequitable justice, and discriminatory employment, all problems endemic in the Mexican American areas of southern California as much as in other parts of the Southwest. In this process CSO became an important and meaningful post-World War II political phenomenon in the Mexican American community.

In general CSO pressed for full and equal rights for Mexican Americans. The new emphasis was the extra appeal for active and increased participation by as many elements of the community as possible. Therefore, in contrast to previous organizations, CSO tended to be more egalitarian. Under the influence of an outside catalyst (Saul Alinsky's Industrial Areas Foundation) it became a group that no longer served as the vehicle of a relatively few and successful Mexican Americans. Although the leadership tended to be new middle class, on the whole it made an effort to recruit members of the working class and other lower-class elements, including new arrivals from Mexico. CSO also had some non-Mexican members, although they were comparatively few.

This idea of an alliance of equals from various strata of Mexican American society became important. In contrast to the paternalism of previous organizations, such as LULAC, there was little concern with the assimilation of lower-class elements into the mainstream of American life. Nor, for that matter, did CSO show any interest in "Mexican culture." The guiding idea of CSO was to cope with concrete and immediate social, economic, and political problems.

The founders of CSO assumed that American institutions were basically responsive to the needs and demands of the Mexican American population. There were no questions about the legitimacy of these institutions; it was always assumed that proper community organization and action would force Anglo institutions to respond to the needs of Mexican Americans. Accordingly, getting Mexicans to exercise the right to vote became a prime CSO objective. Members organized large-scale nonpartisan community drives to register voters. In Los Angeles these registration drives rather significantly increased the number of Spanish-surname voters. The immediate results were electoral victories by Mexican American candidates, there and in nearby communities. Furthermore, CSO pressure on public housing authorities, on the Fair Employment Practices Commission (FEPC), and against police brutality also yielded results. Housing authorities eased discriminatory practices, Mexican American representation was included in the FEPC, and the police department agreed "to go easy on Mexicans" on the Los Angeles East Side.

At the time members considered CSO tactics radical and militant, and throughout the 1950s the CSO remained a politically powerful organization that emphasized direct, grassroots community action. Numerous CSO chapters were organized throughout the state of California, each duplicating the Alinsky approach to community organization.

In recent years CSO has declined as a potent community organization, in part because of the withdrawal of financial support from the Industrial Areas Foundation, and in part because it lost some of its most energetic members.

For example, the single most well-known former member of CSO, César Chávez, split with the urban-centered CSO to organize a union of farm workers. Also contributing to the decline of CSO was the rise of competing organizations of Mexican Americans.

Other organizations in the Southwest reflect the aggressive political style growing after World War II. In Texas, there is the important American G.I. Forum. The G.I. Forum was founded by a south Texas physician, Dr. Hector Garcia; the immediate cause of its formation was the refusal of a funeral home in Three Rivers, Texas, to bury a Mexican American war veteran in 1948. The incident attracted national attention, and the idea of the G.I. Forum spread rapidly not only in Texas but also throughout the Southwest, to several midwestern states, and to Washington, D.C. Although the Forum is concerned with nonpartisan civic action, it has moved increasingly toward more direct and aggressive political activities. In Texas, where its main strength lies, the G.I. Forum launched intensive "Get out the vote" and "Pay your poll tax" drives in the 1950s. Subsequently, it has continued voter registration drives since the repeal of the Texas poll tax. On a number of other issues, the Forum continues to act as a spokesman against the problems that beset the Mexican American community in Texas.

If the CSO and the American G.I. Forum reflect the goals of the immediate postwar years, two political groups founded in the late 1950s show a shift in both the political goals and the resources available in the community. In California the Mexican American Political Association (MAPA), founded in 1958, and in Texas the Political Association of Spanish-speaking Organizations (PASSO) were organized essentially as groups pressuring the political system at the party level. These were not primarily attempts to organize the Mexican American poor to register and vote; they were efforts to use growing middle-class strength to win concessions for Mexican Americans from the Anglo-dominated political parties. Essentially the goal of both associations was simply to get Mexican Americans into political office, either as nominees for elective office in the regular parties or as appointees of elected Anglo officials. Thus the best-publicized effort of either group was the successful deposition of the Anglo political structure in Crystal City, Texas, in the early 1960s. In this venture, PASSO joined with some non-Mexican groups, notably the Teamsters and the Catholic Bishops' Committee for the Spanish Speaking. (Although the victory in Crystal City was short-lived, it was as significant to Texas Mexicans as the more recent victory of a Negro mayor in Mississippi was to the black community.)

Both MAPA and PASSO gain strength by virtue of their statewide connections, which are particularly important in the outlying rural areas where repression has been a norm. Statewide ties give courage and support to local efforts. (At this writing one of the strongest MAPA chapters in California is the chapter in the Coachella valley, a citrus- and date-growing area not far from Palm Springs. The local chairman, a vociferous spokesman for Mexican American laborers, is constantly subject to harassment. He is also constantly in demand outside the immediate area. The intervention of outside elements in a local and rather repressive situation has reduced isolation and repression. As in Crystal City, one of MAPA's victories has been the election of Mexican American officials in the grower-dominated town of Coachella.)

Although both MAPA and PASSO are still largely confined to California and Texas, respectively, there are branches and organizational efforts in other states. The two associations once considered amalgamation into a regional group; but, incredibly, the effort failed because the two groups could not agree on a common name. Texas Mexicans could not afford the then too overt ethnic pride suggested by "Mexican American," and the California group would not accept the euphemism "Spanish-speaking." At these discussions, one disgusted delegate finally proposed "CACA" (a Spanish equivalent of the English "doo-doo") to represent the "Confederated Alliance of *Chicano* Associations." Interestingly, only in such an intensely in-group situation could the name *Chicano* be suggested. At the time this word could not be used for a serious political discussion.

THE CHICANO MOVEMENT

Throughout this chapter we have suggested that Mexican American political activity has often been related to social structural factors. Because much of this political activity was possible only after certain structural changes in Mexican American life, there were seldom any real alternatives beyond simple reaction to Anglo pressure. The importance of the *Chicano* movement as an alternative to pressures from the majority society can hardly be overemphasized. It is a distinctively novel development in the Mexican American community. The *Chicano* movement developed in southern California no earlier than 1966, and it is already a sharp new force in the political expression of Mexican Americans throughout the southwest.

The *Chicano* ideology includes a broad definition of political activity. Ironically, such thinking was possible only for a new generation of urbanized and "Anglicized" (that is, assimilated) young Mexican Americans, who were much less burdened by social and class restrictions than their elders were and whose education had exposed them to new ideas.

The exact beginnings of the movement are obscure. There is some evidence that the *Chicano* movement grew out of a group of conferences held at Loyola University in Los Angeles in the summer of 1966. As originally conceived by its Catholic sponsors, the conferences were to create a fairly innocuous youth organization for the middle-class Mexican students attending various colleges throughout California. Very quickly the movement grew beyond the intent or control of its sponsors (Loyola has never been very noted for its interest in Mexican American education) and it drew in yet others, not students and not middle class, who were attracted by the ideology of *chicanismo.* Thus it cannot be understood as a movement limited to the young, to students, or even to urban areas. It must also be understood as including the followers of Reies Tijerina in northern New Mexico and César Chávez' embattled union of striking farm workers in central California. In 1969 Rodolfo (Corky) González was the principal leader and inspiration of the *Chicano* movement in Denver although his interests were mainly in urban civic action. Moreover, "Corky" has organized regional youth conferences and his influence spreads far beyond the local area. No one leader has yet emerged in southern California or in Texas.

As this wide range of activity shows, the *Chicano* movement is extremely heterogenous, and its elements have different aims and purposes. In this way the movement cuts across social class, regional, and generational lines. Its aims range from traditional forms of social protest to increasingly more radical goals that appear as a sign of an emerging nationalism. It is a social movement, in that it can be described as "pluralistic behavior functioning as an organized mass effort directed toward a change of established folkways or institutions."[9] The dynamic force of the movement is its ideology–*chicanismo.*

The new ideology is advanced as a challenge to the dominant Anglo beliefs concerning Mexicans as well as to the beliefs of Mexican Americans themselves. Although we have emphasized that students are by no means the only element of the *Chicano* movement, we will reconstruct *chicanismo* primarily as it has been developed among students. Actually, this is only one of several ideological strands but it is the most consistently developed, thus the best illustration of the change from protest to nationalism and a synthesis of the ideology of *chicanismo.*

The first student form of the *Chicano* movement coincided with the development of new student organizations in California universities and colleges in 1966 and 1967. Some of these groups were the United Mexican American Students (UMAS), the Mexican American Student Association (MASA), Mexican American Student Confederation (MASC), and Movimiento Estudiantil Chicano de Aztlán (MECHA). More recently the Mexican American Youth Organization (MAYO) has appeared, with particular strength in Texas. (MAYO is also the name adopted by the new organizations of *Chicanos* in California prisons.) These student groups were at first concerned with a rather narrow range of problems in the field of education, particularly those concerned with increasing the number of Mexican American students in college. To the extent that these student groups were active in the Mexican American community, they were involved with various forms of protest against specific and longstanding grievances, such as police brutality and inferior educational facilities, although other forms of community activity also involved political campaigns.

Chicano student groups thus have never repudiated ordinary forms of political activity, although for them such forms as voting constitute only one political alternative. Actually, given the wide range of problems facing the Mexican American community, *Chicanos* view conventional forms of political activity as perhaps the least effective. Instead, they favor forms of confrontation as the most effective means to gain access for the traditionally excluded *Chicano,* even though it has, on occasion, led to violence. In general, this conception of politics contrasts sharply with the ideas of more conservative Mexican American leaders, most of whom adhere to very limited and "safe" politics with an emphasis on voting and "working within the system" to gain political leverage. This is not to say that *Chicanos* reject working for social change within the system; as a matter of fact, much recent activity has focussed on bringing about change in the universities and colleges as well as in the public school systems. Nevertheless, whereas the moderates seek to bring major change in American society through nonviolent means, the more militant speak of the need for "revolutionary activity," though they often leave the details and direction of this revolution unspecified. While they admire the life style and aspirations of revolutionary leaders like Ché Guevara, they have thus far made no systematic theoretical connection between the *Chicano* movement and the general literature on revolution. The theoretical underpinnings of the *Chicano* movement thus often lack a strong direction.

And yet, the advent of the *Chicano* movement does represent a revolutionary phenomenon among Mexican Americans. As we shall see, most of the change from traditional forms lies in (or is reflected in) the ideology of *chicanismo.* Basically eclectic, *chicanismo* draws inspiration from outside the United States and outside the Mexican American experience. The Cuban Revolution, for example, exerts some influence, as do the career and ideals of Ché Guevera. For instance, the Brown Berets (a *Chicano* youth group) affect the life style of this revolutionary. Black Power also offers something of a model. Most recently, *Chicanos* have resurrected the Mexican revolutionary tradition.

Basically, however, *chicanismo* focuses on the life experience of the Mexican in the United States. It challenges the belief system of the majority society at the same time that it attempts to reconstruct a new image for Mexican Americans themselves. *Chicanos* assume that along with American Indians and black Americans, Mexicans live in the United States as a conquered people. This idea allows *chicanismo* to explain the evolution of the *Chicano* as essentially conflictful. In each conflictual relationship with Anglos, the Mexicans lost out and were thus forced to live in the poverty and degradation attendant upon those with the status of a conquered people. This is no better illustrated than by the Mexicans' loss of communal and private property. As a result, they had no choice but to work the land for a *patrón* (usually an Anglo, but sometimes a Mexican, who exploited his own people). When the Mexican was thrown off the land, he was forced to become an unattached wage-earner, often a migrant farm worker; or he might migrate to a city, where the exploitation continued. In any event, *chicanismo* emphasizes that the Mexican was transformed into a rootless economic commodity, forced either to depend on migrant farm work or to sell his labor in the urban centers, where his fate depended upon the vicissitudes of the economy. Ironically, indispensable as Mexican labor was for the economic development of the Southwest, the Mexican got little recognition for his contribution and even less benefit from it.

Chicanos therefore see the economic expansion of the Southwest as essentially a dehumanizing process. They also point out that during periods of economic depression in the United States, when the Mexican became "superfluous" and "expensive," Anglo society had no qualms about attempting to eliminate Mexicans from the United States, as in the repatriations of the 1930s. . . . The repatriations are viewed as a conscious attempt to eliminate the *Chicano* from American society.

The thrust of *chicanismo* is not only economic, but also cultural. In many ways, the exploitation and suppression of his culture is what most angers the *Chicano,* who views the attempt to deracinate Mexican culture in the Southwest as the reason why Mexican Americans are disoriented about their culture and often attempt to deny it. The *Chicano* points out that the Anglo himself often views Mexicans with a great degree of ambivalence. Anglos oftentimes take over aspects of "Spanish" (which is really Mexican) culture and at the same time deny it to the Mexican himself. In this fashion Mexicans were denied the development of a more autonomous cultural life, especially as it touches upon Spanish language use, the arts, and so on. (This was done in spite of the agreements made in the signing of the Treaty of Guadalupe Hidalgo. Early drafts of the treaty contained Mexican government efforts to make formal recognition of language rights for Mexicans who chose to remain in the United States after the Mexican War. These provisions were not approved by the U.S. Senate.)

Worse yet, the ideology goes on, the cultural suppression continues to the present day, reinforced by Anglo institutions, particularly the schools. The extreme position (although by no means infrequent) is represented by the fact that Mexican American students in the public schools are corporally punished for using Spanish, their native language. Under these circumstances, it is understandable that the Mexican American student remains ignorant and often ashamed of his past. When the Mexican is mentioned in textbooks, it is in a romanticized and stereotypically Anglicized version of "Spanish culture" that may be congenial to Anglos but is remote and irrelevant to the Mexican

American. The *Chicano* considers this type of whitewashed "Spanish" culture particularly galling because he feels that while Anglos may selectively choose certain motifs from Mexican culture, the person behind the culture, the Mexican himself, is given neither recognition nor respect.

Chicanismo also focuses on race, and in some ways this emphasis constitutes one of the most controversial aspects of *chicanismo.* It is argued that Anglo racism denies the Mexican his ethnicity by making him ashamed of his "Mexican-ness." Mexican ancestry, instead of being a source of pride, becomes a symbol of shame and inferiority. As a consequence, Mexicans spend their lives apologizing or denying their ancestry, to the point that many dislike and resent being called "Mexican," preferring "Spanish American," "Latin," "Latin American," and similar euphemisms. For these reasons, the term *"Chicano"* is now insisted upon by activists as a symbol of the new assertiveness.

Advocates of *chicanismo* therefore hope to reconstruct the Mexican Americans' concept of themselves by appeals to pride of a common history, culture and "race." *Chicanismo* attempts to redefine the Mexicans' identity on the basis not of class, generation, or area of residence but on a unique and shared experience in the United States. This means that appeals for political action, economic progress, and reorientation of cultural identity are cast in terms of the common history, culture, and ethnic background of *la raza.*

Chicano ideologues insist that social advance based on material achievement is, in the final analysis, less important than social advance based on *la raza;* they reject what they call the myth of American individualism. The *Chicano* movement feels that it cannot afford the luxury of individualism; if Mexicans are to confront the problems of their group realistically they must begin to act along collective lines. Hence, the stirrings of a new spirit of what *chicanismo* terms "cultural nationalism" among the Mexican Americans of the Southwest.

Chicanismo has led not only to increased participation in community activities, but also to a heightened and often intense interest in cultural life. *Chicano* poets, playwrights, journalists, and writers of all varieties have suddenly appeared. There are *Chicano* theater groups in several large cities (often known as the *teatro urbano*) and one nationally known and well-travelled group from Delano, California (*El teatro campesino*), which tells the story not only of the striking California farmworkers but of *Chicanos* in general. Newspapers and magazines also reflect this desire to disseminate the idea of *chicanismo.* Throughout the Southwest numerous *Chicano* "underground" newspapers and magazines publishing literary materials have emerged. There is even a *Chicano* Press Association, a regional association representing *Chicano* publications from Texas to California. Furthermore, because of the strong base in colleges and universities, a serious and generally successful drive to develop "ethnic studies" programs has appeared, especially in California. As part of the drive to spread the idea of *chicanismo* in education, *Chicanos* place an emphasis on Mexican contributions to American society, thus giving *Chicano* college students a new conception of their past and present.

Chicano student groups share an orientation similar to that of black students, and on occasion they cooperate and support each other on similar demands. (There is more mutual support between black and brown students than between their counterparts at the community level.) The alliance between black and brown students, however, has not been close, harmonious, or continuous. *Chicano* student organizations have not yet been significantly involved with Anglo radical student groups, although these groups sometimes claim their support or claim that they are working for the benefit of *Chicanos.*

NOTES

1. The historical material in this chapter is drawn heavily from the historical source materials cited in Chapters Two and Three [of *The Mexican Americans,* by Joan Moore] and also on Walter Prescott Webb, *The Texas Rangers: A Century of Frontier Defense* (Boston: Houghton Mifflin Co., 1935), and on Ralph Guzmán, "The Political Socialization of the Mexican American People" (unpublished manuscript, 1967).

2. Webb, *Texas Rangers,* p. 176.

3. This section draws heavily on Guzmán, "Political Socialization." See also Miguel D. Tirado, "Mexican American Community Political Organization" [reprinted here, article 7] and Robert A. Cuéllar, "A Social and Political History of the Mexican-American Population of Texas, 1929-1963" (unpublished Master's thesis, North Texas State University, Denton, Texas, 1969).

4. Article III, constitution of OSA, cited by O. Douglas Weeks, "The League of United Latin-American Citizens," *The Southwestern Political and Social Science Quarterly,* X (December 1929), p. 260, cited in Tirado, "Mexican American Political Organization," p. 5.

5. Weeks, "League," p. 260, cited in Guzmán, "Political Socialization," p. 355.

6. Mexican American voting was "managed," in V.O. Key's term. For a specific discussion of Texas Mexican American politics see his *Southern Politics* (New York: Vintage edition, Alfred A. Knopf, Inc., 1949), pp. 271-76. Key also puts the Texas pattern into the general Southern political context.

7. Letter published in the *Hidalgo County Independent;* Edinburg, Texas, March 8, 1929, cited in Weeks, "League," pp. 275-76, cited in Guzmán, "Political Socialization," p. 160.

8. The zoot suit riots were a series of racial incidents in Los Angeles during the summer of 1943–later called "race riots"–between U.S. servicemen and Mexican American youth (also called "pachuco riots"). These battles, the humiliation of Mexican Americans, ensuing mass arrests of Mexicans (*not* of the servicemen who were later shown to have provoked them) had a deep impact on the Mexican American community. It resulted immediately in a sharp increase in Anglo discriminations of all kinds against Mexicans and laid the ground for a deep anger and bitterness among the Mexican American community which had been largely impotent to deal with the situation. McWilliams gives an account of the riots in *North from Mexico*.

9. As defined by Abel, in *Why Hitler Came to Power,* as cited in Martin Oppenheimer, *The Urban Guerilla* (Chicago: Quadrangle Books, 1969), p. 19.

B. The Individual (Psychological) Base

IN GENERAL, BEFORE AN INDIVIDUAL WILL PARTICIPATE IN POLITICS, HE OR she must feel relatively secure within his environment. Insecurity, fear, alienation and loss of identity or self-esteem are psychological deterrents to political activity. In addition, before a Chicano can act as a Chicano in politics he must identify positively with a distinctive group of people. These psychological prerequisites to political action have been difficult for the Chicano to attain because of the negative attributes that the majority society has ascribed to him. Even today, negative stereotyping of the Mexican American continues. In order to counteract this portrayal, Chicanos are currently stressing the virtues of *La Raza* and defending and promoting the Chicano culture.

Donald Freeman's interviews with Mexican Americans in South Tucson demonstrate the Chicano's feeling of detachment from the U.S. political system. Also evident in his article is the attachment that the Chicano traditionally has for the Democratic party. This identification with a major political party is one of the most important psychological links of the Chicano to the American political system. As Edgar Litt has pointed out, it serves as a stabilizing or conservative force in politics and tends to preserve the political status quo.[1]

From the selections up to this point it should be clear that the experience of the Chicano in this society has resulted in a negative political socialization. This is borne out in a survey of the political orientations of Chicano children. In a measure of attitudes which favorably predispose an individual to participate in traditional politics, the survey indicates that the Mexican American ranks lower than the Anglo American child. Thus the psychological support conducive to future participation in electoral politics is relatively low among contemporary Mexican American youth.

Some Chicanos have overcome the psychological obstacles and have begun to confront the American political system in a forceful way. The recent success of La Raza Unida party in Texas, for example, seems to have given the Chicano a fortified psyche, a heightened identification with a cause and a people, and the security to challenge the prevailing American ethos. This is evidenced in the article by Armando Gutiérrez and Herbert Hirsch.

NOTES

1. Edgar Litt, *Ethnic Politics in America* (Glenview, Ill.: Scott, Foresman and Co., 1970), pp. 20–28.

4: PARTY, VOTE, AND THE MEXICAN AMERICAN IN SOUTH TUCSON

Donald M. Freeman

SOUTH TUCSON IS AN INCORPORATED CITY, COMPLETELY SURROUNDED BY the city of Tucson. The little municipality (population of 7,004 in 1960, and about one square mile in land mass) is now twenty-seven years old, and apparently South Tucsonians continue to enjoy their separate existence.[1] Incorporation was a tactic to avoid the taxes and regulations of Tucson. Over 60 percent of the population of South Tucson is Mexican American, and Mexican Americans dominate the government of the city today. . . .

South Tucson is made almost entirely of low-income people who are largely outside the social mainstream of middle-class America. The political world of such people is a limited world. As voting studies have demonstrated, most American voters live all their political lives with a limited awareness of issues, parties, politics, and governmental operations. The people who exist at the bottom of the status ladder (by whatever sort of measure you wish to use) attain a level of political knowledge far more limited than that of the mass public. Awareness of functional specialization within the world of politics may well escape the deprived and disinherited in our society. . . .

A drive through South Tucson will quickly convince a social scientist that

Paper delivered at the Annual Meeting of the Southwestern Political Science Association, March 1967. Reprinted by permission of the author.

This study was designed by the author's Graduate Seminar in Survey Research at the University of Arizona in the spring of 1966. The sample was drawn by the seminar, and the early field work was conducted by the seminar. The project was supported by the Institute of Government Research. Earl de Berge, Research Assistant in the Institute of Government Research, contributed greatly to the project, acting as field work coordinator. Carlos Felix of the Romance Languages Department at the University of Arizona translated the interview schedule into Spanish.

he is observing a distinctive sub-population in society. One strip of retail and service establishments runs right down through the middle of the city. The balance of South Tucson is probably best described as humble, simple, or marginal housing. There are a substantial number of trailer dwelling-units in South Tucson. The motels have mixed temporary and permanent residents. There are many small houses in South Tucson which would never pass the building inspection laws of a modern city, but the city should not be described as a slum and a ghetto. It is more appropriate to think of it as a predominately Mexican American enclave, with a number of substandard dwelling-units. Some houses in South Tucson that would have a very low tax evaluation are kept so well that they have a neat and attractive appearance. . . .

Relying on the three best objective measures of socioeconomic status, we can draw a more detailed picture of the social and economic opportunities available to Mexican Americans. Using occupation of the head of the household, we find that only 3.3 percent of the Mexican Americans hold white-collar jobs (professional and technical, managers and officials, self-employed businessmen, clerical and sales), while 24.2 percent of the Others in South Tucson hold white-collar jobs. The largest single occupational category for Mexican Americans is unskilled labor, 28.7 percent. Eighty-two percent of the Mexican Americans hold blue-collar jobs, compared to 63.7 percent of the Others grouping.

The opportunity to break out of the blue-collar occupational category is simply not available to the Mexican American, since the educational background to make the move has not been acquired. Slightly over 10 percent of the Mexican Americans have had no education at all, and a total of 57.4 percent of this ethnic group in South Tucson has had no more than a seventh-grade education. The lack of education at the higher levels for Mexican Americans is even more striking: no Mexican American in our sample has completed college. If you add together all categories of education from completed high school on up, you find that just under 10 percent of the Mexican Americans have a high-school education or better. . . .

Roughly one-third of the Mexican American families have a total income of less than $3,000 a year, and over two-thirds of the families earn less than $7,500 a year.

The Mexican Americans are quite aware of their social and economic condition. One fifty-three-year-old, second-generation Mexican American, who had five grades of school, was described by the interviewer in these terms:

> Respondent had strong feelings about any inequality because of race or wealth. She kept remarking about how no one cares about the poor—they are thrown into jail. And she was often not hired because she was Mexican. "But we are free and have our health, so I can't complain."

She is a housewife and a hospital kitchen aide; her husband is a laborer with Southern Pacific Railroad. For another example, a second-generation Mexican American male, forty-five years old, with one-half a year of education was described by the interviewer in this quote:

> Respondent had very strong opinions and was quite articulate, but he kept apologizing about how he talked. Said he wished he could express himself well, but didn't go to school and felt his English was poor. It really wasn't. He used some words like cooperate, etc., and used them properly. He said the fellows where he worked kidded him about how he talked. Really, most frustrated he was. Said he would like to tell a lot of people how he felt, and was glad to have this interview, but thought he still wouldn't get across what he meant. He is very bitter about government in a way. Said he used to be quite interested, but not any more—all he gets is promises and nobody will help.

In the party response section of this same interview, the respondent was asked "Is there anything in particular that you don't like about the Democratic party?" His answer speaks of his economic condition and reveals something of the operations of the Democratic party in South Tucson:

> Nothing to say against them—But, the guys after us for voting—get elected, and all that, you just talk to me and we'll fix you up—get you work—8 to 10 days a month. They never did—I went to talk to [Mexican American South Tucson Democratic Councilman]—out of work one and one-half years—losing house—sorry nothing for laborer. What's the use of voting if they won't help us—even if he is Mexican, I'd rather go for white people even if I'm a Mexican.

In sum, there is ample evidence to convince the social scientist that the Mexican American is disadvantaged socially and economically by his ethnic status.

POLITICAL PARTIES IN SOUTH TUCSON

The two great political parties in the United States are venerable institutions, with rich images and traditions which permit the voter and even the non-voter to relate through them with the world of politics. In *Political Parties and Political Behavior* this description of the mass public's image of parties appears:

> The images of the Democratic and Republican parties have remained rather stable for three decades. The Democratic party is the party of prosperity, war, creeping socialism, bureaucratic red tape, the little man, the laboring man, the Negro and minority groups generally, the welfare state, Franklin D. Roosevelt and John F. Kennedy, the South, and internationalism. The Republican party is the party of peace, responsible adminis-

> tration, depression, free economy, the businessman, the better classes, the white Protestant of English origins generally, Dwight D. Eisenhower, and Herbert Hoover, "Americanism," and cautious internationalism.[2]

The images of the two political parties for Mexican Americans and South Tucsonians generally fit rather well into research findings on the mass images.[3]

The image of the Democratic party for South Tucsonians and for Mexican Americans is quite positive. For South Tucson as a whole, 181 favorable comments were made about the Democratic party and only 49 unfavorable comments were made, a ratio of better than three favorable to one unfavorable comment. Mexican Americans volunteered 112 favorable remarks to 22 unfavorable ones, a positive Democratic ratio of five to one. Group-Related responses account for 31.9 percent of South Tucson's image of the Democratic party. Traditional ties with the Democratic party (personal, family ties or affective comment) account for 24.5 percent of the remarks, and the Domestic Policies of the party account for another 14.1 percent. It is rather remarkable that Party Leaders drew only 10.1 percent of the volunteered remarks. Government Management is a cipher in the image, evoking about an equal number of positive and negative comments, while the Democratic party's Foreign Policies are a clear liability for its image.

For Mexican Americans only, the image is even more clearly dominated by the Group-Related, Traditional, and Domestic Policy components. Slightly over 70 percent of the Mexican Americans volunteered positive remarks falling into these three categories. Only 21.3 percent of the Mexican Americans volunteered remarks falling in all the other four categories.

The image of the Republican party among people in South Tucson is much weaker in detail, and substantially negative. The number of volunteered negative remarks is greater than the number of volunteered positive remarks, 72 to 50 for all of South Tucson and 35 to 22 for Mexican Americans only. However, the negative feeling toward the Republican party appears to lack intensity—there appears to be an abbreviated or disinterested view of the Republican party. For South Tucson as a whole, the three leading components of the anti-Republican image are Group-Related (11.7 percent), Party Leaders (10.1 percent), and Traditional (6.9 percent). Only the order changes when we talk about Mexican Americans alone: Group-Related (9.8 percent), Traditional (5.7 percent), and Party Leaders (4.9 percent). The pro-Democratic and anti-Republican views are not mirror images of each other, because Domestic Policy is supplanted by Party Leaders when you move from the pro-Democratic to the anti-Republican side of the data. An overwhelming proportion of the Group-Related responses favoring the Democratic party and opposing the Republican party were couched in these terms: the Democratic party is the party of the common man, lower-income people, working-class people, and the average man, while the Republican party is bad for these groups or good for big business, the upper classes, the rich and the powerful.

More than a few Mexican Americans have no knowledge of political parties and politics—they are apolitical. One eighty-one-year-old lady who was born in Sonora, speaks only Spanish, is not a citizen, and is a widow could not distinguish between parties and government. We asked her what she likes about the Democratic party and she replied: "I am very happy in this country. I'm an immigrant and they have treated me with kindness." And some have only a limited view of the parties. For example, here are the statements from a twenty-seven-year-old, second-generation Mexican American (he had seven grades in school, works as a dishwasher in a drugstore, and there are eight adults and seven children in the household he heads):

Like about Democrats: "Some people say it's better than Republicans. I feel the same way as others."
Dislike about Democrats: "Seems all right to me."
Like about Republicans: "No."
Dislike about Republicans: "Just don't like them."

The affection for the Democratic party and the positive image of the Democratic party transcends generational and social differences among the Mexican American people in South Tucson. Below I shall quote the party responses from several Mexican Americans of different circumstances.

I. Female, forty-nine years old, she and her husband are second-generation Mexican Americans, nine grades in school, and she has voted.
Like about Democrats: "Democrats are mostly the poor people—they are more interested in helping the poor people—lots of Spanish-speaking people get jobs from the Democrats—not from the Republicans."
Dislike about Democrats: "No, nothing."
Like about Republicans: "No, I really don't like the Republican party very well."
Dislike about Republicans: "They are the party of the big fish; we are the little fish."

II. Male, fifty-seven years old, he was born in Arizona but his wife was born in Mexico, three grades of school, speaks only Spanish, has voted.
Like about Democrats: "Always provides jobs and supports."
Dislike about Democrats: "No, no idea."
Like about Republicans: No response.
Dislike about Republicans: "Yes, the Republican president in 1929 allowed the people to starve. Ever since then I have always disliked [them]."

III. Male, eighty-three years old, born in Mexico and came to this country in 1890, has been a citizen since 1946, two years of school in Mexico, retired from Southern Pacific Railroad, and has voted. Respondent speaks only Spanish.

Like about Democrats: "Democrats working man's party. Republicans for the rich. Democrats best for him because he is a working man."
Dislike about Democrats: "Nothing in particular."
Like about Republicans: "I don't like a thing. Some speak well of them, but I won't change my affiliation. All candidates promise much but do nothing. Once in office won't comply with campaign promises. All parties' candidates do this, no exceptions."
Dislike about Republicans: "Nothing in particular except they are the party of the rich."

IV. Male, thirty-eight years old, he and his wife born in Mexico, is not a citizen, is trying to learn to speak English but now speaks only Spanish, has six grades of education, he is a laborer with a construction company and has not voted.
Like about Democrats: "It's more on the side of the poor–makes a better chance for one."
Dislike about Democrats: "No."
Like about Republicans: "I don't know. The Democrats pull a little more to the side of the poor–it is convenient for one."
Dislike about Republicans: "No."

V. Male, twenty-nine years old, he was born in Mexico but his wife was born in Arizona, he is not a citizen, speaks only Spanish, has seven years of school, is a mechanic and voted in Mexico but not in the United States.
Like about Democrats: "They give more opportunities to the worker. They help."
Dislike about Democrats: "No."
Like about Republicans: "No. They don't help as much."
Dislike about Republicans: "No."

Political scientists have attempted to measure the voter's relationship with his political party in a variety of ways since the earliest voting behavior research. The most successful technique of measuring the voter's psychological relationship to his party is that designed by the Survey Research Center in Michigan.[4] The SRC party identification scale classifies the voter at one of seven points along a continuum running from Strong Democrat through Independent to Strong Republican, or, if the person completely rejects party as a meaningful concept to him, he is designated as Apolitical. Party identification, as measured by the SRC scale, is a powerful independent variable which explains a substantial proportion of a person's partisan political behavior.

The party identification of Mexican Americans in South Tucson is distinctively pro-Democratic. About one-half of all American voters are strong or weak identifiers with the Democratic party, but roughly two-thirds of all South Tucsonians are strong or weak Democrats. The Mexican Americans are significantly stronger in their identification with the Democrats when compared to either a national sample or the Others group from South Tucson. Forty-three and four-tenths percent of the Mexican Americans are strong Democrats, while only .8 percent of this group are strong Republicans. The proportion of weak Democrats to weak Republicans is 23 percent to 1.6 percent. As might be expected, given the Mexican American's background and lack of socialization in this political system, 13.1 percent of the group is Apolitical, a figure much larger than one could find in a national sample.

The voting consistency of Mexican Americans in all presidential elections reinforces the picture we are drawing of this group's attachment to the Democratic party. Thirty-six and one-tenth percent of the Mexican Americans always vote Democratic in presidential elections, compared to .8 percent of the group that always votes Republican and 8.2 percent which votes for different parties. Mexican Americans are distinctively more Democratic in the consistency of their voting than either the Others group or the SRC 1964 national sample, and they are substantially under the Others group and the SRC 1964 national sample in voting Republican and voting for different parties. The significantly large proportion of Mexican Americans voting Democratic over the years is made even more remarkable by the fact that 47.5 percent of the Mexican Americans have never voted and were thereby not included in the party voting frequency.

The extensive literature on American voting behavior that has developed in the last twenty years has revealed that party attachments for the individual voter are largely inherited from the voter's parents.[5] We asked our respondents about the voting behavior of their parents and found that 72.1 percent of the Mexican Americans either had parents who did not vote or they didn't know whether their parents voted. The socialization literature largely rests on parental party identification, not voting behavior, however there is an indication in our data that much of the party identification of Mexican Americans cannot be attributed to parental political orientation. Only 23 percent of the Mexican Americans had one or both parents who voted Democratic. As our party identification data would predict, only 2.4 percent of the Mexican Americans had one or both parents voting Republican. The Others group divides much as you would expect a low-income population to divide: 45.5 percent had one or both parents who voted Democratic, 6.1 percent had parents who voted for different parties, and 12.1 percent had one or both parents who voted Republican.

There are actually more strong Democrats, 44.4 percent, among those Mexican Americans who said their parents did not vote or didn't know whether their parents voted than there are among those who said that one or both parents had voted Democratic, 42.9 percent. This would lead us to minimally hypothesize that the strong ties of Mexican Americans with the Democratic party flow in part from the ethnic group to which they belong.

VOTING BEHAVIOR IN 1964

The most important observation one can make about Mexican American voting behavior in 1964 is that 51.6 percent were not eligible to vote and 13.9 percent who were eligible did not vote. In other words, roughly two-thirds of the Mexican Americans in South Tucson did not vote. Johnson outpolled Goldwater among Mexican Americans 30.3 percent to .8 percent. About one-fifth of the Others group was ineligible to vote and another fifth was eligible but did not vote. The Others group divided its vote in favor of Johnson, 47 percent to 9.1 percent.

If we consider the voting decision of voters only in 1964, the distinctiveness of the entire South Tucson support for Johnson is quite clear. Johnson drew 97.4 percent of the Mexican American vote and 83.8 percent of the Others vote in South Tucson. The comparable percentage from SRC's post-election reported vote from the nation as a whole was 67.5 percent. At least in South Tucson, Mexican Americans voted for Johnson about as heavily as Negroes across the nation.[6] Even allowing for an over-reporting of vote in favor of the winner in a post-election survey, this is a remarkably high level of support for President Johnson.

When voting behavior in 1964 is checked by party identification, there appears to be a clear relationship between the two variables; however, one must be very careful about interpreting these data since most of the cells in the table [omitted here] are empty or contain very small frequencies.[7] Johnson received the votes of 43.2 percent of those Mexican Americans who identified themselves as either strong or weak Democrats, 11.2 percent of the votes of persons who identified themselves as independent Democrats, Independents or independent Republicans, and none of the votes of the three persons who identified themselves as weak or strong Republicans. The persons who identified themselves as weak or strong Democrats appear to be more clearly integrated into the political system; of all the party identification categories, they have the smallest proportion who did not vote. All of the Apoliticals were ineligible to vote, as might be expected.

POLITICAL PARTICIPATION IN SOUTH TUCSON

One of the simplest measures of the voter's involvement in the political system is the voter's level of interest in politics. The low level of interest in politics on the part of all South Tucsonians is only one indication, among several which we shall now marshall as the conclusion of this paper, of their lack of integration into the American political and party system. There is no statistically significant difference between the Mexican American and Others categories; both have a low level of interest in politics. Just under one-half of both groups say that they are "somewhat interested" in politics. Roughly four Mexican Americans say that they are "not interested at all" in politics to every one who says that he is "interested a great deal" in politics. The Others group does have a substantially larger proportion saying they are "interested a great deal" in politics.

We have checked Mexican Americans against Others in South Tucson on six types of political activity. In every case the Others group has a larger proportion of persons saying they have engaged in the activity. Because of the small frequencies involved in the cells of tables under analysis, there is no significant statistical difference between Mexican Americans and Others in two of the six activities; however, the overall difference between the two groups is impressive. Only 52.5 percent of the Mexican Americans *have voted* at some time in their lives. Eighteen percent of the group have *attended political meetings and rallies.* The same proportion of the Mexican Americans, 13.1 percent, say they have *made a financial contribution to a party* and *worked for a political candidate.* Fifteen and six-tenths percent of the Mexican Americans *have tried to influence another person's voting decision,* and 2.5 percent *have held a government or party office.* The level of political participation of Mexican Americans is quite comparable to the level of political participation of southern Negroes in 1961 on three of the activities: attending meetings and rallies, making a financial contribution, and working for a political candidate. In 1961 only 41 percent of southern Negroes said that they had voted at some time in their lives, significantly lower than the comparable 52.5 percent for Mexican Americans in South Tucson.

The cause of the large non-voting population in South Tucson should be explored, since 47.5 percent of the Mexican Americans and 19.7 percent of the Others group have never voted. Some non-voting exists all through our political system, and the traditional explanations one receives from the non-voter are: illness, not old enough before, military service interfered, work interferes, or my religion forbids any political activity. Only 17.2 percent of the non-voting among Mexican Americans can be explained by one of these traditional "excuses," and the comparable figure for Others is 46.2 percent. Students of voting behavior also expect to find a segment of the public which lacks interest in politics or can give no reason for not voting; 22.4 percent of the Mexican Americans and 30.8 percent of the Others give these explanations. The largest single explanation for non-voting given to us by Mexican Americans is tied directly to the group's ethnic status; they say they are not citizens of the United States, they are immigrants and they don't relate to the system, or that they do not speak English. One of these statements explained non-voting for 41.4 percent of the Mexican American group. Another 3.4 percent are illiterate.

The research design for this study was drawn up with the expectation that Mexican Americans had been barred from the ballot box and had been victims of discrimination against them in the political system. . . . Not one indication of discrimination is to be found in our interviews. Throughout the interview schedules the respondents say they were treated well, fine, or great when they went down to register. Some respondents indicated that the mobile registration unit had come to their home to register them because they were not physically able to go down to register. In the language of one Mexican American respondent, they treated him "well—they gave him full honors—first class." The precincts which serve South Tucson overlap areas of Tucson as well and may be staffed by non-South Tucsonians, however there is excellent evidence here that registrars have not discriminated against Mexican Americans.

There is ample evidence in the data we have already presented to demonstrate that Mexican Americans are poorly related to and only partially integrated into the political system. There is every reason to expect that the Mexican American in South Tucson lacks information about the political system and that the government and its leaders are vague, only partially understood referents in their lives. We sought to test this hypothesis by including a simple political information test in the interview schedule. . . .

On five of the seven questions in the test a substantially smaller proportion of the Mexican Americans answered the questions correctly compared to the Others group in South Tucson. On the other two questions, the proportion of both groups answering the questions correctly was small, and the margin of the Mexican Americans over the Others was 1 and 2 percent. . . . Three Mexican Americans for every one Others group member answered none correctly, and more Mexican Americans than Others answered one correctly, but at each of the other levels, from two correct to six correct, the Others group had a larger percentage of its members answering questions correctly than had the Mexican Americans. . .

CONCLUSION

We have only begun, in this brief paper, to sketch the broad outlines of the political behavior of Mexican Americans in South Tucson. These sketches have been basically descriptive and comparative. Explanatory models of any level of sophistication are absent from this paper.

The picture we have drawn is of a people who are economically and educationally deprived, who see the Democratic party as an aid to the underprivileged and poor, who have a strong commitment to the Democratic party demonstrated in psychological identification with it and in a strong tendency to vote for it, and, finally, who reflect their ethnic background and lack of integration in the political system through low levels of political participation and low levels of political information. All of these components of our picture are true despite the fact that these Mexican Americans have their own city, governed by Mexican Americans, and that there is no indication whatsoever that they have suffered discrimination at the ballot box. Mexican Americans have held public and party offices at every level of Arizona state and local government, but probably not in proportion to their potential or real voting power.

Our data describe South Tucson. Do they describe all of the 3,344,000 Mexican Americans in the Southwest? We don't know. Our social and economic data have been confirmed in other studies,[8] but there has been a fantastic lack of attention to Mexican American political behavior. The behavioral sciences must, in my opinion, turn their research attention to this ethnic group. Research using aggregate data on a large scale is underway; a few small-scale studies based on survey research have been conducted; large-scale, significant research on Mexican American political behavior, using the most powerful research tools and techniques available (and of course calling on our foundations to open their coffers) is certainly in order at this time.

NOTES

1. *The Arizona Republic* (Phoenix), August 14, 1960, p. 12.

2. William J. Crotty, Donald M. Freeman, and Douglas S. Gatlin, *Political Parties and Political Behavior* (Boston: Allyn and Bacon, 1966), p. 334.

3. The section on party images follows the approach used by Angus Campbell, Philip Converse, Donald Stokes, and Warren Miller, *The American Voter* (New York: John Wiley, 1960), pp. 523–538. More directly it follows the type of analysis used in Donald R. Matthews and James W. Prothro, "The Concept of Party Image and Its Importance for the Southern Electorate," in M. Kent Jennings and L. Harmon Zeigler, *The Electoral Process* (Englewood Cliffs, N.J.: Prentice-Hall, 1966), pp. 139–174. . . .

4. For the Survey Research Center staff treatment of this subject, see Campbell, *et al., The American Voter,* pp. 120ff. The use of the party identification scale in virtually all serious work coming out of Ann Arbor is well demonstrated in their latest work; see: Angus Campbell, Philip Converse, Warren Miller, and Donald Stokes, *Elections and the Political Order* (New York: John Wiley, 1966). . . .

5. This literature is becoming too extensive to begin to list here. Certainly Herbert Hyman's work should be cited: *Political Socialization* (Glencoe, Ill.: The Free Press, 1959). . . .

6. The best source of information on the 1964 election currently available is: Philip E. Converse, Aage R. Clausen, and Warren E. Miller, "Electoral Myth and Reality: The 1964 Election," *American Political Science Review* 59 (June 1965), 321–336. For a brief discussion of the voting behavior of Negroes in 1964, see page 330.

7. See "The Impact of Party Identification," in Campbell, *et al., The*

American Voter, pp. 120–145. Our data are illustrative of behavior which squares completely with theory presented in *The American Voter.*

8. See for example: . . . Arthur J. Rubel, *Across the Tracks: Mexican-Americans in a Texas City* (Austin: University of Texas Press, 1966); Walter Fogel, *Education and Income of Mexican-Americans in the Southwest. Advance Report 1 of the Mexican-American Study Project* (Los Angeles: Division of Research, Graduate School of Business Administration, University of California, 1965).

5: MEXICAN AMERICANS AND MODES OF POLITICAL PARTICIPATION: Regime Norm Development in Chicano Children

F. Chris Garcia

THE LAST FEW YEARS HAVE WITNESSED A CONSIDERABLE MODIFICATION IN the American electorate, with perhaps the most significant change being its increased size, youthfulness, and pigmentation. Most of the newly enfranchised are young and/or "colored" due to the constitutional extension of the suffrage to eighteen-year-olds, passage of legislation such as the Voting Rights Act of 1965, adjudication striking down voter qualification requirements, and the general political activation of America's "colored ethnics"—Afro-American, Mexican American, native American and other racial minorities. Many of the most active and vocal of the ethnic minorities are youthful, as some of the older members have found it difficult to break the nonparticipant mold forged by years of political racism.

The fact that the scope of political conflict has been increased by the addition of a largely unknown element poses some provocative practical and theoretical questions. Have these heretofore largely excluded groups been sufficiently socialized to the American political system so that their entrance into the political arena will have only a quantitative rather than a qualitative effect? Will their political energies be directed through conventional channels of political expression, or will less orthodox forms of participation be the mode? Information about the attitudes of these groups' members can provide some clues about their future behavior. Their activity will have theoretical implications concerning the stability of the political system and will be of

This is a revised version of Chapter 5 in *Political Socialization of Chicano Children,* New York: Praeger Publishers, 1973, pp. 108-133.

practical consideration for the system's ruling authorities as well as for emergent group leaders who wish to maximize their political effectiveness.

Adherence to the norms of a political system is considered to have an important stabilizing effect upon its functioning. Members of a polity are expected to conduct themselves in a certain agreed-upon manner which will promote an orderly method of political activity. In a democracy these "rules of the game" include such norms as an agreement upon decision-making procedures, the behavior of a "good" citizen (e.g., interest and participation in political affairs), and a viable relationship between those in public office and the electorate. If a democratic system is to persist, it must inculcate in its politically relevant members these standards of behavior; if substantial numbers of these citizens do not learn the rules of the democratic game, their consequent political behavior is more likely to be disruptive of the system's functioning.[1]

However, while behavior congruent with a system's norms may be desirable from a systemic perspective because of its contribution to stability and system maintenance, it may be that these same normal activities are dysfunctional for some individual members of the political community. For example, members of certain ethnic groups have long participated in the conventional modes of electoral politics and yet have achieved a level of political success less than proportionate to their degree of participation.[2] The normal operating procedures of the American system have been biased against its "colored" minorities to the extent that the members of minority groups have built up negative sentiments toward the rules; these attitudes may then diminish or extinguish further normative behavior. As Michael Lipsky has stated, "[normative] behavior might lead to expressions of apathy and lack of interest in politics or a rejection of conventional political channels as a meaningful area of activity."[3]

Recent activities of various groups in this country have renewed interest in the question of whether or not their participants have been socialized to this system's norms of political behavior. Members of ethnic minorities, such as the blacks, Chicanos and native Americans, while considered almost irrelevant to the system politics in the past, are now seen to be strenuously engaged in political interactions with the decision-makers of the "outside" system. While the most dramatic of these have been in the form of protest marches, sit-ins and other forms of direct confrontation, the more traditional forms of political behavior also seem to be on the increase. Since the "colored" ethnic minorities are bound to have a substantial impact on the functioning of the American political system in the near future, an examination of their orientations toward the norms would seem to be important. Such additional information should be of interest to the system's authorities who are concerned with the stability of the system and the predictability of these groups' political activities as well as to those minority group members who seek to employ the most effective political tactics in line with group dispositions.

In this study we have examined the development of regime norms among members of the second largest non-European minority in the United States—the Mexican American. While a survey of these attitudes among adult Chicanos would be informative and should be given high priority, an inquiry into the development of political standards among Chicano youth is at least as valuable. Childhood orientations provide clues as to the roots of adult attitudes and may also give insights into the future political behavior of adult Chicanos.[4] It is also true that the recent political agitation by Americans of Mexican ancestry, as well as blacks and native Americans, is largely a youth movement.[5] Of course, the presence of attitudes in children which support a particular mode of political behavior does not guarantee that form of political participation when they become adults. However, it does indicate that children are beginning to develop certain expectations concerning the relationships between adult citizens and the political world. If children perceive adults acting in a particular manner, it is more likely that when they themselves become system participants their behavior will be guided accordingly.[6] Our study, therefore, is concerned with the political orientation of Chicano schoolchildren. We have sought to compare the attitudes of a sample group of these children with those of their Anglo classmates. The focus of investigation is upon the democratic regime norm of political involvement, as indicated by the subject's attitudes of political trust, duty, and efficacy.

PREREQUISITES OF POLITICAL PARTICIPATION

The few studies of the political behavior of Mexican American adults that do exist generally reveal that they do not participate to the same extent as Anglos.[7] Many and diverse explanations have been advanced for their lower level of political participation: that they have been discouraged by the discriminatory practices of the larger society, that they have only recently moved to the more politically vibrant cities, that their socioeconomic status is generally low, and that because of certain cultural traits—such as a tendency to accept their situation ("fatalism")—they place less importance on political activism.[8] Unfortunately, the extent of Mexican American participation in politics has been the subject of very little scholarly investigation. Even less attention has been given to antecedent factors shaping their political behavior. The news media do provide regular evidence that Mexican Americans' political participation in the larger society is on the increase.

A multitude of studies have demonstrated that certain attitudes are highly correlated with political participation.[9] Among these are political efficacy—the feeling that one can affect government through his actions; political trust—an attitude of confidence and faith in the activities of governmental officials, and a sense of political duty—the feeling that it is important, *per se*, for a citizen to participate in democratic politics. In our sample groups of Mexican American schoolchildren each of these attitudinal prerequisites to political action has been examined by the use of three attitude scales.[10]

As mentioned earlier, the presence of these attitudes in children does not guarantee that they will participate in system politics when adults, nor does it, by itself, assure support for the political regime. It does, however, indicate that they are at least beginning to acquire orientations that are congruent with regime norms.

POLITICAL TRUST AND CYNICISM

Political trust and its converse, cynicism, have been found to be highly related to political participation. If a person feels distrustful toward his public officials, it is likely that this psychic gap between them would diminish political interest and participation.[11] The adult Mexican American in the United States certainly has cause to distrust the American government. The history of contacts between the Mexican American people and the government of the United States is replete with incidents of prejudice and discrimination against these people who were brought into the American system through conquest.[12] The stipulations of the Treaty of Guadalupe-Hidalgo settling the war between the United States and Mexico and protecting the personal and property rights of Mexican Americans were largely ignored by the U.S. government. Indigenous political and social organizations were destroyed and new social, economic, and political systems were superimposed on the annexed area. Relationships between governmental authorities, particularly law-enforcement agents, and Mexican Americans have historically been abrasive. Even today this minority group's contacts with government agencies, particularly those with a great deal of administrative discretion, is characterized by some mutual suspicion and distrust. The small amount of survey evidence which is available suggests that adult Mexican Americans have a low level of confidence in the general political process.[13] Even though comparable data on the specific dimension of political cynicism is lacking, it is not unreasonable to speculate that the level of trust in government may be low. In turn, this orientation may be passed on to the Chicano child.[14]
Investigations into the feelings of political cynicism among children of other "disadvantaged" minorities have produced findings which would also imply lower levels of confidence among the Mexican American minority. Schley Lyons found fifth- through twelfth-grade Negro students more cynical than their white classmates, and Negro high-school students in Detroit have been reported as less trusting in government than white students.[15] Rural, lower-

class white children of the Appalachian region also have been found to exhibit high levels of political distrust.[16]

For all the foregoing reasons, one would hypothesize that Mexican American children would be more cynical than their Anglo cohorts.

The Political Trust Scale employed in this study consisted of two items on which the agreement or disagreement of the student was requested: (1) "I think that whatever goes on in government is all for the best," and (2) "The government in Washington can be trusted." Persons disagreeing with both items expressing trust in government were judged the most cynical (low trust). Responses to these items indicate that the youngest Mexican American children are very trusting of their government (Table 1); a majority of third-graders agree with both items. As stated, even though one might expect negative evaluations of the government's reliability from their families, this

TABLE 1

LEVELS OF POLITICAL TRUST AMONG MEXICAN AMERICAN AND ANGLO CHILDREN

Grade	*Percentage (N) With Low Trust*	*Percentage (N) With High Trust*	*Total N**
		Mexican Americans	
3	4.3% (6)	57.1% (80)	140
5	6.4 (11)	45.3 (78)	172
7	15.5 (30)	30.9 (60)	194
9	22.6 (40)	19.2 (34)	177
All	12.7% (87)	36.9% (252)	683
		Anglos	
3	6.4 (8)	54.4 (68)	125
5	8.1 (10)	39.0 (48)	123
7	15.4 (21)	30.9 (42)	136
9	21.9 (35)	16.9 (27)	160
All	13.6% (74)	34.0% (185)	544

*Includes *Medium* Levels of Trust

may not be the case, or at least other positive factors override any transmitted parental cynicism. This result might lend weight to Jennings' and Niemi's suggestion that political cynicism is not an attitude transmitted from parents to their children.[17] Their comment that "[r]egardless of parental feelings, children develop a moderately to higher positive view of the trustworthiness of the national government . . ."[18] would seem to hold true for Chicanos. Although it has been suggested that the socialization milieu of the school is an important contributor to the development and maintenance of political trust,[19] our data do not support this. During the formative years of ages nine through fifteen, when schools should be the most influential socializing agent,[20] these Chicano youth (as well as the Anglos) become increasingly distrustful of their government. By the ninth grade more Mexican American youths do not consider the government trustworthy than extend it their confidence.[21]

The effect of social class on Mexican Americans' feelings of trust in government was examined, not only because socioeconomic position is a significant factor in the formation of children's political orientations, but also because the current Chicano *movimiento* is distinguished by its working-class leadership and support. When the Mexican American students are analytically divided into socioeconomic categories, slight variations in each group's political trust is noted. At the stage during which familial influence is the strongest, i.e., at the third-grade level, middle-class youngsters express their greatest trust in government. This may reflect a less negative political evaluation by the more affluent families of these children. During the years when the mental abilities of the child develop rapidly, and when the most influential socializing agents are the school and the peers, the cynicism of both socioeconomic groups increases at a comparable rate. As they approach the age of political adulthood, the declining trust in the middle-class child levels off; however, that of the working class declines even more sharply. Since at this stage, experiences with the "outside world" are the most significant socializing factors, it is not improbable that adverse experiences as a member of an impoverished ethnic minority are reflected in this attitude.

The only comparable study of political cynicism among Chicano students revealed that ninth-grade Mexican American students differed from their Anglo and black classmates in that they were more cynical.[22] Although the study's small sample precluded effective controls for socioeconomic class, Cornbleth hypothesized that " . . . low socioeconomic status . . . may have more strongly influenced these Mexican Americans' political beliefs than did presumed cultural traits."[23] This substantially correlates with the findings of our study which demonstrates that differential levels of trust among Mexican American adolescents are partially a product of class standing. However, regression analysis[24] demonstrates that, for our total sample, ethnicity is still a better predictor of political trust than is socioeconomic class when all other variables are held constant.

Among our Chicano children, the most powerful predictor of this attitude is the degree of Spanish-language usage. This variable is based upon the relative use of Spanish and English by the child and his mother in the home. The level of Spanish usage may be the most accurate reflection of the extent to which a group is culturally assimilated. Therefore, those Chicanos who are least assimilated into the core of American culture in terms of economic status and language are the most distrustful of the system which has not yet incorporated them. Thirty-one percent of the Spanish-speaking Mexican Americans are highly trustful of the government, with a decline in support from 51 to 12 percent from the third to the ninth grade, while 43 percent of the English-speaking Mexican Americans (and 25 percent of these ninth-graders) exhibit high trust in government.

In sum, Mexican American children, as a whole, trust the United States government about as much as do their Anglo schoolmates, but the cynicism level of both groups is quite high. Children of Mexican descent do not seem to possess a low level of trust when they first contact the political system. Growing up in their particular circumstances, however, exerts a tremendous depressive influence on their level of confidence. The six-year developmental pattern evolves from majority trust in the third grade to more cynicism than trust at the ninth grade. Most distrustful are the lower-class, mainly Spanish-speaking Chicanos.

SENSE OF POLITICAL DUTY

Another attitude which can be an important requisite for participation by the democratic citizen is his sense of political duty. A citizen in a democratic society is expected to take part in political activities by at least casting a ballot.[25] While various motivations lie behind electoral participation, the internalized obligation of the voter is certainly a significant orientation.[26] Three items designed to measure the degree of socialization to the norm of political duty through electoral participation were included in the questionnaire.[27]

Mexican Americans in the United States, as a consequence of separation from the larger society, have largely retreated from "outside" politics. To the extent that they do participate politically, it has been primarily within the parameters of the barrio society.[28] Consequently, Mexican American parents might be expected to pass on these feelings of political detachment to their young. In addition, the until recently rural status of Mexican Americans plus their lowly economic position both imply sociological variables correlated with a low sense of electoral participation, making it less likely that Mexican

American youth would have inculcated in them a strong sense of political obligation to the American government.

Research on the sense of civic obligation of children of another distinctive disadvantaged minority, the Afro-American, has concluded that this particular ethnic minority has not been socialized to feel a sense of political duty to the extent of its white counterparts.[29] In fact, of the measures of attitudes conducive to political participation used in this research, political duty has been found to be the one most highly correlated with race.[30]

For all these reasons, one might hypothesize that Chicano children would be less socialized to support the regime norm of citizen (electoral) duty than would their Anglo classmates. As expected, at all grade levels Mexican American youths manifest lower levels of political obligation than do Anglos (Table 2). At both the third-grade and the ninth-grade levels, almost twice the percentage of Chicanos exhibit a low sense of electoral obligation compared to their non-Mexican American cohorts. When high and medium levels of citizen duty are combined, 87.7 percent of the Chicano students feel that it is

TABLE 2

LEVELS OF CITIZEN DUTY AMONG MEXICAN AMERICAN AND ANGLO CHILDREN

Grade	*Low*	*Medium*	*High*	*Total*
		Mexican Americans		
3	27.9% (39)	60.7% (85)	11.5% (16)	100.0% (140)
5	11.9 (20)	57.0 (98)	31.4 (54)	100.0 (172)
7	6.7 (13)	48.5 (94)	44.8 (66)	100.0 (194)
9	6.2 (11)	37.3 (66)	56.5 (100)	100.0 (177)
All	12.1% (83)	50.2% (343)	37.6% (257)	100.0% (683)
		Anglos		
3	15.2% (19)	58.4% (73)	26.4% (33)	100.0% (125)
5	2.4 (3)	50.4 (62)	47.1 (58)	100.0 (123)
7	2.2 (3)	39.7 (54)	58.1 (79)	100.0 (136)
9	3.2 (5)	28.8 (46)	68.2 (109)	100.0 (160)
All	5.5% (30)	43.2% (235)	51.3% (279)	100.0% (544)

important, *per se,* to vote, while 94.7 percent of the Anglos feel the same about the franchise. Perhaps because of the emphasis that civics teachers place on voting,[31] the belief in the significance of the suffrage increases tremendously through the school years. By the time these students are three years from voting age, 56.5 percent of the Chicanos and over two-thirds of the Anglos exhibit very strong dispositions toward the exercise of the suffrage.

Stepwise regression analysis reveals that socioeconomic class produces slightly more variation in the children's rankings on citizen duty scale than does ethnicity. The lowest socialization to this norm occurs among the lower-class third-graders within each ethnic group, there being a much larger gap between the Anglo third-graders of each economic level than between the two Mexican American classes. Among those ranking low on this attitude scale, variations in social status make less difference for Chicanos than for Anglos. The middle classes of both groups display similar patterns of an increasing sense of civic obligation. While middle-class third-grade Chicanos initially rank lower than their Anglo peers, they display a similar developmental pattern of very rapid socialization to this norm, with a leveling off at the seventh-grade level. The lower classes are slower in developing a high sense of electoral obligation and may still be increasing it in the ninth grade. Lowest in their sense of civic obligation at all stages is the Mexican American working class (34.4 percent high obligation). The combined effects of ethnic discrimination plus low socioeconomic status are apparently too great to be overcome by curricular attempts at instilling this sense of civic duty.

Partial correlation analysis also points out that the best of all predictors of orientations toward citizen duty is the degree of Spanish-language usage of the respondent. Thus, the "most Mexican" American children display the lowest sense of civic electoral obligation. Slightly over 30 percent of the more Spanish-speaking feel highly obligated to vote, while 43.5 percent of those who use English are so inclined. Because of the highly supportive results of their responses to other items in this study[32] (not discussed herein), these particular opinions of the Spanish-speakers do not reflect a greater loyalty to another political system, such as Mexico. Instead, the specific nature of the attitude being measured—the importance of participation in elections—must be taken into account. Until a recent court decision overruled the applicable section of California's election code,[33] it had disenfranchised all but those literate in English. Citizens whose language was mainly Spanish could hardly be expected to feel a sense of obligation toward a duty that they had never had the privilege of exercising. In addition, it is estimated that California contains about 250,000 permanent residents who own property, pay taxes and are subject to its laws, but who, because they do not know English, are prohibited from becoming citizens of the United States and California and therefore cannot qualify to vote. While specific data is missing on this point, it is very likely that some of the Mexican American children's parents are not themselves citizens of the United States and are thus ineligible to vote. The estrangement from the suffrage undoubtedly affects the attitudes of Mexican American parents, who in turn probably transmit their attitudes to their children. In view of this absence of attitudinal and behavioral cues supporting electoral participation, the existence of a high-level sense of civic duty in even a comparatively small percentage of children from Spanish-speaking families is surprising.

POLITICAL EFFICACY

The feeling that an individual's political activities have some effect on the political system is one of the most widely investigated regime norms.[34] Most of this research had its precedent in the early works of the voting behavior researchers at the University of Michigan's Survey Research Center, who have defined political efficacy as "the feeling that individual political action does have, or can have, an impact upon the political process . . . that political and social change is possible, and that the individual citizen can play a part in bringing about this change."[35] A sense of political efficacy has been shown to be associated with political interest, increased political participation, positive attitudes toward the political system (i.e., legitimacy), personal trust, education, and income.

The most complete analysis and discussion of children's responses to this regime norm is contained in an article by Easton and Dennis.[36] Five of the items used in previous research were found by them to have the greatest significance for childhood socialization studies, and these were incorporated in the present study to form a scale of political efficacy. Their "most important conclusion" was that children have begun to develop a sense of political efficacy by the third grade.[37] At this early age the child's image of government is quite diffused, and his responses on these items are interpreted as *projective* attitudes about the proper behavior of adults; he is learning to think about adults and politics in a manner which will influence the way he thinks about himself as he matures politically. As Easton and Dennis state: "We can . . . interpret the attitudinal component [political efficacy] . . . as a first but critical step in the child's acquisition of an orientation to political efficacy *as it relates to himself.* He is building up an emotional frame of reference or loose attitudinal structure through which he has come to think about and view expected relationships between adult members of the system and the authorities."[38]

Their article, reporting on the attitudes of a national sample of 12,000 white, middle-class students, revealed that by early adolescence most pupils develop strong feelings of political efficacy, supportive of the regime.[39] However, differences among subgroups in the American population have been found. Children from families of lower socioeconomic standing have been found to lag behind their cohorts of higher status in the development of this norm.[40] Several studies have found that black children feel less efficacious than their white classmates from an early age.[41] However, an investigation which compared the levels of political efficacy of a small sample of "Negro Americans, Anglo-Americans and Mexican Americans" in a common setting, discovered no significant differences among the groups.[42] However, all three groups in the ninth grade felt less efficacious than the white eighth-grade students of the studies reported earlier.

For several reasons, it was hypothesized that Mexican American children would manifest lower levels of political efficacy than their Anglo classmates. As reported earlier, Mexican Americans have been politically, as well as socially and economically, suppressed, with the result that their levels of politicization toward system politics is low.[43] When they have participated in system politics, their efforts have been rather ineffective as measured by favorable governmental response to their needs. The findings of low feelings of political efficacy among the children of similarly subordinated black and lower-class populations increase the probability of finding similar orientations among Chicano children. Additionally, two cultural values ascribed to the traditional Mexican American family might also depress efficacious feelings in the Chicano child. If indeed Mexican Americans do perceive themselves as subjects rather than masters of their destiny,[44] the youngster would be likely to feel less confident or unable to manage political forces. Moreover, children are traditionally relegated to a very subordinate status in the family vis-à-vis adults,[45] a position which could be carried into their later political lives. In any case the family is generally thought to be the agent of socialization having the greatest impact on the early development of political efficacy.[46]

Our hypothesis is supported by the responses of our sample as indicated in Table 3. Mexican American children initially manifest lower levels of political efficacy, and although there is a slight increase through the school years, the increase is less than half that of the Anglos. In fact, the percentage of Chicanos having feelings of low political efficacy is greater in the ninth grade than in the third.[47] Over half of the oldest Anglos feel strongly that citizens can affect their government (high efficacy), while only a little over one-quarter of the Mexican American ninth-graders concur. During adolescence some movement from medium to high levels of efficacy is evident among the Mexican Americans. However, a hard core of low-efficacy attitudes persist through the school years.

Evidence concerning the effect of social class on attitudes of political efficacy in children is mixed.[48] For our sample, when all other independent variables are held constant, social class has less effect on this attitude than ethnicity, which is the strongest predictor of all the variables. The effect that socioeconomic status does have on the orientations of Mexican Americans is

TABLE 3

LEVELS OF POLITICAL EFFICACY AMONG MEXICAN AMERICAN AND ANGLO CHILDREN

Grade	*Low*	*Medium*	*High*	*Total*
		Mexican Americans		
3	17.1% (24)	65.6% (92)	17.1% (24)	100.0% (140)
5	16.9 (29)	65.6 (113)	17.5 (30)	100.0 (172)
7	17.6 (34)	57.1 (111)	25.3 (49)	100.0 (194)
9	18.1 (22)	54.1 (96)	27.7 (49)	100.0 (177)
All	17.4% (119)	60.3% (412)	22.2% (152)	100.0% (683)
		Anglos		
3	12.8% (16)	61.6% (77)	25.6% (32)	100.0% (125)
5	13.8 (17)	43.6 (66)	32.5 (40)	100.0 (123)
7	12.5 (17)	44.9 (61)	42.7 (58)	100.0 (136)
9	9.4 (15)	38.2 (61)	52.5 (84)	100.0 (160)
All	12.0% (65)	48.8% (265)	39.3% (214)	100.0% (544)

revealed by Table 4. The third-grade Chicano of the lower class exhibits a higher level of political efficacy than his middle-class schoolmate. This may be one example of the higher rate of positive, idealistic responses given by the youngest lower-class Chicano to most items in this study. Over the next four years the number of middle-class Chicanos having high efficacy doubles and almost doubles again in the next two years. After an early dip, the lower-class Chicano demonstrates attitudes of higher efficacy at a slow, steady rate, but at the ninth grade he still lags considerably behind the middle-class seventh-grader. This rise in the efficacious orientations of the Chicano working class, after the early decline, probably reflects the influence of the school and its attempt to inculcate democratic norms. Working-class children apparently are more susceptible to such socialization by schools than those of higher economic status.[49] The trend toward increasing feelings of political efficacy is reversed among the most mature middle-class Chicanos. It may be that as they approach adult status they become more quickly aware of the actual efficacy of their people, and their attitudes begin to reflect actual political potency, as gleaned from experience with government and its agencies, rather than an abstract acceptance of a regime norm.[50]

TABLE 4

LEVELS OF POLITICAL EFFICACY AMONG MEXICAN AMERICAN CHILDREN, BY SOCIOECONOMIC CLASS (N=683)

Grade	*Low*	*High*	*Difference*
		Middle Class	
3	10.0%	10.0%	0.0
5	15.0	20.0	+ 5.0
7	16.3	38.8	+22.5
9	17.0	24.3	+ 7.0
		Lower Class	
3	18.2	18.2	0.0
5	16.9	14.5	− 2.4
7	16.9	21.3	+ 2.4
9	17.6	28.0	+10.4

The importance of membership in a distinctive culture as one determinant of feelings of political efficacy may be demonstrated by the finding that, among Mexican Americans, the variable most effecting this attitude is the amount of Spanish-language usage (or degree of acculturation) of the Chicano while among Anglos grade level is the best predictor of responses. Whether this strong effect of subcultural membership is the result of cultural value differences, family relationships, or, more directly, the greater alienation of those least integrated into the American core culture can only be answered by further investigation.

In sum, Mexican American youth feel substantially less confident than Anglos that citizens' activities affect governmental decisions. Unlike their Anglo peers, a majority of Chicano adolescents feel only moderately rather than highly efficacious by the time they are a few years from voting age. Attitudes of non-efficacy prevail through the years for a significant number of Chicanos.

SUMMARY AND DISCUSSION

Ethnicity has been seen to be a very important variable with respect to the development of support for these preparticipative regime norms. In general, although the Mexican American children trust their government about as much as Anglos do, they feel more futile about exerting influence on it and are less motivated to participate in elections than their Anglo peers. In its earliest stages, differences in orientations between the two ethnic groups are generally narrow, with the third-grade Chicanos slightly more trusting but feeling less efficacious and less conscious of electoral duty. However, later socialization produces a divergent and less positive orientation for Chicano youth, particularly those who are of the lower class and are most Mexican. The attitudinal gulf that develops between Mexican and Anglo American children as they mature may indicate that ethnic differences in political orientations may be more the product of the minority's negative experiences with secondary socializing agents than a reflection of familial inculcation of distinctive cultural values.

From the system's viewpoint, the developmental pattern of Chicano socialization toward these regime norms can be viewed with some anxiety, but perhaps mostly with a sense of relief. It is true that young Chicanos are initially much in accord with all regime norms; however, as they mature their attitudes diverge from those of their Anglo cohorts and they become increasingly alienated from the American political tradition. If political authorities were concerned with bringing several million Mexican Americans into the system, they might be disappointed that Chicano adolescents feel less politically efficacious and view elections as less important than do Anglos. On the other hand, Chicano estrangement from system norms can manifest itself in non-participation in political affairs, with the result that this minority need not be of any concern to public officials. After all, it might be an unwise risk to increase the size of the political arena when the outcome of such an expansion is at best ambiguous.[51] If governmental attempts to increase Chicano political behavior were initiated, it is possible that success would be rewarded by "abnormal" and hence threatening political behavior rather than by a marked increase in support for system norms.

Political authorities might be able to guide the direction of newly participating members through efforts toward more positive socialization experiences for the young Chicanos. The finding that their less positive orientations seem not to be deeply embedded in familial patterns of socialization but are largely the products of later experiences offers some hope. If governmental decision-makers become more responsive to the needs of the Chicano community, if visible policy results reinforce the perceived effectiveness of Chicano political participation, and if governmental agents and agencies can operate to decrease their uneasy relationships with the community, then it is likely that the youths' political attitudes will become more supportive.

The findings of this research can also have practical significance for members of the Chicano community who are striving to promote the political participation and, consequently, the political influence of Mexican Americans. Among Chicano adolescents the sense of electoral obligations and the feeling of political efficacy are both quite low, posing a strategical obstacle to political activism, at least of the conventional variety. A great effort will be necessary to encourage electoral participation. Door-to-door registration drives and similar personal encouragement will help, but much energy should be directed at practices such as gerrymandering and voter qualification requirements which have vitiated an increase in participation. In addition to stimulating traditional forms of participation, perhaps reliance on activities such as strikes, boycotts, walk-outs and demonstrations, all very much a part of recent Chicano political activities,[52] is an appropriate strategy for this ethnic group. Attitudinal as well as institutional roadblocks to conventional behavior can thereby be circumvented. Indeed, such tactics have brought more reaction from the decision-makers than members of this neglected ethnic community are accustomed to. Favorable governmental responses to these "abnormal" activities may not only result in more proportionate political influence for the Mexican American community, but, ironically enough, the perceived efficacy of such political participation may also increase support for established regime norms among Mexican Americans.

NOTES

1. As posited by David Easton, *A Systems Analysis of Political Life* (New York: John Wiley and Sons, 1965), pp. 200-204.

2. Stokely Carmichael and Charles Hamilton, *Black Power: The Politics of Liberation in America* (New York: Random House, Vintage, 1967); Chuck Stone, *Black Political Power in America,* rev. ed. (New York: Dell, 1970); Ralph C. Guzmán, "The Political Socialization of the Mexican American People" (Ph.D. diss., University of California, Los Angeles, 1970); California State Advisory Committee to the United States Commission on Civil Rights, *Political Participation of Mexican Americans in California* (Washington, D.C.: U. S. Government Printing Office, 1971).

3. Michael Lipsky, "Protest as a Political Resource," *American Political Science Review* 62 (December 1968), p. 1158.

4. While the exact relationship between children's attitudes and adult behavior is indeterminate and the subject of voluminous debate, all agree that early socialization experiences are influential. For a comprehensive summary of some literature on this linkage, see Edward Zigler and Irwin L. Child, "Socialization," in *Handbook of Social Psychology,* 2nd ed, by Gardner Lindzey and Elliot Aaronson, vol. 3 (Reading, Mass.: Addison-Wesley, 1968), 450-589.

5. Guzmán, "Political Socialization of the Mexican American People," pp. 302-305, 347-355; also, Armando Rendon, *Chicano Manifesto* (New York: Macmillan, 1972), pp. 191-215.

6. This point is elaborated by David Easton and Jack Dennis, "The Child's

Acquisition of Regime Norms: Political Efficacy," *American Political Science Review* 61 (March 1967), 25-38.

7. For example, Leo Grebler, Joan W. Moore, and Ralph Guzmán, *The Mexican American People–The Nation's Second Largest Minority* (New York: The Free Press, 1970), pp. 556-572; Guzmán, "Political Socialization of the Mexican American People," pp. 404-412; Mark R. Levy and Michael S. Kramer, *The Ethnic Factor* (New York: Simon and Schuster, 1972), pp. 77-94.

8. The subject of fatalism as a cultural trait of the Mexican American is an extremely controversial topic of debate among Mexican American scholars. Many Chicanos reject this trait as a derogatory stereotype created by a racist Anglo society. Those admitting the possibility of its existence hold that this is not an attitude peculiar to the Mexican American but rather is found among any group of persons economically depressed or subject to systematic racial discrimination. Evidence has been mustered to support all positions and much of it is presented, along with his own ideas, by David Lopez Lee, "Mexican-American Fatalism–An Analysis and Some Speculations," *Journal of Mexican American Studies* 1 (Fall 1970), 44-53.

9. Although the literature on this subject is vast, a summary of much of it is found in Lester Milbrath, *Political Participation* (Chicago: Rand McNally, 1965); and Robert E. Lane, *Political Life* (New York: The Free Press, 1959).

10. The Political Efficacy Scale (5 items) is that adapted by Easton and Dennis for use in their socialization study from that used with adult respondents by the University of Michigan Survey Research Center. Measurement of Citizen Duty is by a three-item scale modified from a Survey Research Center four-item scale. Two items devised for this study form a scale of Political Trust.

11. Robert E. Agger, Marshall N. Goldstein, and Stanley A. Pearl, "Political Cynicism: Measurement and Meaning," *Journal of Politics* 23 (August 1961), 477-506; and Edgar Litt, "Political Cynicism and Political Futility," *Journal of Politics* 25 (May 1963), 312-323.

12. These have been recounted by Guzmán, "The Political Socialization of the Mexican American People," pp. 106-170. See also Rodolfo Acuña, *Occupied America: The Chicano's Struggle Toward Liberation* (San Francisco: Canfield, 1972).

13. Grebler, Moore, Guzmán, *Mexican American People,* pp. 567-569.

14. Even though some research has shown that a particular norm, such as political cynicism, may not be a value passed from parent to child, e.g., M. Kent Jennings and Richard G. Niemi, "The Transmission of Political Values from Parent to Child," *American Political Science Review* 62 (March 1968), 169-184.

However, others have held that trust in the political system is greatly dependent upon familial socialization. Allman, for example, contends that political trust is more dependent upon primary socialization than on secondary experiences, Joseph M. Allman, "Socialization, Personality and the Orientation Toward Change" (Ph.D. diss. Michigan State University, 1968), p. 142. And a study of Appalachian children also added evidence that political cynicism is transmitted from parents to their children, Dean Jaros, Herbert Hirsch, and Frederic Fleron, "The Malevolent Leader: Political Socialization in an American Sub-Culture," *American Political Science Review* 62 (June 1968), 564-575.

15. Schley Lyons, "The Political Socialization of Ghetto Children: Efficacy and Cynicism," *Journal of Politics* 32 (May 1970), 288-304; Lee H. Ehman, "An Analysis of the Relationships of Selected Educational Variables with the Political Socialization of High School Students," *American Educational Research Journal* 6 (November 1969), 559-580.

16. Jaros, Hirsch, Fleron, "The Malevolent Leader."

17. Jennings and Niemi, "Transmission of Values," p. 179.

18. Ibid., p. 178.

19. M. Kent Jennings and Richard G. Niemi, "Patterns of Political Learning," *Harvard Educational Review* 38 (Summer 1968), 443-467.

20. According to the developmental profile theory formulated by Richard E. Dawson and Kenneth Prewitt, *Political Socialization* (Boston: Little, Brown, 1969).

21. Although his quasi-developmental data is not strictly comparable, the trend toward increasingly cynical attitudes by Mexican Americans is similar to that by Negroes reported by Lyons in 1970. The very similar pattern of development for Anglo children is also noteworthy.

22. Catherine Cornbleth, "Political Socialization and the Social Studies: Political Beliefs of Mexican American Youth," (mimeographed, paper delivered at the annual meeting of the American Educational Research Association, New York City, February 1971).

23. Ibid., p. 8.

24. Multivariate regression analysis was accomplished through the Multiple Classification Analysis computer program in the OSIRIS system constructed at the Institute for Social Research at the University of Michigan. The program measures the statistical effect of a control variable or "predictor" after adjustment for its correlations with other predictors in the analysis. For a full discussion of this technique see Frank Andrews, John A. Sonquist, and James N. Morgan, *Multiple Classification Analysis* (Ann Arbor, Mich.: Institute for Social Research, University of Michigan, 1967).

25. Milbrath ranks voting as a "spectator" activity rated only above "exposing oneself to political stimuli" on a scale of increasing levels of participation, *Political Participation,* pp. 16-22.

26. As thoroughly documented in Barnard R. Berelson, Paul Lazarsfeld, and William N. McPhee, *Voting* (Chicago: University of Chicago Press, 1954); Angus Campbell, Gerald Gurin, and Warren Miller, *The Voter Decides* (Evanston, Ill.: Row, Peterson, 1954); and Angus Campbell, Philip E. Converse, Warren E. Miller, and Donald E. Stokes, *The American Voter* (New York: Wiley, 1960).

27. The children were asked to agree or disagree that: (1) "So many other people vote in the national elections that it doesn't matter much whether or not any one person votes," (2) "A lot of elections are not important enough

for a person to bother with," and (3) "It isn't so important to vote when you know the people you vote for don't have a chance to win."

28. Guzmán, "Political Socialization of the Mexican American People," pp. 145-281.

29. For example, Ehman, "Relationships of Educational Variables"; Kenneth P. Langton and M. Kent Jennings, "Political Socialization and the High School Civics Curriculum in the United States," *American Political Science Review* 62 (September 1968), 852-867; and Alden J. Stevens, "Children's Acquisition of Regime Norms in Subcultures of Race and Social Class: The Problem of System Maintenance" (Ph.D. diss., University of Maryland, 1969).

30. Stevens, "Children's Acquisition of Norms," pp. 56-65.

31. Robert Hess maintains that civics teachers dangerously exaggerate the importance of the individual's vote as a method of influencing government. Robert Hess, "Political Attitudes in Children," *Psychology Today* 2 (January 1969), 24-28; and "Political Socialization in the Schools," *Harvard Education Review* 38 (Summer 1968), 528-536.

32. F. Chris Garcia, *The Political Socialization of Chicano Children: A Comparison With Anglos in California* (New York: Praeger, 1973).

33. *Castro v. California,* 1970.

34. Easton and Dennis in a footnote to an article on the subject list twelve books and seventeen articles dealing with political efficacy. See David Easton and Jack Dennis, "The Child's Acquisition of Regime Norms: Political Efficacy," p. 27, n. 4.

35. Campbell, Gurin, Miller, *The Voter Decides*, p. 187.

36. Easton and Dennis, "Child's Acquisition of Regime Norms," pp. 25-38.

37. Ibid., p. 31. The five items used to measure political efficacy are: (1) "What happens in the government will happen no matter what people do. It is like the weather, there is nothing people can do about it." (2) "My family doesn't have any say about what the government does." (3) "I don't think that people in government care much about what people like my family think." (4) "There are some big powerful men in the government who are running the whole thing and they do not care about us ordinary people." (5) "Citizens don't have a chance to say what they think about running the government."

38. Ibid., p. 32.

39. Also reported by Robert D. Hess and Judith V. Torney, *The Development of Political Attitudes in Children* (Chicago: Aldine, 1967), pp. 68-69.

40. As reported by David Easton and Jack Dennis, *Children in the Political System: Origins of Political Legitimacy* (New York: McGraw-Hill, 1969); Hess and Torney, *Development of Political Attitudes;* and Herbert Hirsch, *Poverty and Politicization* (New York: The Free Press, 1971).

41. Ehman, "Relationships of Educational Variables"; Langton and Jennings, "Political Socialization and Civics Curriculum"; Joan E. Laurence, "White Socialization: Black Reality," *Psychiatry* 33 (May 1970), 174-194; Lyons, "Ghetto Children," and Stevens, "Regime Norms in Subcultures."

42. Cornbleth, "Political Socialization and Social Studies."

43. Grebler, Moore, Guzmán, *Mexican American People,* pp. 557-572.

44. Arthur L. Campa, *Cultural Variation in the Cultures of the Southwest* (Denver: University of Denver, 1965); M. S. Edmundson, *Los Manitos: A Study of Institutional Values* (New Orleans: Tulane University, Middle American Research Institute, 1957); Florence L. Kluckhohn and Fred L. Strodbech, *Variations in Value Orientation* (Evanston, Ill.: Row, Peterson, 1961); William H. Madsen, *Mexican Americans of South Texas* (New York: Holt, Rinehart and Winston, 1964); Lyle Saunders, *Cultural Difference and Medical Care: The Case of the Spanish Speaking People of the Southwest* (New York: Russel Sage Foundation, 1954).

45. Olen Leonard and C. P. Loomis, *Culture of a Contemporary Rural Community, El Cerrito, New Mexico, Rural Life Studies* (Washington, D.C.: U. S. Department of Agriculture, 1941); Edmondson, *Los Manitos;* Mary Ellen Goodman, *The Mexican American Population of Houston: A Survey in the Field, 1965-1970* (Houston, Texas: Rice University Press, 1971); Madsen, *Mexican Americans of South Texas.*

46. The importance of the family to the general socialization of the child is reviewed by Richard E. Dawson and Kenneth Prewitt, *Political Socialization* (Boston: Little, Brown, 1969), pp. 105-126. When the relative influence of each of three major socializing agencies, the family, the school and the peer group, have been compared, the family has the greatest impact on the development of political efficacy. See Kenneth P. Langton and David Karns, "The Relative Influence of the Family, Peer Group and School in the Development of Political Efficacy," *Western Political Quarterly* 22 (December 1969), 813-826.

47. A study of learning models has suggested that political efficacy will necessarily decline from grade nine onward. T. G. Harvey, "Models of the Adolescent Socialization Process" (Ph.D. diss., University of Hawaii, 1968).

48. Elliott S. White has argued that social class is not a significant predictor of feelings of political efficacy among school-age children in his "Intelligence and Sense of Political Efficacy in Chidren," *Journal of Politics* 30 (August 1968), 710-731. But this contention was criticized as being the result of faulty methodology by Robert A. Jackman, "A Note on Intelligence, Social Class and Political Efficacy in Children," *Journal of Politics* 32 (November 1970), 984-988.

49. Such is the hypothesis of Langton and Karns, "Relative Influence of the Family, Peer Group and School." The effect of teaching methods on the political attitudes (including efficacy) of bi-racial classes of students has been investigated by Ehman, "Relationships of Educational Variables."

50. Allman, "Socialization, Personality and Orientation," p. 142, hypothesizes that feelings of efficacy are almost entirely the products of secondary, rather than primary, socialization.

51. E. E. Schattschneider has discussed the point in *The Semisovereign People* (New York: Holt, Rinehart and Winston, 1968).

52. Guzmán, "Political Socialization of the Mexican American People"; Rendon, *Chicano Manifesto;* and Stan Steiner, *La Raza: The Mexican Americans* (New York: Harper and Row, 1969).

6: THE MILITANT CHALLENGE TO THE AMERICAN ETHOS: "Chicanos" and "Mexican Americans"

Armando Gutièrrez and Herbert Hirsch

IF HISTORY IS A FABRICATION OF THE PAST OUT OF THE ACCEPTED MYTHS of the present, then the history of the Chicano has been misinterpreted. Commonly treated as a docile, "sleepy," minority, the history of the Chicano has in fact been a history of political turbulence and political oppression. They have been latently and manifestly oppressed. While scholars seem reluctant to brand as violence the oppression foisted upon a sub-group by the dominant culture, that oppression is nonetheless a form of systemic violence. Controlling the systemic political roles and, therefore, the legitimate use of violence, the Anglo dominated state has systematically repressed any manifest stirrings of Chicano consciousness–even in areas where Chicanos are a numerical majority. This manifest oppression is exemplified by state action of the type which has made the Texas Rangers famous. Founded in 1835 with the purpose of handling the "Mexican problem," the Rangers have been used as an internal police force to "put down" any indigneous stirrings of overt rebellion. In the late 1800's, for example, there was a saying in South Texas that, "Every Texas Ranger has some Mexican blood. He has it on his boots."[1] As late as 1966 a Chicana passes on a story concerning the melon strike of Rio Grande City, Texas as told her by an eye witness.

> When they saw the guns, the men (Chicanos attending a UFWOC meeting) put their hands in the air. They thought the Rangers . . . were drunk. They

---

From *Social Science Quarterly,* 53 (March 1973), pp. 830-845. Reprinted with permission of the *Social Science Quarterly.*

The authors wish to thank Professor David Garza and the Government 370K students who spent their time helping to design the questionnaire and gather the data.

were told to lay on the floor. They (the Rangers) were cursing them the whole time, saying they were going to kill the bastards. Then they proceeded to kick Maddaleno (Dimas, a young Chicano who allegedly committed the crime of yelling "viva la huelga" to a Ranger's face) and smashed the back of his head with a shotgun barrel. He is in the hospital in a critical condition, with a broken rib, concussion, blood clot near the spine.[2]

Latent oppression is harder to conceptualize and even more difficult to confront in the realm of political action. The historic effects of uni-lingual and uni-cultural education–while the policy itself is pursued through vigorous political action–are felt in less overtly political ways. The consequence of such a policy for the Chicano results in the destruction of the culture coupled with the concomitant destruction of individual identity. This identity crisis forced upon a subcultural people by the Anglo dominated state has severe political implications.[3] We know, for example, that an individual's sense of self-esteem is related to the way in which he views the larger world. In a political context, a person with a high sense of self-esteem, i.e., a strong sense of identity, is more likely to be interested and involved in political activity.[4] It was not, for example, until the blacks first began to organize and develop a sense of identity as a black in a white dominated society that they could begin to engage in effective, collective political action. Latent oppression is further manifested through the myth of cultural pluralism.[5] As perpetuated in the United States it would have subcultural peoples believe that it is the "right" of all peoples to engage in political activity. In fact, cultural pluralism exists on only one level. There are, of course, numerous cultural groups residing within the territorial boundaries of this country. Yet, this is not what is meant by cultural pluralism–or at least this is not what the rhetoric tells us. The melting pot concept reigns supreme. All peoples, it states, have equal access to the resources necessary for collective political action and, therefore, all have an equal opportunity to manifest their desires through participation in the systemically defined channels of political action. The predominant pattern, we submit, has been one of cultural domination. This domination destroys identity and inculcates the most repressive of nonconscious ideologies.[6] Racism, as with political oppression may be both latently and manifestly displayed. It is manifest in the case of the white bigot blowing up school buses or aggressing against young blacks on their way to a previously all white school, or through the use of the Texas Rangers to quell strikes. It is latent in the case of the good liberal, i.e., "some of my best friends. . . ." It is even more latent and oppressive in its nonconscious form; when one culture succeeds in socializing another to the extent that the other culture (usually a subculture) believes in its own inferiority and incapacity for political action.[7] Thus we have a Mexican American who states, "Most Latins don't know how to think politically. We complain and complain about what is wrong but very few of us speak up and state exactly what we want. We need to shout our demands instead of whining about our grievances."[8] The latent oppression of which we earlier spoke is manifested in precisely this way. The Anglo dominated state has succeeded in inculcalting a form of self-directed racism, or in our terms, weak self-identity. Latent oppression involves less cost to the dominant culture than manifest oppression. Every time the dominant culture is forced to resort to arms to put down an indigenous uprising it expends certain valuable resources. It is much more efficient, i.e., involves less cost, if the dominant culture can succeed in socializing large numbers of its subcultural citizenry (and for that matter dominant cultural citizenry) to believe not only that they are inferior and therefore must blindly and obediently defer to that dominant leadership, but that the subcultural members are themselves part and parcel of that dominant culture, that they are, in other words, Anglos. Thus, political activity is constrained by the Chicano's very perception of his own identity. This study seeks to examine the influence of racial self-identity upon social and political perceptions and on the implications of these for political activity.[9]

CULTURAL AND HISTORICAL SETTING

Crystal City, Texas occupies, from our perspective, a particularly important position in the history of the Chicano movement. It is the first community in which a majority which has previously been repressed by the state-wide dominant Anglo society has succeeded in turning systemically sanctioned politics to its advantage and has finally become politically what it has always been numerically—a "real majority." Thus we seek to investigate in this paper the effect of political liberation upon the political awareness of Chicano youth in one South Texas community.

The political implications of this investigation are profound. If the Chicano movement is to continue to grow it must politically socialize its young with a strong sense of "Chicano" identity. This study is a preliminary investigation to ascertain at this point in time whether this is in fact occurring.

Crystal City. For the traveler destined for the Gulf Coast, Crystal City would probably be remembered (if at all) for the imposing sign on its outskirts proclaiming the city as the "Spinach capital of the world" and for the Popeye the Sailor statue in the city's square. This small city of 10,000 has only one other distinctive feature. For Chicanos from the West Coast to the Gulf Coast the mention of Crystal City is often accompanied by a raised fist and ringing "vivas." It is here that the Chicano movement has achieved its most significant success. It is to Crystal City that Chicanos throughout the United States look for the glimmer of inspiration which keeps the movement growing.

For a long time Crystal City was much like any other South Texas community. With a four to one proportion of Chicanos to Anglos, the city's government had traditionally been run by the economically dominant Anglos. The schools were no different. As late as 1970 the School Board was made up of five Anglos and two Mexican Americans. The faculty of the school system had some 97 Anglos and only 30 Mexican Americans–this in a setting in which Chicanos constituted some 86 percent of the total school population. To be sure, the Mexican Americans of Crystal City had "taken over" the city once before, in 1963. Control was short-lived, however, and the Anglos quickly re-established their control.

The groundswell began with the 1970 elections for school cheerleaders, which were traditionally chosen by the Anglo-dominated faculty. Given this impetus, and the phenomenal amount of organization, Chicanos were able to take over the city and the school district virtually overnight. The changes which have occurred since this takeover in the spring of 1970 have been staggering. In the year following the takeover, a bilingual education program was instituted for grades 1, 2, and 3. Although no official or unofficial policy was implemented to reduce the number of Anglos in the schools, the number of Anglos in the schools (both as students and as teachers) was cut in half. Later (for the 1971-1972 school year) the Anglo student population had diminished to the unbelievable figure of 18. Anglo teachers were few; administrators fewer. Finally, Chicanos had taken over not only numerically but also spiritually. Classes were conducted largely in Spanish. Chicano culture and heritage were taught freely. Emiliano Zapata's name was heard more often than George Washington's.

At the time of the survey used in this study (May, 1971), Crystal City was in the middle of a metamorphosis that will continue to affect its citizens for years to come. The Chicanos of Crystal City seemed to have taken to heart the words of José Angel Gutiérrez, later to be elected School Board president: " . . . Mexicanos need to be in control of their destiny. They need to make their own decisions. We need to make the decisions that are going to affect our brothers and maybe our children. We have been complacent for too long." In the middle of this situation our survey was administered.

We originally expected that the effects of the Chicano political successes would not yet be completely internalized by our respondents. Hence, we thought that Chicanos would still score low on such scales as self-esteem and political knowledge.[10] After all, these Chicanos (grades 7 through 12) had spent more than half their lives in the schools as they had been run before the takeover. If one is to believe much of the political socialization literature, basic attitudes would have been formed much earlier. It was not, we thought, reasonable to expect the changes which had taken place (even as dramatic as they were) to undo the "fruit" of 12 to 18 years of exposure to Anglo domination. Moreover, the influence of the larger Anglo society could not be completely kept out. Radio, television, newspapers, and magazines continued to present to the Chicano the same messages as before. While there are Spanish language radio and television networks and periodicals, the influence from the "outside" could hardly be expected to cease or be altogether mitigated. Our expectation, therefore, based on the limited amount of work previously done on the Chicano,[11] was to find low self-esteem scores and other characteristics normally attributed to subcultural groups. At the other extreme, there were some who felt that the unique place of Crystal City in the socio-historical map of the Mexican American people would have turned the previous expectations completely around. For the "grito" of Crystal City had been cultural pride. Tired of shuffling about at the feet of the "Magnificent Seven syndrome," the Crystal City Chicano had left the place reserved for him by Anglo society (asleep under the cactus, of course) and not only set about reversing the power structure of that community but had actually pulled it off. The Chicano, contrary to popular belief, had long been "awake," but now he was finally able to use systemic politics to assert himself. Would not such a dramatic physical change (from white to brown councilmen, teachers, administrators) cause great spiritual changes? Would not this change be manifested in the minds of the student? For it was the students themselves who had precipitated the stir. They had led the boycotting of classes. They had worked night and day to get the Raza Unida party slate elected to the local offices. Therefore, it seemed equally logical that attitudinal changes would be manifested in the students. Importantly, it had not been the high school seniors, but the juniors and sophomores, who had led the "uprising." These people, of course, were still in the school when the survey was given. Expectations of high self-esteem, knowledge, etc. also seemed warranted.

METHODS

The Sample. The team of researchers gave questionnaires to all pupils in grades 7 through 12 (786 students). We have no reason to suspect an unusually high or low absentee rate on the day the survey was administered. As a result of hostility and language difficulties, we ended up with a total sample of 726.

This sample consisted of 54 percent males and 46 percent females. In approximately 86 percent of the homes the father was present. An important breakdown which was not as clear as we might have hoped was that between migrants and non-migrants. By the time of the survey most migrants had already gone "up North." Even so, based on the children's place of birth and/or places lived, we determined that some 51 percent were or had been in the migrant stream. Yet, when we tried to use migrant status as a control variable the sample size decreased to 164 and was not useful due to the number of zero cells in the resulting tables.

Regarding the education of the parents, the sample substantiated the general pattern throughout the Rio Grande Valley.[12] The model category for parents' education was that of grade school education. Some 37.8 percent of the students' fathers and 36.1 percent of their mothers had completed grade school. The next largest category were those with no education. The fathers in this group made up 22.3 percent of the sample while the mothers constituted 23.5 percent. Only 6.7 percent of all the students' parents had completed college. The majority (69.4 percent) of the sample did not know their parents' combined income. Of those reporting, 16.0 percent reported their parents' annual income as below $2,999. Of these over 40 percent ranked below the $1,000 category. Only 2.2 percent of the students reported their parents' yearly income as greater than $10,000. Parents' occupation was distributed similar to income. Most students did not know parents' exact occupation, or did not answer the question, making it impossible to use either income or occupation as control variables. Finally, the question was posed to the students as to what language was first learned in the home. Spanish ranked as the first language in 78.9 percent of the cases. This, of course, concurs with the fact that at the time of the sample Chicanos made up 86 percent of the total school population.

The Questionnaire. One of the first questions to arise when the study under consideration was conceived was that concerning the applicability of standard questionnaire methods to Chicanos. The cultural and linguistic problems seemed of paramount importance. Therefore, the help of students in a Mexican American politics course was enlisted. Many of these students were Chicanos and after a painstakingly long process of suggestion, discussion, compromise, and deletion the final version of the survey offered a combination of both standard measures (political cynicism scale, faith in the people scale, etc.) and some original and highly insightful categories applicable to Chicanos alone (part of the questionnaire was taken only by Mexican Americans). Thus, the students were asked to identify such terms as huelga, Cesar Chavez, Chicano, etc. In addition, questions were asked regarding family loyalty and ties. In categories regarding party preference, La Raza Unida party was included. Even with these precautionary measures, some of the students (particularly the seventh graders) seemed to have some difficulty in comprehending the meaning of various questions. Nevertheless, the authors are convinced that the final product offers a uniquely insightful look at the socialization of Chicanos amidst the turmoil of political change at the community level.

Chicano Consciousness. A distinction which is at the base of our hypotheses, regards that made between those students who classify themselves as "Chicanos" as opposed to such terms as "Mexican Americans," "Latin

Americans," and "Spanish Americans." In recent years the term "Chicano" (a derivative of Mexicano) has come to gain wide acceptance throughout the Southwest among those Spanish-speaking who wish to retain their culture and language amidst a society which discourages it. To be sure, many Mexican Americans not only do not identify with the term, but also regard it as degrading. But to the "militant" (be they young or old) Spanish-speaking the term signifies a unique identity and feeling which only one who has suffered the consequences of being Mexican can know. Not only is the term one which the Chicano has created himself but also one which oftens confounds the Anglo. For most Anglos do not know its origin, its meaning, or its correct pronunciation. Instead, Anglos have been most comfortable with such "acceptable" terms as Latin Americans or, more recently, Mexican Americans. Use of the term, "Chicano," much like the refusal to anglicize one's name from Juan to John, is thus in some ways an act of defiance. It signifies a pride in one's culture, heritage and language. If Anglos want to know something about this culture and its customs, they will have to do it on Chicano terms.

Because of the voltage of the term it thus seemed particularly important to make a distinction between those who preferred the other more aceptable terms and those who preferred "Chicano." Of those reporting, 48.9 percent (253) called themselves "Chicanos" while slightly less, 47 percent (212) preferred the term "Mexican American." The rest of the categories yielded a small number of responses. The significance of the distinction between self-identification as a "Chicano" or a "Mexican American" is, as noted above, our particular focus.[13] Thus, we are interested in the social and political awareness (some might wish to call it "consciousness") of the Chicano. The questions we seek to illuminate are: What is a "Chicano"? How does he view certain selected aspects of his social and political world? Finally, what are the consequences for political action of any differences in political perspective?

FINDINGS

The Social World of the Chicano Student. The link explicated earlier between self-identity and social and political perspectives of the Chicano should manifest itself in self perceptions of the possibility for the Chicano child to achieve success in the society at large. Hence, the student's perception of his social world could be expected to differ according to his own self identification as a "Chicano" or a "Mexican American." While our data are not comprehensive, they do focus on selected aspects of achievement orientation and perceptions as to the possibility of realizing these desires.

Students were asked to respond to items reflecting the rhetoric of the open society. Thus, Table 1 illustrates interesting findings.

TABLE 1

SELF IDENTIFICATION AND PERCEPTIONS OF SUCCESS

		Percent	
		Mexican American	*Chicano*
"Anyone can achieve his goal in life by hard work"			
Agree	1	51.0	52.6
	2	19.2	16.5
	3	16.7	13.9
	4	7.6	7.8
Disagree	5	5.5	9.1
Total Percent (N)		100.0(198)	99.9[a](230)
		X^2 = 2.83, gamma = .01	
"Do you think you have the same chance to succeed in life as anyone else?"			
Yes		76.7	76.7
No		23.3	23.3
Total Percent (N)		100.0(202)	100.0(236)
		X^2 = .00, gamma = .001	

[a]Percent does not equal 100 due to rounding.

There are absolutely no significant differences between "Chicanos" and "Mexican Americans" in their acceptance of this portion of the American ethos. Even those whom we expected to demonstrate greater awareness of the barriers imposed against non-white people believe that hard work will lead to success and that they have the same chance to succeed that is offered to "everyone else." The Crystal City students seem to have internalized the "American dream." Like Horatio Alger, they view the United States " . . . as a 'land of promise' where golden opportunities beckon to able and ambitious men without regard to their original station in life."[14] There are a number of possible interpretations that one could place on these findings. It is possible that the Crystal City students believe that they (the individual respondents) will work hard and therefore achieve success while others who do not work as hard have less of a chance. This strikes us as similar to some perceptions of why people remain poor. They are poor because they do not work hard. If they did they could pull themselves up by their own effort. It is also possible that the responses are ego-defensive. That is, the "Chicanos" and "Mexican

Americans" have to maintain their belief in the possibility of success in order to hang on to some sense of self-identity. A third alternative is related to the very special circumstances within Crystal City. If they could gain control of Crystal City after years of being ruled, then hard work can lead to success. However, when one travels outside the limited boundaries of Crystal City itself one's chances in the larger society necessarily begin to decrease. While we cannot substantiate any of these hypothetical conclusions, we do find, as we begin to inquire further, that aspirations and hopes for success remain high. Thus, fully 78 percent of Mexican Americans and 77 percent of Chicano identifiers believe they will at least graduate from high school. Again, this is possibly related to the special circumstances within Crystal City where the schools have, as noted previously, begun to reflect the culture of the Chicano. Yet, their aspirations remain high when we examine further educational hopes.

Crystal City does not contain a college or a university. Despite this, 85 percent of the Mexican American identifiers and 81 percent of the Chicano identifiers want to attend college and 73 percent of the Mexican American identifiers and 72 percent of the Chicano identifiers believe that they will in fact have the opportunity to do so. That these findings persist despite the economic and cultural barriers mitigating against the possibility that they will be able to attend college attests to the power of the "American dream."

The persistence of this perception in the face of overwhelming empirical evidence to the contrary, we hypothesize, leads to heightened rather than lowered political consciousness. To aspire and then have one's aspirations shattered on the sharp realities of everyday life can have, at the very least, two consequences. First, it could lead to frustration, alienation and heightened activity and consciousness. Given the Crystal City context we hypothesize that the more militant identifiers will move in the latter direction because they will be better able, as their sense of themselves as Chicanos develops, to see the holes in the dream. Their perceptions of political reality should be more realistic and they should demonstrate a greater willingness to undertake political action.

The Political World of the Chicano Student. The tentacles of the dominant ethos extend beyond social perceptions and are intimately interwoven into the world of politics. Yet, it is an over-simplification to draw a hard and fast line between the two. Political values overlap in important areas with social values. For example, the rhetoric of equal opportunity tells us not only that all have an equal chance for success in the society—defined, of course, in economic terms—but also that all are equal before the law. We asked a series of questions to ascertain whether there were significant differences between "Chicano" and "Mexican American" identifiers in this regard. Table 2 demonstrates that there are. Students who identify themselves as Chicanos are

TABLE 2

SELF IDENTIFICATION AND EQUALITY BEFORE THE LAW

		Percent	
		Mexican American	*Chicano*
"In the United States, a person, no matter who he is, is always considered innocent before the law, until proven guilty."			
Agree	1	46.5	37.4
	2	19.2	14.8
	3	18.7	17.8
	4	9.6	11.7
Disagree	5	6.0	18.3
Total Percent (N)		100.0(198)	100.0(230)
		$X^2 = 16.39, P < .01$, gamma = .23, $P < .005$	
"If you are poor or not white, you can never achieve freedom in America."			
Agree	1	11.6	18.4
	2	10.6	9.6
	3	19.1	18.0
	4	11.0	16.7
Disagree	5	47.7	37.3
Total Percent (N)		100.0(199)	100.0(228)
		$X^2 = 8.58$, gamma = −.15, $P < .02$	
"If a person has enough money, he can buy his way out of any trouble."			
Agree	1	20.7	29.9
	2	12.6	16.7
	3	21.2	16.2
	4	13.6	11.5
Disagree	5	31.8	25.6
Total Percent (N)		99.9[a](198)	99.9[a](234)
		$X^2 = 7.66$, gamma = −.17, $P < .01$	

[a]Percent does not equal 100 due to rounding.

much more likely to disagree with the classic conceptualization of the United States' system of justice. They do not believe that a person is always "innocent until proven guilty."

Chicanos are more likely to agree that, "If you are poor or not white, you can never achieve freedom in America." Similarly, they are more likely to believe that, "If a person has enough money he can buy his way out of trouble." While cynical, this is a more realistic perception of the Chicano's contact with the dominant judicial system. He is beginning to perceive that there is a gap between rhetoric and practice. The Chicano, in other words, is probably less likely to unquestionably accept the pronouncements of the Anglo society. He may be experiencing a heightening of his political consciousness.

If this hypothesis is accurate, the trend should continue to appear in measures of selected political attitudes. Table 3 does show the continuation of this pattern–and the differences between the two groups are statistically significant. Chicanos score higher on civil liberties and political cynicism than do Mexican Americans. The higher political cynicism of the Chicano is related to the cynical perceptions of the judicial process. The higher civil liberties score is not inconsistent. Heightened political consciousness should lead one to place more rather than less emphasis upon civil liberties. If one has been discriminated against all one's life, then one can easily learn the value of a

TABLE 3

SELF IDENTIFICATION AND SELECTED POLITICAL ATTITUDES

	Percent	
	Mexican American	*Chicano*
Civil Liberties Score		
Low	30.8	18.7
High	69.2	81.3
Total Percent (N)	100.0(172)	100.0(214)
$X^2 = 7.66, P < .01$; gamma $= .32, P < .002$		
Political Cynicism		
Low	1.5	1.7
Medium	48.5	34.6
High	50.0	63.7
Total Percent (N)	100.0(204)	100.0(237)
$X^2 = 8.81, P < .02$; gamma $= .26, P < .002$		

civil libertarian outlook. How else could a minority ever have the potential to mobilize their resources? The items contained in the civil liberties scale used in this study concentrate on the right of unapproved of individuals to speak out or to hold public office–in other words, to attempt to mobilize their resources. Members of minority groups with high political consciousness are able to see the need for the maintenance of such liberties.

Having established, at this point in time, that there is a trend in the direction of heightened political awareness on the part of students who identify themselves as "Chicanos," we must inquire what the possible behavioral implications of this trend are. Are students who identify as "Chicano" more likely to be willing to engage in the more militant forms of political action? The data in Table 4 suggest that they are. Asked to respond to a series of questions regarding the necessity of changing "our form of government" and means to bring these changes about, Chicano students show up as more favorably disposed toward the use of collective political action.

For example, Chicano students are more likely than Mexican American students to agree that "the best way to handle problems is to band together." Moreoever, fully 30 percent of the Chicano respondents disagree with the statement that "there is no sense in forming a third party" while only 16 percent of the Mexican American students feel the same way. Chicanos are also more likely to approve of the use of public marches or demonstrations (38 percent to 22 percent for Mexican Americans) and are less likely to condemn the use of violence as a political instrument.

In short, the pattern remains. Students who identify themselves as "Chicanos" are more likely to approve of and, by extension, engage in collective, political action. In order to achieve a more comprehensive picture of the likelihood of action we administered a series of story completion or "semi-projective"[15] tests to the same group of students. We used three similar stories[16] involving encounters between the police and another person. The stories read the same except that in the first story the culprit was Juan Gonzalez, in the second he was called John Grant, and in the third Beulah Johnson. The purpose of such tests is to allow the respondents to project their own feelings into the contrived situation. In this particular case we hypothesized that students who identified themselves as "Chicanos" would project much more militant emotions into the story than would students who called themselves "Mexican Americans." We were not disappointed for the results provided corroboration of the data previously presented. Thus, following the coding method originated by Greenstein and Tarrow, we separated the responses into three separate dimensions: Initial definition of the situation, outcome of the episode, and norms governing the encounter.

"Chicano" students were more likely to define the situation with regard to the encounter between Juan Gonzalez and the police as involving racial discrimination than were the Mexican American students (16 percent of the

TABLE 4

RACIAL IDENTIFICATION AND THE USE OF COLLECTIVE ACTION

		Percent	
		Mexican American	*Chicano*
"The best way to handle problems is to band together with people like yourself to help each other out."			
Agree	1	41.2	49.6
	2	32.2	24.3
	3	17.6	13.5
	4	6.0	5.6
Disagree	5	3.0	7.0
Total Percent (N)		100.0(199)	100.0(230)
		X^2 = 8.39; gamma = −.08	
"There is no sense in forming a third party to get new laws passed."			
Agree	1	16.9	15.4
	2	21.0	22.0
	3	32.8	20.7
	4	12.8	12.3
Disagree	5	16.5	29.5
Total Percent (N)		100.0(195)	99.9[a](227)
		X^2 = 13.75; $P < .01$; gamma = .13; $P < .03$	
"The best way to get government officials to do something is to organize a public demonstration or march."			
Agree	1	22.5	37.6
	2	18.0	20.5
	3	34.5	26.6
	4	11.0	7.9
Disagree	5	14.0	7.4
Total Percent (N)		100.0(200)	100.0(229)
		X^2 = 15.98; $P < .01$; gamma = −.28; $P < .001$	

TABLE 4 cont.

RACIAL IDENTIFICATION AND THE USE OF COLLECTIVE ACTION

"No matter how bad things may get, one should have faith in our government and never resort to violence."			
Agree	1	32.1	22.1
	2	19.4	20.4
	3	27.6	20.4
	4	10.7	18.1
Disagree	5	10.2	19.0
Total Percent (N)		100.0(196)	100.0(226)

$X^2 = 15.69$; $P = .01$; gamma $= .22$; $P < .001$

Chicano respondents and 6 percent of the Mexican American respondents perceived racial discrimination). On the other hand, 26 percent of the Mexican American students replied simply that the police were doing their job, while only 12 percent of the Chicano students responded in this vein. It is evident that students who identify themselves as "Chicano" are more suspicious of the authority structure of the Anglo society. They are more likely to perceive the subtle institutional forms of discrimination and racism than are students who identify as "Mexican Americans."

When we turn our attention to the respondents' projections regarding the "outcome of the episode" we find a similar pattern. While a large percentage of both types of identifiers perceive the Chicano as being punished (74 percent of the Mexican American students and 83 percent of the Chicano students) the trend is more evident when the stimulus on the story is shifted from Juan Gonzalez to John Grant. In the case where the Anglo is stopped by the police 46 percent of the Mexican American identifiers finished the story by hàving the officer give a ticket to Mr. Grant, while only 29 percent of the Chicano identifiers answered in this way. Students who identify as Chicanos are again less likely to accept the equality before the law argument. They perceive that a white person who is stopped by the police is less likely to be punished than a Chicano. Further evidence can be found in the fact that when the stimulus is shifted to Beulah Johnson 52 percent of the Mexican Americans see the woman as being punished while only 32 percent of the Chicano identifiers noted the same phenomena. As we noted earlier, most of the respondents did not perceive Beulah Johnson as a black woman–they only perceived the sexual dimension. The higher political cynicism or realism of the Chicano identifiers is reflected in that they are more likely to believe that a woman will have a greater chance to get away with speeding than a Chicano. They have, in other words, a less idealized conception of the role of the police. Call it cynicism or a realistic appraisal of the American ethos. Whatever the label, students who are in the process of developing their identity as "Chicano" are more likely to perceive the existence of discrimination.

The last dimension analyzed dealt with the students' projection of norms governing the episode. Again we find Chicano identifiers as more likely to perceive "racial inequality" in the case of Juan Gonzalez than Mexican American identifiers (18 percent of Chicano identifiers as compared to no Mexican American identifiers). Moreover, in the John Grant story Chicano students tended to project that the "Anglo is above the law" (17 percent as compared to 8 percent of Mexican American students). The results of the semi-projective tests are best summarized by the perception of who gets fined. As Table 5 demonstrates, students who identify themselves as "Chicano" are more likely to project a higher fine for Juan Gonzalez than for John Grant or Beulah Johnson. They are also less likely than Mexican American identifiers to project an equal fine for all those stopped by the police. In conclusion, the results of the semi-projective tests corroborate our earlier data on political orientations. Students who identify themselves as Chicanos are more likely to perceive inequality and to project these perceptions in their answers. They are, in other words, more acutely aware of the subtle institutional forms of discrimination and they are more likely to be willing to take direct action to bring about political change.

TABLE 5

SELF IDENTIFICATION AND FINE IMPOSED IN STORY COMPLETION

	Percent	
	Mexican American	*Chicano*
Higher fine for Mexican	37.4	63.6
Higher fine for Anglo	2.6	1.4
Higher fine for Woman	7.0	2.9
All same	37.4	24.3
No fine	15.6	7.8
Total Percent (N)	100.0(115)	100.0(140)

$X^2 = 18.03; P < .01; \text{gamma} = -.40; P < .001$

CONCLUSION

While our data do not enable us to make before and after comparisons between students who self identify as "Chicano" or "Mexican American," we have been able to provide a preliminary description of the differing levels of political consciousness at this point in time.

While the Chicano students of Crystal City do not differ from those who self identify as Mexican American in their perceptions of the American dream, particularly regarding their own possibility for success in this society, the results on the political dimension do form a defineable trend. Crystal City students who self identify as "Chicano" tend to have a higher level of political consciousness than students who self identify as "Mexican Americans."

This higher level of political awareness is manifested by Chicano identifiers in that they are much less likely to unquestioningly accept the usual clichés regarding equality before the law and justice in America. Their level of political cynicism is higher than that of Mexican American identifiers and so are their civil liberties scores. Chicano students, moreoever, express greater readiness to engage in the various forms of collective political action, i.e., marches, demonstrations and the formation of third parties, and they are less likely to reject the use of violence to achieve political ends. Chicano identifiers, as noted in the results from the semi-projective tests, are more likely to be sensitive to the more subtle institutional forms of discrimination. In other words, Chicano identifiers no longer feel that they are at the mercy of their environment. They have begun to develop a sense of identity and a sense that they can control their environment—especially their political environment.

These findings have, it seems to us, important historical-political consequences. If the heightened Chicano consciousness manifested by self-identification as a "Chicano" is a result of the political success of La Raza Unida party in Crystal City, then as Chicanos tend to consolidate their gains, as their successes extend outward into realms other than the political, their social consciousness should also undergo radical revision. Moreover, the continued success should tend to decrease the number of students who identify themselves as "Mexican Americans." This decrease should then manifest itself in further developing the level of political consciousness among Crystal City Chicanos.

Implications such as these extend beyond the territorial boundaries of Crystal City. As Chicanos begin to experience political success in other parts of the country their sense of identity will probably undergo a process comparable to that which we have seen in Crystal City. A strong sense of self leading one to identify oneself strongly with one's cultural-racial group will increase the number of Chicano identifiers and will, therefore, steadily increase political awareness. This awareness should then result in greater political activity. In other words, we have not heard the last from the Chicano movement—we may only have seen the beginning.

NOTES

1. Stan Steiner, *La Raza: The Mexican Americans* (New York: Harper & Row, 1969), pp. 360–377.

2. See Arthur J. Rubel, *Across the Tracks: Mexican-Americans in a Texas City* (Austin: University of Texas Press, 1966) for some vivid personal accounts of the vigilante actions of the Texas Rangers. Also see W. P. Webb, *The Texas Rangers* (Boston: Houghton Mifflin Co., 1935).

3. Robert L. Derbyshire, "Adolescent Identity Crisis in Urban Mexican-Americans in East Los Angeles," in Eugene B. Brady, ed., *Minority Group Adolescents in the United States* (Baltimore: The Williams and Wilkins Co., 1968), pp. 73–110.

4. Morris Rosenberg, *Society and the Adolescent Self-Image* (Princeton: Princeton University Press, 1965), pp. 256–260. The literature on self-esteem is voluminous. For a review of some of the literature on internal and external control, see Julian B. Rotter, "External Control and Internal Control," *Psychology Today,* 5 (June, 1971), pp. 37–42+. Also see the bibliography to this article.

5. Octavio Ignacio Romano-V, "The Anthropology and Sociology of the Mexican Americans," in Octavio Ignacio Romano-V, ed., *Voices: Readings from El Grito* (Berkeley, Calif.: Quinto Sol Publications, Inc.), pp. 26–39.

6. Daryl J. Bem, *Beliefs, Attitudes and Human Affairs* (Belmont, Calif.: Brooks/Cole Publishing Co., 1970), pp. 89–99, defines a nonconscious ideology as "a set of beliefs and attitudes which he accepts implicitly but which remains outside his awareness because alternative conceptions of the world remain unimagined," p. 89.

7. See Louis Knowles and Kenneth Prewitt, *Institutional Racism in America* (Englewood Cliffs, N.J.: Prentice-Hall 1969).

8. William Madsen, *Mexican Americans of South Texas* (New York: Holt, Rinehart and Winston, 1964), p. 110.

9. Our analysis is, of course, constrained because we are unable to make before and after comparisons. Since we were unable to get access to the Crystal City schools until after Chicanos dominated the school board we are unable to say how much of the process we are investigating is the direct result of that political action.

10. For studies using these variables in other cultures see: Dean Jaros, Herbert Hirsch, and Frederick J. Fleron, Jr., "The Malevolent Leader: Political Socialization in an American Sub-Culture," *American Political Science Review,* 62 (June, 1968), pp. 564–575; Herbert Hirsch, *Poverty and Polit-*

icization: Political Socialization in an American Sub-Culture (New York: The Free Press, 1971). There has been a recent increase in the number of good articles on the political socialization of blacks. See, for example, Edward Greenberg, "Children and Government: A Comparison Across Racial Lines," *Midwest Journal of Political Science,* 14 (May, 1970), pp. 249–275; and Schley R. Lyons, "The Political Socialization of Ghetto Children: Efficacy and Cynicism," *Journal of Politics,* 32 (May, 1970), pp. 288–304.

11. Derbyshire, "Adolescent Identity Crisis"; Madsen, *Mexican Americans of South Texas;* Celia S. Heller, *Mexican American Youth: Forgotten Youth at the Crossroads* (New York: Random House, 1968); Anthony Dworkin, "Stereotypes and Self-Images Held by Native-Born and Foreign-Born Mexican-Americans," in John H. Burma, ed., *Mexican-Americans in the United States* (Cambridge, Mass.: Schenkman Publishing Co., 1970), pp. 397–409.

12. United States Commission on Civil Rights, *Mexican-American Study Report #1: Ethnic Isolation of Mexican Americans in the Public Schools of the Southwest* (Washington, D.C.: U.S. Government Printing Office, 1971).

13. Alfredo Cuellar, "Perspective on Politics," in Joan W. Moore, *Mexican Americans* (Englewood Cliffs, N.J.: Prentice-Hall, 1970), pp. 137–156 [reprinted as articles 3 and 30 of this volume].

14. Ely Chinoy, *Automobile Workers and The American Dream* (Garden City, N.Y.: Doubleday & Company, 1955), p. 1.

15. The tests we devised were based upon the work of Greenstein and Tarrow. See Fred I. Greenstein and Sidney Tarrow, *Political Orientations of Children: The Use of a Semi-Projective Technique in Three Nations* (Beverly Hills, Calif: Sage Publications, 1970).

16. The directions and stories read as follows: In answering the following questions you will have to use your imagination. This is not a test and there are no right or wrong answers. You will read the beginning of a story, and then you can finish it in any way you want. Simply imagine how the story would end. Do you understand? It is up to you to decide how to finish the stories and it doesn't matter what answers you give.

1. Juan Gonzalez was driving to work one morning. Since he was late he drove faster than the speed limit. A policeman stopped him. FINISH THE STORY.
2. John Grant was driving. . . .
3. Beulah Johnson was driving. . . .

(We originally conceived that Beulah Johnson would be perceived as a black woman. Most of our respondents, however, simply perceived the sexual dimension.)

C. The Organizational Base

IN HIS TEXT ON ETHNIC POLITICS, EDGAR LITT STATES: "THE PERSISTENCE of American ethnic politics can be traced in part to the activities of organizations capable of mobilizing ethnic sentiments for political objectives."[1] In this section we will examine three of the major organizational bases of Chicano politics: 1) the voluntary association or mutual aid organization, 2) the political party, and 3) the Catholic Church.

Ethnic associations or *mutualistas* have played a very important role in the development of Chicano politics. Contrary to popular belief, the American of Mexican ancestry has throughout his history established organizations for the purpose of rendering assistance both psychological and material. Miguel Tirado refutes the oft-asserted contention that Mexican Americans, unlike other ethnic groups, have not formed political organizations to advance their interests. Although Chicano organizations throughout history have served political purposes, their multifunctional nature has sometimes obscured this fact.

The political party most important to the Chicano up to this stage has been the Democratic party. The Mexican Americans' affinity for the Democrats is documented in the article by McCleskey and Merrill. These investigators show that in Texas (as is also true in the other states of the Southwest) Mexican Americans offer widespread, if somewhat shallow, support for the Democratic Party. The authors also observe that Texas Chicanos thus have a good opportunity to use party politics to help advance *La Causa.* Finally, the well known Chicano leader César Chávez, offers his observations on the important contributions that religious organizations and various religious leaders have made to his part in the Chicano movement.

NOTES

1. Edgar Litt, *Ethnic Politics in America* (Glenview, Ill. Scott, Foresman and Co., 1970), p. 42.

7: MEXICAN AMERICAN COMMUNITY POLITICAL ORGANIZATION
"The Key to Chicano Political Power"

Miguel David Tirado

A COMMON ASSUMPTION OF MUCH OF THE PAST STUDY OF THE MEXICAN American minority has been the belief that this ethnic group is politically apathetic and complacent with respect to participation in community organizations. Such eminent scholars as William D'Antonio and William Form, for example, have concluded that "the Spanish-name community has developed relatively few voluntary organizations. . . ." They argue that this phenomenon is a consequence of the group's low socio economic level and its low levels of internal social integration.[1] This view is also shared by some Mexican Americans concerned with the question of political organization in the Mexican American community. In a letter to the Chairman of the Equal Employment Opportunity Commission, a former Executive Director of the National G. I. Forum, Ed. Idar Jr., argued that "over the centuries, by culture, by history, and even by his own religious convictions, the Mexican American has been 'brainwashed' into a sense of futility, docility, and resignation." "For these reasons, and others," he concludes, "the Mexican American has suffered from lack of leadership."[2]

The intent of this article is first to evaluate these assumptions of Mexican American apathy in the context of community political organization by briefly reviewing the history of Mexican American organizational behavior particularly in the State of California since the beginning of the mass Mexican migration to this country around 1910. Particular attention will next be given to questioning the assumption of D'Antonio, Form, and others that "unlike ethnic groups in northern and eastern cities, the Spanish surname population

Reprinted from *Aztlan: Chicano Journal of the Social Sciences and the Arts,* Vol. 1, No. 1 (Spring 1970), pp. 53-78. Reprinted with permission of the author.

had not formed clubs which could serve their political interests."[3] A counter hypothesis, in turn, will be offered which suggests that many Mexican American community organizations, although not manifesting the traditional attributes of a politically-oriented body, have served a vital function in advancing the political interests of the Mexican American minority, and may therefore be referred to as community political organizations.

The third objective of this essay is to scrutinize the nature of some of those Mexican American community political organizations which have grown faster and persevered longer than others in order to isolate those ingredients which tend to promote stability and vitality in a Mexican American political organization. It is no secret that Mexican American organizational efforts in the past have been characterized by their general inability to create politically concerned community organizations which can continue to thrive once the issue of crisis motivating their original formation has passed. Yet, as Saul Alinsky notes in the following quote, the need for permanent politically concerned bodies in the community is crucial if the minority is to permanently improve its political and economic status relative to the dominant groups in society.

> Recruits without organization, however, are meaningless. That's the basic plague of the civil rights struggle. No one can distinguish between a movement and an organization. You have a march and a lot of speeches, then it pisses out—that's a movement. The operation was a success but the patient died. An organization keeps on growing, keeps on making trouble, keeps on chipping away to get what it wants.[4]

Hopefully the ensuing historical analysis of past Mexican American efforts at community organization will offer some clues on how the current growing political ferment in the Mexican American community can be oriented toward fomenting a solid organizational foundation upon which to establish a constant source of political influence.

1900–1940

Some of the earliest organizations formed by the Mexican community in the United States were mutual benefit and protective associations whose functions were similar to those served by the mutual aid societies set up by earlier immigrant groups to this country. By pooling their meager resources the Mexican immigrants learned they could provide each other with low cost funeral and insurance benefits, low interest loans and other forms of economic assistance. As Paul Taylor notes, these same mutual aid societies called "mutualistas" also provided "a forum for discussion and a means of organizing the social life of the community."[5]

It was in this capacity that several of these early Mexican "mutualistas" assumed a degree of political awareness and concern for social action. One of the best examples of this was the *Alianza Hispanoamericana* and the early activities of its "founder lodge" organized toward the end of the last century in Tucson, Arizona. As Manuel Gamio indicates, "its aims were very clearly political" since its objective was to replace the Texans in control of Tucson politics at the time with native Tucson residents of Mexican descent.[6] After succeeding in this endeavor, it subsequently assumed a primarily mutual aid function with some 275 lodges throughout the Southwest.

Another early example of how many of the Mexican "mutualistas" evolving during the first twenty years of this century took a real interest in social action is the Lázaro Cárdenas Society organized by members of the Los Angeles Mexican community soon after World War I. In addition to providing low rate insurance benefits for the community, Richard Thurston notes that "it also held meetings to discuss and take action on community issues such as the lack of school buses and of other facilities."[7] Recognizing that the municipal facilities available to them were inferior to those found elsewhere in the city, these Mexicans also realized that community organization for social action was the only way to have their grievances remedied.

A similar conclusion was reached about the same time by another group of Mexican immigrants in Kansas City. Faced with the threat of expatriation following the War, the Mexican "colonia" organized a *Liga Protectora Mexicana* to protect the right of residence concomitant with their legal immigrant status. The *Liga Protectora* was a grass roots organization in structure serving during the short two years of its existence a series of functions ranging from finding jobs for the unemployed to providing food and clothes for the needy. With the end of the post-war depression which had provoked the threat of expatriation, the organization lost its major reason for existence and dissolved in 1923.[8]

Although, initially there was a concern for social action and politics among many of the early examples of Mexican community organization in this country, their major concern was providing fundamental social and economic benefits for their members while offering a focal point for entertainment and social activity in the Mexican American community. Cognizance of their minor concern for politics should not lead one to underestimate the importance of such mutual aid societies as *La Alianza Hispano Americana, La Sociedad Progresista Mexicana, Comité de Beneficiencia Mexicana,* and the *Sociedad Unión Cultural Mexicana* in the history of the Mexican minority. For, as Paul Taylor points out, "these societies represent the only continuous organized life among the Mexicans in which the initiative comes wholly from the Mexicans themselves. . . ."[9] In addition, due to their size and popularity they offer a potential source of great political strength in the Mexican community.[10]

ORDEN HIJOS DE AMERICA

Although many of the "mutualistas" in their inceptions participated somewhat in social action and politics, a growing number of Mexican community leaders in the 1920's began to realize that more specialized organizations were needed if the Mexican Americans' interests were to be well defended in American society. One of the first signs of this awakening arose in San Antonio, Texas, where a small group of Mexican American community leaders in 1921 organized the *Orden Hijos de America* (Order Sons of America). Unlike the "mutualistas" which were open to United States citizens and non-citizens alike, the Orden restricted its membership exclusively to "citizens of the United States of Mexican or Spanish extraction, either native or naturalized."[11] This limitation of membership to American citizens indicated a growing realization by Mexican American leaders that political power is essential for the achievement of the minority's aims in this country, and that political power only arises with the organization of a solid voting bloc of citizens. This awakening was evident in the Orden's Declaration of Principles where the founders asserted that members should "use their influence in all fields of social, economic, and political action in order to realize the greatest enjoyment possible of all the rights and privileges and prerogatives extended by the American Constitution."[12]

The Orden's activities, however, were not limited to voter registration but also involved direct political action. One of its earliest acts in the Corpus Christi area, according to Paul Taylor, "was to seek opportunities for qualified Mexican Americans to serve on juries." Previous to this action Spanish-surnamed citizens were automatically dropped from the eligible lists without ever being summoned. As one of the Orden leaders explained, "the first thing we did was to write a request that we be admitted to the jury. I had noticed that in court cases, Mexicans were sent to jail for offenses for which Americans were given suspended sentences or let off."[13]

Due to this political awakening and their successful efforts in remedying the above such inequities, the Orden succeeded by 1928 in establishing seven councils with its most politically active branches located in Corpus Christi and San Antonio. Unfortunately, an organizational split soon developed which was to characterize many subsequent Mexican American political organizations. The division arose over the dissatisfaction of the two more activist councils with the other slower moving elements of the Orden. The result was the secession of the Corpus Christi and San Antonio Councils and their founding of what later was to become the League of United Latin American Citizens.

LEAGUE OF UNITED LATIN AMERICAN CITIZENS (LULACS)

Established in 1929 as the League of United Latin American Citizens, LULACS was originally intended to incorporate the Orden Hijos de América and other interested Corpus Christi and San Antonio Mexican organizations into a single united body of concerned Mexican American citizens. Because of the reluctance of the Orden Hijos de América to subordinate itself to a younger organization, however, LULACS was forced to establish an entirely new membership composed of "native born or naturalized citizens eighteen years of age or older, of Latin extraction." While framing its first Constitution on the general model of the Orden Hijos de América, LULACS placed much more emphasis on their members' absorption into American society and on their commitment to improving the political and economic position of the Mexican American community.

The first LULACS Constitution makes explicit in its first article that a major aim of the organization is "to develop within the members of our race the best, purest and most perfect type of a true and loyal citizen of the United States of America." The Organization's founders simultaneously committed its members and their families to total assimilation into American society, believing that "in order to claim our rights and fulfill our duties it is necessary for us to assimilate all we can that is best in the new civilization amidst which we shall have to live."[14] Toward this end, the Constitution stipulated that English would be the official language of LULACS and each member must pledge himself "to learn and speak and teach same to our children."

This talk of assimilation was facilitated by the fundamentally middle class nature of the membership, which at that time was the only element of the Mexican community that tended to be American citizens anyway. LULACS decision not to become a grassroots based organization, however, was a conscious one in the belief that the entire Mexican American community would be better served if LULACS "remained a small concentrated group unified in purpose and better fitted to fight the battles of the less fortunate."[15] This argument was also predicated on the belief that by remaining middle class and elitest LULACS could do more to reduce the stereotype that many Anglo-Americans held of Mexican Americans as "foreigners" and "unpatriotic."

In spite of this elitest approach to the organization's membership, LULACS from its inception displayed a sincere concern for the well-being of the less fortunate Mexican Americans. This concern led the various LULACS Councils to take an interest in political issues affecting the Mexican American community even though its first Constitution expressly stated that "this Organization is not a political club." The succeeding paragraph in Article II of the LULACS Constitution, however, defends the membership's involvement in politics by advocating that "with our vote and influence we shall endeavor to place in public office men who show by their deeds, respect and consideration for our people."

The apparent contradiction in the above two proclamations of the LULACS Constitution is explicable if one takes into consideration the negative connotation which the term "politics" held and to a certain degree still holds for many Mexican Americans. One explanation for the Mexican American's reticence to refer to their organization's activities as political may be the legacy of disillusionment with politics stemming from the Mexican immigrant's political experiences prior to leaving Mexico. The memory of political corruption and instability in Mexico which provoked many to leave their homeland was so deeply ingrained in their psyches that it was only natural these early immigrants carry this abhorrence for politics with them and transmit it on to their offspring. It is no wonder then that one of the early leaders of LULACS, Alonso Perales, defined a political organization in the following terms:

> If a political organization is understood to be an association of unscrupulous individuals whose sole intention is to elevate to and maintain in public power some leader for the sole purpose of dividing with him the crumbs or scraps of the spoils of office, then our organization is not political.[16]

Although local LULACS Councils are to be found in 21 states of the Union, the organization's strength lies primarily in Texas, the state of its origin. Here efforts have been made to involve the entire family in LULACS activities by means of Ladies' Auxiliaries along with special programs and benefits for the young. The most celebrated of these LULACS Youth Service Programs was their summer school for Texas preschool children which many view as the precursor of the War on Poverty's Head Start program in the Southwest.

Although intended to be a national Organization, LULACS has been less successful in instituting comprehensive community action programs in other states where Councils have been established. Due in part to a lack of sufficient supportive funds and the competition with other Mexican American organizations, California LULACS, organized since 1947, has been slower than some other groups to implement community action programs. Its lack of tight organizational unity, however, has also served to discourage the rise of dictatorial leadership cults by any individual or group of individuals so characteristic of many other Mexican American organizations. The nature of LULACS, nevertheless, is rapidly changing with its co-sponsorship of Operation Service, the federally funded War on Poverty program in the Southwest. For new demands have been placed on LULACS recently both to coordinate its local councils' activities more effectively and to take a more active role in promoting community action programs. One only hopes that these new pressures for change will not unleash in LULACS the same forces of disunity which were seen in the Orden Hijos de América and in such subsequent organizations as the Mexican Congress.

MEXICAN CONGRESS

Organized in 1938 as a federation of Mexican American organizations in the Southwestern states, the purpose of the Mexican Congress was to work for "the economic and social and cultural betterment of the Mexican people, to have an understanding between the Anglo-Americans and Mexicans, to promote organizations of working people by aiding trade unions and to fight discrimination actively."[17] While its efforts in the Southern California area were directed primarily at reducing discrimination, it also took an active interest in politics. The Mexican Congress was instrumental in the Los Angeles Mexican community's unsuccessful attempt to get one of their own, Ed Quevedo, elected to the Los Angeles City Council before the war.

Although at its peak of activity, the Mexican Congress boasted a membership of 6,000, its popularity soon waned until its total disappearance during the Second World War. One reason given for its short existence was disagreement over the major functions of the Congress with the older membership criticizing the organization's activities for being too politically radical.[18] The more basic cause for its demise, however, lay in the fundamentally Mexico-oriented perspective retained by much of the Mexican minority in the Southwest up until World War II. As recent immigrants to the United States, many of them expected ultimately to return to Mexico and had little interest in establishing permanent affiliations with groups in this country. John Burma notes that even many of those who had lived in the United States for twenty years continued to think of themselves as "Mexicans temporarily in the United States."[19]

Some reasons for the persistence of the Mexican community's identification with Mexico and reluctance to establish permanent organizational ties in this country were the geographic proximity of the Mexican "colonias" to the old country and the ease with which the Mexican pattern of life could be preserved in the Southwestern States up until the War. A third reason was the growing atmosphere of hostility in the Southwest against Mexicans fostered by the apprehensions of many Americans about the growing numbers of Mexican immigrants inhabiting the area. This hostility ultimately reached its peak in the 1930's with the repatriation of 500,000 Mexican residents of the Southwest, many of whom were born in the United States and eligible for citizenship.

1940-1970

During the warm days of June, 1943, a sequence of events occurred which exposed the poor condition of community organization and the lack of effective leadership in the Mexican American community of Los Angeles. The events were the Zoot Suit Riots in which Mexican American youth and servicemen clashed in the streets of East Los Angeles climaxing in a full fledged riot and the threat of massive reprisals against the Mexican American minority. In the months following the riots great attention was focused on the problems of the Mexican American minority in an effort to determine and remedy the causes of the disturbances. Organizations both public and private undertook programs to aid the long-neglected Mexican American youth.

When efforts were made to contact the leading spokesmen and community groups of the Mexican American minority, these outside organizations found they had no viable counterparts in the Mexican community. Their surprise was only equalled by the embarrassment of many Mexican Americans who realized the urgent need to organize the "barrio" more effectively for social action and political representation. These men were aware that East Los Angeles was full of small neighborhood groupings and social clubs, but saw with a few exceptions none of them able to offer the political leadership so vital to the Mexican community's improvement.

One of these exceptions was the *Coordinating Council for Latin American Youth,* organized in 1942 for the purpose of directing the attention of public authorities and American society in general to the plight of the Mexican American youth. Representing a multitude of smaller organizations, the Coordinating Council as early as November, 1942, presented to the Los Angeles County Board of Supervisors a petition urging enactment of a list of remedial actions to increase opportunities for Mexican American youth. If this petition had been promptly acted upon by the County officials, it is the opinion of Ruth Tuck that these reforms "might have obviated the events (Zoot Suit Riots) seven months later."[20]

UNITY LEAGUES

In response to the growing need for community organizations particularly suited to achieve political objectives, Mexican Americans of the Pomona Valley (California) founded the first in a series of Unity Leagues. Although aided and encouraged by such educated professionals as Ignacio Lopez (editor, El Espectador) and Fred Ross (organizer from the Industrial Areas Foundation), the Unity League's membership primarily consisted of economically lower class Mexican Americans. In this way, it differs sharply from the traditionally middle-class membership of most of the earlier Mexican American political organizations discussed, and served as the model for many subsequent efforts at grass roots political organization in the Mexican American community.

The Unity League's first political success occurred in Chino, California, with the election of the first Mexican American to a city council seat in years. The campaign organized by the Unity League to get Andrew Morales elected to the city council of Chino is significant for it reveals the degree to which Mexican Americans were learning effective techniques of political organization. Twenty deputy registrars were enlisted from the Mexican community to assure 100 percent Mexican voter turnout with the aid of a block captain system organized throughout the "colonia." A fund raising drive was also inaugurated with even non-citizens contributing to the ultimate collection of $450 in donations.

The result of these efforts was the registration of almost the entire eligible Mexican American community and their near perfect turnout at the polls resulting in the election of Morales by over 100 votes.[21] Crucial to the Unity League's success in Chino was its ability to manipulate into a crisis the issue of no representation on the City Council for the 38 percent of Chino's population who were Mexican American thereby capturing the attention of the entire Mexican community. This same organizing tactic was also employed by Fred Ross in his subsequent efforts to establish Unity Leagues in San Bernardino and Riverside, California. In both cases Fred Ross found a potentially explosive issue upon which to rally the Mexican American community into supporting the efforts of the Unity League to eliminate school discrimination.

COMMUNITY SERVICE ORGANIZATION (CSO)

The end of the War saw the return of a very different Mexican American than had left for War four years previous. Having risked his life for the United States, the returning Mexican American G.I. came back with a desire to participate actively in American society. These American-oriented war veterans were to transform the traditionally Mexico-oriented mentality of much of the Mexican American community into a growing identification with American society and the Mexican Americans' contribution to it. Upon their return from overseas, many Mexican American veterans were also quick to notice the inferior position their minority occupied in relation to the rest of American society. Their desires to improve the conditions of life in the "barrio," however, at first were thwarted by the lack of opportunities for Mexican Americans to assume leadership in the existing assistance programs, since most of the responsible positions in these organizations were already occupied by Anglo-Americans. Cognizance of this fact led a number of these dedicated young Mexican Americans to consider forming their own community organizations.

One of the first of these organizations to be established in California was the *Community Service Organization.* Founded in Los Angeles during September, 1947, by a small group of Mexican American veterans and factory workers, the CSO began attacking a series of problems plaguing the East Los Angeles area from educational reform in the local schools to cases of police mistreatment of Mexican American youth. Starting with a membership of only fifteen, the group's activities soon attracted a grass roots membership of over 250 meeting in open forum in a local elementary school to discuss the issues of concern to the Mexican American community.

As the CSO wrestled with an unresponsive municipal government, the membership soon became aware of the need for Mexican American political representation in City Hall. After the failure to elect a Mexican American by the name of Edward Roybal to the Los Angeles City Council, the leadership of CSO resolved to undertake a massive voter registration drive in the Mexican American community in order to assure Roybal's victory in the next election. Assisted by Fred Ross, who brought with him the experience of the early Unity Leagues, the CSO swore sixty-three of its members in as Deputy Registrars and succeeded in registering 12,000 Mexican American citizens by the end of the year. The struggle to get the first Mexican American elected to the City Council since 1881 had just begun. Using the technique of "House Meetings" in which neighbors invited other neighbors into their homes to listen to a representative of CSO, the organization was able to bring the voter registration in East Los Angeles up to 40,000 and expand its own membership to 3,000 strong.[22] The result of these efforts was the election in 1949 of the first Mexican American to the Los Angeles City Council in 68 years. In addition, a heightened sense of their own political potential was injected into the Mexican American community which was to serve as the basis for the future political mobilization of Spanish-speaking citizens.

In spite of these successes, the CSO soon forsook overt participation in the political arena for a growing concern with providing the Mexican American minority community services of a mutual aid type. This is not to say that the CSO did not continue to work for increased Mexican American voter registration or push for legislation beneficial to the Spanish-speaking community. This change in approach, however, did mean that the CSO would never again publicly support a candidate for political office even though unofficial fund raising functions continued to be held for those candidates responsive to the problems of the Mexican American minority.

The adoption of a mutual aid approach to community organization represented the CSO leadership's response to the question of how does the organization solidify its membership in order to pursue a program of long-term pressure on public authorities to improve the conditions of the Mexican American community? Their motives for reviving this traditional philosophy of mutual aid, so characteristic of the earliest efforts at Mexican American community organization, were best expressed in the following passage from the CSO's Twentieth Anniversary Commemorative publication:

> During the first seventeen-year period CSO, like many crusading groups, was subjected to strong opposition and this was compounded with an unsolidified membership. The L.A. CSO leadership, realizing that these factors could be the seed of its own destruction adopted in 1964 the mutual aid philosophy as the best insurance to solidify its membership and to develop into a strong contending pressure group.[23]

The Los Angeles CSO in recent years has developed a number of mutual benefit programs ranging from the traditional death benefit insurance and credit union to the more innovative Buyers' Club and Consumer Complaint Center. As for the other approximately thirty CSO chapters throughout the State of California, little progress toward coordinating the organization's efforts on a statewide basis has been made due to what Joan Moore calls "the extreme localism of Mexican American leadership and action."[24] The one major exception to the above observation is the CSO's eight year crusade to have the State Legislature pass a bill granting old age pensions to non-citizens. Although their efforts were successful with the bill's passage in 1962, criticism has been directed toward the CSO for its single-minded concern in the political sphere with the problems of the elderly at the expense of other equally crucial problems. The Los Angeles CSO of late has responded to this pressure for a multi-issue orientation with an attack on zoning regulations in East Los Angeles and its advocacy of subdividing City Government into Neighborhood Community Councils for greater citizen participation in government.

AMERICAN G.I. FORUM

The same year that the Community Service Organization was being organized, an increasing number of returning Mexican American veterans in Texas and elsewhere were experiencing discrimination in education, employment, medical attention, and housing. In a manner typical of many Mexican American community political organizations, the American G.I. Forum grew out of one specific incident of discrimination against a war veteran who was refused burial by a funeral home in Three Rivers, Texas. Angered by this and other earlier acts of prejudice against Mexican American G.I.'s, a respected Mexican American physician, Dr. Hector Garcia, and a group of other concerned Mexican American veterans from Corpus Christi, Texas, decided to organize themselves into a veterans organization dedicated to combating such acts of discrimination and improving the status of Mexican Americans in Texas. Calling themselves the American G.I. Forum, they succeeded their first year not only in having the Mexican American G.I. in question buried in Arlington Cemetery with the assistance of then Congressman Lyndon Johnson, but also eliminated discriminatory practices in the Corpus Christi Veterans Hospital. Urged on by their initial achievements in reducing discrimination the G.I. Forum succeeded in establishing over 100 Forums in Texas by the end of 1949. Today the G.I. Forum is organized in 23 states with a membership of over 20,000.

Although officially non-partisan, the organization's members are encouraged to participate actively in politics. Recognizing the dearth of Mexican

American representation in government, the G.I. Forum urges its members to run for political office, and actively recommends Mexican Americans for appointive positions in government. Typical of the G.I. Forum's activist role in promoting Mexican Americans for public office was the organization's chastizing of Kansas Governor William Avery for failing to reappoint a Mexican American to the State's Civil Rights Commission at their 1965 Convention in Kansas City.

The G.I. Forum's period of greatest success in promoting political reform and social action benefiting the Mexican American community was during the 1950's, at a time when other groups timidly shrank from adopting an activist posture for fear of being called Communist. This unique role of the G.I. Forum during the 1950's was made possible by its leaders' skillful manipulation of patriotic symbols and their veteran status to combat accusations that the organization was advocating leftist programs. Although the organization is now criticized by some for being too status quo oriented, the G.I. Forum's effective use of American symbols to cloak such political action as their opposition to the importation of agricultural laborers from Mexico assured the existence of at least one organization committed to protecting the rights of Mexican American citizens during those tense years.

The G.I. Forum has also been active in providing community services to the Mexican American minority. Some examples of its benefit programs are its "back to school" drives, scholarship programs, and more recently low-cost housing through their cosponsorship of Operation Ser. Of special interest is the G.I. Forum's deliberate attempt to involve the entire family in its activities. Recognizing that members' competing obligations to both the organization and their families has spelled the downfall of many Mexican American organizations, the Forum established both a Ladies' Auxiliary and Junior G.I. Forums for the youth. In addition, the local chapters of the Forum have attempted to meet the social needs of their members' families by sponsoring dances, picnics, and annual Queen contests. By attempting to fulfill a series of varied functions for its members, the G.I. Forum has succeeded in solidifying its membership and remaining a "strong contending pressure group" for Mexican American rights.

MEXICAN AMERICAN POLITICAL ASSOCIATION (MAPA)

Although all of the Mexican American community organizations discussed at one time or another have taken an active interest in politics, most have hesitated to openly admit the political nature of many of their activities for some of the reasons discussed earlier. One of the first organizations in the Mexican American community, however, to formally declare its primary function as political is the *Mexican American Political Association.* Organized on a statewide basis throughout California in 1958, MAPA grew out of the realization by many concerned Mexican American leaders that their community no longer could depend upon the Democratic Party structure to champion the political cause of the Mexican American in California. Shocked by the defeat of Edward Roybal for Lieutenant Governor in 1954 and Henry Lopez for Secretary of State in 1958 during a year of otherwise Democratic landslide, these leaders came to recognize the need for an organization solely dedicated to advancing the political interests of the Mexican American in California.

Constitutionally committed to a bi-partisan stance, MAPA is concerned primarily with electing Mexican Americans to public office and supporting candidates for both parties who are dedicated to bettering the status of the Mexican American minority. Due in part to MAPA's efforts to increase Mexican American political representation in California, two state assemblymen, one Congressman, three Superior Court Judges and three Municipal Court Judges of Mexican American descent were subsequently elected. In the political arena, MAPA has also pressed for legislation beneficial to the Mexican American and has undertaken voter registration drives and programs of political education such as "floating seminars" throughout the state.

In the sphere of social action, individual MAPA chapters have also taken the initiative in promoting the interests of the Mexican American community. Numerous examples exist of MAPA chapters coming to the defense of Mexican Americans over all sorts of issues ranging from police malpractices to school discrimination. A case in point was the Compton, California Chapter's successful efforts to improve the educational conditions at a local public school where 90 percent of the students are Mexican American.[25] In its efforts to meet the various needs of the minority, MAPA also encourages family involvement in many of its activities. This is stimulated through a system of dual membership for wives of members at no extra cost, and by the organization's recruitment of women for positions of responsibility in MAPA.

The efforts of MAPA to promote political organization and social action among the economically lower class Mexican Americans have been hindered in the past by the predominantly middle class membership of the organization. As Ralph Guzman noted, this class consciousness among the Mexican American community has prevented many of the organizational achievements of the Mexican American middle class from serving to increase community participation among lower class Mexican Americans.[26] One reason for this has been up until recently the Mexico-oriented perspective of the poorer Mexican American compared with the assimilative orientation of the middle class Mexican American. Each group, in turn, has been aroused by differing symbols with middle class organizations such as LULACS emphasizing American symbols of patriotism while such "grass roots" organizations as the early "mutualistas" employed Mexican names and emblems to satisfy the greater ethnic consciousness of the Mexican American poor.

Recognizing the need to bridge this gap between their middle class members and the poorer Mexican American if MAPA is to achieve its stated objectives, the organization's leadership recently has attempted to increase lower class participation in MAPA by intensifying the organization's ethnic identification and by facilitating the poor's access to MAPA functions. The former tactic involves the implementation of ethnically-charged symbols in public statements and closer collaboration with such highly ethnic-conscious young Mexican American groups as the United Mexican American Students (UMAS). The lower class Mexican American's access to MAPA functions has been facilitated by recent attempts to locate MAPA Conventions and other events in close proximity to poorer Mexican neighborhoods. As explained by the current President of MAPA, "this . . . was done in order that we might attract more of our barrio poor who in the past have been excluded from our conventions." He goes on to say that "we must eliminate this in our organization if we ever hope to gain the respect and understanding from those who do not participate due to their economic status."[27]

A second difficulty plaguing previous Mexican American organizations which MAPA's founders strove to avoid was the danger of dictatorial leaders ("Liderismo") assuming control of the organization and perpetuating their rule by encouraging a personality cult of loyal followers ("cultismo"). Recognizing the Mexican Americans' susceptibility to personalistic leadership in which the individual's loyalty is first to his chosen leader and second to the organization, the framers of MAPA's Bylaws sought to decentralize the organization's structure enough to assure the autonomy of each chapter within its respective Assembly District. As the major author of the Bylaws explains, "the State Executive Board (of MAPA) is provided with no powers to initiate or make local endorsements, which field is reserved to the locally chartered assembly, congressional and county district organizations."[28]

The fact that the State Executive Board of MAPA does insist that all state-wide political endorsements for such offices as Governor be reserved to the annual state-wide MAPA Conventions in which all chapters are represented does not obliterate the fact expressed by Manuel Ruiz that "the basic elements in MAPA are the practical realities of local political autonomy."[29] The original MAPA leadership recognized that only by conscientiously respecting the autonomy of its local chapters could they assure organizational vitality and the participation of all its members. Under no circumstances was the decentralization of its structure intended to discourage strong leadership in MAPA. Rather they hoped through local autonomy to assure the blessings of dynamic leadership without the curse of either "liderismo" or "cultismo."

EFFORTS TO COORDINATE MEXICAN AMERICAN ORGANIZATIONS

After discussing the benefits of a decentralized organizational structure, the question now arises whether efforts to unite all Mexican American community organizations under one permanent coordinating body have been successful. One attempt to establish such a united front in California dates back to 1953 when the *Council of Mexican American Affairs* was founded in Los Angeles. As a "non-partisan, non-sectarian, and non-profit citizens organization dedicated to the development of leadership among Americans of Mexican descent and to coordinating the efforts of all the various organizations and groups concerned with the betterment of the Mexican American in the Los Angeles region," CMAA began with 44 member organizations.[30]

With the above goal of coordinating all other existing Mexican American organizations in mind, CMAA maintained an office and full-time executive director who organized conferences on issues of concern to the community and provided member organizations with assistance in the form of information and new channels of communication. Unfortunately, CMAA's laudatory efforts to unite the multitude of organizations in the Mexican American community met with failure due to the member organizations' refusal to pay their dues and their lack of sufficient financial resources to accomplish such a task.

After a period of dormancy, the CMAA in 1963 was revitalized under new leadership and with a completely new approach to serving the Mexican American community. Instead of attempting to coordinate the grass-roots organizations in the community for a more unified Mexican American voice in civic affairs, CMAA has accepted the role of a small elitest organization of successful Mexican American professional and businessmen functioning as a high-level pressure group for the Mexican American minority. By organizing political banquets and community forums in which public officials are invited to address the Mexican Americans in public office and pressure other public officials to take a greater concern for the minority.

The failure of CMAA to coordinate the various organizations in the Mexican American community during its earlier years is due in part to the significance of class homogeneity for the success of a Mexican American community organization. As mentioned earlier, organizations with a middle class membership seldom hold much attraction for lower class Mexican Americans. Since most of the efforts to unite community organizations stem from the middle class segments of the Mexican American minority, it naturally follows that these attempts would hold little interest for the poorer members of grass-roots Mexican American organizations. Dr. Ernesto Galarza refers to this problem in discussing the possibility of organizing the minority into a national organization:

> The higher one goes toward national organization the greater the preference of Mexican Americans to express themselves in English and to use symbols that mean something only to English-speaking people. Reverse the direction and one finds the more intense symbolism and greater use of Spanish at the grass-roots. This weakens both the organizational strength and the emotional strands upon which organization depends.[31]

A more recent attempt to organize the Mexican American minority into a unified national body was undertaken by the *Political Association of Spanish Speaking Organizations* (PASSO). Founded in the early 1960's in Texas as an outgrowth of the Viva Kennedy Movement, PASSO was dedicated to organizing the Mexican Americans of the Southwest into a united national political organization capable of exerting political pressure at all levels of government. After experiencing great success in organizing chapters among the Mexican Americans of Texas, PASSO's leadership then attempted to organize chapters in Arizona as part of the larger goal of a national organization. The Arizona Mexican American community, however, was unresponsive to the overtures of PASSO preferring what Juan Martinez describes as "an organization more suited to the needs of the Arizona Spanish-speaking." In response to this demand for an Arizona-based organization, the *American Coordinating Council on Political Education* (ACCPE) was established with a paid membership of 2500 Mexican Americans and chapters in ten of Arizona's fourteen counties.[32]

The failure of PASSO to expand successfully into Arizona reflects a second major obstacle confronting efforts to coordinate the organizational activities of Mexican Americans. This is the intense "localism" or emotional identification with a local region so prevalent among Mexican Americans living in different areas of the Southwest. As Joan Moore notes, "tactics defined as rather cautious in one setting may be viewed as "trouble making" in another, with the attendant withdrawal of support by other Mexican Americans in either situation." She goes on to say that "these 'local' variations may occur even within the same metropolitan area."[33]

One recent organizing effort which is displaying an awareness of these above obstacles in its attempts to coordinate the activities of Mexican American organizations is the *Southwest Council of La Raza.* Established in 1968 as a non-profit corporation of Mexican Americans, dedicated to "assisting local Mexican American community efforts to organize themselves more effectively," the Council respects the autonomy and integrity of the local community organizations it is working to assist. As its First Annual Report reiterates, "it is not a mass-membership organization nor was it created for the purpose of giving any one organization a "base." Rather all of the Council's efforts "are aimed at the development of the barrio through the organization and encouragement of local cooperative community groups in the barrio," with its own activities "being supportive in the broadest sense."[34]

In order to avoid the divisions arising from middle class control over grass-roots operations and intense "localist" sensitivities, the Southwest Council has encouraged the formation of "action-oriented local councils," composed of representatives from the "barrio." It is the function of these local councils to advise and assist the Southwest Council in its efforts to appreciate and meet the needs of community organizations. Unlike the earlier efforts of the Council of Mexican American Affairs, the Southwest Council has not had to depend upon its participant members for financial support due to a $630,000 grant from the Ford Foundation. The future success of the Southwest Council as a self-sufficient body will, therefore, depend upon its leadership's willingness to reject what Ernesto Galarza calls "ready-made patterns" of national organization for methods more suited to the personality of the Mexican American community.[35]

HISTORICAL LESSONS

One of the results of the preceding historical analysis is a refutation of the assumption that the Mexican American minority has been politically apathetic and slow to develop community action organizations. Rather, the above historical study leads to the conclusion that major elements of the Mexican American community have consistently expressed an interest in politics and have organized themselves over the years into community action groups for the purpose of improving the minority's relative status in American society. The Mexican American minority, however, has expressed this concern for politics and desire for social action in a very different way than other segments of American society. As Arthur Rubel observes, "Chicanos seem no less interested in political issues than do Anglos."[36] By overlooking this fact, many observers erroneously have concluded that the Mexican American was politically unconcerned since they were unable to detect in the Mexican American community any political organizations comparable to the ones used in the Anglo American community for political expression.

Unlike the Anglo American, the Mexican American traditionally has not developed highly specialized organizations for the sole purpose of political action. Rather he has preferred to establish undifferentiated multi-purpose organizations which will serve not only his political needs but also his economic, social, and cultural ones as well. Considering the previously discussed Mexican reticence to describe one's activities as "political" due to the negative connotations the term holds for the Mexican American community, it has also been customary for such all-purpose organizations to avoid using the term "political" either in their title or statement of purpose. The fact that these Mexican American community organizations do not refer to themselves or their activities as political in nature does not in any way, however, negate their willingness to undertake political action in the form of pressure on public officials or support of legislation when the need arises. Julian Samora and Richard Lamanna confirm this in the following quote from their study of Mexican Americans in East Chicago, Indiana:

> With the exception of the associations ancillary to the religious institutions and the strictly recreational groups . . . all associations have a *political*

> *overtone,* and urgent need for unity, a sense of contributing to the adjustment of its members to the community, a feeling that through the effort of the association the community is made aware of the presence and the needs of the Mexican American.[37]

In addition to exposing the unfamiliarity of many non-Mexican American observers with the actual nature of organizations in our community, the previous historical analysis has also revealed the Mexican American's ignorance about the nature of his own organizations and what makes them prosper. For the one major indictment to be thrown at Mexican American efforts at political organization on the "grass-roots" community level is their generally short-lived nature. Originally organized in response to a crisis or specific case of discrimination, these community action groups often fade away as the crisis passes, leaving the community just as unprepared when the next crisis develops. Some formula to assure the continued vitality of Mexican American community political organizations, therefore, is needed if the Mexican American community is to develop and maintain what was referred to earlier as "strong contending pressure groups" in the struggle for social, political, and economic quality.

From our analysis of those Mexican American organizations which have endured longest while maintaining much of their original vitality, five clues emerge to how a Mexican American community political organization can best retain both its membership and vigor for years of political combat and social action.

1. Multi-Functional

As mentioned above, most Mexican American community political organizations in the past have been characterized by their willingness to serve many different functions for their membership. Most successful Mexican American political organizations, for example, also seem to offer mutual aid benefits of some sort to help their members in time of financial need. They attempt to meet the social needs of their community by sponsoring dances, picnics, banquets, etc. Mexican American political organizations that ignored these various other needs of their members have often found it difficult to retain the interest and support of their membership after a political issue or crisis has ceased to be current.

In their multi-purpose orientation these Mexican American community organizations resemble the political organizations of the early European immigrants to this country who, experiencing the same poverty as the Mexican American today, were forced to rely on their own organizations for services they otherwise could not afford. In this sense, the multi-functional attribute of successful Mexican American political organizations may be more characteristic of any organization of poor people rather than a uniquely Mexican phenomenon.

2. *Family Involvement*

Related to the quality of multi-functionalism is the second attribute of those Mexican American community political organizations demonstrating greater longevity and vitality. This is their provision for the involvement of members' families in the activities of the organization, either through the establishment of women's and young persons' auxiliaries or through regular group social activities in which the members' families can participate. In the case of MAPA, dual membership for both husband and wife was found to be an effective technique for incorporating the family in MAPA's activities. No matter how achieved there is little doubt that family involvement is crucial to the success of a Mexican American organization. Emanating from a culture that places great emphasis on loyalty to family, a Mexican American political organization member will experience a conflict in his obligations to family and to the organization he belongs to with the former usually winning out unless provision is made by the latter to reduce the tension. The best way to reconcile these demands on the individual member is to encourage the family's equal identification with the organization.

3. *Single Issue Area Crisis Approach*

Most voluntary political organizations in the Mexican American community develop initially around a crisis issue or series of related issues of crucial importance to the community. As the crisis passes or the issue fades in importance, the organization is confronted with a decline in membership and support unless its leadership has learned to either provoke or capitalize upon another series of crises. As the previous study of successful Mexican American political organizations reveals, the crisis orientation and its perpetuation is essential until the "grass roots" membership has developed enough political sophistication to actively support the organization even during periods of relative calm.

One of the dangers in this "crisis issue" approach, however, is the strain that is places upon the organization's limited resources of manpower and money. For as the organization's reputation for success grows, so also does the community's demand for it to undertake newer and larger tasks. One possible solution to this dilemma may be an attempt to limit the organization's scope of responsibility to a specific "issue area" such as discrimination in education or housing where the organization's limited resources can effectively cope with the crises that develop. The success of such a "single issue area approach" depends, however, upon the degree to which other "single issue" oriented community organizations emerge to attack the other areas of concern to the community. If these other bodies do not appear, the organization will be forced by community pressure to undertake tasks unrelated to its original scope of responsibility thereby running the risk of overextending its resources and failing. To avoid this, many of the successful Mexican American political organizations discussed have satisfied the pressure upon them to expand their activities by taking on one issue area at a time in a sequential manner, thereby concentrating enough of its resources on each crisis to assure success.

4. Personalistic Consensual Leadership/Decentralized Structure

The most often observed characteristic of Mexican American political behavior is its emphasis on personalism or the need to personally identify with a candidate or leader. Whereas many will support a candidate primarily based on their intellectual agreement with his beliefs, the Mexican American voter has been observed to support more often that candidate whose personality he can identify with and relate to. As Arthur Rubel notes, "unlike Anglo Americans, Chicanos vote for persons with whom they can establish relationships amenable to personalistic instrumental activities."[38]

This subjective criteria for political leadership also arises in the Mexican American's selection of a community organization leader. The success of a Mexican American political organization, therefore, depends upon leadership by a man who not only can capture the devotion of the membership but also will respect the personalities and opinions of the other members. In short, the type of leader best suited for promoting organizational longevity and vitality is one with a magnetic personality who recognizes the need for developing a consensus of opinion among the membership before acting.

Unfortunately, this combination of personal magnetism and respect for the sensibilities of other members is difficult to find in a leader and attempts to promote it frequently have led to dictatorial leadership and a reign of cultism. Recognizing these dangers of strong personalistic leadership, several successful Mexican American organizations already discussed have discovered a safeguard against dictatorial leadership and greater assurance of a consensual decision making approach in the form of a decentralized administrative structure. By distributing leadership responsibilities among several elected officers, or among its local chapters in the case of a larger body, an organization can protect against its domination by an autocratic leader. The tactic of decentralizing power in the organization also encourages the development of experienced younger leadership for the future.

5. Ethnic Symbolism

In our discussion of the effect of class differences on the nature of Mexican American political organizations, it was observed that differing symbols were used to attract various segments of the Mexican American community to membership in organizations. The G.I. Forum, and LULACS, for example, effectively used the symbols of American patriotism to attract assimilative conscious middle class Mexican Americans to their ranks. In turn, one sees such newer organizations as the *Crusade for Justice* in Colorado and the *National Farm Workers Association* in California employing ethnically charged symbols such as "La Raza" to induce poor Mexican Americans to join them. The above success of "Corky" Gonzalez and Cesar Chavez in attracting supporters through the effective use of ethnic symbolism leaves little doubt that any attempt to organize successfully the Mexican American community especially at the grass roots level must involve a strong appeal to ethnic loyalty.

In conclusion, the above five ingredients for Mexican American organizational success should not be construed to be either exclusive or inclusive. Rather they should simply be viewed as some clues to why certain Mexican American political organizations in the past have prospered and why some may have failed to endure. The five hypotheses may also serve as a useful formula in evaluating the potential effectiveness and longevity of recently established Mexican American organizations. For until those currently involved in the political organization of the Mexican American community begin to study the earlier organizing efforts of equally dedicated Mexican American leaders, they are destined to perpetuate many of the same conditions which have inhibited the effective political organization of the Mexican American minority in the past.

NOTES

1. William V. D'Antonio and William H. Form, *Influentials in Two Border Cities, A Study in Community Decision-Making,* 1965, p. 30.

2. Letter from Ed. Idar, Jr. to Franklin Roosevelt, Jr., published in Albert Pena, Jr., "Needed: A Marshall Plan for Mexican Americans" *The Texas Observer,* April 15, 1966, p. 1.

3. D'Antonio and Form, *op. cit.,* p. 246. See also Alphonso Pinckney, "Prejudice Toward Mexican and Negro Americans," *Phylon,* Winter 1963, no. 24, p. 358.

4. John Gregory Dunne, *Delano, The Story of the California Grape Strike,* 1967, p. 55.

5. Paul Taylor, *Mexican Labor in the United States,* 1928; p. 45.

6. Manuel Gamio, *Mexican Immigration to the United States,* 1930, p. 133.

7. Richard Thurston, *Urbanization and Socio-Economic Change in a Mexican American Enclave,* Ph.D. Thesis, UCLA, pp. 36-37.

8. Paul Ming Chang-lin, *Voluntary Kinship–Voluntary Association in a Mexican-American Community,* Master's Thesis, University of Kansas, pp. 93-94.

9. Paul Taylor, *op. cit.*

10. The Sociedad Progresista Mexicana organized in 1929 has 18,000 members and 65 lodges throughout the State of California alone.

11. Article III, Constitucion y Leyes de la Orden Hijos de América in O. Douglas Weeks, "Lulacs" in *Southwestern Political and Social Science Quarterly,* December 1929, pp. 260-261.

12. Section I, Declaration of Principles, *ibid.*

13. Paul Taylor, *An American Mexican Frontier, Nueces, County, Texas,* 1934, p. 247.

14. Quote of J. Luz Saenz, LULACS Founder, from *El Paladin,* Corpus Christi, Texas, May 17, 1929, in O. D. Weeks, *op. cit.*, p. 274.

15. O. D. Weeks, *ibid.*, p. 272.

16. O. D. Weeks, *ibid.*, p. 275.

17. John Burma, *Spanish Speaking Groups in the United States,* 1954, p. 103.

18. *Ibid.*

19. *Ibid.*, p. 104.

20. Ruth D. Tuck, "Behind the Zoot Suit Riots," *Survey Graphic,* August, 1943, p. 316.

21. Interview with Ignacio Lopez (editor of *El Espectador* and founder of the Unity Leagues), April 28, 1969, Los Angeles, California.

22. Fred Ross, *Get Out If You Can, the Saga of Sal Si Puedes,* California Federation for Civic Unity, 1953, pp. 12-13.

23. Community Service Organization, *20th Anniversary Commemorative Publication,* March 25, 1967, p. 18.

24. Joan Moore, *Mexican American Problems and Prospects Special Report,* University of Wisconsin, 1966, p. 54.

25. "MAPA and the Community," *The Voice* (Official MAPA publication), December 31, 1965, Vol. 1, No. 3, p. 3.

26. Lecture by Ralph Guzman, Fall Quarter 1968, California State College, Los Angeles.

27. Abe Tapia, Welcoming Address to the Ninth Annual Convention of MAPA, Pico Rivera, California, June 29, 1968.

28. Letter of Mr. Manuel Ruiz to former MAPA President Edward Quevedo, December 18, 1963.

29. Letter of Mr. Ruiz to Mr. Bert Corona (a former President of MAPA), June 13, 1967.

30. Paul M. Sheldon, "Community Participation and the Emerging Middle Class," in Julian Samora, *La Raza, Forgotten Americans,* p. 39.

31. Ernesto Galarza, "Program for Action; The Mexican American, a National Concern," *Common Ground,* Summer 1949, published as a pamphlet by the Common Council for American Unity, p. 37.

32. Juan Martinez, "Leadership and Politics," in Julian Samora, *La Raza, Forgotten Americans,* 1966, p. 54.

33. Joan Moore, *op. cit.*, p. 55.

34. Southwest Council of La Raza, *First Annual Report,* February 1968 to February 1969, pp. 2-3.

35. Ernesto Galarza, *op. cit.*, p. 37.

36. Arthur Rubel, *Across the Tracks, Mexican Americans in a Texas City,* 1966, p. 139.

37. Julian Samora and Richard A. Lamanna, *Mexican Americans in a Midwest Metropolis: A Study of East Chicago,* Mexican American Study Project, Advance Report 8, UCLA School of Business Administration, p. 65.

38. Arthur Rubel, *op. cit.*

8: MEXICAN AMERICAN POLITICAL BEHAVIOR IN TEXAS

Clifton McCleskey and Bruce Merrill

THE CURRENT EXPANSION OF SCHOLARLY INTEREST IN THE MEXICAN American population is a development long overdue. . . . we are steadily improving our understanding of many dimensions of the Mexican American experience. In the realm of politics, however, our knowledge of this group lags badly. Still in short supply are basic data of the sort long available not only for Anglos but also for blacks, Jews, and other minorities. What follows, then, is an attempt to augment that scanty body of literature by reporting some data on Mexican American political behavior in Texas. Since the significance of a given pattern of ethnic behavior is often relative to the patterns characteristic of other groups, we have placed considerable emphasis on comparing Mexican Americans with Negroes and Anglos.

THE MEXICAN AMERICAN IN TEXAS

Although almost one out of every five Texas residents (18.4 percent) is of Spanish origin, members of that group are not evenly distributed across the state. They constitute a majority of the population in only 21 of the state's 254 counties, and comprise between 25 and 50 percent of the population in only 27 others.[1] There are another 31 counties which had 2500 or more Mexican American residents in 1970.

Three major and two minor population clusters can be discerned, though there is some overlap among them. First, Mexican Americans in Texas increasingly are to be found in the cities, with more than 60 percent of them

From *Social Science Quarterly,* 53, No. 4 (March 1973), pp. 783-798. Reprinted by permission of the *Social Science Quarterly.*

located in the seven Standard Metropolitan Statistical Areas associated with San Antonio, El Paso, McAllen, Houston, Brownsville, Corpus Christi, and Laredo. A second concentration is along the Mexican border and in the counties south and southwest of San Antonio. Extending out from that base and running up the Gulf Coast is a third cluster of counties with sizeable Mexican American populations. A thin string of counties in central Texas between Waco and San Antonio and a scattering in the intensive agricultural areas of the South Plains complete the geographical picture. Except in the major cities, particularly Houston and San Antonio, there is not much overlap of the Mexican American population with Negroes.

From what has been said elsewhere about the depressed social and economic status of Mexican Americans, one could only expect that they have been subjected to considerable discrimination. Segregation in the use of public facilities was not imposed on Mexican Americans by state law, but it was a widespread practice at local levels until fairly recently, often on the basis of official action by local authorities.[2] So far as state government is concerned, the prevailing attitude has been one of neglect and indifference. Policy changes of special interest to Mexican Americans have been few in number, limited in scope, and recent in origin. A Legislative Council study in 1968 found Mexican Americans (and blacks) to be grossly under-represented on the state payroll, especially in middle and upper echelons. Even the symbolic pay-off has been meager. Governor Connally's appointment of Roy Barrerra as Secretary of State in the closing years of his administration drew considerable comment precisely because it was such an extraordinary thing for a Mexican American to hold a major state office. On the rare occasion when one has sought an elective state office, he has been poorly rewarded for his efforts, as is illustrated by the defeat of state Senator (now Congressman) Henry B. Gonzalez in the Democratic gubernatorial primary of 1958 and in the special Senate election of 1961, and of state Representative Lauro Cruz in the Democratic primary for state treasurer in 1972.[3]

Yet these generalizations do not fully depict the political status of Mexican Americans in Texas. Unlike Negroes, they were never officially barred from the Democratic primaries, though local rules and informal discouragement sometimes stood in their way. Also unlike blacks, Mexican Americans quite early aligned themselves with the Democratic party, developing in South Texas political organizations capable of delivering a sizable bloc vote.[4] In the areas of Mexican American concentration, local and district offices have long been filled by members of that group, though seldom in proportion to population.[5] Thus in some respects Mexican Americans have traditionally had a place in Texas politics long denied to blacks.

In order to delineate that role more clearly, and to assess better the prospects for change, we present the following data on the political behavior of Mexican Americans.

ELECTORAL PARTICIPATION

The lore of Texas politics has it that Mexican Americans usually have not qualified and voted in the same proportion as the rest of the citizenry. Contrary to that lore, Shinn found in some years no significant correlation, and in other years, a positive correlation between *registration* and percent Spanish surname population.[6] However, he found the expected negative correlation between *turnout* and Spanish surnames. The same pattern emerges from the data presented in Table 1, which shows that registration rates in the 15 counties with a Mexican American majority in the 1960s were at about the same levels as, or were sometimes higher than, the state as a whole. On the other hand, the turnout of registered voters in the Mexican American counties was usually 5 to 15 percent below that of the entire state.

TABLE 1

VOTER REGISTRATION AND TURNOUT IN TEXAS AND IN PREDOMINANTLY MEXICAN AMERICAN COUNTIES, 1960–1970 (IN PERCENTAGES)

	Voter registration[a] as percentage of adult population[b], 1960		*Voter turnout as percentage of registered voters*	
Year	*State*	*Mex. Am. counties[c]*	*State*	*Mex. Am. counties[c]*
1960	46.9	46.5	89.1	79.0
1962	42.9	44.3	63.6	65.4
1964	50.5	51.4	87.1	76.0
1966	48.3	53.2	48.1	40.6
1968	64.0	65.1	75.6	60.7
1970	63.2	69.6	53.9	47.9

Source: Calculated from data obtained from the office of the Secretary of State.

[a]Registration for years prior to 1966 is based on poll tax payments and exemptions. Since exempt persons living outside cities of 10,000 or more did not have to get exemption certificates, the figures in the table understate the number of qualified voters and hence the registration percentage for those years.

[b]"Adult population" figures for 1960 and 1970 are from Census data. The figures for the interim years were derived by interpolation.

[c]This category consists of 15 counties in South Texas in which the Spanish-surname population *in 1960* was 50 percent or more of the total. They are: Brooks, Cameron, Dimmit, Duval, Frio, Hidalgo, Jim Hogg, Jim Wells, La Salle, Maverick, Starr, Webb, Willacy, Zapata, and Zavala.

A somewhat different pattern of participation was reported by McCleskey and Nimmo for Mexican Americans in Harris County (Houston).[7] Their findings reveal a much lower rate of registration for Mexican Americans, particularly under the poll tax system. The end of the poll tax in 1966 improved their registration levels, but did not bring proportionality with Anglos and blacks. However, that same study showed that Mexican Americans, once qualified to vote, had a rate of turnout almost as high as that of the other two groups. Thus the limited data at hand indicate that Mexican American electoral participation is somewhat below the Texas average, but there is conflicting evidence as to whether it is due to failure to register or failure to turn out on election day.

In addition to registration and voting, electoral participation may include other activities such as holding party office, contributing money or labor to a campaign, attending rallies, and talking politics with friends.[8] In all cases except the first it appears from Table 2 that Anglos have the highest participation rates and Mexican Americans the lowest, with blacks in between but closer to the Mexican Americans. The much lower rates for the latter group may reflect such broad factors as socioeconomic status, language barriers, and different political styles, but another contributing factor may be the lessened efforts of Texas' political parties to mobilize Mexican American

TABLE 2

POLITICAL PARTICIPATION IN TEXAS, NOVEMBER, 1969 (IN PERCENTAGES)

	Anglo *(N=797)*	*Negro*[a] *(N=419)*	*Mexican American*[a] *(N=375)*
Held party office	2	1	2
Given money to campaign	24	16	11
Attended political rallies	32	18	22
Worked for candidate	24	21	13
How often do you talk politics with your friends?			
Frequently	27	23	14
Sometimes	27	31	32
Seldom	35	28	32
Never	9	16	22

Source: Survey described in footnote 8.

[a]Identification by surname, observation and when necessary by asking for indication of lineage.

voters. Thus, 22 percent of all Anglo respondents and 15 percent of the Negroes reported that they had been asked to work for the Republican party, compared to 9 percent of the Mexican Americans. Similarly, 20 percent of the Anglos and 29 percent of the blacks had been asked to work for the Democratic party, compared with 16 percent of the Mexican Americans.

Since the possession of political information is largely a function of educational achievement, it is not surprising to learn from Table 3 that Anglos are most likely to be able to name or identify their U.S. senators (though unreported here, a similar pattern holds for identification of the governor and other state officials). However, it is interesting that Mexican Americans can recall and identify the names of both Texas senators more often than blacks, although the latter have already been shown in general to have higher rates of participation. Particularly noteworthy is the fact that, compared to blacks, Mexican Americans show a greater capacity to *recall* the names of Texas senators; the higher the reported level of education, the greater the difference in recall capacities of the two groups. This anomaly may reflect a tendency on the part of Mexican Americans to have more political interest and concern, or it may simply indicate that there is a difference in the quality of education provided the two groups.

PARTY IDENTIFICATION

Table 4 amply confirms the attachment of Mexican Americans to the Democratic party, for no less than 86 percent identify themselves as "Democratic" to some greater or lesser degree. That identification with the Democratic party began in the mid-nineteenth century when the South Texas political system was first given shape. It was reinforced by the development of the one-party system in Texas, and further cemented by the class, ethnic, and religious appeals of the national Democratic party from Franklin Roosevelt to the present.

But it is interesting to note that this pronounced attachment of Mexican Americans to the Democratic party is overshadowed by that of blacks. Among the latter, 63 percent identified themselves as "Strong Democrats," whereas "only" 45 percent of the Mexican Americans so identified themselves. In the context of such overwhelming Democratic strength, the attachment of Anglos to that party (23 percent "Strong Democrat," 30 percent "Weak Democrat") seems rather puny, though in fact it compares favorably with national patterns of party identification.

The Republican Party almost draws a blank so far as the two minorities are concerned, for the "Strong" and "Weak" Republican categories combined account for only 2 percent of the blacks and 3 percent of the Mexican Americans. It fares better with Anglos, for one out of four identify with the

TABLE 3

VOTER IDENTIFICATION OF TEXAS SENATORS, BY EDUCATIONAL LEVEL (IN PERCENTAGES)

		Total Sample		*Less than H.S.*		*H.S. Graduate*		*College*	
	Anglos (*N*=797)	*Mex. Am.* (*N*=370)	*Negro* (*N*=407)	*Mex. Am.* (*N*=182)	*Negro* (*N*=213)	*Mex. Am.* (*N*=111)	*Negro* (*N*=111)	*Mex. Am.* (*N*=62)	*Negro* (*N*=78)
Recall Yarborough[a]	42	38	32	32	28	44	37	64	45
Identify Yarborough[a]	49	35	28	29	34	38	41	27	33
Total Yarborough	91	73	60	61	62	82	78	91	78
Recall Tower[a]	41	32	25	26	22	31	27	62	35
Identify Tower[a]	45	32	28	35	27	39	31	21	31
Total Tower	86	64	53	61	49	70	58	83	66

[a]Recall was measured by asking respondents to name their two U.S. senators. Identification was measured by asking individuals who could not name the senators to pick their names from a list of several persons.

TABLE 4

PARTY IDENTIFICATION OF THE TEXAS ELECTORATE IN 1969
(IN PERCENTAGES)

Party Identification[a]	*Total state-wide (N=1591)*	*Anglo (N=797)*	*Negro (N=419)*	*Mex. Am. (N=375)*
Strong Democrat	41	23	63	41
Weak Democrat	29	30	27	45
Independent, leaning Democrat	2	3	1	2
Independent	7	11	2	5
Independent, leaning Republican	3	5	1	1
Strong Republican	6	10	1	1
Weak Republican	8	15	1	2
Don't Know	4	4	4	4
	100	100	100	100

[a]Question: "Generally speaking, do you usually think of yourself as a Republican, a Democrat, an Independent, or what? (If Republican or Democrat) Would you call yourself a strong (R) (D) or a not very strong (R) (D)? (If Independent) Do you think of yourself as closer to the Republican or Democratic Party?" See John P. Robinson, *et al., Measures of Political Attitudes* (Ann Arbor: Institute for Social Research, 1968), p. 495.

GOP. Anglos are also much more likely to classify themselves as an "Independent" of one sort or another.

These relative patterns of party identification carry over into the reported voting habits of our respondents (Table 5), albeit with some shrinkage of Democratic margins. Thus, 83 percent of the blacks and 68 percent of the Mexican Americans report that they vote mostly or entirely Democratic, compared with 38 percent of the Anglos. Conversely, the two minorites usually give only one or two percent to the Republican party whereas 18 percent of the Anglos vote mostly or entirely for the GOP. Anglos are also more likely to split their tickets to some significant extent, for 49 percent of them reported doing so, compared with only 27 percent of the Mexican Americans and 13 percent of the blacks.

These data indicate that the GOP in Texas is indeed composed mostly of Anglos. While strong Republican candidates fare better than the percentages in Tables 4 and 5 might suggest (due to the higher turnout of Republican

TABLE 5

USUAL VOTING HABITS OF TEXAS VOTERS, BY RACE AND ETHNICITY, 1969 (IN PERCENTAGES)

Usual vote of respondent	*Anglo (N=797)*	*Negro (N=419)*	*Mex. Am. (N=375)*
Only Democratic	16	53	35
Mostly Democratic	22	30	33
More Democratic than Republican	14	6	9
Equally Democratic and Republican	27	6	17
More Republican than Democratic	8	1	1
Mostly Republican	10	1	1
Only Republican	3	1	–
Other, DK, NR, etc.	–	3	5
	100	100	100

voters and to the Republican tendencies of many "independents"), the implication is clear that the GOP in Texas is destined to remain the minority party as long as Mexican Americans and Negroes continue overwhelmingly to identify with and to vote for the Democratic party.

That assessment assumes, of course, that there is no major realignment of the party system in Texas. We will have more to say on that later, but it is worth noting now that Merrill's analysis indicates the possibility of a new alignment pitting liberal Anglos, Mexican Americans, and blacks against conservative Anglos formerly divided between the two major parties.[9] In other words, some overriding emotional issue (busing?) might realign the parties on axes tangential to positions regarding civil rights and race relations, drawing enough conservative Anglos into the Republican party to enable it to become the majority party without black or Mexican American support. There are, however, indications that Republican leaders and candidates are not waiting for a major realignment. Armed with the knowledge that Mexican Americans are less strongly identified with the Democratic party, they have begun a cautious courtship of that group.[10]

ISSUE ORIENTATION

Although there is considerable research indicating that ideology is meaningful only for a small segment of the United States electorate,[11] the notion is widespread among activists and observers in Texas that there is an underlying liberal-conservative dimension to state politics (symbolized by, but not limited to, the factionalism in the Democratic party). In pursuit of this ideological dimension we asked our respondents to place themselves, then-Senator Ralph Yarborough, and then-Congressman George Bush (the Republican nominee in the 1970 Senate race) along a conservative-liberal continuum as indicated in Table 6.

Apart from the fact that considerably more members of the minority groups than Anglos were unable to classify themselves, the most notable aspect of the self-classification question is once again the intermediate position of the Mexican Americans. Forty-seven percent of the blacks identify themselves as liberal, compared to 29 percent of the Mexican Americans and 18 percent of the Anglos. Similarly, 40 percent of the Anglos described themselves as conservative compared to 23 percent of the Mexican Americans and 14 percent of the Negroes.

When our respondents were asked to classify Senator Yarborough on the conservative-liberal continuum, there were no striking inter-group differences. Almost the same percentage of each sub-population (26-28 percent) was unable to place the Senator on the continuum and the remainder in each group did not differ greatly in their ideological assessment. From 35 to 47 percent considered him liberal while from 13 to 18 percent considered him conservative. Interestingly, Mexican Americans saw Senator Yarborough as less liberal and more conservative than did either blacks or Anglos. With respect to George Bush, who was much less familiar to Texas voters, approximately one-half of the Anglos (47 percent) and Negroes (52 percent) and two-thirds of the Mexican Americans (65 percent) were unable to classify him. However, those respondents who made the effort classified Bush in much the same way, regardless of the group to which they belonged.

Inasmuch as our questions about liberalism and conservatism elicited responses from all three groups that tend to conform to "reality" (most expert observers would agree that Anglos are more conservative than the minorities, and that Yarborough is more liberal than the moderate Bush), it seems fair to conclude that a substantial portion of the Texas electorate is capable of making distinctions based on that dimension. Unfortunately, our data shed no light on whether voters in any of these three ethnic groups do in fact make decisions by weighing liberal and conservative considerations. Conceivably, they may be aware of the ideological dimension but do not act upon it.[12]

POLITICAL EFFICACY AND ALIENATION

It may be that the most significant thing about the data on political efficacy reported in Table 7 is the generally low levels that prevail–levels that

TABLE 6

IDEOLOGICAL PERSPECTIVES OF TEXAS VOTERS, BY RACE AND ETHNICITY, 1969 (IN PERCENTAGES)

Ideological classification	*Anglos (N=797)*			*Negroes (N=419)*			*Mex. Am. (N=375)*		
	Self	*Bush*	*Yarborough*	*Self*	*Bush*	*Yarborough*	*Self*	*Bush*	*Yarborough*
Liberal	10	4	33	36	4	35	18	4	23
Somewhat liberal	8	7	12	11	8	13	12	4	15
Moderate	34	20	14	21	14	12	28	13	16
Somewhat conservative	20	14	9	6	11	6	9	8	9
Conservative	20	8	6	8	11	7	14	6	9
Don't know	8	47	26	18	52	27	19	65	28
	100	100	100	100	100	100	100	100	100

TABLE 7

POLITICAL EFFICACY[a] AMONG TEXAS VOTERS BY RACE AND ETHNICITY (IN PERCENTAGES)

Degree of efficacy	*Anglo (N=797)*	*Negro (N=419)*	*Mex. Am. (N=375)*
High	24	8	10
Medium	49	46	46
Low	27	46	44
	100	100	100

[a]The efficacy scale is that set forth by Angus Campbell, Gerald Gurin, and Warren E. Miller, *The Voter Decides* (Evanston: Row, Peterson and Co., 1954), pp. 187–189.

should be worrisome to any person concerned with the health of the body politic.[13] Given the fact that Anglos dominate the Texas political system, it is not surprising that they also report higher levels of efficacy than do members of the other two groups. What is a bit puzzling is that the levels of efficacy for Mexican Americans are almost exactly the same level as for blacks, for in most other dimensions treated here the Mexican Americans have occupied a position intermediate between blacks and Anglos.

When alienation is considered we return to that familiar pattern (Table 8).[14] More than one-half (52 percent) of our Negro respondents scored high on the alienation scale, compared to 36 percent of the Mexican Americans and "only" 25 percent of the Anglos. Presumably that pattern is broadly reflective of the differences in the experiences and general status of the three groups in Texas, though class is likely to be a factor as well. In any case, the existence within any social group of a low level of efficacy combined with a high degree of political alienation portends a volatile, potentially disruptive situation. As has been pointed out elsewhere, when social groups such as blacks or Mexican Americans are unhappy with their share of society's scarce resources and when they feel that it is impossible to otherwise alter that distribution, violence may be their only recourse.[15]

CONCLUSIONS

The implications of these findings for the future of Mexican Americans in Texas depends heavily on how one tries to explain the causes of their present

TABLE 8

POLITICAL ALIENATION[a] AMONG TEXAS VOTERS BY RACE AND ETHNICITY (IN PERCENTAGES)

Degree of alienation	*Anglo (N=797)*	*Negro (N=419)*	*Mex. Am. (N=375)*
High	25	52	36
Medium	30	34	38
Low	45	14	26
	100	100	100

[a]See John P. Robinson and Phillip R. Shaver, *Measures of Social Psychological Attitudes* (Ann Arbor: Institute for Social Research, 1969), pp. 172–176.

status. As summarized by Almaguer, four distinct lines of interpretation have been developed: (1) deficiencies of the group (i.e., Mexican Americans are held back by their own cultural values and traditions); (2) racism and discrimination; (3) class domination; and (4) internal colonialism. Our present knowledge is such that in all likelihood we cannot safely embrace or reject any one of the above,[16] but the point is that acceptance of any one of these explanations implies that–barring a revolution–change for Mexican Americans will come primarily through economic and social rather than through political processes.

This may be so, but one should not dismiss the possibility that politics can be an independent or at least an intervening variable capable of shaping the social and economic status of a group. Even if so, we must still ask whether Mexican Americans in Texas can turn electoral politics to greater advantage. They have several important assets. One is numbers, for they constitute around 15 percent of the electorate. As noted earlier, there is considerable geographical concentration, thus facilitating the building of a political base around the control of local offices. Their intermediate political status, discussed above, would seem to give them flexibility in the formation of coalitions and the development of the "swing" capacity needed to play a balance of power role in elections. From our data there appears to be enough ideological feeling (liberal) to provide a degree of consensus on goals. It would appear, then, that there is indeed an unrealized potential for increasing the political power of Mexican Americans.

But the path to attainment of that power is by no means clear. In addition to the inevitable problems of resources, organizations, and leadership, there is the dilemma familiar enough to blacks: Is it better to pursue liberal Democratic coalition politics with all the compromises, sharings, and delays that it entails, or to go it alone with all the rocks and shoals associated with minor party activity? Not surprisingly, Mexican Americans elected to legislative and local offices on the Democratic ticket see coalition politics as the preferred path, as do other Democrats who need Mexican support for their ticket. And indeed it is true that in some cases the withdrawal of Mexican American support for liberal Democratic candidates will ensure the election of more conservative officials, at least in the short run.

But the strategy of "going it alone" has its supporters too, and hence the formation in 1970 of a new political party, La Raza Unida. It began by contesting local (legally) nonpartisan elections in the Crystal City area and subsequently expanded into other South Texas counties. Then, in 1972, it offered candidates for state office as well. There is some reason to believe that LRU in 1972 withdrew enough votes from the Democratic primary to cause the defeat of several liberal candidates, including one Mexican American state senator. On the other hand, in the general election, LRU won several local offices. More importantly, for a time it appeared to have split off enough votes from the Democratic gubernatorial nominee to bring about the election of the first Republican governor since Reconstruction (eventually the Democratic candidate emerged with about 48 percent, the Republican with about 45 percent, and LRU's candidate with about 6 percent).

That election illustrates quite well the possibilities and the pitfalls of the minor party strategy. If LRU is able to play successfully a balance of power role, it may be able to improve the policies of the major parties toward Mexican Americans, regardless of what it can get for itself in the way of tangible rewards. By improving the prospects for a GOP victory, such a role for LRU might also help to bring about a realignment of the party system by speeding the shift of conservative Anglos from the Democratic to the Republican party. But to the extent that LRU reduces Mexican American participation in the Democratic party, it shrinks the prospects for a successful liberal coalition and increases the likelihood of continued conservative control of the state (indeed, the Republican gubernatorial candidate who was almost elected in 1972 because of LRU's role was far more conservative than the eventual Democratic winner).

At this stage, it is not at all certain which alternative Mexican Americans will or should pursue; it may be that some of each is the answer. What does seem clear is that there are improved opportunities for a larger role for Mexican Americans in Texas politics. We like to think of the data reported above as a kind of bench mark which in the years ahead we can periodically consult to measure the rate and direction of political change in Texas.

NOTES

1. U.S. Bureau of the Census, Census of Population: 1970, *General Social and Economic Characteristics,* Final Report PC (1) C45 Texas (Washington, D.C.: U.S. Government Printing Office, 1972).

2. For interesting examples of the situation in the 1940's in Texas, see Pauline R. Kibbe, *Latin-Americans in Texas* (Albuquerque: University of New Mexico Press, 1946).

3. Interestingly enough, the Republican party has a much better record than the Democratic party for nominating Mexican Americans for state office. The GOP nominated Rudy Garza for Comptroller of Public Accounts in 1966, Manuel Sanchez for Treasurer in 1968, and Edward Yturri for Attorney General in 1970. (All fell short of winning.) Though we have not made a systematic check, it seems unlikely that *any* Mexican American has been nominated for state office by the Democratic Party, certainly not in the twentieth century.

4. The development of political machines in South Texas has been chronicled by O. D. Weeks, "The Texas-Mexican and the Politics of South Texas," *American Political Science Review,* 24 (Aug., 1930), pp. 606-627.

5. A study by José Angel Gutiérrez (unpublished paper, Department of Government, University of Texas at Austin) showed more than 700 elected Mexican American officials in Texas in 1971, most of them holding county, district, and school offices. In the same year there probably were not more than 50 elected black officials in Texas, though the black population is about two-thirds that of Mexican Americans.

6. Allen M. Shinn, Jr., "A Note on Voter Registration and Turnout in Texas, 1960-1970," *Journal of Politics,* 33 (Nov., 1971), pp. 1120-1129.

7. Clifton McCleskey and Dan Nimmo, "Differences Between Potential, Registered, and Actual Voters: The Houston Metropolitan Area in 1964," *Social Science Quarterly,* 49 (June, 1968), pp. 103-114; Nimmo and McCleskey, "Impact of the Poll Tax on Voter Participation: The Houston Metropolitan Area in 1966," *Journal of Politics,* 31 (Aug., 1969), pp. 682-699.

8. The behavioral data presented in the remainder of this paper are taken from a statewide, multistaged, proportionately stratified (population and race), random probability sample conducted by Merrill Research of Dallas, Texas. The study was initially sponsored by Sam Wyly Foundation and the authors gratefully acknowledge their contribution. One thousand five hundred and seventy-one (1,571) respondents were interviewed during the last two weeks of November, 1969. Five callbacks were made and 81 percent of the original sample was interviewed. A substitution technique was used to replace people not interviewed so data cells would be large enough during the analysis phase of the study. The confidence interval for the sample when P=.50 was calculated to be ± 2.7 percent (effective N=1273).

One significant limitation should be kept in mind when interpreting this data. Only individuals who were registered to vote or who indicated to our interviewers they definitely would vote were interviewed. Thus, the data generalizes only to the actual Texas electorate in 1969 and not to the entire potential electorate.

9. See Bruce Merrill, "Party Realignment and Social Class: 1958-1970" (unpublished doctoral dissertation, University of Michigan, 1971).

10. The existence of such strategy is deduced from newspaper accounts of recent meetings in South Texas featuring Republican party leaders and candidates.

11. See for instance, Angus Campbell, *et al.*, *The American Voter* (New York: Wiley and Sons, 1960), pp. 188-215. But see also Gerald Pomper, "From Confusion to Clarity: Issues and American Voters, 1956-1968," *American Political Science Review,* 66 (June, 1972), pp. 415-428.

12. For an effort to get at the existence and influence of liberal-conservative attitudes, see Lloyd Free and Hadley Cantril, *The Political Beliefs of Americans: A Study of Public Opinion* (New York: Simon and Schuster, 1968). While they found the liberal-conservative dimension meaningful for ideological and for operational purposes, they conclude that self-identification was not a very helpful indicator.

13. "Sense of political efficacy may be defined as the feeling that individual political action does have, or can have, an impact upon the political process, i.e., that it is worthwhile to perform one's civic duties. It is the feeling that political and social change is possible, and that the individual citizen can play a part in bringing about this change." Angus Campbell, Gerald Gurin, and Warren E. Miller, *The Voter Decides* (Evanston, Ill.: Row, Peterson, 1954), p. 187. For a review of the salient findings on political efficacy, see Lester Milbrath, *Political Participation* (Chicago: Rand McNally, 1965), pp. 56ff.

14. Alienation and cynicism imply a more active and hostile orientation towards politics and government than the passive withdrawal and detachment of anomie. As with anomie, the overwhelming majority of the existing evidence indicates that those who are alienated tend towards political withdrawal. Also they more than likely find little to be proud of in the political system. They more than likely have little faith in majority rule. They more than likely regard politicians as corrupt or inept or both." Don R. Bowen, *Political Behavior of the American Public* (Columbus, Ohio: Charles E. Merrill, 1968), p. 112. For a more extended discussion of alienation, see Milbrath, *Political Participation,* pp. 78-81.

15. William Gamson, *Power and Discontent* (Homewood: Dorsey Press, 1968).

16. Tomás Almaguer, "Toward the Study of Chicano Colonialism," *Aztlan,* 2 (Spring 1971), pp. 7-22. He concludes that the fourth explanation is the only viable one.

9: THE MEXICAN-AMERICAN AND THE CHURCH

César E. Chávez

THE PLACE TO BEGIN IS WITH OUR OWN EXPERIENCE WITH THE CHURCH in the strike which has gone on for thirty-one months in Delano. For in Delano the Church has been involved with the poor in a unique way which should stand as a symbol to other communities. Of course, when we refer to the Church we should define the word a little. We mean the whole Church, the Church as an ecumenical body spread around the world, and not just its particular form in a parish in a local community. The Church we are talking about is a tremendously powerful institution in our society, and in the world. That Church is one form of the Presence of God on Earth, and so naturally it is powerful. It is powerful by definition. It is a powerful moral and spiritual force which cannot be ignored by any movement. Furthermore, it is an organization with tremendous wealth. Since the Church is to be servant to the poor, it is *our* fault if that wealth is not channeled to help the poor in our world.

In a small way we have been able, in the Delano strike, to work together with the Church in such a way as to bring some of its moral and economic power to bear on those who want to maintain the status quo, keeping farm workers in virtual enslavement. In brief, here is what happened in Delano.

Some years ago, when some of us were working with the Community Service Organization, we began to realize the powerful effect which the

From *El Grito* I, no. 4 (Summer 1968), pp. 9-12. Reprinted by permission of Quinto Sol Publications, Inc. and the United Farm Workers, AFL-CIO.

The article was prepared by Mr. Chávez during a 25-day "spiritual fast" and was presented to a meeting on "Mexican-Americans and the Church" at the second Annual Mexican-American Conference in Sacramento, California on March 8-10, 1968.

Church can have on the conscience of the opposition. In scattered instances, in San Jose, Sacramento, Oakland, Los Angeles and other places, priests would speak out loudly and clearly against specific instances of oppression, and in some cases, stand with the people who were being hurt. Furthermore, a small group of priests, Frs. McDonald, McCollough, Duggan and others, began to pinpoint attention on the terrible situation of the farm workers in our state.

At about that same time, we began to run into the California Migrant Ministry in the camps and fields. They were about the only ones there, and a lot of us were very suspicious, since we were Catholics and they were Protestants. However, they had developed a very clear conception of the Church. It was called to serve, to be at the mercy of the poor, and not to try to use them. After a while this made a lot of sense to us, and we began to find ourselves working side by side with them. In fact, it forced us to raise the question why OUR Church was not doing the same. We would ask, "Why do the Protestants come out here and help the people, demand nothing, and give all their time to serving farm workers, while our own parish priests stay in their churches, where only a few people come, and usually feel uncomfortable?"

It was not until some of us moved to Delano and began working to build the National Farm Workers Association that we really saw how far removed from the people the parish Church was. In fact, we could not get any help at all from the priests of Delano. When the strike began, they told us we could not even use the Church's auditorium for the meetings. The farm workers' money helped build that auditorium! But the Protestants were there again, in the form of the California Migrant Ministry, and they began to help in little ways, here and there.

When the strike started in 1965, most of our "friends" forsook us for a while. They ran—or were just too busy to help. But the California Migrant Ministry held a meeting with its staff and decided that the strike was a matter of life or death for farm workers everywhere, and that even if it meant the end of the Migrant Ministry they would turn over their resources to the strikers. The political pressure on the Protestant Churches was tremendous and the Migrant Ministry lost a lot of money. But they stuck it out, and they began to point the way to the rest of the Church. In fact, when 30 of the strikers were arrested for shouting Huelga, 11 ministers went to jail with them. They were in Delano that day at the request of Chris Hartmire, director of the California Migrant Ministry.

Then the workers began to raise the question: "Why ministers? Why not priests? What does the Bishop say?" But the Bishop said nothing. But slowly the pressure of the people grew and grew, until finally we have in Delano a priest sent by the new Bishop, Timothy Manning, who is there to help minister to the needs of farm workers. His name is Father Mark Day and he is the Union's chaplain. *Finally,* our own Catholic Church has decided to recognize that we have our own peculiar needs, just as the growers have theirs.

But outside of the local diocese, the pressure built up on growers to negotiate was tremendous. Though we were not allowed to have our own priest, the power of the ecumenical body of the Church was tremendous. The work of the Church, for example, in the Schenley, Di Giorgio, Perelli-Minetti strikes was fantastic. They applied pressure—and they mediated.

When poor people get involved in a long conflict, such as a strike, or a civil rights drive, and the pressure increases each day, there is a deep need for spiritual advice. Without it we see families crumble, leadership weaken, and hard workers grow tired. And in such a situation the spiritual advice must be given by a *friend,* not by the opposition. What sense does it make to go to Mass on Sunday and reach out for spiritual help, and instead get sermons about the wickedness of your cause? That only drives one to question and to despair. The growers in Delano have their spiritual problems . . . we do not deny that. They have every right to have priests and ministers, who serve their needs. BUT WE HAVE DIFFERENT NEEDS, AND SO WE NEEDED A FRIENDLY SPIRITUAL GUIDE. And this is true in every community in this state where the poor face tremendous problems.

But the opposition raises a tremendous howl about this. They don't want us to have our spiritual advisors, friendly to our needs. Why is this? Why indeed except that THERE IS TREMENDOUS SPIRITUAL AND ECONOMIC POWER IN THE CHURCH. The rich know it, and for that reason they choose to keep it from the people.

The leadership of the Mexican-American Community must admit that we have fallen far short in our task of helping provide spiritual guidance for our people. We may say, "I don't feel any such need. I can get along." But that is a poor excuse for not helping provide such help for others. For we can also say, "I don't need any welfare help. I can take care of my own problems." But we are all willing to fight like hell for welfare aid for those who truly need it, who would starve without it. Likewise we may have gotten an education and not care about scholarship money for ourselves, or our children. But we would, we should, fight like hell to see to it that our state provides aid for any child needing it so that he can get the education he desires. LIKEWISE WE CAN SAY WE DON'T NEED THE CHURCH. THAT IS OUR BUSINESS. BUT THERE ARE HUNDREDS OF THOUSANDS OF OUR PEOPLE WHO DESPERATELY NEED SOME HELP FROM THAT POWERFUL INSTITUTION, THE CHURCH, AND WE ARE FOOLISH NOT TO HELP THEM GET IT.

For example, the Catholic Charities agencies of the Catholic Church has millions of dollars earmarked for the poor. But often the money is spent for food baskets for the needy instead of for effective action to eradicate the causes of poverty. The men and women who administer this money sincerely want to help their brothers. It should be our duty to help direct the attention to the basic needs of the Mexican-Americans in our society . . . needs which cannot be satisfied with baskets of food, but rather with effective organizing at the grass roots level.

Therefore, I am calling for Mexican-American groups to stop ignoring this source of power. It is not just our right to appeal to the Church to use its power effectively for the poor, it is our duty to do so. It should be as natural as appealing to government . . . and we do that often enough.

Furthermore, we should be prepared to come to the defense of that priest, rabbi, minister, or layman of the Church, who out of commitment to truth and justice gets into a tight place with his pastor or bishop. It behooves us to stand with that man and help him see his trial through. It is our duty to see to it that his rights of conscience are respected and that no bishop, pastor or other higher body takes that God-given, human right away.

Finally, in a nutshell, what do we want the Church to do? We don't ask for more cathedrals. We don't ask for bigger churches or fine gifts. We ask for its presence with us, beside us, as Christ among us. We ask the Church to *sacrifice with the people* for social change, for justice, and for love of brother. We don't ask for words. We ask for deeds. We don't ask for paternalism. We ask for servanthood.

II. Accommodation Politics

THE POLITICS OF ACCOMMODATION ARE THE "CONVENTIONAL" OR "traditional" politics that white ethnic groups have generally used to carve their niche in the American political system. Accommodation politics is well suited to a culturally pluralistic social system or a melting-pot society. But, since neither of these social systems exist in regard to the Chicano in the U.S., his use of accommodation politics may not be an optimal strategy. Accommodation politics generally involves working within the system, that is, employing strategies which are considered to be within propriety by the majority society. These are the politics of the electoral process, the politics of pressure groups, of lobbying, of political parties, of writing letters to elected representatives. The essential and characteristic process of accommodation is that of negotiation, log-rolling and compromise.

In accommodation politics, the demands presented to the political decision-makers are not "radical" demands, i.e., existing institutions are not challenged, nor is a basic redistribution of power sought. The direct involvement of masses of people seeking both a widespread distribution of material benefits and the preservation or promotion of intangible or symbolic values does not fall within the conventional political norms. Instead, persons or groups involved in an accommodative political process operate within the generally accepted institutional and value framework of the American core culture. Accommodationists are generally willing to accept the system as is, and only desire entrance and acceptance into the system. While it is sometimes difficult to ascertain whether a particular political move is accommodative or not, perhaps the best "rule of thumb" is whether or not it is deemed acceptable, right, and proper by the majority of people.

Accommodation politics therefore does not usually result in comprehensive policy changes. In fact, comprehensive or radical change involving a widespread redistribution of power probably cannot occur using this type of politics exclusively. Policy changes are most likely incremental and the redistribution of power is slow in coming about if it ever does.

In this section we will examine three types of accommodation politics: 1) the politics of recognition, 2) collective welfare benefits politics, and 3) preferments and secondary benefits. These are listed in order of increasing importance, each succeeding type being more likely to accomplish a basic or an important change in the distribution of political power between the core culture and the Chicano people.

A. Recognition

RECOGNITION IS THE LOWEST ORDER OF ACCOMMODATION POLITICS. IN this style of politics, individual ethnics can achieve a position of political significance and thereby reap some material benefits. However, few, if any, material benefits are rewarded to the masses. The individual ethnic who succeeds politically is one who is acceptable to the current power structure. This means that the ethnic, although he may be representative of his group from the perspective of the core culture, cannot be *too* ethnic, that is, not so ethnic that he is not acceptable to the majority society.

A major characteristic of recognition politics, therefore, is that a particular ethnic group is recognized by the core power structure as being important enough to warrant one of their members taking a place in the political system. However, the individual ethnic in this case owes his position not to the strength of his own ethnic constituency, but instead is beholden to the power structure. This strategy of recognition may be devised to buy off more substantive demands by the ethnic masses through the substitution of psychic rewards to the ethnic community. The community, then, is supposed to exult in the fact that one of theirs has been chosen for a seemingly important position and that they, as a group, are important enough to be noticed by the powers that be.

Thus the politics of recognition often involves "token" appointments—appointments of ethnics to positions which are more a showpiece for the politician in power than they are an actual increase in the political influence of a particular ethnic group. While providing some psychological rewards to the ethnic group, the politics of recognition can drain off native leadership from the ethnic community and thereby retard the building of an ethnic political power base.

The articles in this section demonstrate that Chicano political leadership has often been the result of recognition politics. The first selection, comprised of three newspaper articles written before and after the 1972 presidential election, provides a recent example of the way in which recognition strategies may be employed by the major political parties. Chicano "leaders" (those recognized as such by the Anglo community) often are not truly representative of their ethnic community. The Watson and Samora article, first published in 1954, illustrates how native leadership is often of a subordinate nature in a community containing both core culture and native ethnic individuals, and hypothesizes about the reason for this situation. Factors intrinsic to the "Spanish American" culture are discussed as well as the probably greater effects resulting from decades of Anglo domination. A Chicano leadership which stems from a power base in the Chicano community itself is crucial to the Chicano's political destiny—yet the dependent position of the Chicano makes emergence and development of effective leaders very problematic.

10: THE "CHICANO RECOGNITION" STRATEGY OF A NATIONAL PARTY

Tony Castro

WHILE CESAR CHAVEZ FIGHTS THE farming lords in California, while Jose Angel Gutierrez struggles with his Raza Unida party in Texas and while Reies Tijerina spearheads his people's movement in New Mexico . . .

While the Chicano or Brown Power revolution smolders and occasionally catches fire, a more sensitive and almost obscure Mexican-American revolution is quietly evolving in federal offices in the Southwest and Washington, D.C.

In the vernacular of the Nixon administration, it is a revolution that perhaps can best be described as the Republicanization of the Mexican-American.

For in the last three years, Mexican-Americans have been placed in more federal government jobs and named to higher government positions than ever before in their history.

In the last year alone, President Nixon has:

- Named Phillip V. Sanchez, a defeated GOP candidate for Congress in California, as national director of the Office of Economic Opportunity.
- Appointed Mrs. Romana A. Banuelos, a Los Angeles businesswoman, as treasurer of the United States, becoming the first Mexican-American woman named to such a high government post.
- And revived the long-slumbering Cabinet Committee on Opportunities for Spanish Speaking People with the appointment of Henry M. Ramirez, an educator from the President's home town, as its chairman.

The administration's appointments, the dispersion of jobs and the sudden interest in Mexican-American affairs all point to the obvious:

President Nixon, often accused of being a habitual campaigner, is politicking to woo the Mexican-Ameri-

Reprinted with permission of the *Dallas Morning News.*

cans, the country's second largest minority group, which some observers feel may determine whether Mr. Nixon goes down in history as a 1- or 2-term President.

Most of the estimated 11 million Mexican-Americans live in five Southwestern states–Texas, California, Colorado, New Mexico and Arizona–where their votes are considered the swing votes between the Democratic and Republican tickets.

Altogether, these five states are worth 86 electoral votes, almost a third of the number needed for re-election.

And thus with re-election time a little more than 10 months away, the President's strategy in appealing to Mexican-Americans has become as exposed as his Southern Strategy was in 1968.

Republicans, Democrats and Mexican-Americans all generally admit that a Chicano Strategy is under way.

"The President has had a fight with labor and he has no credibility with the blacks," said Texas GOP Chairman Dr. George Willeford. "He's got more credibility with Mexican–Americans than with any other one special-interest group."

But what makes the President's Chicano Strategy even a bigger threat to the Democrats is its timing, coming when Mexican-Americans are openly disgruntled with their lack of progress within Democratic party ranks.

Mexican-Americans who have succeeded in the Democratic party are few. And those who have been elected to public office as Democrats have come from areas where Mexican-Americans are a majority of the population.

Texas State Rep. Paul C. Moreno of El Paso, a Democrat, is an example, and he firmly believes his people "are going to have a definite effect on the results of the next election."

"We're fed up with the promises we've been getting from the Democrats," he said. "The Democratic party just hasn't delivered (for the Mexican-American) . . . I see a definite political revolt into the Republican party unless something drastic comes around among Democrats."

Part of the Mexican-American disenchantment with the Democratic party already has manifested itself in the creation of La Raza Unida party, which is expected to have considerable impact in South Texas.

But the Nixon administration's strongest tool in appealing to Mexican-American voters is its decision to place Mexican-Americans in high position and then to show off its appointees to the public.

Henry M. Ramirez, for instance, visited Dallas earlier this month when the U.S. Civil Rights Commission released its second report on Mexican-American education in the Southwest.

Ramirez, formerly chief of the commission's Mexican-American division, directed the $1-million federal study.

At a news conference, however, he went to great lengths to emphasize that he now is head of the President's Cabinet committee for Spanish-speaking people.

"As I move throughout the country," Ramirez said in an earlier interview, "I find the Spanish-speaking people saying they are now more than ever in a position to evaluate what both parties have to offer.

"They are taking a good close look at the Nixon administration with an eye to possibly giving more support than they did before—which was very little—based on performance."

Republicans are measuring the President's performance on the number of brown faces which the administration has placed in government positions.

"We know that if the Democrats win (next year) we'll all be replaced," said one Mexican-American federal employee in a Dallas regional office. "What we want to see, though, is if we're replaced by other Mexican-Americans.

"The Nixon administration has a track record for having put a great number of us on the government payroll, more than ever under the Democrats. If the President is beaten, it will at least be a test of how much the Democrats will do for our people."

The decision to place more Mexican-Americans in the administration has marked a reversal for President Nixon, whose ardor toward Mexican-American appointees probably cooled after his first top one—Small Business Administration chief Hilary Sandoval Jr. of El Paso—became entangled in corruption within the SBA.

Democrats, for the most part, sidestep the issue of unkept promises that have been made to the Mexican-American.

Minnesota Sen. Hubert H. Humphrey, the 1968 Democratic presidential nominee, and others criticize the Nixon administration for its opportunistic approach to the Mexican-American.

Humphrey, who is strongly considering making a bid for renomination by the Democrats, has intimated that the President's interest in Mexican-American affairs is only political and that it probably would taper off after next November.

The fact that the appointments of Mexican-Americans to high-ranking administration positions have been made within the last year gives credence to Humphrey's argument, as does the story of the administration's sudden reawakening of the Cabinet Committee on Opportunities for Spanish Speaking People.

Created during the Johnson administration, the Cabinet Committee began a 2-year siesta when President Nixon took office.

The law that created the committee required that the committee chairman meet with members of the President's Cabinet and that an advisory council be established.

But the Nixon administration failed to carry out the law. Both Committee Chairman Martin G. Castillo and Executive Director Henry Quevedo resigned their positions, reportedly under pressure from the White House.

And as late as last spring, a committee spokesman said, "Word has filtered down that we shouldn't even try to get near the White House."

The administration, according to the spokesman, was disturbed by the heavy Democratic vote by Mexican-Americans in the California and Texas senatorial elections in which President Nixon and the Republican candidates were rebuffed.

Last August, however, President Nixon appointed Ramirez to the long-vacant position of committee chairman and appointed an advisory council.

The White House action on the Cabinet committee was followed by the appointment of Mrs. Banuelos as U.S. treasurer, a position whose chief function is to sign all U.S. currency.

The appointment of Mrs. Banuelos, however, cost the administration some mileage when it was discovered that her $5-million-a-year food business employs a high number of illegal Mexican aliens who are hired for cheaper wages than she will pay Mexican-Americans.

But the administration's major political stroke in its Chicano Strategy was the appointment earlier this year of Phillip V. Sanchez as national director of the Office of Economic Opportunity, the administrative arm of the War on Poverty.

In his position, Sanchez is the highest-ranking Mexican-American in the administration.

A close look at OEO's role within the administration, however, indicates, as one White House critic put it, that "Sanchez is a chief without much of a tribe."

In the last three years, the administration slowly has been switching anti-poverty programs from OEO to other departments and it eventually hopes to make it a research and evaluation agency.

President Nixon also has opposed some of OEO's activist programs that have attacked local governments, and earlier this month he vetoed the controversial Child Development bill that incorporated measures to continue OEO funding and establishing an independent legal services corporation.

Like Ramirez, Sanchez has not hesitated in selling the Republican party to the public.

"Mexican-Americans are flocking to the Republican party," he said in an interview while in Dallas recently. "They (Democrats) have completely taken the Mexican-American for granted.

"They come to the fiestas and to woo us when it's election time and then you'll never hear from them again. What we need is a massive Mexican-American shift to the Republican party to show both the Democrats and Republicans a lesson."

Sanchez, however, reportedly now has found himself in an embarrassing situation with the White House over the appointment of a Mexican-American to the OEO Southwest regional office in Dallas.

In a copyrighted story Nov. 24, The Dallas News reported that the appointment was about to be made and that it was closely tied with President Nixon's strategy for winning Texas' 26 electoral votes in 1972.

The administration announced two weeks ago, the appointment of Samuel R. Martinez as the OEO Southwest regional director. But the previous week the White House had surprisingly delayed Sanchez's formal swearing-in ceremony.

A delay of a scheduled swearing-in ceremony is unheard of in Washington, and reliable sources indicated it may have been the administration's way of showing its displeasure with Sanchez's office, on whom it blames the news leak.

The swearing-in ceremony, according to the sources, is to take place soon, now that the Martinez appointment has been officially announced.

Texas thus emerges as a good example of how President Nixon hopes to utilize the Chicano Strategy in his re-election bid.

More than 2 million Mexican-Americans make up about 15 per cent of the state's population and are expected to comprise some 700,000 of the state's registered voters next year.

An estimated 3 per cent of the registered Mexican-American voters in Texas voted for the Republican ticket in 1968 when President Nixon lost the state by about 40,000 votes to Sen. Humphrey.

Theoretically, a shift to the Republican party of another 3 per cent of the Mexican-American voters in 1972 would make up the 40,000-vote difference.

Democrats and some Mexican-Americans argue that the Republicans are facing an uphill effort in trying to convert Mexican-Americans to Republicanism. Mexican-Americans traditionally have voted Democratic.

Republicans admit the difficulties of the Chicano Strategy, but interestingly enough they concede there is some selectivity to the plan.

"I don't see any way of courting the entire Mexican-American bloc vote," said State GOP Chairman Willeford. "We want to appeal to the middle-class Mexican-American that is emerging today."

In some respects, the middle-class Mexican-American group is one that the Republican party awakened to after the 1968 election.

"After 1968," said Dallas County GOP Chairman Tom Crouch, "it was the general consensus that one of the target areas for new voter potential was among the Mexican-Americans."

Texas Republicans have established an advisory committee on Mexican-American affairs, and they say the number of Mexican-Americans who have registered as Republicans in the last three years has surprised even the party.

Among the most loyal of the party's Mexican-American members are the government employes, many of them having reached middle-class status within the last three years.

In the past Mexican-Americans have complained that while they have made up some 7 per cent of the nation's population, they composed less than 3 per cent of the federal government work force.

"The idea of giving high-level jobs to Chicanos will take its toll against the Democrats," said State Sen. Joe Bernal, himself a Democrat.

That middle-class, organization mindedness of today's urban Mexican-Americans is demonstrated by the recent Houston mayor's race.

In the runoff election, Louie Welch, who had the support of Republican precinct organizations, got more than half the Mexican-American vote. Meanwhile, challenger Fred Hofheinz, who had the minority-liberal-labor election apparatus, garnered 94 per cent of the black vote—indicating that minority support is by no means monolithic.

Many Mexican-Americans also have remained miffed at the Democrats since 1966, when a Rio Grande Valley farm workers march on the State Capitol was snubbed in Austin by then—Gov. John B. Connally.

Instead of meeting the marchers in Austin, Connally along with then Atty. Gen. Waggoner Carr and Ben Barnes, who was state House speaker at the time, met the farm workers in New Braunfels to tell them he would not greet them in Austin.

Conally rejected the demands being made by the marchers, and he angered the farm workers even more when they interpreted his remarks as meaning he could not lend the dignity of the governor's office to greeting them at the Capitol.

Carr was running for the U.S. Senate that year and later was decisively beaten by Sen. John G. Tower, who got the votes of countless numbers of liberals, blacks and Mexican-Americans who chose not to support the conservative Democrat candidate.

A question now hanging is what effect the Nixon Chicano Strategy will have on other races in the state. Sen. Tower again is up for re-election, and the governor's race includes what will be a bitter Democratic primary battle.

Making the Texas Democrats' position even more precarious is new State AFL-CIO President Roy Evans, who has vowed to support only candidates sympathetic to labor and minority positions.

Mexican-Americans traditionally have sided along with labor, and the AFL-CIO's new posture could present difficulties for several Democrats, including Lt. Gov. Ben Barnes, who is running for governor.

State Sen. Bernal believes the Democrats "are going to have to humanize a little bit."

"They are going to have to start thinking in serious terms that the party is going to need the Chicano vote and the black vote," he said.

Democrats like Dallas County Chairman Earl Luna, however, discount the seriousness with which Mexican-Americans are contemplating a switch to the GOP.

"I think they (Mexican-Americans) recognize this as a tokenism type thing which is simply an attempt to get some votes from some people for whom the Republican party has never produced," Luna said.

"The so-called wooing by the Republican party is wishful thinking."

Epilogue:

LATINOS LEFT OUT IN COLD

Peggy Simpson

WASHINGTON (AP)–Leaders of the Spanish-speaking community are complaining that despite a record vote for President Nixon, Latinos are getting neither the programs nor the top-level jobs they want from the administration.

"You have been used and you have been deceived and you have been lied to," Rep. Henry B. Gonzalez, D-Tex., told one gathering of Latino leaders.

"Spanish-speaking voters gave the President a vote of confidence, and we've been left out in the cold," said Tony Gallegos, national chairman of the American GI Forum, a Mexican-American organization.

An administration official, Fred Malek, said there will be more appointments for Mexican-American and other Spanish-speaking citizens in the next month or two.

But so far in the second Nixon administration no Spanish person has been named to a high position.

During the campaign, The Nixon re-election committee courted the Spanish minority with elaborate bilingual brochures and films; and with frequent banquet circuit tours by latin-Americans in the administration, including treasurer Romana Banuelos and antipoverty chief Philip V. Sanchez.

Since the election, Sanchez has been removed as head of the Office of Economic Opportunity, and Carlos C. Villarreal eased out as head of the Urban Mass Transportation Administration. Mrs. Banuelos was asked to stay, but her tenure is expected to be brief.

The Latin Community had expected representation in undersecretary and assistant secretary posts, but most of them have now been filled. And some programs

Reprinted from the *Albuquerque Journal,* February 21, 1973, with permission of the Associated Press.

aimed at the nation's second largest minority are being phased out.

A group named SER-Service Employment Redevelopment—which is a joint venture of two Latino groups—got a 50 per cent money increase in a contract signed by Nixon in a ceremony last fall. Soon afterward, SER received a telegram saying there would be no increase. Now there are indications the group will be cut off altogether.

Malek, a former special assistant to the President, says there will be no erosion of Latino influence.

"When the dust all settles you'll probably find more Mexican-American and other Spanish-speaking in high positions than you did before the election," Malek said in an interview. He now is deputy director of the Office of Management and Budget.

Malek said Nixon himself set the tone for hiring more Spanish-speaking and that is why he is convinced it will continue.

Even though one or two Latinos are leaving, he said, other appointments are in the mill.

"Anybody who suggests that they're not being rewarded simply isn't letting us have a chance to demonstrate that we care," he added. "We're not looking simply at which groups gave us the vote increase but at those who are best going to serve the public interest and we recognize a large untapped reservoir in the Mexican-American community."

Alex Armendariz, a Chicago economist who headed the Hispanic campaign for Nixon, said the vote shift to Republicans was dramatic in the Latino community. He breaks it down into three categories: the Mexican-American vote moved from 10 per cent Republican in 1968 to 36 per cent in 1972; the Puerto Rican vote, from 17 to 27 per cent; and the Cuban vote, from 60 to 70 per cent.

Armendariz is among those who believes there will be an upturn in Latino fortunes. He said Nixon's post-election reorganization is unprecedented in its scope and appointments are thereby being delayed.

At election time there were 49 Latinos in supergrades—people who need presidential appointments for the $25,000-and-over jobs. Since then with no new appointments, these changes have occurred:

—Sanchez, removed as head of the OEO, is destined for an ambassadorship, probably to Panama. Persons close to Sanchez say he is unsure whether his political ambitions—let alone his finances—can survive a term as ambassador to such a hot spot nation.

—Villarreal, eased out as administrator of the Urban Mass Transportation Administration, is being offered other jobs but, apparently, not the right one yet.

—Rodolfo Montejano left his California law practice to accept Nixon's nomination last June to the Interstate Commerce Commission. The Senate didn't get around to confirm him and he was serving an interim appointment when he learned early this year Nixon apparently has decided against resubmitting his name.

–Horacio Rivero, the only Spanish-speaking ambassador yet named by Nixon, is reportedly on the verge of being recalled from Spain. Rivero was confirmed only in September.

–Carlos Conde and Antonio Rodriguez have worked in the White House on jobs apparently to be dropped in Nixon's executive reorganization. They may be offered replacement jobs but this clears the White House staff of Spanish surnamed "advocates."

–Henry Ramirez, chairman of the Cabinet Committee on Opportunities for Spanish Speaking Peoples, doesn't know yet whether he'll be staying. There have been reports the administration would like to dismantle the agency.

WASHINGTON (AP)–Former antipoverty chief Philip Sanchez is expected to be named ambassador to Honduras this week, but four others with Spanish surnames in federal policy positions have lost their jobs.

They are Ed Aguirre, who was regional director of the Dept. of Labor in San Francisco; Sam Martinez, regional director of the Office of Economic Opportunity in Dallas; Pete Mireles, chief of the migrant division of OEO; and Antonio Rodriguez, a White House aide.

Presidential counselor Anne Armstrong said the erosion will be short-term only and that announcements will be coming soon of important government positions for more members of the Spanish-speaking minority.

One appointment she apparently had in mind was that of Sanchez as ambassador to Honduras.

On election day last fall, 52 Spanish-surnamed persons held "supergrade" positions in the Nixon administration.

The Nixon re-election campaign committee had noted this in bilingual appeals to the more than 10 million Spanish-surnamed citizens, most of whom have been Democratic stalwarts in the past.

Martinez's departure was expected in some circles because of the elimination of the Dallas-Southwestern OEO region. He plans to return to private life in Denver.

Mireles' migrant division is being moved intact, however, to the Housing and Urban Dept. and he had wanted to go with it.

Rodriguez has been on the federal payroll since early in the Nixon administration. Recently he had been on the State Dept. rolls but worked mostly out of the White House, recruiting Spanish-surnamed persons for federal jobs.

Reprinted from the *Albuquerque Journal,* March 14, 1973, with permission of the Associated Press.

11: SUBORDINATE LEADERSHIP IN A BICULTURAL COMMUNITY: An Analysis

James B. Watson and Julian Samora

IT IS HELD IN THE PRESENT PAPER THAT THE ABILITY OF A SUBORDINATE group to generate effective leadership in its relations with a dominant alien people is a critical aspect of dominant-subordinate group relationships. The subordinate group in question here is the Spanish of the Southwest. We wish to see the Spanish leadership in its autonomous setting, to see it in relation to the intercultural system which is emerging between Spanish and Anglo-Americans, and to consider leadership and some of its acculturational consequences.

REGIONAL BACKGROUND OF THE CASE

The Spanish-speaking people are one of the largest United States ethnic minorities, and are concentrated principally in the southwestern part of the nation. Those whose forefathers were in the area in 1843 when the United States acquired the territory are also among the oldest ethnic groups, although many others have entered the region from Mexico over the intervening years. The Spanish-speaking are not powerful politically, a fact closely related to the perennial lack of leadership among them. They are seen by some authorities as surprisingly undifferentiated, compared to other large American ethnic groups, in schooling, in occupation, in income, and in degree of acculturation.[1] Perhaps the most outstanding fact about the Spanish, besides their lack of leadership is their low rate of acculturation. The special historical status of the Spanish may have a bearing upon the two facts, and the broad historical context suggests linkages between the leadership question and that of low assimilation.

From *American Sociological Review* 19 (1954), pp. 413-421. Reprinted by permission of the American Sociological Association.

The Southwestern Spanish[2] were a separate society when they came into contact with, and in a sense were conquered by Anglo-Americans, or "Anglos." Speaking a separate language and practicing separate customs, they were highly visible culturally. They represented nevertheless a modified branch of European civilization, unlike the Indians from whom they had received many influences, and unlike African slaves. In contrast to many Europeans who migrated to the United States, however, they had not voluntarily elected to adopt the lifeways of the dominant group. Moreover, they were more "native" and ecologically more adapted to their habitat in the Southwest than the dominant group. In these two respects they were more like Indians than immigrants. In the growing similarity of their goals with those of the dominant group, the Spanish are comparable to the present United States Negro, though their cultural similarity to Anglos is much less. In the sense of being a "conquered people" enslaved by their conquerors, the Spanish are somewhat like colonial people but more strictly comparable to the French of Canada. They differ from the French, however, in having smaller numerical strength relative to the dominant group, and they did not occupy the beachhead and focal areas of the Anglo-American culture and society. Their relative isolation (1650-1900) from the parent culture as well as from the Anglo culture is also an important factor with respect to assimilation.

Hence, historically having less motivation toward assimilation and deeper environmental and traditional roots than most U. S. immigrants, less commitment to and a less exclusive need for identification with the dominant cultural system than U. S. Negroes, but smaller numerical strength and less strategic position than the Canadian French, the Spanish as a group might be expected, more than others, to sense ambivalences about assimilation. Again, beside the fact of an increasing struggle for status in the Anglo system, one must place the opposing fact—peculiar to the Southwestern Spanish—that they have at their backs an effective reservoir of Spanish language and national Mexican culture to help reinforce and stabilize any tendency toward cultural separatism.

All of these broad, contradictory factors probably play their part in the default of Spanish leadership, as well as the more specific factors discussed below. In the larger Southwestern setting ambivalence about nativism *vs.* assimilation would obscure the direction Spanish leadership should take and thus hamstring the development of effective leadership.

Turning to the present, there is singularly little controversy concerning whether Spanish leadership is weak, regardless of the point of view of different commentators. Agreement is all but unanimous among scientific investigators,[3] among social workers and public and private agencies interested in the Spanish-speaking people, among Anglo politicians, and among the people themselves. The Spanish of "Mountain Town," the subject of the present paper, are no exception.

THE COMMUNITY STUDIED

In the summers of 1949 and 1950, students from the Department of Sociology and Anthropology of Washington University, under James B. Watson's direction, carried out part of an intended long-range study of a small Anglo-Spanish community. Samora further pursued field work in the community, relating particularly to the question of Spanish-speaking leadership and organization, in the spring and summer of 1952.[4] It is largely with the findings from this biethnic community that we propose to explore the question of weak leadership, but with the general background of the region always in mind.

Mountain Town, as we have called the community, is located in a high mountain valley of southern Colorado. It is at about 7000 feet above sea level, in an area of mixed truck farming and cattle and sheep ranching. Its 1950 population was close to 2500, comprising approximately 58 per cent Spanish-speaking and 42 per cent Anglos. (Hence the Spanish-speaking are not numerically a "minority" in the community itself, and will not be so called.) Founded around 1870, Mountain Town developed as a community of Anglo miners, storekeepers, and homesteaders. There were at the time but few "Old Spanish" families in the area, and they did not precede the Anglos by more than a decade or two. Mountain Town, hence developed differently from the older established Spanish communities to the south which Anglos have come to dominate. The difference may have a bearing in the discussion which follows.

Descendents of original Spanish settlers still live in or near Mountain Town. It is probable that at least some of them could have been classed as *Patrón* families. Two or three are still landowners. However, the vast majority of Spanish-speaking families in Mountain Town came at a later date, many possibly around 1920. Much of this migration was from the Spanish villages of northern New Mexico, and kinsmen can often still be traced to or from that area. Practically none of these people are landowners, except for house plots; nor are they often proprietors in any other sense. The largest number are still seasonal wage workers, unskilled or semiskilled "stoop labor." Some of the women work as domestics, but many more work in the fields or produce-packing sheds. As a group, the Spanish-speaking depend for employment on the prosperity of local agriculture.

While the foregoing generalizations stand, some Spanish are now making their way slowly up the socioeconomic ladder as store clerks, garage or filling station employees, a few as operators of small groceries or oil stations, and several as salaried clerical personnel. There has been a gradual increase over the last 25 years in the number of Spanish-speaking who have eighth grade schooling, and gradually more go on or complete high school.[5] The war industries of the Pacific Coast attracted a number from Mountain Town and materially raised their economic level, and service in the armed forces broadened the ethnic outlook of not only Spanish but also of some Mountain Town Anglos. There is no question of palpable Spanish acculturation. Bilingualism, to mention an important facet, now prevails among a majority of the Spanish and increasingly one finds older people the only strict monolinguals.

Many older Anglo residents of Mountain Town feel that they have seen a definite change in the social and economic status of the Spanish-speaking, but there is no denying that traditional attitudes and traditional ethnic relationships still generally prevail. The Anglo and Spanish-speaking groups are sharply distinguishable as to religion, economic status, occupational status, language, surnames, residence, and usually physical appearance. Ethnic distinctions along these lines are made by nearly all members of both groups. The Spanish are nearly all nominally Catholic and the Anglos are nearly all nominally Protestant. Political and economic control of the community is in the hands of the Anglos. There is not the slightest question of their superordinate position in relation to the Spanish as a whole, though certain individuals of Spanish background clearly receive personal respect and prestige well above that of many Anglos.

The Anglo-Spanish relationship has some of the properties of a caste system. Spanish and Anglo are practically endogamous. Religious participation is mostly along ethnic lines, and many Anglo Protestants would not want the conversion of non-Protestants at the expense of any sizeable Spanish attendance in their churches. Although somewhat ill defined, there is residential distinctness in Mountain Town, and distress is felt by some Anglos at having close "Mexican" neighbors. The Spanish are excluded almost completely from Anglo social and civic organizations (*e.g.*, lodges, Volunteer Firemen, Chamber of Commerce, Junior C of C, Rotary), except, to some extent, the P.T.A. and a veterans' group. In the cases of many of these organizations, the vast majority do not qualify for membership (*e.g.*, in Rotary), but the lack of qualifications appears to be largely incidental. Parties, dancing, picnics, and visiting are uniformly intra-ethnic, as are bridge, sewing circles, teas, and bazaars. As in a true caste system, obviously the sharp differentiation of interaction is not simply the will and doing of one group by itself. The Anglos, for example, find out, when they decide to broaden the membership of the Parent-Teachers Association, that it is not easy to enlist Spanish parents or to have them assume office.

SPANISH DISUNITY

The disunity among the Spanish group is quite evident in Mountain Town. Disunity does not mean the existence of factionalism, it refers, rather, to the lack of common action and to limited group cohesion. When an issue of import to the members of the group comes up, few people will do anything about it. This has been proved many times in such things as politics, school segregation, employment, arrests, welfare aid, and in general discrimination.

Considering the distinctness of sociocultural boundaries, the disunity of the Spanish group is striking, for the rigid exclusiveness of the Anglos might theoretically be a strong factor in their cohesion. Nor can Spanish disunity find its explanation in any wide socioeconomic disparity within the group. Nevertheless, Spanish cohesion seldom transcends such verbalizations as *nosotros* ("we") or *la raza* ("our people"), a generalized resentment of Anglo dominance and discrimination, and a readiness to perceive injustice in Spanish-Anglo dealings.

Disunity is a large factor in the lack of political power of the Spanish. In Mountain Town numbers do not explain the failure of the subordinate group—a majority—to put people they trust into critical offices. The Spanish are not wholly indifferent about certain elective offices, the sheriff, for example, who, if prejudiced, may enforce the laws quite one-sidedly. The school board offices are also thought to be ethnically critical or sensitive because of constant fear of segregation. But the election of an avowedly pro-Spanish candidate is rare indeed. Perhaps few Anglo politicians have understood the basic disunity of the Spanish, but a good many have at least recognized it. Occasionally, however, a direct appeal is made to the Spanish as Spanish. The results in Mountain Town bear out the cynical who feel it is better to ignore the ethnic issue. "They will not even vote for their own people" is commonly asserted, and this is bitterly conceded by most Spanish.

The failure of unity and leadership in politics is not the only type of weakness of the Spanish group. There is, of course, a more informal type of leadership in inter-ethnic relations. The "spokesman", as he is often called, is a leader to whom politicians or others may turn for advice and commitments on matters seen as affecting the interests of the ethnic group. There are two or three Spanish individuals in Mountain Town—one in particular—whom most Anglos consider to be spokesmen. The same individuals were cited by the majority of the Spanish when asked by Samora who were the leaders of their group. Yet these individuals usually make commitments for their group only at great risk. Actually, they generally refuse to do more than express an opinion or give very general advice. Investigation failed to show that any individual among the Spanish, including those most mentioned as leaders by Spanish and by Anglos, was willing to assume the responsibilities of a real spokesman for the group. There was no reason to believe that any of the persons mentioned could actually keep significant commitments if he made them.

But if a distinction is made between the inter-ethnic leadership described above and intra-ethnic leadership,[6] is the picture of the latter more favorable? Investigation was made by the junior author and his wife of 16 *sociedades* and *mutualistas*, lodges and mutual benefit organizations, which exist in Mountain Town with exclusively Spanish membership and objectives, as well as of lay societies ancillary to the Roman Catholic Church. The findings, reported in detail elsewhere, were rather uniform.[7] On the whole, the non-church associations were characterized by ineffectual leadership, very poor attendance, irregularity of procedure and schedule, lack of decisive action—even in inducting new members, and often a precarious existence. Careful comparison of the church-sponsored sodalities (*e.g.*, Altar Society, Family Society) revealed the priest as central to their direction and probably instrumental in their better showing compared to the secular groups. Even when the priest tried to play a less prominent role, circumstances, if not his own inclinations, tended to thrust him into a position more beside than behind the figure in the chair. Lay leadership, by the priest's admission, from observation of the members, and by their testimony, was not considered adequate.

The facts about the Mountain Town Spanish suggest deficiency, then, both as to leadership in inter-ethnic relations and as to leadership of purely ethnic organizations, except those ancillary to the Church. Yet strong factors for cohesion unmistakably exist—Anglo exclusiveness, a relatively undifferentiated Spanish group, a common ethnic tongue, Spanish group concepts, recognition of group-wide grievances, their majority voting position, and even some Anglo political attempts to unify the Spanish vote. In the light of such factors, we may ask why leadership is so ineffectual among the Spanish.

THE HYPOTHESIS OF LEADERSHIP DEFICIENCY

It is the contention of this paper that four principal conditions account for the inadequacy of Spanish leadership in Mountain Town and probably to some extent among the Spanish of the larger Southwest.

(1) Traditional forms (patterns) of leadership, which functioned well enough in pre-Anglo-Spanish culture, have been unadaptable and possibly a handicap to the development of adequate patterns of group leadership in the contact situation.

(2) Increasingly, the status goals of the Spanish group as a whole lie in the direction of Anglo culture; for the achievement of such goals, hence, leaders relatively well adapted to the Anglo system are increasingly indicated.

(3) General ambivalence and suspicion are accorded individuals of Spanish

background who are "successful" since the terms of success are now largely Anglo terms (viz. (2) above), and it is widely assumed that success is bought by cooperation with the outgroup and betrayal of one's own.

(4) Although caste-like enough to give sharp definition to the two groups, Anglo structure is relatively open to competent Spanish and thus permits the siphoning off of potential Spanish leadership, individuals relatively well adapted to the Anglo system.

The net result of these conditions is that, in the lack of adaptable traditional types, the only potential leaders who might be qualified to provide the kind of leadership indicated today are by virtue of their very qualifications absorbed into the larger body politic and are disqualified in the minds of their own fellows.

DISCUSSION

(1) The conclusion is widespread that what can be said about traditions of authority in Mexico, and even Latin America, applies on the whole to the Spanish of the Southwest. If so, the pre-Anglo-Spanish picture was one of strong authoritarian roles, the padre, the *patrón,* and the *jefe de familia.*[8] The *caudillo* is of course a classic Latin American type. In fact, a suggestive interpretation can be made of these roles in Spanish culture as variations on the same fundamental theme, strong and decisive authority, and F. R. Kluckhohn has commented that the Spanish-American is quite systematically trained for dependence upon such authority.[9] Such a pattern would scarcely appear by itself to be an impediment to the existence of effective Spanish leadership in inter-ethnic relations.

But the traditional pattern of local, secular authority among the Spanish is of the wrong kind. First, in many places, the *patrón* pattern was simply unable to survive the innovations of Anglo contact. In Mountain Town the *patrón-peón* relationship has no strong personal relevance for the majority of Spanish. They probably still possess some cultural adjustments to the pattern, but many lack deep roots in the community and hence lack any long-standing familial connection with local *patrón* lineages. Moreover, there is relatively little tenant or even employee relationship nowadays except with Anglo landlords or employers. Crew bosses and labor middlemen exist, to be sure, but these intercultural agents are usually themselves committed to Anglo employers.

Yet there are two *patrón*-like figures in Mountain Town, and these were the ones most often mentioned as leaders by the Spanish Samora interviewed. There was some ambivalence about them, however. Many who named these "leaders," apparently in default of anyone else, declared that they could not be counted on in a pinch or that they would not do all that they could for the Spanish people.[10] Investigation showed that these pseudo-*patrones,* when called upon, usually served their fellow Spanish in limited and personal ways. They might give an individual help in the form of advice or instructions. They sometimes helped him fill in an official form or make out an application. They might, though rarely, intercede, using their personal influence with some governmental (*i.e.*, Anglo) agency, typically the County Welfare bureau. Intercession in these cases would almost never be insistent; in fact, it is ordinarily reluctant. The pseudo-*patrones* were not reported by anyone as ever attempting to organize their people for some lasting and broadly based social action.

Interestingly enough, leadership in approximately these limited terms matches fairly well the authors' understanding of the older *patrón* pattern. The *patrón* did not form committees, found organizations, or often refer formally to his followers for common assent to social decisions. He bound them to him on a personalistic basis, with advice and counsel and by providing assistance to those lacking other resources. Such paternalistic leadership could function in the status system of colonial Mexican culture; it cannot function very extensively where the *patrón* cannot assure his followers of security in reward for their loyalty—they work for Anglos—and where even the status of the *patrón* himself is guaranteed by no *latifundium* manned with loyal retainers. Too often his status depends—even more than that of successful Anglos, he feels—upon the sufferance and approval of those in dominant positions. In such a situation erstwhile leader and follower can do little for each other in the traditional terms which were the very core of the *patrón-peón* relationship.

It may be relevant to add that the *patrón* himself was usually identified with the same general social class as those who held most of the important formal offices in the government. Ties of kinship were traditionally common between *patrón* and official. It is probably not going too far to suggest that the *patrón* himself tended in many instances to act informally as an agent of government in relation to the *peones*—"His word was law." To the extent that *patrón* status was adjusted to fit such an identification with and informal extension of governmental authority, it would likely not be an adaptable form of leadership when kinship and status identification with the dominant group were made ambivalent or impossible through their replacement by aliens.

It will be recalled that the church-sponsored societies in Mountain Town are generally the most effective ones among the Spanish. The lack of interethnic leadership by the church certainly cannot be blamed, like that of the *patrón*, on any local restriction of the church's ability to function, nor probably on any intrinsic maladaptation of church leadership. Rather, the reason is probably that the Roman Church in the United States is only indirectly political and that not all its communicants are Spanish. In any event the church does not attempt to provide local leadership for the Spanish as a group in their common struggle for status. A special factor in Mountain Town is the national origin of the priests, who come from Spain. This factor may be of no consequence, however, as Southwestern Spanish parishes with American-born priests may have no greater church leadership than Mountain Town in inter-ethnic relations.

(2) No attempt will be made to argue that traditional Spanish culture everywhere in the Southwest approximates that of Anglos in all its basic values. The case to the contrary has been effectively presented elsewhere, *e.g.*, concerning time orientation and the value attached to formal schooling.[11] Even with only superficial observation it is clear that "go-getter" tendencies are much less typical of Spanish than of Anglos, and there may be some basis in fact for other traits ascribed to the Spanish in the Anglo stereotype, as well as *vice-versa*.

Nevertheless, it is possible to carry the emphasis of Spanish-Anglo cultural differences to the point where certain obvious and growing similarities of goal and value are overlooked or omitted. Generalizing, necessarily, the Spanish in Mountain Town are interested in better jobs, better pay, and more material things, such as automobiles, housing, and appliances. There is increasingly a concern for having children complete at least grammar schooling and learn at least moderately fluent English. Measures taken by the school system, which either are, or are interpreted by the Spanish to be, attempts at segregation (such as a special first grade for English-deficient children), are strongly resented, as is discrimination in hiring and firing in employment, and alleged inequality in the administration of Old Age Pensions. The Spanish in Mountain Town, however, as we are emphasizing, are not very effective in changing conditions as they would.

It may be that the Mountain Town Spanish differ somewhat as to goals from those in other parts of the Southwest. They are almost entirely landless, and are predominantly low-paid agricultural labor, a kind of rural proletariat. Yet they are resident, not essentially a migratory group. However, we are not convinced that Mountain Town is markedly unrepresentative of Spanish elsewhere in the Southwest.

The Spanish goals sketched lie in the direction of Anglo goals and for their realization a mastery of Anglo techniques and behavior patterns is necessary. Insofar as advancement toward such goals involves groupwide status, Spanish leader qualifications must necessarily include such skills as literacy, relatively high control of the English language, and knowledge of social, political, and legal usages primarily based on the dominant culture. Few Spanish in Mountain Town possess such thorough adjustment to and broad familarity with Anglo culture, dependent as it largely is upon extensive schooling.

(3) Only a handful of eight Spanish individuals in Mountain Town possess the necessary qualifications in markedly higher degree than their fellows. As a matter of fact, it is essentially individuals with proven ability in Anglo culture

who are singled out for mention as "leaders" in the survey conducted by Samora. What, then, if anything, keeps these persons from exercising the leadership functions so generally desired by the Spanish? As was mentioned, a good deal of ambivalence exists concerning these people (almost all men) in the minds of most Spanish questioned. It is often stated that these "leaders" will not really accept an active part in directing a struggle for Spanish equality; they will only do such things for their fellow Spanish as they think will not antagonize the Anglos. They are even frequently accused of working for the Anglos and not for *la raza.* And not a few feel that such leaders could only have achieved their–usually modest–socioeconomic position at the expense of "selling out to the Anglo" or "by climbing over their own people." They are referred to as "proud" (*orgullosos*). Another adjective has been coined in Spanish especially to describe such relatively successful members of the Spanish community. Samora found that they are called "*agringados*"–"gringoized."

Here, then, is the dilemma: that the very traits which would qualify an individual to provide the sort of leadership called for are such as to cast suspicion upon his loyalty in the eyes of many he would lead. Is it that the qualified "leaders" make little effort to lead effectively because they feel–perhaps correctly–that they would have difficulty in getting an effective followership? Or is it that they get no effective following largely because of their own reluctance to exert leadership? No simple answer to the question will do, of course, particularly as leadership and followership are reciprocal roles and the lack of either precludes the other. It may be hard to say if there is a causal priority in Mountain Town between the two factors, but something more like a vicious circle is suggested by the frequent testimony of Mountain Town Spanish: many agree, on the other hand, that the relatively assimilated "leaders" are "proud" (*orgullosos*) but admit, on the other, that the people are "envious" (*envidiosos*) and are themselves unable to "follow" (*seguir*) anyone. It appears to be the case both that the hypothetical leaders are unwilling to lead and that the hypothetical followers are unable to accept followership.

(4) The factors so far suggested for the default of Spanish leadership clearly have their inter-cultural aspects, though they appear in some respects intrinsic to the Spanish culture. The fourth factor is more completely extrinsic to the Spanish side of the picture. It is that the ranks of the Anglo social structure are not completely closed to the exceptional Spanish individual who achieves appreciable mastery of Anglo culture. There is obviously no question about discrimination against individuals of Spanish background for equally competent Spanish and Anglos do not have an equal probability of success. But Anglo discrimination is paradoxically not rigid enough, in a sense, for the "good" of the Spanish as a group. That is, those able to deal with Anglos on their own terms frequently have a chance to do so–as individuals. Hence,

they are not completely frustrated, embittered, or thrust back into their own group where they must either quit the struggle altogether or turn their energies and skills to leading their people in competition with the Anglos. Instead, although against greater obstacles than an Anglo, the unusual person frequently achieves a degree of success to some extent commensurate with his abilities relative to those of his fellows.

From the standpoint of leadership the Spanish situation is not helped by Anglo mythology. The Anglo social myth recognizes two racial types among the Spanish-speaking. One is the "Real Spanish," with higher intelligence, industry, and dependability, while the other is the "Mexican," a term frequently preceded by opprobrious adjectives according to the context. The latter type, according to the Anglo, lack ambition, and generally possess just the qualities which lodge them where they are found in the social order.

The Spanish themselves make no distinction between "Real Spanish" and "Mexicans." When referring to themselves in Spanish they use the term "*mejicanos*"; when referring to themselves in English they use the term "Spanish." When the Anglos refer to them, the Spanish prefer that they use the term "Spanish" rather than "Mexican," because of the derogatory connotation of the latter term.

There is greater social acceptance of the "Real Spanish" by Anglos, particularly when they show mastery of Anglo culture–which tends to corroborate the myth. This divisive effect of Anglo mythology on the Spanish group, although difficult to assess, is nonetheless real.

The net result of these characteristics of the Anglo system is to lower the motivation of qualified persons to lead, and perhaps to contaminate the successful individual in the view of his group. His partial acceptance by the Anglo gives seeming verification to Spanish suspicions of disloyalty. The intercultural source of this effect on subordinate leadership is dramatically underscored by the Mountain Town evidence.

The three most overtly successful Spanish individuals in Mountain Town confirm in every major respect mentioned what has been said above. They are much more competent and successful in the Anglo system than most Anglos; they are given a social acceptance by the Anglo group which, although far from unqualified, sets them markedly apart from the great majority of the Spanish; they are predominantly regarded by Anglos as "spokesmen" for the Spanish group, although by no means are they themselves willing to play the role intensively; they are mentioned with the highest frequency by the Spanish interviewed as "leaders" and the only people of their own to whom one could turn for certain kinds of assistance; but they are complained against as *orgullosos,* as being unwilling to do as much for the *raza* as they easily might, and as being subservient to the Anglo and unwilling to risk offending him. These individuals are, then, leaders largely by default and would not otherwise be mentioned as leaders. Although almost uniquely qualified in some respects to lead, they do not. In a situation where adequate inter-ethnic leadership would call for the exercise of organizing skill and close indentification of the destines of leader and follower, these individuals largely limit themselves to personalistic functions roughly comparable to those of the *patrón* of yore, and a social distance tends to be kept which is in some respects as great as between *patrón* and *peón*. Though the comparison with traditional patterns is suggestive, we need not, as has been discussed, hark back to the *patrón* system to explain everything in the situation found today. Inter-cultural factors in the Spanish relationship with Anglos are of strategic importance in explaining leadership deficiency.

NOTES

1. Leonard Broom and Eshref Shevky, "Mexicans in the United States: A Problem in Social Differentiation," *Sociology and Social Research,* 36 (January, 1952), pp. 150-158).

2. The term "Spanish," used throughout the paper refers to "the Spanish-speaking people."

3. Cf. Robert C. Jones, "Mexican Youth in the United States," *The American Teacher,* 28 (March, 1944), pp. 11-15; Olen Leonard and C. P. Loomis, *Culture of a Contemporary Rural Community, El Cerrito, New Mexico,* Washington: USDA, BAE, 1940; R. W. Roskelley and C. R. Clark, *When Different Cultures Meet,* Denver: Rocky Mountain Council on Inter-American Affairs, 1949; George I. Sanchez, "The Default of Leadership," in *Summarized Proceedings IV,* Southwest Council on the Education of the Spanish-Speaking People, Fourth Regional Conference, Albuquerque, New Mexico, January 23-25, 1950; Ozzie G. Simmons, *Anglo Americans and Mexican Americans in South Texas, A Study in Dominant-Subordinate Group Relations* (Ph.D. Thesis, Harvard University, 1952); Ruth D. Tuck, *Not With The Fist: Mexican-Americans in a Southwest City,* New York: Harcourt, Brace and Company, 1949.

4. Julian Samora, *Minority Leadership in a Bi-Cultural Community* (Ph.D. Thesis, Washington University, St. Louis, 1953).

5. James B. Watson, *Preliminary Observations Based On the Community of Mountain Town* (Unpublished manuscript, Washington University, St. Louis, n.d.).

6. Julian Samora, *op. cit.,* p. 52.

7. *Ibid.,* pp. 13-51.

8. Cf. R. L. Beals, *op. cit.,* pp. 8-10; and O. Leonard and C. P. Loomis, *op. cit.,* p. 15.

9. F. R. Kluckhohn, "Dominant and Variant Value Orientations," in C.

Kluckhohn and H. A. Murray, *Personality in Nature, Society, and Culture,* 2nd ed. rev., New York: Knopf, 1953.

10. Julian Samora, *op. cit.,* pp. 74-76.

11. Cf. F. R. Kluckhohn, *op. cit.,* pp. 352-4; R. L. Beals, *op. cit.,* pp. 5-13. Arthur Campa, "Mañana is Today," in T. M. Pearce and A. P. Thomason, *Southwesterners Write,* Albuquerque: University of Mexico Press, 1947.

B. Collective Welfare Benefits

THE POLITICS OF COLLECTIVE WELFARE BENEFITS HAVE BECOME INCREASingly important to "colored ethnics" in general and to the Chicano people in particular. These politics involve two major groups of political actors: 1) the administrators or bureaucrats whose job it is to provide various welfare services to their clientele, and 2) the ethnic masses, that is, the segment of the ethnic community receiving social services from governmental agencies. This style of ethnic politics differs from the politics of recognition in that mass action and consequent mass material rewards are involved rather than individual benefits and mass psychic rewards. Historically, the old-style politics of material benefits was usually directed by the urban party organization. This strategy kept the mayor, ward boss and petty local bureaucrats as power brokers dispensing their tangible rewards to various ethnic groups that were dependent upon governmental largesse in return for electoral support. Since the Chicano is at the bottom of most socioeconomic rankings, he has been placed in a position of dependency to the federal, state, and local service agencies. However, since the welfare or service functions of government have, over the past few years, gravitated toward Washington, D.C., most of the politics of *collective* welfare benefits are now between ethnic masses seeking visible material benefits and the federal bureaucracy.

The colored ethnic minorities, including the Chicano, are now faced with the problem of employing political strategies that will have a maximum favorable effect on federal bureaucrats. Traditional-style electoral and pressure group politics have often failed to have much effect on the vast, non-responsive bureaucratic inertia even when employed by those members of the dominant society possessing traditional political resources and operating within the conventional political norm. How much more difficult it is for a relatively powerless ethnic minority, such as the Chicano, to secure not only tangible benefits to the masses based on their needs, but also to achieve direct participation in the decisions allocating both resources and values. Chicanos, like other ethnic minorities, have often had to resort to new-style, non-conventional politics, usually in the form of mass protest activities, in their attempts to change the relationship between themselves and the bureaucracies. However, as Litt states: "[c]ollective ethnic benefits are capable of accommodating the demands of ethnic minorities [only] as long as the premises on which these benefits rest are not politically volatile. . . . [A]s long as dependent relations with welfare agencies were accepted as a necessary element of social service, the allocation of collective benefits was accommodating." "But," he continues, "values such as 'integration' and 'participation' run contrary to the ecology of party organization and to the rationale of collective benefits."[1]

Therefore, the politics of collective welfare benefits can at best provide only immediate and limited tangible payoffs to ethnic minorities. Moreover, demands for such intangibles as self-determination, cultural pride, and community participation cannot be met by this kind of politics.

Typically, the relationship of the Chicano people to government agencies has been an unpleasant and abrasive relationship. This is graphically pointed out in the selection from the UCLA Mexican American study project. Chicano contacts with government administrators such as border and immigration officials, social welfare workers, and law enforcement agencies have probably led to generally negative attitudes on the part of both Chicanos and government personnel. On the other hand, the study by Comer, Steinman, and Welch indicates that, at least in some cases, Chicanos have found satisfaction with government services. More importantly, the authors contend that Chicanos' satisfaction or dissatisfaction with public welfare services bear practically no relationship to their general orientation toward the political system. However, because of the special nature of the sample, the results of this study may be an exception rather than the rule. In fact, another study[2] has perceived Chicano contacts with government service agencies as forming the most likely stimulus for further collective political action by the Chicano. This study, cast in a more typical setting, dealt particularly with the Chicano's response to the shortcomings and inadequacies of the current health care service provided him.

Whatever the case, in our increasingly bureaucratized society it has become extremely important for ethnic minorities to learn well the game of bureaucratic politics.

NOTES

1. Edgar Litt, *Ethnic Politics in America* (Glenview, Illinois: Scott, Foresman, 1970), p. 71.

2. Jerry L. Weaver, "Health Care Costs as a Political Issue: Comparative Responses of Chicanos and Anglos," *Social Science Quarterly* 53 (March 1973), 846-854.

12: CONTACT WITH GOVERNMENTAL AGENCIES

Leo Grebler, Joan Moore, and Ralph Guzmán

FOR MANY NEW IMMIGRANTS FROM MEXICO THE ONLY CONTACT WITH THE Anglo world beyond the employer has been with a government agency. Historically, this contact has nearly always been strained. Whatever the present degree of tension–and it varies from place to place and agency to agency–an understanding of the distinctive quality of these contacts is important for an understanding of the total experience of Mexican Americans. . . .

Generally, Mexican Americans have made very few attempts to modify the government agencies' operation. There have been school desegregation cases, and, as we shall discuss below, some suits against law enforcement agencies. But this slender record of challenge to authority does not mean that the Mexican Americans have defined the administration of government programs as just. In part, the quietude has stemmed from a widespread and diffuse fear of authority. Challenging even a "helping" agency such as the school may bring–and has brought–criminal indictments. Also, in the past the Mexican government has concerned itself with certain violations of civil or social rights of Mexican Americans, and this interest by a foreign government created an ambiguous atmosphere.

This article suggests that lower-status Mexican Americans developed a generalized subcultural "coping pattern" in their contact with official agencies. It is a pattern that emphasized withdrawal. The few cases that came to *be* cases (in the sense that a dialogue was established with the agency) were in fact deviant cases, illuminating the larger "coping pattern" by their exceptional quality.

These observations may apply to any subordinate group. Hence, our discussion draws on the general literature on the relationship between low-status people and government agencies or bureaucracies. Government agencies, of course, *are* bureaucracies, and it has been cogently argued that the rationality, impersonality and specificity of *all* bureaucracies in dealing with lower-class individuals in some wasy exacerbate the problems they are designed to cure.[1] Problems of communicating the agency's desiderata—always present with lower-class clientele—are aggravated when the bureaucrat speaks no Spanish and the client no English. These persistent problems have been aired in the past literature. Government agencies, in addition, have the implicit coercive power of the society behind them. This also probably affects all subordinate groups. However, the Mexican-American experience shows some special qualities stemming both from the high visibility of many of the poor and from the fact that poor Mexican Americans are often defined by Anglos—notably government officials—as "probably foreign." In fact, the propensity of government officials to question their legal status—and their special relations with a Federal agency devoted to testing citizenship—form an important part of this Mexican-American experience.

THE BORDER PATROL

From the earliest part of the twentieth century Mexican immigrants were viewed as only temporary visitors to American society. They were seen as people who could benefit the Southwest by providing labor and who in return would ask nothing more than a small paycheck as they went contentedly home to Mexico. (Whether or not they perceived of Mexico as "home" was rarely questioned.) The growers during the 1920s firmly believed that Mexicans returned home after their stint in the fields.[2] Those who did not go back to Mexico or who wanted to be in the United States at an inconvenient time or place were handled by a variety of local and Federal agencies. Of these the U.S. Border Patrol was the most important. . . .

Border Patrol operations have become not only technically but also socially more sophisticated [since its inception in 1904]. Basically, however, they are of three kinds. First is the watch over the border itself, which now involves complex methods of tracking, with air and ground observation of sand traps and drag trails (smoothed-out surfaces in strategic areas to show footprints), traffic checks, transportation-terminal checks, and so on. All of these techniques are designed to apprehend aliens at entry. The second operation is an elaborate set of apprehension activities after entry. Finally, of course, there is the deportation of illegal entrants. . . .

Mexican Americans appear to feel no special hostility to the Border Patrol in its role as guardian at the border. Would-be illegal entrants know the risks and take their chances. However, the circumstances of operations at the border mean that United States citizens of Mexican descent are subject to harassment. Indignant stories about this harrassment are extremely common, particularly among middle-class Mexican Americans who try to come back to the United States from a trip across the border to Mexico. The term "harassment" is not used loosely; hours of delay and embarrassing and degrading questions may be entailed. Resentment and resistance are taken as suspicious conduct. (There is always, particularly at the border, the problem of contraband and suspicion of contraband, especially narcotics, to complicate the problem of legality of entry.) This experience can be particularly upsetting when it occurs to a third-generation Mexican American. To the Border Patrol official such procedures, and the search of ranch and farm lands near the border, appear fully justified. To the law-abiding Mexican American they often do not.

It is their apprehension of illegal entrants that has made the Border Patrol synonymous with obtrusive Anglo authority for many Mexican Americans, primarily because it involves raids and interrogations in areas of heavy Mexican-American concentration which also normally harbor large numbers of illegal aliens. At present these checks occur mainly in two kinds of areas–those with many work opportunities, such as agricultural centers, and those which are transportation nexuses. . . .

Raids and interrogations are also conducted in settled urban communities, with many Mexican Americans stopped and queried closely about their nativity status. Informers are used to locate "illegals"–hardly a practice that makes for intra-ethnic solidarity. . . .

The most extensive effort to apprehend illegal entrants was known as Operation Wetback.[3] By the early 1950s it had become evident that large numbers of Mexicans were continuing to cross the border illegally, despite the existence of the *bracero* program. Growers strenuously resisted proposals to make it a crime to employ "illegals," and normal control measures did not seem to work. Widespread alarm about the "wetback invasion" led to official recommendations to Congress that the United States Army be called upon to "stem the tide."[4] In fact, Operation Wetback was conducted by a retired general, and was organized with military precision by an expanded and better-equipped Border Partol. The roundup effort–raids and interrogations–got under way in June 1954. A special mobile force concentrated first on California and then on Texas, and extended to points as far from the border as Spokane, Chicago, Kansas City, and St. Louis.

Expulsions under this program reached vast proportions. The number of apprehensions rose from 875,000 in the fiscal year 1953 to 1,035,282 the next year. As Operation Wetback was phased out, it fell to 256,290 in 1955 and 90,122 in 1956.[5] In mid-1955, the Immigration and Naturalization Service reported that "for the first time in more than ten years, illegal crossing over the Mexican border was brought under control."[6] In the first half of the 1950s as many as 3.8 million expulsions of Mexican aliens were recorded. (These include multiple counts of men who had entered and been expelled more than once.)

The sweep included persons of long residence in this country as well as those of only a few weeks' tenure. United States-born children were known to have been expelled with their parents. Many American-born adults were stopped and asked for proof of citizenship in cities far removed from the border—and some, reacting with anger as well as amazed incredulity, came into conflict with the officers. Because of its large scale and allegations of rough treatment, Operation Wetback became one of the most traumatic recent experiences of the Mexican Americans in their contacts with government authority. No Mexican-American community in the Southwest remained untouched. . . .

Organized or organizing labor has generally been in alliance with the Border Patrol, whereas growers' associations are reported to have lobbied in Washington to keep the agency's budget as small as possible.[7] That organizing labor is often Mexican American means that their feelings about the Border Patrol's activities are deeply ambivalent: On the one hand, wetbacks jeopardize union efforts, but on the other hand many have wetback relatives and friends. The same deep and probably unresolvable ambivalence is evident in many Mexican Americans' discussions of restricting even legal immigration from Mexico.

THE WELFARE REPATRIATIONS OF THE DEPRESSION

Operation Wetback may have been even more traumatic because it echoed a similar experience of some twenty years earlier. The equivocal citizenship status of Mexican Americans and the consequences for their relations with governmental authority are nowhere more evident than in the actions of welfare agencies during the Great Depression of the 1930s. During those years of sharply curtailed immigration, many individuals returned to Mexico. Some went entirely by their own volition, and many were deported as Federal authorities responded to unemployment by increasing the raids and other enforcement activities of the Border Patrol. But there was another kind of return movement, organized by local authorities in conjunction with private welfare agencies and assisted by the Republic of Mexico itself. During this period, many American cities were perilously close to bankruptcy. It became evident that money could be saved in relief expenditures by removing Mexicans from the welfare rolls. Massive efforts were undertaken to send Mexican welfare recipients back to Mexico. This strategy was congruent with the general American view of the time that Mexicans were really better off "home," irrespective of the wishes or legal standing of the individuals involved. In many cases these individuals were actually United States citizens—a possibility that was apparently never conceived of at the time.

In Los Angeles, unemployed Mexicans had been a burden on the local relief budgets as early as the late 1920s.[8] Many more applied after 1929. The city's economic rationale for "repatriating the Mexicans" is vividly described by Carey McWilliams, who observed the process at close range:

> It was discovered that, in wholesale lots, the Mexicans could be shipped to Mexico City for $14.70 per capita. The sum represented less than the cost of a week's board and lodging. And so, about February 1931, the first train-load was dispatched, and shipments at the rate of about one a month have continued ever since. A shipment, consisting of three special trains, left Los Angeles on December 8. The loading commenced at about six o'clock in the morning and continued for hours. More than twenty-five such special trains had left the South Pacific Station before last April.
>
> The repatriation programme is regarded locally as a piece of consummate statescraft. The average per family cost of executing it is $71.14, including food and transportation. It cost Los Angeles County $77,249.29 to repatriate one shipment of 6,024. It would have cost $424,933.70 to provide this number with such charitable assistance as they would have been entitled to had they remained—a saving of $347,468.41.[9]

Between 1931 and 1934 the Los Angeles Department of Charities launched 15 special trainloads averaging 1,000 Mexicans each.[10] The records of the Los Angeles County Board of Supervisors—their negotiations with Mexican railroads, their careful accounting—cover many pages. There is practically no mention in these pages of the reaction of Mexicans involved—nor of their friends and relatives, who witnessed the "repatriations." Some of our field interviews with Mexican Americans, however, have suggested the depth of the shock, and perhaps even more important, of the sense of impotence and helplessness among those affected.

We have a record of the procedures involved in only one case, the city of Detroit. There the Department of Public Welfare established a Mexican Bureau in 1932. All Mexicans applying for aid were referred to the Bureau. The policy was instigated at the suggestion of and enthusiastically supported by the Mexican Consul and Diego Rivera, who was in Detroit at the time. The Mexican Bureau chartered trains to carry Mexicans to the border at $15 a person including food. The movement was far from benevolent. On the basis of case records, Humphrey comments:

> At the "Mexican Bureau" discussion occurred which was designed to evince a forthright declaration of the intentions of the Mexican family head regarding his return to Mexico. When knowledge of the actual functions of this agency became widespread in the colony, resistance appeared even to the point of refusals to go to the agency. . . . Referral was made to the Mexican Bureau, despite frequent protestations by

> families that repatriation was not desired. . . . Persons who were naturalized citizens, and children who were born citizens, were subjected to scrutinizing inquiry for purposes of "repatriation." In one case the worker strongly insisted that the possibility of continued dependence was grounds for repatriation, despite the fact that the head of the family had been naturalized. . . . Children might oppose this move for the same reason. . . . The rights of American-born children to citizenship in their native land were explicitly denied or not taken into account.[11]

Pressures exerted by the Detroit case workers included "threats of deportation, stoppage of relief (wholly or in part, as, for example, in the matter of rent), or trampling on customary procedures. Thus, placing a family on the 'cafeteria list' meant that it would not receive 'out-door relief' in its home, but would have to troop to a commissary for meals." . . .[12]

To the present-day observer, the procedure of those days, with all of its bureaucratic overlay, is painfully reminiscent of the later removal of the Japanese from the West Coast during World War II. There was no institution aiding those who wanted to stay in the United States. Almost no voice of contemporary dissent by Anglos was heard. The ethnic community seems to have been so intimidated that there is no record of organized protest. Only the informal record—for example, of *corridos* (epic ballads)—suggests the depth of the distress.[13]

It is impossible even to arrive at an estimate of the numbers of individuals involved, or even of all of the cities that instituted the procedure. The unusual situation led the Commissioner General of Immigration to comment in 1931:

> An unrecorded but impressive number of Mexicans have returned home in the past year, with the help of the Mexican Government itself or through the efforts and aid of cities, towns, and charitable organizations. . . . The Immigration Service had not the facilities to keep count of this hegira, but with the purpose of laying the groundwork for future readmission without expense or trouble, many of the aliens sought to impress upon our officers that they were leaving the country but temporarily. It is certain that nearly all will seek to return when employment and business conditions improve.[14]

The scale of the exodus is indicated by a decline in the Mexico-born United States population from 639,000 persons in 1930 to little over 377,000 in 1940.

In fact, many individuals did try to return to the United States. Among those "repatriated" were United States citizens, and if they had had the resources or the information, they could have challenged their removal on constitutional grounds. . . .

The welfare repatriations of the 1930s differ legally and economically from Operation Wetback in the 1950s. During the Depression the focus was on the indigent Mexican; in the 1950s it was on the "illegal" Mexican. But both deportation programs shared important functional characteristics. Both emphasized the foreignness of the Mexican Americans. This was particularly evident during the Depression, when it was an operating assumption of the welfare agencies that the people they deported were aliens. It was further evident in their alacrity to reject Mexican Americans as part of the normal American community welfare obligation. (Of course, this did not apply in the case of the charter-member "Spanish Americans" in Colorado and New Mexico, where "the majority . . . became directly dependent upon the Federal government" during the Depression.[15]) Both programs were massive in their impact, removing not isolated individuals but large groups. Both involved Mexican as well as United States authorities. Both were grim reminders that for low-status members of the group a claim to the rights of citizenship is always subject to question.

WELFARE, HEALTH, AND CONSERVATION

Little information is available on how the equivocal status of their citizenship affects Mexican-American willingness to use the social agencies of local and state governments. That Mexican Americans now turn to welfare agencies for money is evidenced in the surveys of Los Angeles and San Antonio: Approximately six percent of the Los Angeles respondents and five percent of the San Antonio respondents received welfare payments from local sources (exclusive of unemployment and Federal Social Security benefits). But the evidence on more general attitudes is scanty except for a notable concern with what social workers and ethnic spokesmen define as "failures to reach" the Mexican-American clientele. Most frequently, such shortcomings of welfare, health, and other social agencies are interpreted as failures of cultural communication. It is seen as the clash of the rational culture of the bureaucrat and the personalism of the Mexican. Few bureaucrats or researchers realize that these agencies exercise coercive as well as "helping" power. Among those few are the authors of a small-scale study of Anglo-Latin problems perceived by Texas public service personnel. In addition to many attributions of cultural difference, the study mentions that "several workers reported . . . a 'fear of authority,' which . . . created, seemingly, a barrier of suspicion and distrust toward all outsiders."[16] Suspicion and distrust may also be based on demonstrated abuses by the agency of its functions. In recent years, for example, state employment service branches dealing with agricultural labor have offered jobs at below-minimum wages. Rumors about such corruptibility of government-agency officials in the service of growers and at the expense of Mexicans play an important role in the reluctance to utilize agency services.[17]

Another illustration may be drawn from the public health agencies. The problems of these agencies with Mexican-American clientele are severe enough to have generated a number of research studies. By and large the studies focus on the "chasm" in cultural understanding between the folk-like poor Mexican American and the Anglo health practitioner. However, amongst the description of cultural conflict about the causes and treatment of disease appears a usually underplayed but recurrent theme—the sense of distrust of Anglo authority and fear of Anglo power represented by the health worker. Though there are many hints in the literature and in our own field interviews that the problems of cultural conflict are being ameliorated, partly through the recommendations of studies such as Saunders', Hanson's, and others,[18] some of the sources of distrust are evident. For example, tuberculosis cases can be hospitalized, that is, removed from the home and taken to a remote place despite family feelings. Immunization programs (which the Mexican-American poor resist far less than the Negro poor in Los Angeles[19]) cause pain and show no apparent benefit. The past "failures" of the public health agencies, interpreted generally in terms of violation of cultural beliefs, can also be interpreted as violation of norms regarding social relations. Mexican Americans often lack conviction about the helping power of such programs, and in the absence of such conviction the latent coercive power of the agency becomes more salient. Implicitly recognized in many studies, this point is made explicit by Margaret Clark:

> Several factors of the public health worker's status maintain social distance between him and the people with whom he deals: First, he is a government worker and as such is related to other government workers—law enforcement officers, tax assessors, immigration authorities, truant officers, building inspectors, FBI agents, and public prosecutors—all of whom are viewed as potential threats to the security of barrio people.
>
> . . . The second factor which maintains the gulf between medical workers and Spanish-speaking clients is that most public health people are Anglos. Aside from the communication barriers that result from this difference, there are also conflicts resulting from historical group tensions between Anglos and Mexican Americans in California and parts of the Southwest.
>
> . . . Those who are not actually hostile may at least feel uncomfortable with English-speaking persons, fear discriminatory treatment, and remain acutely sensitive to Anglo criticism.[20]

Among the many service agencies coming in contact with Mexican Americans, the U.S. Forest Service would hardly appear to be a source of friction. Yet, the discrepancy between the minority view and the general view of the agency is enormous. To the middle-class Anglo, the Forest Ranger in his flat hat immediately calls up images of Smoky the Bear, surrounded by redwoods, birds, and lovable small animals. To the New Mexican villager, however, according to one among many responsible observers, "it is not uncommon for the native population to see the forest ranger in his olive drab uniform as an American occupational trooper guarding the spoils of the Mexican-American War. The injustices of the past are manifested in the attitudes of the northern New Mexican commoner. There is an enemy in those hills. It is that forest ranger."[21] A service agency to most Anglos, the Forest Service is a coercive agency to the Spanish Americans.

As discussed extensively by Nancie González,[22] the charter-member Spanish-American minority of northern New Mexico came into conflict with conservationists early in the history of their contact with the American society. The villagers were not attuned to conservationist arguments and saw not the overgrazing of their ancestral lands (the Anglos' point) but the erosion of their livelihood as grazing permits in national forest areas were reduced or as the grazing season was shortened. Their almost total dependency on the forest lands for subsistence led to desperate measures, as in the attempt to burn and regain parts of the Carson National Forest in 1967. Resentment against the Forest Service and its personnel reached a peak when it was "learned that forest personnel were used to guide police and National Guard patrols searching for Spanish Americans involved" in the short-lived "Tijerina Rebellion" in Tierra Amarilla, New Mexico.[23]

Though this illustration may seem bizarre to middle-class Anglos accustomed to the recreational use of national forest lands, it is precisely the recreational use that adds insult to the injury perceived by Spanish-American people. Throughout the Southwest, the Forest Service's expenditures for recreation surpass by a wide margin its expenditures for range and revegetation purposes, and the implication is clear to the Spanish-American villager that the rich men play while he starves.[24] The villager is dispossessed, he feels, not for the cause of conservation but for the pleasure of the Anglo. The rifle fire and arson encountered by the Forest Rangers in the forests of New Mexico and Colorado is a consequence of this perception; accurate evaluation of their weak bargaining position makes some ethnic leaders feel that violence is their only means of reaching beyond the government agency to the wider audience of American public opinion. Tijerina's actions and many similar though less broadly organized protests are the desperate expedients of angry rural people who see a "helping" agency as an intransigent opponent of what they define as their collective welfare.

In brief, if service agencies worked ideally they would perform functions that would help counteract the inegalitarian forces in society. The heritage of suspicion attaching to *all* government services, however, probably inhibits their effectiveness. Such agencies not only provide services but they possess and exercise coercive power. For a population whose right to live in this society has been continually under question, the heritage of suspicion of government agencies is justified in those agencies' current operations. Even if their programs were designed for a minimum of *cultural* friction, their effectiveness in "reaching" Mexican Americans would depend on their effectiveness in changing their operations so as to reduce the actual exercise of coercive power.

LOCAL POLICE AGENCIES

If the coercive power of the state is implicit or latent in the operations of service bureaucracies, it is explicit in the case of local police agencies. In general, law enforcement units operate in a spirit of rather diffuse morality. This is perhaps more true in the Southwest with its recent vigilante tradition than elsewhere. Enforcing the law, of course, means protecting or avenging the law-abiding. Very early in the history of most law-enforcement agencies came the discovery that the probability of locating a law-breaker is maximized if attention is focused on the poorer areas of the towns.[25] Thus, suspicion is attached to those who are or look poor. In the case of the visible minorities, such as Negroes and Mexican Americans, the suspicion is easily extended to all members of the group. There has long been a widespread conviction that Mexican Americans are not only poor, but also inherently prone to violence and thus particularly dangerous.

This conviction appears in its pseudoscientific form in the so-called Ayres Report prepared for the Los Angeles County Grand Jury in 1942 after the zoot-suit riots which gave rise to exceptional tension between the police and the Mexican-American population. It said that " . . . his (the Mexican's) desire is to kill, or at least let blood. . . . This inborn characteristic . . . has come down through the ages."[26] This racist report was endorsed by the chief of the Los Angeles Police Department in a letter to the foreman of the Grand Jury: "Lieutenant Ayres of the Sheriff's Department, gave an intelligent statement of the psychology of the Mexican people, particularly, the youths. He stated many of the contributing factors that caused the gang activities."[27]

The persistence of a racist perception of Mexican Americans among police is indicated by the testimony of the chief of the Los Angeles Police Department as recently as 1960:

> The Latin population that came in here in great strength were here before us, and presented a great problem because I worked over on the East Side when men had to work in pairs—but that has evolved into assimilation—and it's because of some of these people being not too far removed from the wild tribes of the district of the inner mountains of Mexico. I don't think you can throw the genes out of the question when you discuss behavior patterns of people.[28]

In addition to the fact that Mexicans thus obviously qualify as members of the "poor and dangerous" classes, police have had two special reasons for close scrutiny of Mexican Americans. For one thing, the suspects may be "illegal." Second, until very recently the traffic in narcotics was defined in many areas of the Southwest almost entirely as a Mexican problem. Thus, Mexican-American lower-class communities have been liable to generalized suspicion on three grounds, and by three law enforcement agencies concerned respectively with general crime, narcotics, and illegal aliens. The latter two frequently conduct raids and use informers. All three agencies often work together.

The effects of such vulnerability on the relations of Mexican Americans with law enforcement agencies must be seen in historical context.* The longest contact has been with the Texas Rangers, a group of law enforcement officers organized in 1835 to protect the frontier and reduced to a token force of 40 men exactly 100 years later. Despite its present-day numerical insignificance, the Texas Rangers ("*los Rinches*") remain a symbol of Anglo control, perceived by the Texas Mexican Americans as a "force which was *designed* to curb and crush any sign of progress or independent action" by Mexican Americans.[29] Its reputation was earned not only during the frontier conflicts of the nineteenth century, but by incidents in the twentieth century as well. The border region of Texas was in constant turmoil in the years 1912-1920, during the Mexican Revolution. German propaganda efforts in Mexico during World War I raised the old questions of Mexican-Americans' loyalty to the United States. As Webb comments in his definitive history of the Rangers: "After the troubles developed the Americans instituted a reign of terror against the Mexicans. . . . In the orgy of bloodshed that followed, the Texas Rangers played a prominent part. . . . The reader would not be interested in a list of a hundred or more clashes, raids, murders, and fights that occurred between 1915 and 1920." But he goes on to supply the context: "In passing judgment one must not forget the psychology of fear and racial antagonism that made the Rio Grande a battle-line and the border a battle field. On one side of the river the slogan was 'Kill the Gringos,' on the other it was 'Kill the Greasers.' "[30] The atrocities committed by the Rangers against Mexican Americans finally came under fire from a Mexican-American state legislator, J. T. Canales—one of the rare instances in which this population has met excesses with something other than withdrawal. Among the effects of the Canales investigation was the decision to reduce the size of the Rangers.[31] . . .

In the 1920s an investigation revealed that basic legal rights were often denied to Mexican Americans arrested in communities of the Southwest. Informants in the Rio Grande Valley reported to Paul S. Taylor that police practiced a double standard of law enforcement, protecting the rights of arrested Anglos while treating their Mexican counterparts with violence.[32] In

*The historical portions of this section were developed from materials prepared by Paul Fisher and John V. Kelly.

complete subversion of Texas law, Dallas police frequently made arrests without cause, denied prisoners legal counsel and maintained a cell in which prisoners were indefinitely held incommunicado. Denver police adopted similar procedures, and Los Angeles police were accused of employing various third-degree tactics ranging from beatings to marathon interrogation sessions.[33]

In the 1930s the vigilante tradition came to life again in the troubled agricultural areas, most notably in California. The San Joaquin Valley cotton strike of 1932 is representative of these encounters between growers and striking workers, and most particularly of the role of the police as a force intervening in a partisan manner. In this strike Mexicans accounted for approximately three-quarters of the work force. As the strike gained enough support to disrupt the harvest, growers began arming themselves. With deputies at their sides, they evicted strikers from farm labor camps. Local police assured the growers of their right to protect their property and undertook a program to keep the peace by strictly enforcing anti-picketing ordinances and arresting strike agitators. Strikers were unarmed; the growers were never disarmed, and local sheriffs deputized additional local officers. Of these new deputies an analyst comments: "The special deputies which numbered more than a hundred in the three counties were even more inexperienced in handling strikes than the sheriffs and their judgment was continually in danger of being warped by their prejudices. Many of the deputies were ranchers, ranch managers, and gin employees."[34]

In the violence which shortly broke out, several strikers were killed. To prevent further bloodshed the Governor of California ordered a large contingent of the State Highway Patrol into the area. The subsequent investigations concluded that "without question, civil rights of strikers have been violated."[35] A local under-sheriff revealed the basic assumptions of the law-enforcement forces about local social structure and about their own role: "We protect our farmers here in Kern County. They are our best people. They are always with us. They keep the county going. They put us here and they can put us out again so we serve them. But the Mexicans are trash. They have no standard of living. We herd them like pigs."[36]

The tradition of law enforcement by "emergency forces" of untrained and partisan men recurs in the history of Mexican-American labor disputes in isolated mining communities during the early years of the twentieth century, and in the fields beginning with the 1928 strike of the *Confederación de Uniones Obreras,* and subsequent strikes in 1934, 1936, and 1941.[37]

Conflict between police and workers has been endemic in the most recent and well-publicized of the agricultural strikes. In the 1966-1967 melon strike in Rio Grande City, Texas, the ubiquitous Rangers appeared to "protect the harvest." Their indulgence in violence led to considerable public protest. In California, the Delano police chief went so far as to change the color of his officers' uniforms so that grape strikers could distinguish between the "friendly" local men and the "less considerate" officers from other forces.[38] Early in 1968, resentment among the grape strikers against law enforcement officers hovered increasingly close to violence. Cesar Chavez, in a remarkable effort to reaffirm the nonviolent nature of the movement, went on a prolonged fast, with serious after-effects on his health. It is probably due largely to his personal influence that this most long-drawn-out, most widely known of the agricultural organizing efforts has been so notably free of violence between police and strikers.

These cases reflect the situation in small communities. Strikes represent a very real threat to the established social system; they vehemently call into question the rationales and the mutual myths by which local ethnic stratification is maintained. Whether or not civilians are deputized in such strikes, the local law-enforcement agencies know, in the words of the earlier-mentioned Kern County under-sheriff, "who put them there," and they know who are the "best" people and who are "trash."

Large city police operate under different circumstances. Far more bureaucratized, they may share the racist assumptions of the small-town policemen, as the earlier quotations indicate, but their operating procedures differ. Mexican Americans did not begin to flock to the cities in large numbers until comparatively recently, and it is difficult to put their experiences there in meaningful perspective. The sense of outrage, the continual references to police brutality, the anecdotes, the picketing, the many harrowing incidents which never become formal cases and thus never permit any chance of redress—all of these give an overwhelming impression of the problems in police relations with Mexican Americans in one city after another. But the police system in cities is far more complex, and its relation to the larger system is far more difficult to disentangle than it is in the smaller towns.

Police tactics in Los Angeles, documented in connection with Mexican-American youth activities in the late 1930s and early 1940s, definitely appear to have departed from tactics used in dealing with other populations. According to one study, "prejudicial treatment" and arrest procedures which employed "indiscriminate, wholesale . . . 'dragnet' methods" were widely used. These procedures, in turn, helped account for a higher arrest-conviction ratio among minorities. Thus, in 1938 the Los Angeles Superior Court records showed a ratio of 5.3 arrests to each felony conviction for Mexican Americans, compared with only 2.7 for Anglos. Furthermore, the same study showed that Anglos, if convicted, had almost three times as good a chance for probation as Mexican-American offenders.[39] Mass arrests continued to be a major police tactic in Los Angeles during the increasingly serious race tensions of the 1940s. It was a major means of control used to suppress what police in 1942 defined as an "imminent" crime wave by youth gangs, which in 1943 "broke out" in the "zoot-suit riots." (Both situations were clearly entangled with racial issues. The zoot-suit riots, in particular, were definitely Anglo-initiated race riots, though the media at the time did not define them as such.[40] The tactic of mass arrests, which was widely publicized, was felt by a relatively detached observer to "almost inevitably intensify the already serious bitterness between the Mexican colony and the remainder of the community."[41] In Los Angeles, intensive police control procedures were used against a population of which a larger proportion was comparatively new on the urban scene and which had neither self-help institutions nor influence on the political process. A number of interviews have suggested that the zoot-suit riots, with the accompanying sensationalized news, left a deep residue of shame and anger among Mexican Americans. Their importance clearly transcended Los Angeles.

It is perhaps significant that in the late 1940s and early 1950s Mexican-American war veterans, age peers of those who had been arrested in the early 1940s, were prominent among those who formed the Los Angeles Community Service Organization (CSO), one of the earliest political associations in the area. And it is also significant that one of the CSO's principal activities was to marshal complaints of police malpractice: It conducted 35 formal investigations between 1947 and 1956.[42] During the same period, another major Mexican-American organization, the Alianza Hispano Americana, developed a program to initiate court action in civil rights violations throughout the Southwest. In the 1960s, the Los Angeles-based Council on Mexican-American Affairs took up the cause. Numerous *ad hoc* groups were formed—and are still formed—in communities when particularly outrageous events occurred. . . . Efforts to achieve more responsible law enforcement thus have moved from "normal" channels to political organization to judicial relief—all without much effect. The condition in the Los Angeles area is duplicated in many places throughout the Southwest.

The problem is compounded by the unwillingness of Mexican Americans to file complaints. As a document issued by the Council on Mexican-American Affairs concludes, Mexican-American "complainants were very reluctant to take their grievances to law enforcement."[43] This is substantiated by the fact that of 1,328 complaints alleging police brutality presented to the U.S. Department of Justice between January, 1958 and June, 1960, only ten were from persons known to be of Mexican descent.[44]

Information on day-to-day details of police practice in areas of heavy Mexican concentration is very poor. A study in the mid-1960s showed Mexican Americans in San Diego to believe that

> In San Diego police "exist for the protection of the . . . Anglo community," and they have only "restraining and punitive" functions [in the minority areas]. . . . Several police practices were singled out for unfavorable comment. It was felt that police are discriminatory, condescending, and paternalistic. This is evidenced by indiscriminate stopping and frisking

> of both minority adults and juveniles; the use of degrading terms, such as "pancho," "muchacho," and "amigo"; and excessive patrolling within the Mexican-American community.[45]

These complaints, according to our interviews, barely scratch the surface of discontent with the police: Condescension may be irritating, but brutality terrifies and enrages.

Post-arrest judicial processes, in turn, are almost totally unanalyzed.[46] At this writing, a motion challenging the constitutionality of indictments returned by the Los Angeles County Grand Jury was being heard; it attacked the jury as grossly under-representing the Mexican-American population. The many complexities of court procedure and of lawyer-client interaction, so critical to the outcome of a case, have barely been studied. These processes, interestingly, have *not* been a significant source of protest by Mexican-American groups. Thus, the operations of the courts, one of the most sensitive government functions, must be left unexplored, though it may be one of the potentially explosive points of contact between Mexican Americans and the government.

IMPLICATIONS OF GOVERNMENT CONTACT

The data available on Mexican-American contact with government agencies are least deficient for those agencies which are directly concerned with law enforcement. Accordingly, we have concentrated on these agencies. It may be objected that data on police practices do not give information about Mexican relationships with "helping" agencies. But the coercive power explicit in the law-enforcement agencies, such as the police and the Border Patrol, has always intruded into the so-called "helping" agencies. This intrusion was most dramatic during the Depression, when many of the city welfare agencies became functionally indistinguishable from law-enforcement agencies directly involved in deportation. The intrusion is continuously latent in all government agencies. Frequently it is manifest. We suggested at the outset of this [article] that many immigrants from Mexico have had contact with American society only through their employers and through government agencies. (Government agencies have, of course, proliferated during the twentieth century and are far more significant in the experience of the present-day newcomer to the United States than they were to the nineteenth-century immigrants coming from Europe.) If our analysis in this [article] is borne out by further research, the confusion of welfare and police functions in the operation of government agencies might be a very significant element in the historical reluctance of Mexican Americans to become attached to this society. Further, it may help explain the alienation and "hard-to-reach" orientation of many Mexican Americans in the present. Thus the Border

Patrol and its actions cannot be dismissed as merely of historical interest. Its past activities have, indeed, left a residue of hatred that influenced all subsequent relationships of Mexican Americans to other agencies. This residue continues to affect the Border Patrol because the Patrol still has much to do with the lives of individuals and the conditions of life in Mexican-American communities. On the other hand, the welfare "repatriations" of the 1930s are of more historical than contemporary relevance. But their rationale and their procedures have a contemporary echo, and they remind us that though the administration of social-welfare funds in the present is not so blatantly coercive as in the past, it nonetheless carries a coercive and degrading quality.

Until World War II government agencies easily could, and did, define Mexican Americans as "probably foreign." Along with most citizens of the Southwest, they added to this legal definition the notion that Mexican Americans were permanently "alien" in behavior. It was this combined definition that permitted the welfare repatriations of the 1930s as a similar definition of another ethnic group, the Japanese Americans, "legitimated" even more extreme government action in California a decade later. It is this legal and social definition that continues to permit the Border Patrol to examine Mexican Americans to see if indeed they *are* foreign and deportable. The "probably foreign" definition of Mexican Americans thus has exposed them to harassment of a very special nature. It has also exposed them to unusual administrative arbitrariness. Under the immigration rules, the burden of proof of citizenship is on the individual rather than on the government. As court cases involving the nationality laws attest, the amount of administrative discretion in this crucial matter is extraordinary. More than most law-enforcement agencies, the Border Patrol initiates action; it does not merely react to citizen complaints.[47] Administrative arbitrariness also characterizes much contact with police and other law-enforcement agencies and has frequently resulted in special discrimination against Mexican Americans.

This [article] has been concerned primarily with government bureaucratic functions and with some of the special relations of Mexicans to these bureaucracies. In recent years the meaning of government to minorities has been changed by the proliferation of a variety of *ad hoc* agencies, particularly those funded by the Office of Economic Opportunity (OEO). They have appeared in local neighborhoods as special-function agencies for minorities, and they have appeared at the state-wide and regional level with similar special mandates to serve hitherto neglected citizens. As such they have provided in some instances a real impetus for local change; in other instances their impact at the local level has been insignificant. But in many places and situations they have provided a specific focus for minority discontent with government agencies in general. Thus, the beginning of an upsurge of militancy among Mexican-American associations coincided with a mass walkout of Mexican-American representatives to a 1966 meeting called by the Equal Employment Opportunities Commission. The meeting, paradoxically, was called by the Commission in response to previous complaints that there had not been enough attention to Mexican-American needs in administration of antidiscriminatory regulations. The Cabinet-level meetings held on Mexican-American problems in 1967 met essentially the same reception from a wide variety of Mexican-American leaders. Failure to meet minority needs is especially irritating in an agency whose sole job it is to meet those needs. However, such special-function agencies do permit the legitimation of protest by minority members. The protest can then spill over to other agencies of government.

An analysis of the role of such agencies in focusing the more diffuse anxiety and resentment of Mexican Americans vis-à-vis government agencies in general would be very useful. In rare instances, such as that of the California Rural Legal Assistance offices, OEO programs have even provided the means for modifying the operations of "normal" local government agencies.[48] Because the roles of government at all levels are changing so rapidly, our discussion here can provide no more than a prologomenon to research in this highly significant area as well as to policy intervention in the status of minorities.

Inquiries into such ostensibly egalitarian institutions as the schools and the welfare agencies generally show persisting structural relations that maintain social inequalities as well as those that work toward their eradication. This is particularly true when these inequalities are related to social visibility, as with poor Mexican Americans. Recently the politicization of contacts between client and agency has shown how clearly the client sees the agency as a combination of welfare and coercion. This politicization has appeared nationally with the welfare rights organizations. It can be viewed as the client counterpart of the agency's combination of welfare and coercion. It has not yet advanced very far among Mexican Americans. In time this politicization, combined with direct political action, may begin to find the solutions to minority problems that men . . . felt were to come from American society at large as natural extensions of the citizenship role.

NOTES

1. Sjoberg, Brymer, and Farris discuss these problems in an analytic review of the literature which includes illustrations from a long-range study of Mexican Americans in San Antonio. Gideon Sjoberg, Richard A. Brymer, and Buford Farris, "Bureaucracy and the Lower Class," *Sociology and Social Research,* L (Apr., 1966), pp. 325-337.

2. See Carey McWilliams, *Factories in the Field* (Boston: Little, Brown and Company, 1939).

3. This discussion was developed from Leo Grebler et al., *Mexican Immigration to the United States: The Record and Its Implications* (Mexican-American Study Project, Advance Report 2, Graduate School of Business Administration, University of California, Los Angeles, Jan., 1966), pp. 33-35.

4. *Reorganization of the Immigration and Naturalization Service,* Hearings before the Subcommittee on Legal and Monetary Affairs of the Committee on Government Operations, House, 84th Congress, first session, March 9 and 17, 1955, p. 3.

5. *Annual Report of the Immigration and Naturalization Service,* 1956, p. 8.

6. *Annual Report of the Immigration and Naturalization Service,* 1955, p. 10.

7. Ernesto Galarza, *Merchants of Labor: The Mexican Bracero Story* (San Jose, Calif: The Rosicrucian Press, Ltd., 1965), p. 61.

8. *Mexicans in California: Report of Governor C. C. Young's Mexican Fact-finding Committee* (Sacramento: 1930), pp. 191-194.

9. Carey McWilliams, "Getting Rid of the Mexicans," *American Mercury,* XXVIII (Mar., 1933), pp. 322-324.

10. We are indebted to Ronald Lopez for calling our attention to the records of the Los Angeles County Board of Supervisors, from which these figures are drawn. Interestingly, simultaneous efforts were made to get Mexicans on the city's relief rolls into agricultural labor. In 1933, the *Los Angeles Citizen* (an AFL official publication) noted that 4,000 Mexican families on welfare had been shipped to the valleys to harvest the cotton crop, which growers contended was in danger of loss from the winter rains (issue of Nov. 10, 1933).

11. Norman D. Humphrey, "Mexican Repatriation from Michigan—Public Assistance in Historical Perspective," *Social Service Review,* XV (Sept., 1941), pp. 505, 507, 509.

12. *Ibid.,* p. 505.

13. See the *corrido* "El Deportado," reproduced in Nellie Foster, "The Corrido: A Mexican Culture Trait Persisting in Southern California" (unpublished Master's thesis, University of Southern California, 1939), p. 182, cited in Armando Morales, *Historical and Attitudinal Factors Related to Current Mexican American Law Enforcement Concerns in Los Angeles* (mimeographed manuscript, Council of Mexican American Affairs, 1967), p. 9. The welfare repatriations were connected in the Mexican-American definition of the situation with the stepping up of raids by immigration authorities, according to Foster (p. 8).

14. *Annual Report of the Commissioner-General of Immigration* for the fiscal year 1931, p. 9.

15. Nancie L. González, *The Spanish Americans of New Mexico: A Distinctive Heritage* (Mexican-American Study Project, Advance Report 9, Graduate School of Business Administration, University of California, Los Angeles, Sept., 1967), p. 88.

16. Glenn V. Ramsey and Beulah Hodge, "Anglo Latin Problems as Perceived by Public Service Personnel," *Social Forces,* XXXVII (May, 1959), p. 346.

17. Ismael Dieppa, lecture at the University of California, Riverside, 1969, referring to such abuses in Santa Cruz County, California.

18. Lyle Saunders, *Cultural Difference and Medical Care* (New York: Russell Sage Foundation, 1954); Robert C. Hanson and Lyle Saunders, with the collaboration of Marion Hotopp, *Nurse-Patient Communication–A Manual for Public Health Nurses in Northern New Mexico* (Boulder, Colo. and Santa Fe, N. Mex.: Bureau of Sociological Research, Institute of Behavioral Science, University of Colorado and New Mexico State Department of Public Health, 1964). See also A. Taher Moustafa and Gertrud Weiss, *Health Status and Practices of Mexican Americans* (Mexican-American Study Project, Advance Report II, Graduate School of Business Administration, University of California, Los Angeles, Feb., 1968).

19. Glenn D. Mellinger, Dean I. Manheimer, and Marianne T. Kleman, "Deterrents to Adequate Immunization of Preschool Children" (Los Angeles County Health Department, 1967), p. 26.

20. Margaret Clark, *Health in the Mexican American Culture* (Berkeley, Calif.: University of California Press, 1959), pp. 232, 233.

21. Tomas C. Atencio, "The Forest Service and the Spanish Surname American," presented at Cabinet Committee Hearings on Mexican American Affairs, El Paso, Tex., 1967.

22. González, *op. cit.*

23. Clark S. Knowlton, "Recommendations for the Solution of Land Tenure Problems Among the Spanish American," presented at Cabinet Committee Hearings on Mexican American Affairs, El Paso, Tex., 1967.

24. Atencio, *op. cit.*

25. See Allan Silver, "The Demand for Order in Civil Society: A Review of Some Themes in the History of Urban Crime, Police and Riot," in David J. Bordua (ed.), *The Police: Six Sociological Essays* (New York: John Wiley & Sons, Inc., 1967). Silver discusses the development of techniques–urban and rural–for dealing with the "dangerous classes" of nineteenth-century England. He comments that the "vigilantism" of rural England at the time exacerbated the latent class conflict, and that the urban pressure for the bureaucratization of police functions operated to insert a "third force," the force of the state, into the situation of developing class cleavage.

26. Cited in Carey McWilliams, *North from Mexico* (New York: J. B. Lippincott Company, 1949), p. 234.

27. C. B. Horrall, letter to Foreman Oliver.

28. *Hearings before the United States Commission on Civil Rights,* San Francisco, Jan. 27, 1960 (Washington, D.C., 1960).

29. Arthur J. Rubel, *Across the Tracks* (Austin, Tex.: University of Texas Press, 1966), p. 47; emphasis added.

30. Walter Prescott Webb, *The Texas Rangers: A Century of Frontier Defense* (Boston: Houghton Mifflin Company, 1935), pp. 479 and 486.

31. *Ibid.,* pp. 513-515.

32. Paul S. Taylor, "Crime and the Foreign Born: The Problem of the Mexican," in National Commission on Law Observance and Enforcement, *Report on Crime and the Foreign Born* (Washington, D.C., 1931), VI, p. 219.

33. National Commission on Law Observance and Enforcement, *Lawlessness in Law Enforcement* (Washington, D.C., 1931), XI, p. 138 (Dallas), p. 141 (Denver), and pp. 143, 144 (Los Angeles).

34. Paul S. Taylor and Clark Kerr, "Documentary History of the Strike of the Cotton Pickers in California–1933," in U.S. Congress, Senate, *Education and Labor Committee Hearings: Violation of Free Speech and Rights of Labor; Part 54, Agricultural Labor in California,* 1940, p. 19947.

35. *Ibid.*, p. 20005.

36. *Ibid.*, p. 19992. Also quoted in McWilliams, *North from Mexico,* p. 191, whose treatment of labor troubles reflects the progressive biases of his era.

37. Galarza, *op. cit.,* p. 39.

38. John Gregory Dunne, *Delano* (New York: Farrar, Straus & Giroux, 1967), p. 114.

39. Edwin M. Lemert and Judy Rosberg, "The Administration of Justice to Minority Groups in Los Angeles County," in R. L. Beals, Leonard Bloom, and Franklin Fearing (eds.), *University of California Publications in Culture and Society,* vol. II (Berkeley, Calif.: University of California Press, 1948), pp. 3, 12.

40. See McWilliams, *North from Mexico,* for an analysis of both the Sleepy Lagoon arrests and the later zoot-suit riots.

41. Paper by Guy T. Nunn, field representative of the Minority Groups Service of the War Manpower Commission (read in a meeting of the Special Mexican Relations Committee of the Los Angeles County Grand Jury, Oct. 8, 1942), p. 17. This was two months following the arrest of more than 600 Mexican youths following the Sleepy Lagoon incident. Nunn also reported the hysterical Anglo reaction to the exaggerated news reports:

> Shortly after the mass arrests of several weeks ago complaints began to reach my agency from communities over a hundred miles away, alleging a sudden increase in discrimination against Spanish-speaking people; many times in localities relatively free of it in the past, as a direct out-growth of events in Los Angeles and of the sensational publicity afforded them. Mexicans were denied access to movies, public parks, and recreational facilities, restaurants. At the same time there was a sharp increase in employment discrimination (*ibid.*).

42. Morales, *op. cit.,* p. 12.

43. Morales, *op. cit.,* p. 15.

44. *1961 Report of the U.S. Commission on Civil Rights,* U.S. Department of Justice.

45. Joseph D. Lohman et al., *The Police and The Community,* U.S. President's Commission on Law Enforcement and Administration of Justice, Field Survey no. 4 (Berkeley, Calif.: 1966), p. 55.

46. A study of court personnel and procedures and an analysis of arrest, arraignment, and bail records has been under way at the University of

Southern California. The study, conducted by the Western Center on Law and Poverty, was sponsored by the United States Civil Rights Commission, and included six places–East Los Angeles, San Bernardino, San Diego, Fresno, San Jose, and Monterey County.

47. See Albert J. Reiss, Jr. and David J. Bordua, "Environment and Organization: A Perspective on the Police," in Bordua, *op. cit.,* for an analysis of the consequences of the predominantly reactive strategy of most police work. Proactive strategy is made difficult in most police work since it usually entails access to private places. Reiss and Bordua argue that the reactive nature of police work means that the social system of the complainer dominates their work. The difference between normal police work and Border Patrol work, where there is usually no complainant, is evident. The consequence has generally been to expand the license of the Border Patrol as its mandate is enlarged to that of enforcing a national ideal.

48. For an account of the operations of the California Rural Legal Assistance in central California–largely on behalf of Mexican Americans–see Calvin Trillin, "U.S. Letter: McFarland," *New Yorker,* XLIII (Nov. 4, 1967), pp. 173-181.

13: SATISFACTION WITH GOVERNMENT SERVICES: Implications for Political Behavior

John Comer, Michael Steinman, and Susan Welch

THIS PAPER HAS A TWOFOLD PURPOSE: TO ANALYZE SOME ASPECTS OF political behavior among Mexican-Americans and, at a more general level, to re-examine some hypotheses about the relationship between satisfaction with government services and support for the political system.

Herbert Jacob has recently pointed out that a neglected element in the literature on political participation is the manner in which individuals enjoy the fruits of their participation.[1] More explicitly, this focus concerns the degree to which individuals obtain valued goods and services from government. In short, it treats individuals as consumers of government services. The so-called consumer role is not only distinct from the more widely researched citizen role; but, in addition, the consequences that flow from one's experiences as a consumer of government services may be more important in terms of creating support for government institutions.

The consumer role differs from the citizen role in that an individual's contact with the political system as a consumer is more personal and direct. For example, individuals as passive consumers are asked to account directly to government for their behavior.[2] The consumer role also includes more activist behaviors. Here, individuals take the initiative themselves. In both instances, the relationship between the individual and government is significantly different from the citizen role. Behaviors included under the citizen

From *Politics 1973: Minorities in Politics,* edited by Tinsley E. Yarbrough. Greenville, N.C.: East Carolina University Publications, 1973, pp. 65-82. Reprinted by permission of John C. Comer and East Carolina University Publications.

The authors wish to thank Alan Booth, John Contu, Dave Dorpat, and John Sahs for their assistance at various stages of the project. Funds for the project were provided by the Comprehensive Health Planning Division and the Mexican-American Commission of the State of Nebraska.

role, such as voting, demonstrating, or working for a candidate, bring the individual into less intimate relation with political authorities than actions related to consumer activities. In acting out the citizen role, an individual typically is much less certain about the effect of his behavior on decision-making and less likely to develop an appreciation of decision-making processes.

In contrast, an individual filling the consumer role is confronted directly with publicly allocated values and frequently with the public officials responsible for their application and enforcement. Not only can the individual typically determine for himself the desirability of a particular policy, but he has a greater opportunity for understanding the dynamics of the situation. That is, he can learn or become associated with the political and administrative procedures involved and anticipate in an approximate way what decisions will be made and by whom. The proximity and clarity of this process permit the individual to assess the degree to which his interests are satisfied. The applicant for welfare benefits, for example, can assess the amount of satisfaction he will receive more precisely and accurately than the individual voting for a particular candidate. The payoffs, positive and negative, in the latter situation are more remote, intangible, and vulnerable to alternative interpretations. There is, in addition, a point at which system outputs may be more immediate to consumer demands. That is, a person acting as a consumer may realize value allocations relating to his inputs in a shorter period of time than one acting as a citizen.[3]

One can anticipate that experience as a consumer also influences reaction to government and politics. It is not as voters, demonstrators, or candidates but as consumers that most experience government. Depending on the nature of the experience, consumer behavior may be related to regime acceptance and, under special circumstances, regime stability.[4] For example, Almond and Verba point out that satisfaction with government output is one factor which leads to support for the political system. Moreover, they suggest that high levels of satisfaction are likely to foster political stability.[5] The concern raised here is particularly important for individuals who have not experienced the more typical patterns of political learning, the person who has not established diffuse loyalties to the political system, or the person who has not internalized the dominant political culture. In Almond and Verba's terms, these people have developed subject orientations, but not, according to the authors, the more vital participant orientations.[6] In the United States, these are likely to be, according to the authors, persons of less education. One might also expect subject orientations among the poor and many members of minority groups, e.g., blacks, Mexican-Americans. Subjects can be expected to behave in system maintaining ways as long as the system treats them reasonably well. However, common parlance suggests that this is nearly never the case. Experiences of the poor and members of minority groups with government are generally less than satisfactory.[7] Experience as consumers may also be important because it can lead to the types of citizen participation noted above.

This paper examines levels of satisfaction and differences in satisfaction with selected government services among a sample of Mexican-Americans. Further, it relates satisfaction to more general political attitudes and behavior. In so doing, it re-examines some hypotheses concerning the relation between satisfaction with government outputs and orientations toward the political system.

I. A REVIEW OF THE LITERATURE

The California studies as well as others dealing with the relations of Mexican-Americans with government and government services suggest some general patterns of behavior. First, it is clear that in some areas Mexican-Americans do not make extended use of government services.[8] This reflects a past experience with the Anglo political world limited almost exclusively to the coercive "hand" of government bureaucracy. In response, Mexican-Americans have adopted a "coping pattern" in their contact with government agencies. The pattern emphasizes passivity and withdrawal. Rarely and with little success have Mexican-Americans involved themselves in attempts to modify or influence their treatment at the hands of government authority. They prefer to leave government alone, and in turn, to be left alone. Moreover, relations with government have been aggravated by differences in language between Mexican-Americans and government officials, and by the reaction of many Anglo authorities to Mexican-Americans, namely the presumption that Mexican-Americans are foreign and in the United States illegally.[9]

Much of the antagonism of Mexican-Americans toward government authority has developed in response to the tactics of the U.S. Immigration and Naturalization Service. In an effort to control illegal entry into the United States from Mexico, immigration authorities, past and present, have subjected many Mexican-Americans who are citizens to harsh and hostile treatment. In some cases, Mexican-Americans who represent third and fourth generations in the United States have been forced to produce evidence of citizenship. The bitterness generated as a result of these encounters has, in many instances, extended to other areas of political and social life.[10]

There is also a considerable body of evidence which suggests that Mexican-Americans have not fared very well at the hands of local law enforcement.[11] For example, early Mexican migrants were subjected to harassment by Texas Rangers and, while the threat has been removed, hostility toward the Rangers remains widespread among Mexican-Americans in the Southwest.[12] In other areas, local law enforcement personnel use harsh and frequently unlawful methods to break strikes of Mexican-American migrants. This pattern of discrimination is not limited to law enforcement in sparsely populated rural areas. One study in a large city of Mexican-Americans' perceptions of law enforcement suggests that police are viewed in largely negative terms.[13] Another study in a large city reveals that Mexican-Americans are more likely to be arrested and convicted for major crimes and less likely to be paroled than Anglo-Americans.[14] In a word, the available evidence suggests that Mexican-American experience with federal and local law enforcement has not been very satisfying.

Mexican-American experience with service agencies reflects a similar pattern. Welfare agencies, for example, are viewed with suspicion and distrust in many areas. This may reflect, among other things, the fact that welfare agencies were instrumental in transporting many impoverished Mexican-Americans, some of whom were United States citizens, to Mexico during the Depression.[15] That impressions of events such as this have hung on is suggested in the small number of Mexican-Americans who avail themselves of welfare services. In Los Angeles, for example, only six percent of the Mexican-American population receive welfare payments.[16] In the area of health care, services very often have been dispensed with little regard for family or community feelings. There is little recognition that many Anglo health practices conflict with the personal beliefs of Mexican-Americans.[17] Insensitivity of both welfare and health agencies has led many Mexican-Americans to view them as an extension of the coercive Anglo society that they have come to know in other areas. Here, too, the Mexican-American experience has not been very satisfying.

The consequences for Mexican-Americans of contact with government agencies, apart from suspicion and distrust of those agencies, are difficult to assess. This paper examines the hypothesis that negative interactions with government agencies lead Mexican-Americans to develop negative orientations toward the political system. More specifically, it is expected that negative interactions lead to disaffect toward government, a low feeling of political efficacy, and withdrawal from the political system. Evidence reported by others supports these hypotheses. For example, the slowness of Mexican-Americans to attach themselves to American society, reflected in lower rates of naturalization than other ethnic groups, is frequently linked to their unsatisfactory experience with government agencies.[18] Lack of participation in politics may reflect Mexican-American experience with bureaucratic authority. One study reports voting of Mexican-Americans in the 1964 general election in Los Angeles and San Antonio to be lower than the average in those cities.[19] Mexican-Americans generally do not feel very efficacious when it comes to politics. Seventy-five percent in Los Angeles and 79 percent in San Antonio respond that government is too complicated. Thirty-five percent in Los Angeles and 40 percent in San Antonio do not feel they have a great deal to say about government. A sizable proportion (44 percent in Los

Angeles and 47 percent in San Antonio) feel that public officials do not care about their constituents.[20] Our own data reveal that our sample is somewhat less politically competent (perceived ability to influence government) than a national cross section of the American people.[21] While many factors account for these differences, many have suggested that Mexican-American distrust of political authority in the context of public bureaucracy plays a significant role. While these studies are interesting and revealing, they do not assess the relationship between governmental output and political support. This is what the present study attempts to do in an exploratory way.

II. METHOD

Data for this paper are taken from a larger study of Mexican-Americans. Interviews were conducted in four communities in two of the four counties that are centers of the Mexican-American population in Nebraska.[22] Sampling was done randomly in five Census Enumeration Districts within the four communities. The size of the communities ranged from a few hundred to over 30,000; the percentages of Mexican-American households in each district ranged from 13 percent to 50 percent.[23] All households designated by the sampling design were screened for Mexican-American residents and all eligible respondents were then offered a choice of taking the interview in Spanish or English; 22 percent chose Spanish.[24] The interviewing was done by three types of interviewers: Professional Anglo interviewers, paired professional Anglo and Mexican-American interviewers, and specifically trained Mexican-American interviewers working alone. Extensive analysis of responses indicated no difference in response to the three types of interviewers.[25] Refusal rate was extremely low (two percent) and only five percent of the households could not be contacted with three callbacks. Comparison of social and economic characteristics of our sample with studies of Mexican-Americans in other parts of the country suggests that our group is not substantially different.[26] Mexican-Americans are not in Nebraska because they have assimilated more, but because agricultural and other work brought them or their parents to Nebraska from Texas, Wyoming, or Colorado.[27]

III. MEXICAN-AMERICAN EXPERIENCE WITH SELECTED GOVERNMENT SERVICES

Much of the literature reviewed above suggests that Mexican-Americans do not take advantage of services provided by the government. Our study dealt with this topic in limited fashion. We asked our respondents whether they were using or had ever used each of the following: food programs, job training and employment services, public aid, and health services. The four categories are not exhaustive and not very precise. They represent general

TABLE 1

MEXICAN-AMERICAN EXPERIENCE WITH SELECTED GOVERNMENT SERVICES

	Food Programs	*Job Training and Employment Service*	*Public Aid*	*Health Services*
Use of service	49% (173)	22% (171)	37% (172)	24% (168)
Service is helping	90% (86)	70% (36)	95% (63)	87% (38)
Agency understands personal problems	90% (78)	92% (31)	98% (57)	100% (33)
A lot to say about agency treatment	30% (80)	22% (36)	25% (57)	19% (36)
Agency asked about treatment	1% (80)	8% (36)	12% (59)	6% (32)

[28] Richard Gilliland, "Food Stamp Participation in Nebraska," State Technical Assistance Agency, Lincoln, 1970. (Mimeographed.)

categories for numerous government services. This is not particularly important; we are not interested in specific programs, but with mapping Mexican-American experience in general. Further, the programs analyzed here are chiefly "helping" programs. The emphasis on helping programs was guided by the fact that government involvement is fairly obvious, yet not overly coercive. In addition to use, we were also interested in the level of satisfaction with each program.

The extent to which Mexican-Americans report that they participate in the four programs is striking. Nearly 50 percent of our sample indicate that they use food programs. When one considers that a positive response refers primarily to the food stamp program, the figure is even more impressive. Participation in the food stamp program in the state of Nebraska among those eligible is only about 20 percent.[28] Furthermore, only 60 percent of our sample of Mexican-Americans is eligible. Use of the remaining services by Mexican-Americans is not as high, but still quite impressive.

What may be a more significant finding is the large number of respondents who indicate that the service they are receiving is helping them. Approximately nine out of ten who use food programs, public aid, and health services respond that the service is helping them. Seventy percent of those using job training and employment services report that the service is helping. This finding by itself says nothing about the ability of government agencies to relate to Mexican-Americans. It may only reflect Mexican-American assessment of the dollar or other value placed on services. We also asked whether respondents felt that the agency where they receive government aid really understands their personal problems. Here again, the overwhelming majority respond positively.

The results represent quite a departure from findings of other studies. Not only is participation in government programs among Mexican-Americans reasonably high, but most feel that the efforts of the government are helping them and that the government understands their personal problems. One can imagine several explanations for these findings. First, it may be that Mexican-Americans are not responding truthfully, that is, they are unwilling to give responses which they feel would be unfavorably received by the interviewer. However, an extensive analysis of responses failed to detect any evidence that Mexican-Americans were not telling the truth.[29] Second, Mexican-Americans may be misperceiving the situation. It may be difficult for Mexican-Americans to rely on government assistance and at the same time feel they are mistreated. Third, Mexican-Americans may be simply taking advantage of government services which are dispensed in a reasonably satisfying manner. The latter may well be the case. Welfare agencies in both areas, for example, are rather small but fairly professional organizations, and appear to be efficiently run. The welfare organization in one county has a Mexican-American on the staff and the other has a Mexican-American working as a secretary. Fourth, Mexican-Americans may be comparing their treatment with past worse experience in the Southwest where discrimination against them is more pronounced.[30]

Respondents were also asked whether they had a lot to say regarding their treatment by various agencies and whether agencies had ever inquired concerning how the respondent was treated. No more than 30 percent respond that they have a lot to say about how they are treated. Fewer still report that agencies have ever asked how they are treated. This finding does not suggest agencies overly concerned with client relations. Treatment here, however, probably does not mean personal courtesy, but more likely, continued government assistance. In many respects, this is out of the control of local agencies. State and federal agencies establish procedures and rules for eligibility. Local agencies may refrain from asking clients about such matters because the agencies can do very little about them. Furthermore, it is doubtful if clients could understand the legal distinctions which provide assistance to some and deny it to others. What is perhaps the more important finding, however, is that lack of input (for lack of a better term) does not seem to influence one's reaction to the agency.

As noted above, the programs examined here are helping agencies. No direct data were obtained for interactions with police. However, many have noted the bad experience that Mexican-Americans have with police. Several questions were asked which provide some sense of how well Mexican-Americans in our sample relate to police agencies in the communities. Thirty-four percent report that if they took a problem to the police their point of view would be given serious attention; 39 percent indicate that their point of view would be given a little attention; and 23 percent report that their point of view would be ignored. In response to the question "would you be treated better, about the same or worse than most people by the police if you were accused of a crime?" seven percent say better, 70 percent report about the same, and 22 percent report worse. Significantly, about one-fourth of the sample feel the police would neither listen to them nor treat them as equals with other citizens. This is not the level of hostility toward the police revealed in other studies, but it is somewhat less positive than responses to programs and services noted above. The less positive attitudes toward the police may reflect the coercive character of law enforcement. Mexican-Americans are particularly suspect of agencies that wield coercive authority.

One might ask why response to the police is more favorable in Nebraska than, for example, in the Southwestern United States or Southern California. For one thing, encounters with the police are probably much less frequent. The primary reason for Mexican-American hostility toward the police, citizenship of Mexican-Americans, is much less a concern of local police agencies in Nebraska. Moreover, the treatment by police may be better in Nebraska because Mexican-Americans, a rather small minority, represent less of a threat. Still further, Mexican-Americans in our sample are reasonably well established in their communities. They are fairly well integrated into the community and probably more permanent. Many (43 percent) own their own home.

IV. SOCIAL VARIABLES AND EXPERIENCE WITH GOVERNMENT SERVICES

In this section we are interested in differences in use of and satisfaction with government services. We have aggregated into single scales the responses to each of the services treated in the previous section. For example, individuals who report that they use one service are given a score of one, individuals who report that they use two services are given a score of two, and so on. Other scales are derived by subtracting the total number of negative references from the total number of positive references to each of the various services. For example, individuals who use two services and report one is helping them and the other is not helping them are scored zero. Correlations between each of the scales and several social variables are contained in Table 2.

With respect to use, income and employment status bear the strongest relationship. While the correlations are not very high, they are in the expected direction. Those with lower incomes who are unemployed are more likely to participate in government programs than those with higher incomes who are employed. The size of the correlations probably reflects the large number of

TABLE 2

RELATIONSHIPS BETWEEN SOCIAL VARIABLES AND SELECTED GOVERNMENT SERVICES

(Coefficients are Pearson product-moment correlations)

	Using Services	*Services are helping*	*Under-stands Problems*	*Say About Treatment*	*Asked About Treatment*
Income	−.13**	.23**	−.13**	−.01	.07
Education	.01	.00	−.16*	.01	−.03
Age	−.12*	.07	.21*	.00	.00
Employment status	−.16*	−.18*	.00	−.08	.05
Years resident in county	−.10**	.03	.17*	−.07	−.08
Years resident in U.S.	−.04	−.03	.26*	−.16	.06
Number in household	.10**	−.17*	−.16*	−.02	−.06
Member political group	.04	.01	.09	−.16**	−.20*
Member nationality group	.09	.15**	−.07	−.15**	−.05
Language of interviewer	.00	−.14**	.04	.03	−.15**
Attitude toward government assistance:					
Rely more on individual initiative	.01	.04	−.07	.32*	.14**
Government stay out of local problems and let community solve them.	−.02	.17*	.13	−.10	.16**

*Significant ⩽ .05.
**Significant ⩽ .10.

Coding: Employment status: employed=2, unemployed=1; member of nationality or political group: member=2, nonmember=1; language of interviewer: English=2, Spanish=1; attitude toward government assistance: agreement with statement (anti-welfare)=1, disagreement with statement (pro-welfare)=0.

poor and uneducated people who do not take advantage of government programs. Other variables related to use are age, years resident in the county, and number in household.

It may be interesting to point out that attitudes toward government assistance are unrelated to use of government services. This suggests that how one feels about government aid has no influence on whether he will participate in government programs. It may mean that the government has succeeded in reaching people whose basic attitudes toward government assistance are negative. It may also mean that Mexican-Americans have not adopted what many feel is a middle class Anglo perspective on government assistance.

Contrary to other studies, neither length of residence in the United States nor facility with English are related to use of government services. This is probably explained in that most in our sample have been in the United States for a considerable length of time, and several agencies in at least one of the counties in which our survey was conducted have Mexican-Americans on the staff who can assist Mexican-Americans who cannot or prefer not to speak English.

Income, employment status, and number in household are related in the expected direction to belief that government services help. The belief that the federal government should stay out of local problems and let local communities handle them is also related to this scale. More interesting is the finding that those who belong to a nationality group and those interviewed in Spanish are more likely to respond that government services help them. The latter finding may be explained in that those who speak Spanish may have lower expectations than those who speak English. That members of nationality groups are more likely to report government programs are helping them may be explained in terms of relative deprivation.[31] Members of nationality groups may be more conscious of the plight of their neighbors and more likely to recognize that government programs are responsible for maintaining them at somewhat higher socio-economic levels.

Some interesting patterns are observed with respect to belief that agencies administering services understand personal problems. Age and years resident in county and the United States are positively related to this index. Income, education, and number in household are inversely related to belief that agencies understand personal problems.

In addition to the one government assistance item, the only variables that are related to belief that one has a lot to say about his treatment by government agencies is membership in nationality and political groups. No doubt those who are members of such groups are aware of organizational efforts on their behalf. Individuals may observe what local organizations are doing and from this conclude that they have some influence over agency operations. Whether organizational activities actually influence agency procedure is another matter. Agency inquiry concerning client treatment is negatively related to membership in a political group, facility with English, and both government assistance items.

V. POLITICAL VARIABLES AND EXPERIENCE WITH GOVERNMENT SERVICES

Here, we are concerned with variables that are influenced by experiences with government services. While it is difficult to be precise about the direction of causality, the argument as it is developed in the literature suggests that large numbers of Mexican-Americans are influenced in their social and political behavior by their experiences with government agencies. Furthermore, while a strong relationship will not demonstrate causality, the lack of a strong relationship must necessarily cast doubt on the hypothesis that negative attitudes toward government services and bureaucrats produce negative attitudes toward government and aspects of the political system.

Table III points out that only two variables are significantly related to use of government services. Those who use government services are more likely to report that the federal government has a good effect on their lives. This is interesting because of the alleged relationship between treatment at the hands of bureaucracy and unwillingness to attach oneself to the nation. Here we find the opposite. Those who have used services are more likely to report that the federal government has a good effect. The reversal must be related to the nature of the treatment Mexican-Americans receive. This finding is also interesting because it suggests that, even though services are dispensed through local bureaucracy, many are aware of the federal government's role in providing them. The other significant correlation obtains for one item of the efficacy scale: "People like me do not have much to say about what the government does." Interestingly enough, the efficacy and participation in politics scales are unrelated to use of government services. Nor is the belief that one is represented related to use of government services.

Belief that the federal government has a good effect is also related to the belief that government services help. Likewise, the belief that one is represented at the state and federal levels of government is related to the belief that government services help. Participation in politics is negatively related to this scale. This may mean that those who deal with bureaucracy and believe that they are being helped feel that there is no need to participate, while those who do not feel that they are being helped continue to press for assistance and improvements in other ways. In any case, the result is contrary to what others have pointed out. Bad experiences with bureaucracy are presumed to diminish participation. Those who respond that government services help them are also more likely to report that they would be given serious attention if they took a problem to the police. This may suggest a slight tendency to generalize favorable experiences with government in one realm to another realm. Support for this point is evident in the variables correlated with belief that government agencies understand personal problems. Favorable responses to government treatment as well as both items dealing with the police are positively related to belief that government agencies understand problems. While correlations are not high, they suggest that government bureaucrats should be aware that their treatment of clients may have repercussions beyond their own agency.

Several items are related to belief that one has a lot to say about his treatment by government agencies. First, belief that one is represented at the local and state levels is positively related to this scale. This may mean that local agencies are considered by some to be either state or local government. Both the participation scale and several items in the efficacy scale are negatively related to belief that one has a lot to say about treatment. This suggests that political efficacy is a many faceted dimension. Individuals probably feel different degrees of efficacy toward different levels of government as well as different institutions at the same level. It also suggests that particular kinds of efficacy do not necessarily lead to political participation. Only one item is related to responses concerning agency inquiries about treatment. People who indicate that agencies asked about treatment are less likely to report that a problem taken to the police would be given serious attention.

VI. CONCLUSION

While the findings in this study are necessarily tentative, owing to the small sample size, its rather narrow geographical focus, and the narrow range of government services treated, we can conclude with caution that the pattern of experience of Mexican-Americans with government services and bureaucrats portrayed in most of the literature is not general. Rather than avoiding government services, Mexican-Americans in our sample are using them to a high degree and with a reasonably high degree of satisfaction. Mexican-Americans do not, however, perceive that they have a great deal to say about their treatment by agencies administering services or that such agencies inquire about treatment.

In seeking explanations for these patterns, we are struck by the failure of demographic and social variables to explain much of the variance in use and satisfaction. It is particularly surprising to find that status variables (income and education) are either unrelated or only slightly related to use of government services among this group. The services examined in this study are specifically designed to reach low income, less educated persons, but our data suggest that the low income and less educated are hardly more likely to use government services than those with higher incomes and more education. Several explanations may be offered for this finding. First, the very poor and

TABLE 3

RELATIONSHIPS BETWEEN POLITICAL VARIABLES AND EXPERIENCE WITH GOVERNMENT SERVICES

(Coefficients are Pearson product moment correlations.)

	Using Services	*Services are Helping*	*Understands Problems*	*Say About Treatment*	*Asked About Treatment*
Federal government has good effect on living conditions	.16*	.17*	.17*	−.13	.04
Represented at County level	−.01	.09	.10	.21*	.07
Represented at State level	.06	.15*	.07	.12*	.00
Represented at Federal level	.04	.19*	.16*	.06	−.05
Participation in politics	−.02	−.11**	−.15	−.17*	−.05
Problem with Government	−.05	.10	.21*	.13**	.05
Problem with police	.02	.12**	.19*	.04	−.13**
Trouble with police	−.07	.10	.22*	.09	.05
Political efficacy	.00	−.05	.10	−.10	.08

Efficacy items:					
A lot to say about government	.12*	−.09	−.04	−.21*	.05
Government officials care what people like us think	−.07	−.08	.10	−.02	.09
Government too complicated for a person like me to understand	.02	−.06	.09	−.15*	.02

*Significant ⩽ .05.

**Significant ⩽ .10.

Coding: Federal government has good effect: 1 = worse, 2 = no effect, 3 = better; represented at county, state and federal levels: 0 = no, 1 = yes; participation in politics represents summation of yes responses to the following activities: talk to people, talk to public officials, work for a candidate, demonstrate, belong to political club, collect money, place bumper sticker on car, attend political rally, picket or boycott, and riot or engage in violent demonstration; problems with government, police: 1 = less consideration than most, 2 = same consideration, 3 = more consideration; trouble with police: 1 = treated worse than most, 2 = treated the same, 3 = treated better; political efficacy represents efficacious responses subtracted from non-efficacious responses to efficacy items; efficacy items: efficacious response = 1, non-efficacious response = 0.

uneducated are likely to be unaware of these services and their eligibility for them. They are likely to be out of the communications mainstream and apprehensive about dealing with government agencies. Second, in our sample, while over 25 percent had a family income of more than $7500, very few had an income that would put the family into the middle middle or upper middle class by the standards of the larger society. If this upper income group has been oversampled, correlations between income and usage would have undoubtedly been higher. Third, the method of analysis, testing for only linear relationships, may obscure a more complex association between status and use and satisfaction with services.

The findings concerning use and satisfaction with government services in relation to attitudes toward the political system and participation in the political system are more clear cut. We find that use and satisfaction bear little, if any, relationship to attitudes of Mexican-Americans toward the political system. This is both contrary to intuition and the findings of others. These data suggest that under certain conditions, at least, even minorities of rather recent vintage in the United States have firm dispositions regarding the political system, and that these are unlikely to be influenced, at least in the short run, by how the system performs. There may be a plausible explanation for these findings. Many people may have trouble linking their own individual situation to events and activities of the larger polity. One's treatment by the local welfare office may not be generalized to the political system. Most are probably unable to make the connection between these two discrete entities. Only those who are politically sophisticated or who are explicitly made aware may be able to make this type of generalization. This is hardly a surprising finding, as years of futile community organization can testify. An individual may attribute poor treatment by government officials or poor services to himself or to a specific bureaucrat or agency. Thus, feelings toward the system as a whole, in the short run, are not seriously affected.

To conclude, while we find a small correlation between use of and satisfaction with services and attitudes toward the federal government and one measure of political efficacy, these relationships are not of the strength expected. This casts some doubt on the tendency to attribute system support to system outputs among the most deprived groups in society. Perhaps these groups, along with most other groups in American society, are part of the general political culture to the extent that even unsatisfactory system outputs are not enough to challenge basic beliefs about the rightness of the political system in general and their place in that system in particular.

NOTES

1. Herbert Jacob, "Contact with Government Agencies: A Preliminary Analysis of the Distribution of Government Services," *Midwest Journal of Political Science,* XVI (February, 1972), pp. 123-46.

2. *Ibid.*, p. 125.

3. *Ibid.*

4. Bureaucracy as an instrument for satisfying consumer demands has also been a concern of scholars interested in political development. See Joseph LaPalombara, "An Overview of Bureaucracy and Political Development," in *Bureaucracy and Political Development*, ed. by Joseph LaPalombara (Princeton: Princeton University Press, 1963), pp. 3-33; see also Gabriel A. Almond and G. Bingham Powell, Jr., *Comparative Politics: A Developmental Approach* (Boston: Little, Brown and Company, 1966), pp. 190-212.

5. Gabriel A. Almond and Sidney Verba, *Civic Culture* (Boston: Little, Brown and Company, 1965), p. 192.

6. *Ibid.*, pp. 17-20.

7. Leo Grebler, Joan W. Moore, and Ralph C. Guzman, *The Mexican-American People* (New York: Free Press, 1970), pp. 517-41; Angus Campbell and Howard Schuman, "Racial Attitudes in Fifteen American Cities" in *Supplemental Studies for the National Advisory Commission on Civil Disorders* (Washington: U.S. Government Printing Office, 1968), pp. 39-45; and U.S. Commission on Civil Rights, *Mexican-Americans and the Administration of Justice in the Southwest* (Washington: U.S. Government Printing Office, 1970).

8. Grebler, *Mexican-American People*, p. 527.

9. *Ibid.*, p. 518.

10. *Ibid.*, pp. 519-23.

11. *Ibid.*, pp. 519-23, 529-34; Joan W. Moore, *Mexican-Americans* (Englewood Cliffs: Prentice-Hall, Inc., 1970), pp. 89-94; David Bayley and Harold Mendelsohn, *Minorities and the Police* (New York: Free Press, 1968); and U.S. Commission on Civil Rights, *Mexican-Americans and the Administration of Justice.*

12. Grebler, *Mexican-American People*, pp. 530-31; Moore, *Mexican-Americans*, p. 89.

13. Joseph D. Lohman, *et al.*, *The Police and the Community*, U.S. President's Commission on Law Enforcement and Administration of Justice, Field Survey No. 4 (Berkeley, California: 1966), p. 55.

14. Grebler, *Mexican-American People*, p. 533.

15. *Ibid.*, pp. 523-26.

16. *Ibid.*, p. 527.

17. *Ibid.*, p. 527; Moore, *Mexican-Americans*, p. 95.

18. Moore, *Mexican-Americans*, p. 49; on immigration of Mexican-Americans to the U.S., see Grebler, *Mexican-American People*, pp. 60-81; and Leo Grebler, "The Naturalization of Mexican Immigrants in the United States," *The International Migration Review I* (Fall, 1966), pp. 17-32.

19. Grebler, *Mexican-American People*, pp. 563-67.

20. *Ibid.*, pp. 567-68.

21. Susan Welch, John Comer, and Michael Steinman, "Political Participation Among Mexican-Americans: An Exploratory Examination," *Social Science Quarterly* (forthcoming).

22. Lincoln County, with a population of about 1000 Mexican-Ameri-

cans, and Scottsbluff County, with over 5500. Source: *1970 Fourth Count Census Data*.

23. Because *Fourth Count Census Data* does not release information on Spanish speaking populations by Enumeration District, location of the Mexican-American population within the cities was done by the informant method. Four to seven informants in each community, ranging from Anglo welfare directors to leaders of Mexican-American rights organizations, were interviewed as to their impressions of the location of Mexican-Americans in the community, and the proportion of total population in that area they believed to be Mexican-American. Estimates of location were extremely similar among the informants, although the estimated proportions varied considerably. Interviewing was done in those districts where mean estimates of the proportion of Mexican-Americans was 15 percent or greater. Every house in the district was enumerated and assigned a random number. Each house under a specified number was called on and respondents screened until a specified quota of Mexican-Americans in each district was reached. Screening was done by combination of Spanish surname or self-report as a Mexican-American.

24. This is approximately the same percent as Freeman found in a survey of Mexican-Americans in South Tucson. Donald Freeman, "A Note on Interviewing Mexican-Americans," *Social Science Quarterly,* XLIX (March, 1969), pp. 909-18.

25. For a full report of the data analyzed from this perspective, see Susan Welch, John Comer and Michael Steinman, "A Research Note on Interviewing in a Mexican-American Community: An Investigation of Some Potential Sources of Response Bias," *Public Opinion Quarterly* (forthcoming).

26. Welch, "Political Participation. . . ."

27. Two-thirds of the two-thirds who are not native Nebraskans said that they came to Nebraska from one of the three states mentioned.

28. Richard Gilliland, "Food Stamp Participation in Nebraska," State Technical Assistance Agency, Lincoln, 1970. (Mimeographed.)

29. Welch, "A Research Note on Interviewing. . . ."

30. Forty-four percent of our sample came from the Southwest originally.

31. This concept is discussed in Robert Merton, *Social Theory and Social Structure,* 3rd ed. (New York: Free Press, 1968), pp. 279-334.

C. Preferments and Secondary Benefits

THE THIRD TYPE OF ACCOMMODATION POLITICS, PREFERMENTS AND secondary benefits, is the highest order of the three types. In preferment politics, the ethnic group actually gains real political power by playing a participative role in the decision-making process itself. Litt says about preferment politics: "to be in on the decision-making process—the formation of core myths used to justify political power—and the structuring of basic institutions is to indeed occupy a preferred political status."[1] For a Chicano community this would mean having their own leaders in positions where they can make important decisions benefiting the community. These leaders would be responsive and responsible to their co-ethnics.

To win a preferred position in the political system is not an easy task, particularly for a colored ethnic minority. Preferments are not lightly surrendered by those in power. Indeed, these preferments must be wrested by the efforts of the ethnic minority. The resistance put up by those who hold power is largely determined by the extent to which these dominant groups have secured other preferments outside of their political positions. If an ethnic minority such as the Chicano is making its bid for political power before others who have recently won these positions are ready to relinquish them and move on to perhaps social, economic, or educational positions, a significant level of conflict will probably result. As U.S. society has matured and developed, fewer nonpolitical rewards have been readily available. Chicanos, then, can expect to find at least as much resistance as other ethnic minorities have in turn encountered.

Chicanos are sorely underrepresented in positions of political power. Only one U.S. senator and four members of the House of Representatives are of Mexican-Spanish ancestry. No large southwestern city has elected a Chicano mayor or majority of the city council. Los Angeles, containing almost a million Chicano people, has no Chicano representative on the governing board of the city or county. Thus Chicanos have fared poorly in the game of preferment politics, primarily due to their exclusion from the process through gerrymandering, restrictive electoral laws, direct intimidation, and other forms of discouragement.[2]

George Rivera has developed a typology of strategies by which Chicanos may successfully engage in preferment politics most suited to the particular social setting. Indeed, Chicanos have been making some dramatic advances the last several years. Their success in Texas under the banner of La Raza Unida party is a good example. One of the founders of that party, José Angel Gutiérrez, stresses the necessity of Chicanos controlling their own destiny, i.e., engaging successfully in preferment politics by supporting their own "third" party. Antonio Camejo recounts the Crystal City, Texas, success story. The rise of El Partido La Raza Unida throughout the Southwest is an important recent development in the Chicano political movement, one which bears close watching and seems to offer a great chance for political victories.[3]

That Chicanos can provide the mass block voting support that is necessary to win elections is demonstrated by the voting behavior patterns research by Mark Levy and Michael Kramer. Unfortunately, since the New Deal the Chicano vote has been so easily garnered by the Democratic party that it has too often been taken for granted. Rudolph de la Garza's research into ethnic voting in El Paso reveals that reciprocal support for Chicano candidates by Anglo Democrats has not been forthcoming. That apparently racist (anti-Chicano) feelings among Anglo voters overrode their Democratic party identification provides an important lesson on ethnic group cohesiveness and electoral "system" politics for Chicanos. If opting to remain within traditional electoral politics, it seems that Chicanos must either become much more independent and flexible when choosing between the two major parties, or else they must rally behind the banner of La Raza Unida or some other third party.

NOTES

1. Edgar Litt, *Ethnic Politics in America* (Glenview, Ill.: Scott, Foresman and Co., 1970), p. 72.

2. These and other forms of "political racism" have been documented by the California State Advisory Committee to the United States commission on Civil Rights, *Political Participation of Mexican Americans in California,* August, 1971.

3. Richard Santillan has recently provided a detailed and comprehensive chronicle of the rise and accomplishments of La Raza Unida party throughout the Southwest. See Richard Santillan, *La Raza Unida* (Los Angeles: Tlaquilo Publications, 1973).

14: NOSOTROS VENCEREMOS: Chicano Consciousness and Change Strategies

George Rivera, Jr.

It is better to die standing
Than to continue living on one's knees
Emiliano Zapata

INTRODUCTION

CHICANOS FIRST BECAME VISIBLE TO THE NATION IN THE SIXTIES, THROUGH the Delano (California) Grape Strike. Mexican Americans were never invisible; they were simply ignored in a decade when the glamor of the civil rights struggle focused upon Black America. Mexican Americans became, to use George Sanchez' (1967) term, the "forgotten people." Even Martin Luther King forgot Mexican Americans until late in his life, and Stokely Carmichael began to understand the "Latino" problem only when he visited Cuba. Most of the Sixties was a time when Black Panthers rarely shook hands with Chicano activists. To blacks, Chicanos were white—though the Mexican American experience proved otherwise to Chicanos living in the Southwest. Thus, the civil rights movement in the Sixties was primarily a black movement. If Chicanos desired social change, they would have to turn toward creating their own independent movement.

The Chicano Movement emerged, to the surprise of many social scientists, in direct contradiction to the "passive, apathetic" image of the Mexican commonly held in sociological and anthropological circles. Today, many of these Anglo "experts" on Mexican American life are being replaced by young

Reproduced by special permission from *The Journal of Applied Behavioral Science,* 8, No. 1 (Jan.-Feb. 1972), pp. 56-71 and from George Rivera, Jr.

Chicano scholars who possess relevant perspectives on the problem. Things are as they should be: Chicanos are speaking for themselves.

Though *barrio* voices have always existed, as omnipresent as the "Echo of a Scream" in the Siqueiros painting, a Chicano intellectual presence has only recently begun to be felt. Educational opportunities have always been poor for the Mexican American. One major difference between the Chicano Movement and the Black Movement is that blacks, though they had segregated, inferior colleges, nevertheless did have access to higher education. In such institutions, intellectual critics could ponder diverse ideologies and positions in order to articulate their own position on society. Why is there no Mexican American W. E. B. Du Bois, Ralph Ellison, or James Baldwin? Because Chicanos had been systematically deprived of higher education. However, limited but increasing opportunities in education are now giving rise to a Chicano consciousness that is being felt throughout the Southwest.

This paper proceeds with a brief discussion of change strategies producing Chicano consciousness and of the conditions which best seem to suit particular strategies. One condition in particular, the presence of a Chicano majority in a rural *pueblo* (town), has recently led to breakthroughs in Chicano participation. What took place in Crystal City, Texas, . . . exemplif[ies] what can happen when Chicanos organize themselves into a political party "to play the gringo's game." I believe the Chicano Party, La Raza Unida, will become a force to be dealt with in American politics. . . . Help in organization and support in numbers are both needed, and will be taken from well-intentioned experts as well as from those who feel the forces of American oppression. Opportunities for such coalitions are discussed.

CHANGE STRATEGIES TO DATE

Chicano consciousness made success possible in the Cesar Chavez-led Delano Grape Strike. The families in the fields were supported by Mexican Americans as well as by sympathetic Anglos in generating an economic boycott of undreamed-of proportions. The philosophy of nonviolent protest gained widespread support for the movement. At the other end of the continuum of change strategies evolved by the Chicano Movement is Reies Lopez Tijerina's armed courthouse raid in Tierra Amarilla, New Mexico: a militant attempt to regain thousands of acres of stolen land.

The struggle continues. At least one effective urban leader has emerged: Rodolfo "Corky" Gonzales, head of the Crusade for Justice in Denver, Colorado. Gonzales has been instrumental in creating the Chicano Youth Liberation Conference held every year in Colorado, and has been actively involved in Chicano politics and Chicano draft resistance. Gonzales has recently helped in setting up an all-Chicano school—Tlatelolco. Opened in October 1970, it offers day care, preschool, elementary, secondary, undergraduate, and adult basic education, as well as vocational training. This past year [1971] Tlatelolco graduated three Chicanos and educated over 150 students, many of whom were victims of Anglo schools–the so-called "push-outs."

Where Chicanos comprise a substantial percentage of the populace, it should be possible to express Chicano consciousness through the established democratic political system. However, throughout the Southwest there are areas where Chicano cultural and/or ethnic majorities are governed by a white numerical minority who are nevertheless an economic majority. Until recently democratic processes were impervious to Chicano participation and/or influence under these conditions.

The efficacy of any change strategy is ultimately dependent on sociological conditions. At least four conditions occur to me, each implying a different strategy for the expression of Chicano consciousness. These conditions are named in Table 1 and described below.

Type I. Pueblo Milieu

A rural area with a Chicano numerical majority best exemplifies Type I. Many of these areas are highly agricultural and can be found in *pueblos* in most of south Texas, north central New Mexico, two locations at the southern border of Arizona (Nogales in Santa Cruz County and Douglas–a mining area–in Cochise County), and two counties in southern Colorado (Conejos and Costilla). The potential for political change in these areas is very high, since a Chicano numerical majority could possibly win control of school board, city, and county offices.

The change strategy which holds the most potential for the *pueblo* milieu

TABLE 1

A TYPOLOGY OF AREAS FOR POTENTIAL CHICANO POLITICAL ACTIVITY

	Numerical Ethnic Composition	
Area	*Chicano Majority*	*Chicano Minority*
Rural	Type I Pueblo Milieu	Type II Calle Milieu
Urban	Type IV Ciudad Milieu	Type III Barrio Milieu

is seizure of the democratic process. (The Crystal City case . . . exemplifies the effectiveness of this strategy.) Though Chicanos in *pueblos* are in a numerical majority, change by ballot or other legitimate channels (courts) sometimes does not occur. In such locales, violence has been known to erupt (e.g., the Tierra Amarilla Courthouse Raid in New Mexico).

Type II. Calle Milieu

An area which is rural and contains a Chicano numerical minority has perhaps the least potential for political change. In such areas, Chicanos are usually found residing on segregated *calles* (streets); and since there are usually not many *calles,* one cannot categorically call the area a *barrio.* Many Chicanos in these areas can also be found scattered on small farms outside the town. Since Chicanos are generally highly urbanized, the proportion of Chicanos in these areas is relatively small. However, countless areas throughout the Southwest exemplify this type.

Since Chicanos are not in a numerical majority in the *calle* milieu, farm worker concentrations provide the germinating seeds for change. Cesar Chavez' strike in Delano is an impressive example of the Type II potential for nonviolent change. However, there are innumerable areas of rural minority where Chicanos do not have union potential. For example, in Glidden and Columbus, Texas, most Mexican Americans work in diffused locations such as gravel pits or in service stations. These areas are not likely to produce collectives striking for change, and thus it probably will be a while before the mores of small-town America are modified, at least as they relate to Mexican Americans.

Type III. Barrio Milieu

An urban area where Chicanos are in a numerical minority is the most characteristic sociological condition in the Southwest. Since these areas contain highly concentrated Mexican American subcommunities (*barrios*), the potential for political activity is very high, in terms of gaining some representation. The biggest threat to organizational efforts in the *barrio* milieu is the problem of gerrymandering and redistricting. The two most politically explosive areas of this type are Los Angeles, California and San Antonio, Texas. Other areas which characterize Type III are Corpus Christi, Texas; Albuquerque, New Mexico; Denver, Colorado; Fresno, California; Tucson, Arizona; Houston, Texas; and numerous other areas throughout the Southwest (Grebler, Moore & Guzman, 1970).

Change strategies in the *barrio* milieu have manifested themselves in the form of urban confrontations. The threat of violence is high in these areas; violence has in fact already occurred in the form of police overreactions to peaceful Chicano demonstrations (e.g., the Chicano Moratorium police riot in Los Angeles and the police raid on the Crusade for Justice headquarters in Denver). The trick will be to turn this threat around so that it is the Chicano community which threatens those who would deprive us of fair representation. Present outbreaks of violence hurt the wrong community.

Type IV. Ciudad Milieu

Type IV is rare in the Southwest since there are relatively few cities with Chicano majorities. This type, known as a *ciudad* (city) can be found only in southern Texas along the border: in Laredo, Brownsville, and El Paso. The potential for Chicano political power in these areas is undoubtedly quite high since Chicanos can elect local officials and also state representatives.

Since Chicanos are in a numerical majority in these areas, strategies for change have taken the route of the democratic process. However, many "establishment" Mexican Americans control the political offices, which could ultimately mean intraminority conflict. If the people's needs are not heard and if *their* representatives are not elected, new change strategies will have to emerge to make the *ciudad* representatives of *all* of the people, and not just another stronghold of the Mexican American middle class.

There are many opportunities for political activity to develop in the Chicano Movement. Texas probably represents the state with the greatest potential, since it has many cities and towns with Chicano majorities (Types I and IV). Since the Chicano constituencies in Texas are poor and uneducated, it is probable that poverty and substandard education will become the rallying points for Chicano action.

To date, political change in the *barrio* has taken the direction of building an independent Chicano political party. In Colorado, Chicanos ran candidates as high as the gubernatorial level on a La Raza Unida Party ticket in 1970. None of their candidates was elected. However, the campaign was primarily *educational,* using the "equal time" ruling of the FCC to convey Chicano perspectives and alternatives to present *barrio* life. Similarly, Chicanos in California and Arizona have taken steps to place La Raza Unida Party on the ballot for 1972. And there is one area where La Raza Unida sponsored successful candidates and accomplished major change through the democratic political process. This took place in Crystal City, Texas, under conditions I consider a *pueblo* milieu. Chicanos in Crystal City expected to win; the spirit had been with them since 1963. . . .

LA RAZA UNIDA PARTY AND ITS FUTURE

Experiences in Zavala County, south Texas, demonstrate how the development of La Raza Unida Party constitutes a major step in Chicano political consciousness. The Chicano vote can no longer be taken for granted. A report (Camejo, 1971) on a study by the League of United Latin American Citizens (LULAC) and the Mexican American Bar Association suggests that an all-out campaign to get Chicanos in the states of Texas, California, Illinois, and New Mexico to register and block vote could result in determining the outcome of the 1972 Presidential election. If the total Chicano vote in the Southwest and Midwest is to have such political potency, and if La Raza Unida Party is going to mobilize this potency, party organizers must begin now to cope with philosophical issues and problems in organization.

Political Machismo

The Chicano Youth Conference of Aztlan held in Denver, Colorado, in March 1969 issued a political position in *El Plan Espiritual de Aztlan* which read:

> Political liberation can only come through an independent action on our part. . . . Where we are in a majority we will control; where we are in a minority we will represent a pressure group; nationally, we will represent one party: La Familia de La Raza.

In June 1971, the Chicano Youth Conference Political Workshop passed a resolution stating that "La Raza Unida will support only La Raza Unida candidates, and under no circumstances will it support either the Democratic or Republican parties."

The disillusionment of Chicanos with existing political parties cannot be overstated. But organizational efforts, especially in the *barrio* milieu, will probably meet resistance from Mexican Americans who are Democrats. To abandon the Democratic Party completely is difficult for some Mexican Americans (e.g., the case of the Mexican American Political Association (Camejo, 1971). Though leading Chicano politicians, such as Albert Peña of San Antonio, have announced that they will probably run as La Raza Unida candidates in future elections, it is doubtful whether other Mexican American politicians can make the transition from the Democratic Party to La Raza Unida Party. Certainly, Representative Henry B. Gonzales (D-Texas) will not make the transition. Thus, the question remains: How will La Raza Unida mobilize already-elected Mexican American Democrats who are cautious about abandoning the Democratic Party?

Coalitions. La Raza Unida Party organizers have been primarily interested in mobilizing Chicanos to political action. Many white liberals will interpret this to mean that whites, or *gabachos,* are not wanted in the Chicano Movement. This is simply not true. What is true is that racist *gringos* are not wanted in the Chicano Movement. For example, in Crystal City, a *bolillo,* Bill Richey, played an instrumental role in helping to develop La Raza Unida Party in south Texas. In fact, he was recruited by José Angel Gutierrez and was later successfully recommended by Gutierrez for the position of City Manager when Chicanos gained control of the city council. Support from white liberals, when genuine, is invited.

Coalition with blacks represents a different problem to be dealt with, especially in the *barrio* milieu. Though some Mexican Americans are reluctant to take steps toward coalition, most Chicanos accept its inevitability, if both groups coalescing have equal power. Whatever cautions exist stem from the competitiveness between minority groups created by the dominant society, and by the fact that in the past coalition with blacks has meant playing a secondary role to blacks. Furthermore, in a coalition where all three groups are involved (blacks, Chicanos, and whites), white liberals tend to support blacks over Chicanos. Such bias probably stems from white guilt, but will have to change considerably if Chicanos are to participate effectively in a coalition.

Candidates and staff for the Movement. The need for educated leaders and trained organizers could prove a limiting factor to Chicanos in organizing counties and communities. In Crystal City (*pueblo* milieu), most of the Mexican American-elected officials' educational attainment was low. Although one should not assume that education is a necessary prerequisite for holding public office, it nevertheless is helpful in the administration of public affairs.

What will happen when Gutierrez, the one leader with organizing skills, decides to leave? Moreover, what will happen in other counties and communities if La Raza Unida Party gains control but lacks skilled organizers? For the present, this problem is not acute, but may prove so when future Chicano candidates take power.

Finances and legal fees. How will the organizational activities of La Raza Unida Party be financed? It cannot continue to grow and still be solely financed from small contributions and honoraria from Chicano leaders' speaking engagements. Such funding may have been sufficient for activities in Crystal City, but will it be sufficient when political activity spreads to other areas?

Though white liberals are eager to support black organizations financially, they rarely recognize that other minority organizations are struggling to stay solvent. This might change, but it will not happen until whites become cognizant of the needs of other minorities. Another possible source of funding could be foundations, like those which actively support black voter registration efforts in the South. Outside funding, though, always poses the question: Will strings be attached?

Since court procedures are often used as social control measures, volunteer legal counsel is also needed. Though the Mexican American Legal Defense and Educational Fund (MALDEF) exists, it cannot handle all of the Movement cases. Though white liberal lawyers sometimes volunteer their time, on occasion they handle critical cases too lightly. If white lawyers do become involved, they must realize that losing a case for Chicanos means losing a means to survival. One case comes to mind: it was a liberal white legal firm in Texas that handled La Raza Unida's case in the courts when La Raza Unida Party was attempting to get on the ballot for the county elections in Crystal City. That defeat in the courts cost Chicanos two more years of waiting to get *representation* at the county level, when two more years could have meant *control* of the county.

CONCLUSIONS

The potential for the development of Chicano political power is quite high in many rural areas of the Southwest, as well as in the urban *barrios* of the West. It is highest in areas which we have labeled *pueblo, ciudad,* and *barrio* milieux. The rise in Chicano consciousness is creating new opportunities for political change.

Though we discussed a situation where nonviolent change occurred, the threat of violence is always present. If Chicanos are not able to realize social change through legitimate means within the system, violence will inevitably erupt as the last resort for changing intolerable conditions. La Raza Unida Party cannot solve all of the Chicano's problems, but it can begin to implement tangible changes for the poor. It can begin to give hope where there once was none. Even before the exploits of Cortez, an Aztec chieftain, upon his election, spoke hopefully in prayer:

Grant me, Lord, a little light,
Be it no more than a glowworm giveth
Which goeth about by night,
To guide me through this life,
This dream which lasteth but a day,
Wherein are many things on which to stumble,
And many things at which to laugh,
And others like unto a stony path
Along which one goeth leaping.*

La Raza Unida Party members, like the Aztec Chieftain, believe in "a little light"; otherwise they would not have supported attempts by the Chicano community to penetrate the political abyss of American politics.

*From Simpson, Lesley Byrd, *Many Mexicos.* Berkeley and Los Angeles, Calif.: Univer. of California Press, 1969. P. xi.

REFERENCES

Browning, H. L., & McLemore, S. D. A statistical profile of the Spanish-surname population of Texas. Austin: Bureau of Business Research, Univer. of Texas, 1964.

Camejo, A. A report from Aztlan: Texas Chicanos forge own political power. Speeches by Mario Compean and José Angel Gutierrez. *La raza unida party in Texas.* New York: Pathfinder Press (Merit Pamphlet), 1970.

Camejo, A. MAPA weighs political action for la raza. *The Militant,* August 6, 1971, pp. 11 and 30.

Conde, C. Crystal City gave PASO the pilot project it needed. *The Dallas Morning News,* May 7, 1963, pp. 17-18.

Grebler, L., Moore, J. W., & Guzman, R. *The Mexican American people.* New York: Free Press, 1970.

Look Magazine. Other Texans: The last angry Americans. October 8, 1963, 68-70.

McKnight, P. How they stole la raza unida party's vote. *The Militant,* November 20, 1970, p. 6.

Martinez, J. R. Leadership and politics. In J. Samora (Ed.), *La raza: Forgotten Americans.* [Notre Dame, Ind.: University of Notre Dame Press, 1966.] Pp. 47-62.

Procter, B. H. The modern Texas Rangers: A law enforcement dilemma in the Rio Grande Valley. In M. P. Servin (Ed.), *The Mexican American: An awakening minority.* Beverly Hills, Calif.: Glencoe Press, 1970. Pp. 212-227.

Sanchez, G. I. *Forgotten people–A study of New Mexicans.* Albuquerque, N. M.: Calvin Horn, Publisher, 1967.

U.S. Commission on Civil Rights. *Mexican Americans and the administration of justice in the Southwest.* Washington, D.C.: G.P.O., March 1970.

15: MEXICANOS NEED TO CONTROL THEIR OWN DESTINIES

José Angel Gutiérrez

AS YOU KNOW, THERE IS A NEW POLITICAL PARTY IN SOUTHWEST Texas. It's called La Raza Unida Party. The history of this party is rather interesting.

For years the Chicano farmworker has made up the majority of the population in the South Texas counties. But he goes trucking across this country on his summer vacation (laughter), and so he's never there to vote. Yet this is precisely the time the primaries are held–in May. And he is already vacationing in his resort area by the time the runoffs are held in June. So, you see, we are in fact not even able to vote.

We have had other problems which we have known about for a long time. For instance, the fact that the mexicano can't cope with the culture of the monolingual creatures that abound in South Texas. You see, we're literate in Spanish, so we can't recognize the name of John Waltberger on the ballot, but we sure as hell recognize Juan Garcia. (Laughter)

Supposedly in this kind of a democratic society the citizenry is encouraged to participate in the political process–but not so in South Texas.

Someone asked me recently whether I thought any type of system other than the American political system could work in South Texas. I thought about it for a minute and suggested that the question be reworded because we ought to try the American system first. (Applause)

They accuse me and mexicanos in Cristal [Crystal City], in Cotulla and

From *La Raza Unida in Texas* (New York: Pathfinder Press, 1970), pp. 10-15.

These are excerpts from a speech delivered at a May 4, 1970 meeting in San Antonio by José Angel Gutiérrez, leader of La Raza Unida party, shortly after his election as president of the Crystal City school board.

Carrizo Springs, of being unfair. One gringo lady put it very well. She was being interviewed around April 6, right after the school board elections and before the city council elections. The guy from *Newsweek* asked her to explain the strange phenomena that were occurring in these counties: a tremendous voter turnout and a tremendous amount of bloc voting. She said, "Well, this is just terrible! Horrible! A few days ago we elected a bunch of bum Mexicans to the city council." And the reporter said, "Well, they are 85 percent of this county." And she replied, "That's what I mean! They think they ought to run this place!"

By all these little things you can begin to understand how to define the word "gringo," which seems to be such a problem all the time. It's funny, because the mexicano knows what a gringo is. It's the gringos themselves that are worried about what the hell it is. (Laughter) Let me elaborate on it.

I'm not going to give you a one sentence thing on them; I feel they deserve at least two sentences. (Laughter) The basic idea in using the word "gringo" is that it means "foreigner." The gringos themselves say, "It's Greek to me." So the mexicano says, "It's griego [Greek] to me." That is one explanation of its origins, according to Professor Americo Paredes of the University of Texas. Another is, of course, the traditional one about the United States troops coming into Mexico with "green coats." The mexicanos would say, with our own pronunciation, "Here come the 'green coats.' " And there are other explanations.

The word itself describes an attitude of supremacy, of xenophobia–that means you're afraid of strangers. I pick up a fancy word here and there. This attitude is also found in institutions, such as the Democratic Party. It's in policies like the one that says you can't speak Spanish in school because it's un-American. It's in the values of people who feel that unless Mexican music is played by the Tijuana Brass or the Baja Marimba Band it's no good. You can't eat *tacos de chorizo* [sausage tacos] around the corner for 20 cents. You've got to go up there to La Fonda [fancy anglo-owned Mexican restaurant] and eat a $3.50 Mexican plate that gives you indigestion. (Applause and laughter)

The formation of this party came about because of the critical need for the people to experience justice. It's just like being hungry. You've got to get food in there immediately, otherwise you get nauseous, you get headaches and pains in your stomach.

We were Chicanos who were starved for any kind of meaningful participation in decision making, policy making and leadership positions. For a long time we have not been satisfied with the type of leadership that has been picked for us. And this is what a political party does, particularly the ones we have here. I shouldn't use the plural because we only have one, and that's the gringo party. It doesn't matter what name it goes by. It can be Kelloggs, All-Bran, or Shredded Wheat, but it's still the same. . . .

These parties, or party, have traditionally picked our leadership. They have transformed this leadership into a kind of broker, a real estate guy who deals in the number of votes or precincts he can deliver or the geographical areas he can control. And he is a tape recorder—he puts out what the party says.

A beautiful example of this is Ralph Yarborough [Democratic senator from Texas]. The only thing he does for Chicanos is hire one every six years. He's perfectly content with the bigoted sheriff and Captain Allee [Texas Rangers] and the guys that break the strikes in El Rio Grande City and with [Wayne] Connally [brother of former Texas governor John Connally] and all these other people. Well, he gets beaten, and he knows why. The Republicans, the Birchers, the Wallaceites and all these people went over to support Bentsen in the primaries. Yet I just read in the paper this afternoon that he said, "As always, I will vote a straight Democratic ticket in November." . . .

Four years ago, when the guy who is now running for commissioner in La Salle County in La Raza Unida Party ran in the Democratic primaries, it cost him one-third of his annual income! That's how much it costs a Chicano with a median income of $1,574 per family per year. With the third party it didn't cost him a cent.

On top of the excessive filing fees, they have set fixed dates for political activity, knowing that we have to migrate to make a living. We are simply not here for the May primaries. Did you know that in Cotulla, Erasmo Andrade [running in the Democratic primary for state senator in opposition to Wayne Connally] lost by over 300 votes because the migrants weren't there? In the Democratic primaries you're not going to cut it. In May there are only 16 more Chicano votes than gringo votes in La Salle County. But in November the margin is two and one-half to one in favor of Chicanos.

So you can see that what's happening is not any big miracle. It's just common sense. The trouble is that everybody was always bothered and said, "We can't get out of the Democratic Party. Why bite the hand that feeds you?" Well, you bite it because it feeds you slop. (Laughter and applause) Others say, "Well, why don't you switch over and join the Republican Party?" Well, let's not even touch on that one.

Why can't you begin to think very selfishly as a Chicano? I still haven't found a good argument from anyone as to why we should not have a Chicano party. Particularly when you are the majority. If you want to implement and see democracy in action—the will of the majority—you are not going to do it in the Democratic Party. You can only do it through the Chicano party. (Applause)

But you see there is another, more important, reason, and that is that mexicanos need to be in control of their destiny. They need to make their own decisions. We need to make the decisions that are going to affect our brothers and maybe our children. We have been complacent for too long.

Did you know that not one of our candidates in La Salle County had a job the whole time they were running, and that they still can't get jobs? The same thing happened in Dimmit County. In Uvalde this is one of the reasons there's a walkout. They refused to renew the teaching contract of Josue Garcia, who ran for county judge. That's a hell of a price to pay. But that's the kind of treatment that you've gotten.

You've got a median educational level among mexicanos in Zavala County of 2.3 grades. In La Salle it's just a little worse–about 1.5 grades.

The median family income in La Salle is $1,574 a year. In Zavala it's about $1,754. The ratio of doctors, the number of newspapers, the health, housing, hunger, malnutrition, illiteracy, poverty, lack of political representation–all these things put together spell one word: colonialism. You've got a handful of gringos controlling the lives of muchos mexicanos. And it's been that way for a long time.

Do you think things are going to get better by putting faith in the Democratic Party and Bentsen? Or that things are going to get better because you've got a few more Chicanos elected to office now within the traditional parties? Do you think that things are going to get better now that the U.S. Commission on Civil Rights has officially claimed that there is discrimination against mexicanos? They've finally found out it's for real–we're discriminated against! (Laughter) Do you think that things are going to get better simply because kids are walking out of schools–kids who can't vote, who in many cases can't convince the community to stand behind them?

No, it's not going to get better. We are going to have to devise some pretty ingenious ways of eliminating these gringos. Yet they don't really have to be too ingenious. All you have to do is go out there and look around and have a little common sense.

It stands to reason that if there are two grocery stores in town and we are the ones who buy from them, then if we stop buying from them they are going to go down. If you talk about transferring the wealth, that's how you do it. . . .

In 1960 there were 26 Texas counties in which Chicanos were a majority, yet not one of those counties was in the control of Chicanos. If you want to stand there and take that you can. You can be perfectly content just like your father and your grandfather were, *con el sombrero en el mano* [with hat in hand].

That's why most of our traditional organizations will sit there and pass resolutions and mouth off at conventions, but they'll never take on the gringo. They'll never stand up to him and say, "Hey, man, things have got to change from now on. *Que pase lo que pase* [Let whatever happens happen]. We've had it long enough!"

This is what we've got to start doing. If you don't go third party, then you've got to go the independent route, because there is no other way you are going to get on the November ballot. And don't try to put in a write-in candidate. That never works. . . .

The recent elections here in April for school board and city council demonstrated something that many people knew was a fact. It was almost like predicting that the sun is going to come up in the morning; if you can count, you know what the results are going to be. But an interesting factor is going to enter in now. We won in an off year in the nonpartisan races, which means that we were able to elect a minority to these positions. So now the establishment has all summer long to figure out how to stop the mexicano. This is where we get back to the old tricks and lies of the gringo. They tried the "outside agitator" bit on me but it didn't work because I was born in Crystal City. So they changed gears. Then they tried the "communist" one for a while—until they found out I was in the U.S. Army Reserves. (Laughter and applause) Then somewhere they dug up my "kill a gringo" thing of about a year ago when I said that I would kill a gringo in self-defense if I were attacked. . . .

Another lie is the white liberal approach. "I like Mexican food. Oh, I just love it!" And this is the kind of guy who's got the *molcajete* [Aztec mortar and pestle for cooking] sitting as an ash tray in his living room. (Applause and laughter)

This kind of character is one that cautions you, "Be careful. Don't be racist in reverse. It's bad enough that gringos don't like 'Meskins' and 'Meskins' don't like gringos. You have to talk things over. You have to turn the other cheek. You've got to be nice. You've got to be polite. You have to have a constructive program."

They ask us, "What are you going to do for the schools in Crystal City?" And when we answer, "Bring education," they don't know what the hell we're talking about.

You see, that's another thing about the liberal. They always love to make you feel bad. And oh, my God, we hate to hurt the feelings of a good anglo liberal, don't we? Well, hell, tell them the truth!

We've been hurting for a long time. They think we've got education, but we know different. How come we have 71 percent dropouts in Crystal City? It's miseducation. We ain't got teachers down there, we've got neanderthals.

These are the kinds of problems we are going to be faced with by the time November comes along. But a lot of people ain't going to buy it. The kids in the schools aren't going to stand for it. They see what this whole gringo thing has done to their parents, what it's done to our community, what it's done to our organizations. And nothing is going to prevent them from getting what is due them.

There's no generation gap in Crystal City. To the old people who are experienced this is nothing new. The older people in Crystal City, who have experienced years and years of humiliation and blows to their dignity, know what's going on. There was a problem for a while with the 25- to 45-year-olds who were trying to be gringos. But that's no longer true. You see, those are the parents of these kids, and these kids got their parents straight very early in the game. (Applause). . . .

You know, civil rights are not just for those under 21. They're for everybody–for grandma, for daddy and mama, and *los chamaquitos* [children] and *primos* [cousins] and sisters, and so on. We've all got to work together. That means that all of us have to pitch in. And this is why in Crystal City you no longer hear "Viva La Raza" and "Chicano Power" and "La Raza Unida" all over the place. We don't talk about it anymore because it's a reality. You see, there *la familia mexicana esta organizada* [the Mexican family is organized]. Aztlan has begun in the southwest part of Texas. (Prolonged applause)

Our actions have made "La Raza Unida" more than just a slogan. Beginning with the walkout, we began organizing and moving in to counterattack every time the gringo tried to put pressure on the mexicano. Boycott his store. Point the finger at him. Expose him for the animal that he is. Bring in the newspapers and photographers and the tape recorders. Let the world see it. . . .

So don't let anybody kid you. We are the consumers, we are the majority. We can stop anything and we can make anything in South Texas if we stick together and begin using common sense.

This third party is a very viable kind of alternative. It's a solution. For once you can sit in your own courthouse and you don't have to talk about community control because you are the community. And we are not talking about trying to run for Congress because you are sitting on the school board and then four years from now you're going to run for county judge. That's not the name of the game either.

We are talking about bringing some very basic elements into the lives of mexicanos–like education and like making urban renewal work for mexicanos instead of being the new way of stealing land. We got screwed once with the Treaty of Guadalupe-Hidalgo and now we're getting it under "Model Cities" and urban renewal. (Applause)

You can be as imaginative as you want and do almost anything you want once you run units of government. I'll give you an example. Everyone publicizes the fact that the Panthers are feeding kids all over the country. And everybody pours out money at cocktail parties and gets very concerned about little kids eating in the morning.

Well, the gringos in Cristal pulled out another one of their gimmicks and just a few days before the elections they decided to experiment with a pilot program of feeding kids in the morning. It was going to last for six weeks and feed 30 kids. They were going to watch them. They were going to experiment, study, conduct a survey to see if they grew an inch. (Laughter)

Well, right now in Crystal City any kid who wants to eat can eat. Free breakfast in all the schools. You can do that, you see. You can also be very, very friendly to your opposition. You can rule them out of order when they get out of hand. You can slap them on the hand: "That's a no no!"

They can't hold an illegal meeting–like they tried yesterday with the school board while I was out of town. They tried to take advantage of the fact that I was out of town to hold a special meeting. But the law says you must give three days' notice. So the gringos failed in their attempt to hire a principal to their liking. We don't need to be experts in parliamentary procedure. All we have to do is follow the book and tell them, No, no! You can't do that!" (Laughter and applause)

Let me be serious for a few minutes, because I think we have laughed enough. Mario was talking about having a third party in Bexar County by 1972. Good luck, Mario. (Applause)

It doesn't matter if you don't agree with MAYO because this thing is no longer just MAYO. The response that we've had to this third party in all sections of our communities has been overwhelming. You saw the results. You can count votes just as I did.

The third party is not going to get smaller. It's going to get bigger.

You have three choices. First, you can be very active in this thing. For once we are not talking about being anti-Democratic or pro-Republican or pro-Democrat and anti-Republican. We are talking about being for La Raza, the majority of the people in South Texas. So there are a lot of things you can do and be very actively involved in.

If you don't choose that route, you can stay home and watch baseball and just come out and vote. But otherwise stay home. Don't get in the way.

The third thing you can do is lend your support, your general agreement. Often we are too critical of ourselves, and the gringo misunderstands that. He says, "You're disorganized, there's no unity among you." Hell, he can't understand an honest discussion when he hears one.

So, you've got these three roles that you can play. Or you can get very, very defensive and say, "This is wrong, this is un-American because you're bloc voting." But don't forget that the Democrats do it too. You can say that this is racism in reverse, but don't forget that we are the majority. And you can say that this is going to upset the whole situation in the state of Texas because we will never be able to elect a senator, because we're segregating ourselves and cutting ourselves apart and that this is not what we should be trying to do, that we should be trying to integrate, etc., etc. Well, before you go on your warpath or campaign, come down and tell that to my sheriff. Tell him how much you like him. Or, better yet, move on down the road a bit and tell it to Ranger Allee himself.

Build your constituency, build your community–that's how we will be electing three and possibly four congressmen in the very near future. There's going to be another congressman in Bexar County, and there's not room for all of them on the North side [anglo section of San Antonio]. (Laughter and applause) So we have some very interesting developments coming up. . . .

16: A REPORT FROM AZTLAN: Texas Chicanos Forge Own Political Power

Antonio Camejo

THE FORMATION OF LA RAZA UNIDA PARTY, AN INDEPENDENT CHICANO political party, has raised the Chicano struggle for self-determination to a higher level.

On April 4, 1970, the slate of La Raza Unida Party swept the school board elections in Crystal City, Texas, defeating the candidates of the Democratic Party. Although the elections were officially "non-partisan" the party affiliations were known to all.

Jose Angel Gutierrez, 25, a founder and former state chairman of the Mexican-American Youth Organization (MAYO), headed a slate of three Chicanos. Elected with Gutierrez were Arturo Gonzales, 21, a gas station attendant, and Miguel Perez, 31, operator of a Chicano dance hall. . . .

On April 7, 1970, La Raza Unida candidates again swept to victory in the city council elections in three cities. In Carrizo Springs, Company D headquarters of the Texas Rangers, Rufino Cabello was elected first Chicano mayor in the city's history. In Cotulla, Raza Unida candidate Alfredo Zamora was elected mayor. In both cities, an additional Raza Unida councilman was elected. In Crystal City two Raza Unida councilmen were elected to the five-member city council, which for several years has been half Chicano.

The racist anglo ruling class in Crystal City (or gringos as they are referred to in Texas) pretty much gave up trying to run their own people for the city council there eight years ago. Their tactic has been to run *vendidos,* or coconuts (brown on the outside, white on the inside)–Chicanos who think like gringos. That is why the city council was composed of four Mexican-Americans and only one gringo.

From *La Raza Unida Party in Texas* (New York: Pathfinder Press, 1970), pp. 3-8.

How did it come about that in these elections young militant Chicanos were able to defeat the gringo and *vendido* candidates of the Democratic Party who were backed up by the ranchers and the other monied interests?

To understand this we must look at the city of Cristal, as the Chicanos there refer to Crystal City. Cristal is 85 percent Chicano and 15 percent gringo, with a small number of anglos friendly to La Raza Unida Party. The people there are primarily migrant laborers who must follow the harvest north into Colorado, North Dakota, Minnesota and Wisconsin each spring, work for miserable wages throughout the summer and return home in the fall.

In many cases, families are forced to put all their possession into hock to raise enough money for the trip to the beet fields. The small amount of money they bring back barely gives them enough to get out of hock and survive the winter months.

Median family income in Zavala County where Cristal is located, is $1,754 per year. The median educational level is 2.3 grades, which is lower than some impoverished Latin American nations. All the agricultural land is owned by gringos, 95 percent of the businesses in the city are also owned by gringos.

In 1962 an attempt was made to give the *mexicano* in Cristal some political representation. PASO (Political Association of Spanish-speaking Organizations) got some Mexican-American Democrats together and ran them for office against the gringo incumbents. In the 1963 elections they succeeded in throwing out the gringo mayor of some 38 years in Cristal, as well as creating the all-Chicano city council. They also had successes in other counties.

PASO, which had not built up any kind of an independent mass movement, became frightened by the unexpected victory. It abandoned the candidates, eventually losing almost all posts within four years. PASO today is the Texas version of the California Mexican-American Political Association (MAPA)—vote getters for the Democratic Party.

But in 1970 something new was added to the picture. La Raza Unida Party came out of a mass movement which developed as a result of the school walkouts in Cristal. Secondly, unlike PASO, La Raza Unida Party does not view itself as simply an electoral coalition to elect candidates, but as a political party in the full sense of the word—participating in strikes, boycotts of gringo-owned businesses, and the fight for community control of the schools.

In the spring of 1969, Cristal students raised a series of demands for improvement of the schools. The school board and administration, however, succeeded in intimidating the students into capitulation.

The resentments and desire for change were not dissipated, however, and remained under the surface until December when again the Chicano students rallied around demands calling for bilingual education, participation in federal programs, such as a lunch program, better physical plant conditions, Chicano counselors, scholarships, the right to bring whatever literature they wanted into the schools, and an end to racist practices in selection of cheer leaders.

The result was one of the best organized and most successful school walkouts in Texas, and probably in the Southwest. Approximately 1,700 out of 2,300 students in grades one through 12 walked out, virtually closing all the schools in the city.

During the Christmas holidays, teachers came from surrounding areas, Chicano restaurants and beer halls closed and turned over their facilities for classroom space and workers used their trucks for buses to transport students to a Chicano freedom school.

Many of the students who at first were not very political quickly began seeing things in their true light. The assistant principal of the high school, a Chicano, was mayor of the city. But it wasn't until they saw his reactionary role during the strike that they made the connection that he was also a *vendido* Chicano. Likewise with the Chicano teacher who also served on the city council. Thus, the real basis for the independent campaign of La Raza Unida Party came out of the desire of the parents and students to throw out the existing racist school board and city council.

But the involvement of the Chicano community quickly went beyond the issue of the schools. Students who were fired from their jobs in local stores for participating in mass marches and rallies were quickly backed up by the entire community which proceeded to boycott those stores.

But they didn't stop there. They contacted the parent company and applied for their own franchises to compete with the gringo stores. This resulted in the opening up of community-controlled Chicano businesses. Much of the financing for La Raza Unida Party and other community projects has come out of these small businesses.

Furthermore, to show their attitude toward Chicano *vendidos,* they boycotted the cleaners owned by the *vendido* Chicano school board member.

For about a week, the community went to the gringo cleaners in town to drive home the point that they would not tolerate one Chicano exploiting another. They then proceeded to set up a community cleaners. As a result of these actions no more students were fired from their jobs.

Students put a coat of brown paint on a statue of Popeye, symbol of the spinach industry, that stands in front of City Hall. After two and a half months (17 actual school days) the school board capitulated.

This would have been a resounding victory in itself. But the Chicano community was not about to let up on its initiative. The high school students, together with the adults, mounted a voter registration campaign which put La Raza Unida Party on the ballot in three counties and netted an almost 100 percent registration among *mexicanos.*

This was a first in the history of Texas and without doubt in all of Aztlan. Maximum voter registration had varied from 15 to 30 percent, as is the case throughout Texas. The power of this burgeoning movement rightly frightened the local ruling class (100 percent gringo) who desperately tried to hinder the party legally.

Pablo Puente, Raza Unida candidate for city council, was ruled off the ballot in Cristal on the basis on a municipal law requiring candidates to own property. But they succeeded in having the law ruled unconstitutional in the federal courts. Puente was placed on the ballot and subsequently won the election along with Ventura Gonzales, Jr.

La Raza Unida Party also succeeded in forcing the Civil Rights Commission to come to Cristal to observe the elections so that the ranchers and agri-businessmen could not blatantly intimidate people with threats of violence, loss of job for voting, or tamper with the ballots.

The real significance of the electoral victory for the Chicano community in Cristal was apparent at a board of education meeting I attended May 11. The meeting was held in the high school cafeteria, which was packed to overflowing with at least 250 people, predominantly Chicano.

While the board had previously consisted of five gringos and two Chicanos, it now consisted of three Raza Unida Party members, three gringos, and a Chicano who decided to move to the left, giving La Raza Unida Party a majority.

Jose Angel Gutierrez, new president of the board by a 4-3 vote, called the meeting to order.

Among the points discussed were the following: The school district would build houses for school employees, but rent would be based on a percentage of the individual's salary. From now on the school buses had to patronize all gas stations equally, including the Chicano gas stations, such as the one where board member Arturo Gonzales works (previously all business had gone to anglo-owned service stations). Employment of personnel for school maintenance must reflect the composition of the community which is 85 percent Chicano.

On all controversial points such as the denial of contracts for the fall to two racist teachers, the vote was four Chicanos, *si*, three gringos, *no*.

The most controversial point, however, was reflected in the minutes of a special meeting of the school board held on April 27. At this meeting Gutierrez suggested that Cristal accept transfers from the Uvalde School District. The motion itself was routine and harmless enough—on the surface. It touched off a heated fight and a lawsuit.

Uvalde is a town similar to Cristal about 40 miles to the north. It had been the scene of a militant strike by Chicano students around 14 demands such as: the right of teachers to be politically active without intimidation (Jorge Garcia, candidate of La Raza Unida Party for county judge, was fired from his teaching job); bilingual education; Chicano studies; more Chicano teachers; the right to bring any literature into the schools; revision of racist text books; and amnesty for striking students upon returning to school.

As in Cristal last December, the Uvalde school board refused to accept the demands of the students and used every means of intimidation, such as arrests, and denial of graduation to seniors, in an attempt to break the walkout.

The students in Uvalde, many of them MAYO activists, turned to Cristal for aid. Attorney Jesus Gamez, now the official attorney of both the Cristal school board and the city council, represented the students before the Uvalde board.

But aid was even more direct. Gutierrez held that if Uvalde wouldn't graduate the striking seniors, then Cristal High School would. The vote: four Chicanos, si, three gringos, no.

The defeated minority on the board then took the board of education to court. Jesus Gamez as the attorney for the board successfully won the case in court, and at the May 11 meeting, Gutierrez matter-of-factly presented the superintendent, a gringo at least twice his age, with a bill for $2,500 for services rendered by Attorney Gamez and told him, "See that it's taken care of."

The complete defeat and humiliation of the gringo board members evoked a very apparent manifestation of pride and elation in the Chicano audience.

Toward the end of the board meeting, Armando Trevino, brother of walkout leader Mario Trevino, pointed out to the board that in a school that was 85 percent Chicano, 20 out of the 25 chosen for the National Honor Society were anglos. (The five Mexican-Americans were considered vendidos by the Chicano students.)

One anglo teacher denied that there had been any discrimination, that it was only because more Chicanos "weren't qualified." Armando Trevino replied, "This happened when I was in school, and it is still happening that qualified students are not elected by teachers . . . I would like the school board to look into it."

One of the gringo board members, typically, objected to discussing this point because it wasn't on the agenda. But this was a new school board now, a Chicano school board. Gutierrez quickly responded: "If there is any problem that any one student or parent has we will always incorporate it into the agenda."

He then added, "This board is not going to stand for any kind of discrimination. And any time an allegation of this nature is made we are going to look into it." A committee headed up by Gutierrez was formed on the spot to investigate the charge.

One could not help but be overcome by what was occurring in that room in South Texas. For the first time, the majority of the people, the Chicano people, were running the schools and beginning to mete out justice to racist teachers and administrators. The Chicano community was being heard before its own school board, rather than being insulted by a gringo board representing a tiny minority.

This reality has already resulted in important gains for the entire Chicano community. By a simple motion of the Chicano board, for example, free breakfast is now provided for every child in every school.

Gutierrez aims to improve the schools and make the education there relevant to Chicanos and thus cut down the 71 percent dropout rate.

The Chicano community has been faced with difficult problems from the beginning of this endeavor. Over thirty anglo faculty members, including some administrators, have resigned from the schools because of the victory of La Raza Unida Party and the actions taken by the board. In spite of this, the school board is moving ahead. Since the candidates of La Raza Unida Party assumed office on April 15, 1970 the following programs have been instituted in the Crystal City Independent School District:

1. Complete bi-lingual education from kindergarten through third grade.
2. A free breakfast and lunch program for every student in every school.
3. Banning of the use of the culturally biased I.Q. tests and English Proficiency tests.
4. The use of relevant texts in the classroom, even though they are not "state approved," which relate the true contributions made to society by Chicanos. *El Espejo,* an anthology of Chicano writings, will be used as a high school English book, and Stan Steiner's *La Raza* will be a high school reader, as only two examples.
5. Student records have been declared *completely* confidential. Crystal City High School is the first secondary school in the United States which will no longer provide the Selective Service Board with any information. This is a reflection of the growing anti-war feelings of Chicanos who suffer one of the highest death rates in Vietnam. Crystal City suffered one of the first casualties when U.S. troops invaded Cambodia and Laos this past May.

All the changes in the schools would be too numerous to list here. Chicanos are being hired to fill vacancies at all levels from teachers, counselors, band director, to vice principals and principals. Even the school song has been changed to "Jalisco." Bi-cultural education (Chicano studies) will now become a reality in Crystal City. For the first time in its history Cristal has the possibility of providing real education for Chicano youth and adults alike.

The City Council in Cristal has also been taking action to improve the living conditions of the *mexicano*. The jurisdiction for law enforcement by the State police and the Texas Rangers has been revoked by the council. This will seriously hinder the ability of these two racist "law and order" outfits to harass the people of Crystal City within their own city limits. The all Chicano city police force is now required to undergo a community involvement training program headed up by La Raza Unida Party.

. . . Chicanos will be in the position of determining priorities for city improvement. At present at least one-third of the Chicano community has no sewage service or paved streets. Also, when citizens now appear before the city council to ask for action on these and other problems they will find official business conducted in both Spanish and English, so that they may use their native tongue. Likewise in school board meetings. . . .

At almost every meeting of the school board since the elections, anglo lawyers, from as far away as Dallas and Houston, have been present in the hope of catching La Raza Unida board members on something. But the Chicano community is standing firm. An oppressed people have gotten a little taste of freedom and they are not about to let that go without a fight.

Rather than being intimidated, the new Chicano party is projecting an ambitious organizing drive which could see the party on the ballot in 26 South Texas counties by 1972.

As the result of an open nominating convention of La Raza Unida Party May 2, the gringo power structure (i.e., the Democratic Party) will face some 40 Chicano candidates in the Nov. 3 elections. La Raza Unida is running a full slate of candidates in the counties of Zavala, La Salle, Dimmit and Hidalgo for all county offices.

The giant step that has been taken in South Texas is an example of what can be done throughout Aztlan. There are scores of cities in Aztlan where the Chicano is a majority. But even in cities where the Chicano makes up only 10 or 20 percent of the population, significant gains can be made by breaking politically from the two capitalist parties. The fight for community control can be a dynamic force if properly led by an independent Chicano political party.

What is needed, however, is to *mobilize* people into action around such demands as community control of the schools in the Chicano community.

What is needed are Raza Unida parties everywhere throughout Aztlan. Such a party will have to continually struggle against those who want to channel every movement for social change into support of the gringo ruling class through the Democratic Party, on the one hand, and those ultra-leftists who consider electoral activity "meaningless" and therefore give a free hand to capitalist politicians in keeping the Chicano and Latino communities under illusions and "under control."

The success of La Raza Unida Party in South Texas should be an inspiration to create two, three, many Cristals. As Gutierrez pointed out on May 4, 1970: "Aztlan has begun, in the southwest part of Texas."

17: PATTERNS OF CHICANO VOTING BEHAVIOR

Mark R. Levy and Michael S. Kramer

RECENTLY, THE LEAGUE OF UNITED LATIN AMERICAN CITIZENS AND THE Mexican-American Bar Association of California issued a white paper entitled, "The Electoral College and the Mexican-American: An Analysis of the Mexican-American Impact on the 1972 Presidential Election." The document argued that a shift in Mexican-American voting patterns could alter the outcome of the upcoming Presidential election in three states of the Southwest, and in Illinois. Like similar documents put out by other ethnic groups, this one somewhat overstated the case. There are two sides to the Spanish-speaking* Presidential vote: high percentages for the Democratic candidate, yet generally declining turnouts.

In 1960, John Kennedy won 85 percent of the Chicano vote. "Viva Kennedy" organizations sprang up throughout the Southwest as Kennedy sought to woo Spanish-Americans, and the Chicano vote was vital for Kennedy in two states, New Mexico and Texas. In New Mexico, Kennedy needed Chicano votes to win; he did not receive 50 percent of the "Anglo" vote. Seventy percent of the Chicano vote went for Kennedy, a 20,000-vote plurality, and the Senator carried New Mexico by only 2,000 votes. In Texas, Chicano votes also made the difference, as the ticket was significantly aided by Texan Lyndon Johnson, a long-time friend of the Chicanos. Kennedy-Johnson did not win a majority in "Anglo" precincts, but in Chicano neighborhoods the ticket took a remarkable 91 percent of the vote (a 200,000-vote Chicano plurality as Kennedy-Johnson carried Texas by fewer than 50,000 votes).

From *The Ethnic Factor,* Touchstone Books. New York: Simon and Schuster, Inc., 1973, pp. 73-85, 248-251. Reprinted by permission of Simon and Schuster.

*[The terms *Spanish-speaking* and *Spanish-American* generally include Puerto Rican, as well as Mexican, Americans.–Ed.]

. . . In three states, Arizona, California and Colorado, Kennedy lost to Nixon by margins of 35,000 to 71,000 votes. Kennedy won substantial Chicano pluralities over Nixon in those states and at least 75 percent of the Chicano vote, but not enough Chicanos had registered (and voted) to tip the balance in Kennedy's favor.

While the 1960 election revealed the potential for Spanish-American Democratic pluralities, the 1964 election showed the beginnings of a profound weakness in the Spanish-American vote, a disintegrating turnout. Lyndon Johnson won 90 percent of the Chicano vote, and 86 percent of the Puerto Rican vote, while carrying all the Spanish-American states but Arizona, the home of his G.O.P. opponent, Barry Goldwater. But the turnout in Chicano and Puerto Rican precincts dropped from 1960. In some Chicano precincts of New Mexico, for example, nearly 15 percent fewer voters turned out.

The drop-off in Chicano votes saved Goldwater in Arizona. The Senator carried his state by only 5,000 votes, while Johnson won 86 percent of the vote in Chicano precincts. In some Chicano sections of Tucson and Phoenix the vote was off by one third, and that was lucky for Goldwater. Had Chicano turnout equaled its 1960 mark, L.B.J. would have had a victory in Goldwater's backyard. . . .

The pattern of shrinking Spanish-American electoral participation continued in the Presidential election of 1968, while the Democratic percentage remained strong. Hubert Humphrey received 87 percent of the Chicano vote and 83 percent of the Puerto Rican. Richard Nixon took 10 percent of the Chicano vote and 15 percent of the Puerto Rican vote, while less than 2 percent of Chicanos and Puerto Ricans voted for George Wallace. Yet turnout for both groups reached its low for the decade. In Chicano precincts of Arizona, for example, there were one third fewer votes than in 1960, and in some precincts of Colorado the number of voters dropped nearly as much. (The Vice-President's percentages in those two states were 81 and 75 respectively.) . . . Humphrey won six out of every seven votes cast in the Chicano precincts of California, but turnout was off by one sixth compared to 1960.

Texas was a glittering exception to the rule of Chicano turnout decline in 1968. Following the abolition of the poll tax in 1966, the Texas A.F.L.-C.I.O. and other liberal groups had registered many thousands of Mexican-American voters. In the election of 1968, contrary to the national trend for Spanish-American voters, turnout in Texas rose by more than twenty points from 1960. Ninety-three percent of the Chicano vote went for Humphrey, and he beat Nixon by more than 300,000 votes in Chicano areas alone. Humphrey carried Texas by only 39,000 votes.

Although Nixon's overall Chicano percentage fell 5 points from 1960, he did make one substantial gain. In New Mexico, Nixon won almost four out of every ten votes cast in Chicano precincts—a good showing that came on the coattails of incumbent Republican Governor David F. Cargo, a popular figure with New Mexico's Chicano voters. Nixon's inroads with the New Mexican Chicanos helped him carry the state as Humphrey came out of Chicano precincts leading Nixon by only 10,000 votes, a margin which the former Vice-President quickly overcame in "Anglo" precincts of Albuquerque.

During the 1960s, the Spanish-American vote lost ground, although its Democratic affiliation held firm. At a time when black voters in the South were making great strides toward equality at the ballot box, Spanish-Americans, both Chicanos and Puerto Ricans, were voting less. With only a handful of notable exceptions, there were fewer Chicano and Puerto Rican Presidential voters by decade's end—a decline which inevitably meant shrinking Democratic pluralities.

CHICANO CANDIDATES, THIRD PARTIES AND "LIBERAL" STRATEGIES

Southern blacks will go out of their way to vote for black candidates, even if it means voting a third-party line. Blacks use the ballot to reward candidates, Democrats and Republicans alike, who hold moderate racial views. The Chicano voter fails to show this same degree of political sophistication; Chicanos do not display interest in third-party candidacies, even when fostered by their own. In addition, the Chicanos have failed to make effective use of split-ticket voting.

First, a mixed bag. In 1970, in New Mexico, Chicano voters cast critical ballots for Joseph M. Montoya, the only Mexican-American in the Senate. Montoya's Republican opponent was Anderson Carter, an unsuccessful former senatorial candidate and a conservative. Montoya, who had been in public life for thirty-five years, expected to win an easy victory. Registered Democrats outnumber Republicans two to one in New Mexico, and Montoya had strong support from the local A.F.L.-C.I.O. and other liberal groups. Carter, who waged an aggressive and well-financed campaign, said that Montoya was one of those "ultraliberals" that Spiro Agnew wanted defeated. Carter lost but by only 16,000 votes.[1] Chicano votes made the difference for Montoya. Turnout in Chicano precincts was strong for an off-year election, and Montoya won better than 77 percent of the Chicano vote, a respectable but not overwhelming performance. Carter garnered 21 percent, and William Higgs, the candidate of the People's Constitutional Party, a Chicano group, polled just about 2 percent of the Chicano vote.[2] Montoya's 77 percent equaled L.B.J.'s record Chicano vote in 1964 and gave Montoya a plurality of more than 25,000 votes. Since the Senator won only 47 percent of the "Anglo" vote, his statewide margin of 16,000 came from his fellow Chicanos.

Now the more typical case. The Chicano vote failed a fellow Chicano in a race for the governorship of New Mexico in 1968. Democrat Fabian Chavez, Jr., was opposed by the Republican incumbent David Cargo and by Jose Maestas, the P.C.P. nominee replacing Reies Tijerina, who had been ruled off the ballot because of a felony conviction. Chicano voters found themselves in a difficult position. On the one hand, Chavez was one of their own; but so was Maestas, and he was associated with the heroic Tijerina. Cargo too was not at all unpopular among the Chicanos; his wife was a Spanish-American, and during his first term in office he appointed many Chicanos to state jobs.

A year before the election, Cargo had sent special state police to put down a disturbance caused by Tijerina's land-grant-claims group, and no one knew how this would affect the Governor's standing in the Chicano community. Chicano turnout was light for a Presidential year, with some precincts casting one third fewer votes than in 1960. Cargo won by 3,000 votes as the Chicano community split 67 percent for Chavez, 33 percent for Cargo, and less than one percent for Maestas.

New Mexico's Chicanos had stayed with the two major parties in overwhelming numbers and Cargo's Chicano showing was only 5 percentage points from its record high in 1966. Chavez won only 46 percent of the "Anglo" vote, and he needed more than his 17,000-vote Chicano plurality to win. The combination of low turnout and Cargo's relatively strong performance in Chicano precincts spelled defeat for Chavez.

Chicano voters again let down a Mexican-American candidate in the 1970 gubernatorial election in Arizona. Democrat Raul Castro (a former United States Ambassador to El Salvador and no relation to the Cuban Castro), ran against two-term Republican incumbent Jack Williams, a conservative, heavily financed by the state's Goldwaterites. Castro had won the Democratic nomination in an upset, and he had little organization or financial backing. In the fall election campaign, Castro stressed his Mexican ancestry in an attempt to stir up support among Arizona's Chicanos, who make up 15 percent of the state's population. He need not have bothered. For although drawing nearly 90 percent of the Chicano vote for a plurality of 35,000, Castro lost to Williams by 7,000 ballots. Turnout in Chicano precincts was low, approximately half of those registered, compared to a statewide turnout of nearly 70 percent. If fewer than 10,000 more Chicanos had voted, Castro could have become Arizona's first major Mexican-American officeholder.

The way Chicanos treat "their own" running as Democrats looks spectacular, compared with Chicano support of Chicanos on third-party lines. Chicano voters showed little interest in the candidates of the People's Constitutional Party as William Higgs (who considered Montoya a "Tio Tomas") captured less than 2 percent of the Chicano vote in New Mexico's 1970 senatorial contest while his gubernatorial running mate, Wilfredo Sedillo, did only half as well (thus paralleling the nearly nonexistent vote for Jose Maestas for governor in 1968). Other electoral contests are similarly instructive. In

California's 1970 gubernatorial contest, Ricardo Romo, a United Farm Worker organizer, ran on the Peace and Freedom Party ticket. Romo had traveled extensively throughout California on behalf of Chicano unity, and he expected to run well in Chicano precincts. But Romo's organizing skills did not bring him an electoral payoff. Liberal Democrat Jesse Unruh won nearly five out of every six votes cast in Chicano precincts, incumbent Governor Ronald Reagan took 16 percent, and Romo received the support of less than 2 percent of his fellow Mexican-Americans.

It was much the same story in Colorado,[3] where Albert Garrule [sic] ran for governor as the candidate of the Raza Unida, or United Race, party. Garrule, a twenty-seven-year-old community organizer, said he wasn't bothered by Colorado's law which requires governors to be thirty years old, since he did not expect to win. Instead Garrule claimed he was running only to increase the political awareness of Colorado's Mexican-Americans. Given the election results, his success was questionable. The real contest was between two-term incumbent Republican John Love and Democrat Mark Hogan, the Lieutenant Governor. Love beat Hogan by nearly 50,000 votes, with Garrule managing 12,000, or less than 2 percent. In Chicano precincts, Democrat Hogan captured better than two thirds of the vote, Love took a respectable 23 percent, and Garrule won only one out of every twelve Chicano votes.

Chicano voters are wedded to the two major parties, and particularly to the Democrats. In fact, Chicanos are so strongly tied to the Democratic party in some states that often they vote blindly Democratic when there is good reason not to.

By failing to vote off the Democratic line for either governor or senator in Texas in 1966, the Chicano vote squandered the impact liberal strategists had sought. In the senatorial contest, archconservative Republican John G. Tower, who had been elected in 1961 to fill L.B.J.'s seat, was opposed by Democrat Waggoner Carr, an equally conservative Democrat, who was then the Texas Attorney General. In the gubernatorial election, two-term incumbent Democrat John B. Connally was opposed by conservative Republican T. E. Kennerly. Texas liberals, including the state A.F.L.-C.I.O. and many black and Chicano organizations, were displeased with the Connally Democrats for running two conservatives. Carr, for example, opposed repeal of Section 14b of the Taft-Hartly Act, and Connally had snubbed Chicano farm workers when they marched on the state capitol demanding a minimum wage of $1.25 an hour.[4] The "liberal" strategy called for a protest vote against the Democrats, and *for* the Republican candidates. Most Chicano voters did not get the message. In the Senate election, Democrat Carr won 82 percent of the Chicano vote, or only 10 percent less than Texas Democrats usually won from Chicanos; and Connally won 90 percent of the Mexican-American vote—just about as well as he always did. Carr lost to Tower by nearly 200,000 votes statewide, and Connally beat Kennerly by more than 669,000.

Four years later, Chicanos reinforced their consistent, undeviating support of Democratic candidacies with their behavior in the Texas race for the United States Senate. The liberal-conservative split in the Texas Democratic party reappeared with a vengeance in the primary campaign. Incumbent Senator Ralph Yarborough, leader of the party's liberal wing, was challenged by Lloyd Bentsen, Jr., a conservative millionaire who was backed by the Connally forces. Bentsen took the standard conservative line, attacking Yarborough for voting against Nixon's Supreme Court nominees and for "compulsive spending of taxpayers' money." Yarborough emphasized his powerful committee positions–chairman of the Senate Labor Committee and an important member of the Appropriations Committee–and said he could do more for Texas in Washington. Yarborough was counting on a strong grass-roots campaign to win him renomination and he expected Texas' Chicano voters to help him as they had done in the past. Although he lost the primary by 89,000 votes, Chicano voters gave the Senator solid support. Yarborough won more than 80 percent of the vote in Chicano precincts and the turnout was high. In some precincts, the Chicano primary vote was nearly equal to the 1968 Presidential totals, an extremely impressive performance for a primary election. Yarborough lost not because Chicanos let him down, but because he won far less than half of the "Anglo" vote.

After the divisive primary, some political observers wondered whether the Democrats would unite in time for the general election. Bentsen had a tough opponent in George Bush, a "New Breed" Republican, and some pro-Yarborough forces, most notably the Texas Teamsters union, endorsed the G.O.P. Congressman. If the Chicanos had lost a good friend in Yarborough, they did not hold a grudge against Bentsen, and he beat Bush statewide, but by only 155,000 votes. Chicano turnout was strong, and almost 83 percent favored the conservative Bentsen. That Chicano support resulted in a Chicano plurality of 185,000 votes–Bentsen's victory margin and then some.

SPANISH-SPEAKING VOTES FOR
PRESIDENT, 1968 AND 1972

	Nixon	*McGovern*	*Nixon gain from 1968*
California	26%	74%	+14%
New Mexico	43%	57%	+ 5%
New York	20%	80%	+ 5%
Texas	20%	80%	+14%
Nation	27%	73%	+15%

Source: Broadcast reports; newspaper accounts; private polls.

On balance, Chicano voters seem to lack the political acuity which marks the Southern black voter. Years of political neglect have made the Chicano voter apathetic. Even when a Chicano politician stands on the verge of a political triumph, Chicano voter response is often lackadaisical. Further, Chicano voters are generally disinterested in attempts to create third-party movements that would speak directly to their needs or force the powers that be into dealing with Chicano problems. No third-party Chicano candidate has done well with his own people, and Chicano voters appear little interested in ideology. They are, almost without exception, straight Democratic party voters. The Chicano vote of the Southwest has a long way to go before it can claim to be a powerful, informed and influential voting bloc.[5] . . .

NEW PARTIES, NEW POWER

Viewed objectively, America's Spanish-speaking citizens are certainly no better off than this nation's blacks, and in terms of dollar incomes, less well off. Like blacks, Chicanos and Puerto Ricans "should" be part of the Democratic party's natural constituency. They are–but a little less so than blacks.

Nationwide in 1972, Spanish-Americans voted almost three-to-one for McGovern, a solid bloc for the Democrat, but nevertheless twice as strongly for Nixon as blacks. In California, the Chicano vote doubled for Mr. Nixon, compared to 1968, but since the President had won only 12 percent that year, doubling his strength still meant a 48 percent Chicano margin for McGovern. . . .

President Nixon's strongest Spanish vote–and it was by no means a majority–came in New Mexico, where three out of every seven Chicanos voted for him. For many years, New Mexico's Republicans have worked to win the Chicano vote, and although they rarely do, Republican candidates often run well enough in Latin precincts to hurt the Democrats. In 1972, for instance, Republican Senatorial candidate Pete Domenici took a strong 48 percent of the Chicano vote, cutting sharply into Democrat Jack Daniels' Chicano potential. Domenici beat Daniels statewide by only 31,000 votes, so if Daniels had been able to win 75 percent of the Chicano vote–a difficult but not impossible task–he and not Domenici would have been elected.

The Chicano vote made its presence felt in a slightly different way in Texas. For the first time, the Chicano-based La Raza Unida Party was running its own candidates for the U.S. Senate and for Governor. As it turned out, the Chicano vote didn't matter all that much in the Senate race–incumbent Republican John Tower swept to an easy win over Democrat Barefoot Sanders–but the contest for the statehouse was much closer, and Chicano voters held the balance of power.

Conservative Democrat Dolph Briscoe beat Republican Henry Grover

CHICANO VOTERS, TEXAS
SENATOR AND GOVERNOR, 1972

U.S. Senate		*Governor*	
Sanders (D)	75%	Briscoe (D)	61%
Tower (R)	14%	Grover (R)	6%
Amaya (La Raza Unida)	11%	Muniz (La Raza Unida)	33%

Source: NBC News.

statewide by a meager 81,000 votes. Among Chicanos, Briscoe won 61 percent: Ramsey Muniz of La Raza Unida was second with one-third of the Mexican-American vote. Since Republican Grover took only 6 percent among Chicanos, Briscoe came out of Latin precincts with a 55 percent plurality of 150,000 votes or nearly twice his statewide margin. If Muniz had not run, Briscoe would have won statewide by at least 52 percent. But even more significantly, if 60 percent of the Chicanos had voted for their co-ethnic Muniz, then Briscoe would not have won at all. In the years ahead, La Raza Unida's candidates may well gain more strength in the Chicano community. Their votes will become even more important, especially in close elections. That fact alone ought to assure La Raza Unida a sympathetic hearing in the councils of the conservative Democratic oligarchy of Texas.

While Spanish-Americans voted a shade less Democratic than they had in 1968, their vote for Democratic House candidates remained as strong as ever. In 1960, 86 percent of Spanish-Americans voted Democratic for the House; in 1972 virtually the same proportion (85 percent) cast Democratic ballots. Democratic strategists in the Southwest, California, and New York should take comfort in this continuing high level of support, and should step up their efforts to build a substantially enlarged pool of registered Spanish voters. For

SPANISH-SPEAKING VOTE IN
NATION, PRESIDENT AND HOUSE OF
REPRESENTATIVES, 1960 TO 1972
(Percent Democratic)

	1960	*1964*	*1968*	*1972*
House of Representatives	86%	87%	85%	85%
President	85%	90%	87%	73%

Source: NBC News sample precincts; Oliver Quayle Survey.

the Republicans, the best strategy seems to be to follow the lead of New Mexico, attempting to cut Democratic Chicano pluralities wherever possible. Either way, the politicians will be paying more attention to the needs and problems of Spanish voters, a good thing for them and for the nation.

All ethnic Americans are becoming increasingly sophisticated in their voting behavior. They remain largely Democratic in party affiliation but they are not blinded by party label. Defections to the Republicans are possible, even likely, when they perceive Democratic candidates as not in sync with their interests. That is the lesson of 1972.

NOTES

1. In 1964, when Montoya was first elected to the Senate, he beat Republican Edwin Mecham by 31,000 votes and won 74 percent of the Chicano vote.

2. The P.C.P. nominee for governor, Wilfredo Sedillo, ran even worse in Chicano precincts, winning less than one percent. Sixty-nine percent of the Chicano vote went to Democrat Wayne [sic] King, and 30 percent to Republican Peter Domenici.

3. In addition to New Mexico, these two states, California and Colorado, are bilingual; their constitutions require state laws to be published both in English and in Spanish.

4. Ironically, Connally owed his first election as governor to Chicano votes. In the 1962 election, Connally did not win a majority of the votes in Texas' "Anglo" precincts; but he did win 93 percent of the Chicano vote, for a margin of nearly 150,000 votes over Republican Jack Cox.

5. The most impressive Chicano political organization is in Texas, where La Raza Unida (United Race party) won a series of elections in 1970 in Crystal City, Carizzo Springs and Cortulla, all farm towns southwest of San Antonio, with large immigrant worker populations. La Raza was born in 1967, after a 400-mile march to Austin (the state capital) to demonstrate for a minimum wage of $1.25. The party is headed by José Abgel [sic] Gutierrez, who was also elected chairman of the Crystal City Board of Education. San Antonio itself appears ripe for Chicano political activity. Its official population is 41 percent Chicano (with over 50 percent believed to be Chicano).

18: VOTING PATTERNS IN "BI-CULTURAL EL PASO": A Contextual Analysis of Mexican American Voting Behavior

Rudolph O. de la Garza

EVENTS OF THE 1950s AND 1960s FORCED AMERICAN SCHOLARS TO ABANDON the myth of the melting pot and seek new ways to explain the place of minority groups in U.S. society, especially groups such as the Mexican American about whom so little was known. As scholars turned their attention to an analysis of the social and political behavior of Mexican Americans, it became evident that much of the existing literature had little validity: with few exceptions existing studies ranged from being irrelevant to fostering stereotypes used to justify racist public policies.[1] Unlike other social sciences, however, political science made no contribution to this body of literature. "Of all the social sciences, however, political science is perhaps the only discipline that has almost totally ignored the Chicano. . . ."[2] Although recently there has been a substantial increase of studies explicitly on Chicano political behavior[3] much more work is needed in order to understand and explain the political behavior of Mexican Americans. It is hoped that this paper will make a contribution to this end.

This study is divided into three sections. The first describes the context of Mexican American political life. The second section empirically tests the validity of this description through an analysis of Mexican American and Anglo American voting patterns in El Paso, a major southwestern city.

Reprinted from *Aztlan: Chicano Journal of the Social Sciences and Arts* 4, no. 2. By permission of the author.

The author wishes to thank James Lamare, Rudolph Gomez, and Richard Calkins, whose critical comments and assistance were most helpful. He is also grateful to José Medina, his research assistant, and to the Cross-Cultural Southwest Ethnic Studies Center of the University of Texas at El Paso for its support of this project.

Section III speculates as to the implications of the findings presented in Section II.

Because the empirical analysis presented here is limited to 1972 El Paso elections, it is impossible to generalize from this to other settings. The findings presented here, however, should suggest insights into Chicano (and Anglo) political behavior in other southwestern communities. At the very minimum, this study should provide hypotheses for testing in cities throughout this region. Moreover, observation of and familiarity with politics in Colorado, California, New Mexico, Arizona and Texas suggests to this writer that the pattern explained here exists throughout these states.

I

Mexican Americans are the nation's second largest minority.[4] They share with native Americans the distinction of being the only territorial minorities in the United States.[5] Mexican Americans had developed viable social and political institutions prior to the Anglo American invasion of the Southwest, and rather than voluntarily become a part of Anglo America, Mexican Americans fought to protect the society they had developed.[6] Defeated in battle, Mexican Americans (formerly Mexicans) nonetheless have maintained many of their cultural characteristics, most particularly language, while Anglo American institutions have oppressed the Mexican American people, depriving them of social and political rights and self-respect. Thus, the position of the Mexican American in the U.S. is not comparable to that of other ethnic groups except native Americans. It is best understood within the framework of colonialism, that is, Anglo America conquered and colonized the Southwest,[7] and the Mexican American people suffer from the legacy of that colonial experience.

However valid the colonial model is to describe the historical experience of the Mexican American people, most scholars and politicians would deny that Mexican Americans continue to suffer under a colonial system.[8] Indeed, it must be admitted that changes in U.S. political practices such as civil rights legislation and the McGovern reforms of the Democratic party, diminish the continued applicability of the colonial model. These changes, however, have not substantially altered the position of Mexican Americans in American society, and a review of their economic, educational and political attainments suggests that while Mexican Americans have more control over their political and economic lives than is true of colonized peoples, they are second-class citizens.

Mexican Americans do not enjoy a proportional share of this nation's wealth. The median income for Mexican American families–$7,486–is substantially lower than the median income of the total U.S. population–$10,285. Furthermore, Mexican Americans are significantly overrepresented among low income groups. Thirteen percent of the total population 14 years and over are classified as below the low-income level; 29 percent of Mexican Americans fall in this category. In the Southwest, 31 percent of all Mexican Americans are in this category.

Mexican Americans are also educationally deprived. While 5 percent of the total population over 25 had completed less than five years of school, 27 percent of Mexicans are so handicapped; while 58 percent of the total population had at least a high school degree, only 26 percent of Mexican Americans had completed four years of high school. In Texas, 52 percent of all Mexican Americans over 25 have only four years of school, and a mere 11 percent has gone to high school. In 1969 the El Paso city manager admitted that over 44 percent of Mexican Americans in El Paso were functionally illiterate. Even more appalling, the 1960 census showed that 20 percent of adult Mexican Americans in Bexar County, Texas, had *no* years of schooling at all.[9]

Perhaps the best indicator of second-class citizenship is the lack of Mexican American elected and appointed political officials. The Mexican Americans are significantly underrepresented in all political decision-making arenas, and sometimes Chicanos are totally absent from decision-making arenas, and sometimes Chicanos are totally absent from decision-making bodies. In California there are five state assemblymen and no state senators.[10] Of 15,650 federal, state, county, and city officials in California in 1970, 310 or 1.98 percent are Mexican American.[11] Chicanos have only slightly higher representation in the four other southwestern states.[12] Lacking their own representatives, Mexican Americans must rely on Anglo spokesmen to articulate their interests. However well intentioned, such spokesmen have mixed constituencies, and therefore are unlikely to be in a position to defend vigorously the interests of the Chicano people. Clearly, then, it would appear that there is at best a minimal Mexican American input into political decision making.

Traditionally, scholars have concluded that the reasons for these low levels of economic status, educational attainment, and political representation reflect the Chicano's culture. Simply stated, the argument is that Mexican Americans lack the Protestant ethic and thus accept their plight as *lo que manda Dios* rather than attempt to improve their lives.[13] If Mexican Americans became culturally mature and sophisticated, continues this argument, they would develop mutually beneficial relationships with politicians and officeholders and thus be in a position to effect changes in institutions and discriminatory practices without the need to assault frontally such institutions.[14]

An alternative view is that the American political process—the manner in which values are authoritatively allocated in this society[15]—functions to restrict the participation of Mexican Americans in U.S. society. American institutions deny Mexican American people access to material and symbolic rewards: as a group Mexican Americans enjoy neither status nor wealth; to the contrary, they endure prejudice, discrimination and poverty. Mexican Americans, aware of their inferior status and cognizant of the potential of political activity as an agent of change have attempted to utilize the political system to effect meaningful changes. This study will attempt to show that the failure to achieve these changes is less a function of cultural traits than of systemic variables beyond the control of the Mexican American people.

A major characteristic of Mexican American political participation is affiliation with the Democratic party. Identification with the Democratic party is so widespread that this is usually considered one of the principal handicaps facing the Mexican American. Critics contend that the Democratic party takes the Chicano vote for granted, and that Chicanos must learn to flirt with both parties and give their support to whichever proves itself the more dedicated suitor.[16] Those who make this argument appear to ignore well-established patterns of ethnic political participation and also disregard the milieu within which Mexican Americans live. As ethnic communities became large enough to be considered a political resource, political bosses and party leaders endeavored to win the support of these groups.[17] The urban machines exchanged jobs and symbolic values for votes. In time, the ethnic groups were no longer dependent on the party leaders for employment or other benefits, yet the new generations remained faithful to the party affiliations of their forefathers.[18] The Mexican American has followed this same pattern.

Like most ethnic groups in the United States, the Mexican American was first recruited into politics through the Democratic party. Many of the programs initiated by President Franklin D. Roosevelt benefitted the Mexican American community, and from these "Deep loyalties developed among many families–loyalties that became traditional, a family heirloom. . . ."[19] These loyalties were reenforced through the control the Democratic party exercised at state and local levels throughout the Southwest. During these years the Democrats controlled politics in California, Colorado, Texas, Arizona and New Mexico. Thus it was predictable that as Mexican Americans became politically active that they would do so within the Democratic party.[20] Once recruited into the party, it was also predictable that Chicanos would follow the pattern of ethnic groups and remain loyal to it even after the reasons for remaining loyal had disappeared.

Although Mexican Americans have given their support to Democratic candidates they have not been oblivious to the treatment they receive at the hands of Democratic leaders. For example, Mexican Americans are unenthusiastic in their support of the Democratic party. Although 88 per cent of Mexican Americans in Texas identify as Democrats, only 30 per cent identify as strong supporters.[21] Furthermore, it was because Mexican Americans were dissatisfied with the policies of the Democratic party that Chicano organizations such as the Mexican American Political Association (MAPA) and Raza Unida developed. " . . . [A] ctivist Mexican American politicians found their efforts to become part of the party hierarchy rebuffed. Many became convinced that Democratic leaders took them for granted."[22]

It should also be noted that Mexican Americans had nowhere else to turn. Republicans have for years written off the Mexican American vote.[23] They "are conscious of the futility of appeals to the Mexican-American electorate and therefore make only halfhearted gestures in promising programs on their behalf."[24] Indeed, when Mexican Americans began supporting Republicans during the 1968 presidential campaign, rather than welcome their support President Nixon's reaction seemed designed "purposely to break up Mexican American forces in the [Republican] party."[25] In 1970 the Republican National Committee filled its national slot of Special Assistant on Spanish Speaking Affairs with a Guatemalan rather than a Mexican American. In 1972 President Nixon promised funding and support to the Mexican American community, but in the months since his reelection he has not only withdrawn the funds he promised but has also dismissed many of those Mexican Americans he had appointed to national office.[26]

A second characteristic of Chicano political life is that Mexican Americans are less politically active than the general population.[27] From this generalization is deduced the proposition that Mexican Americans are apathetic. " . . . [T] he people who might be expected to want the most from an active city government–the poor Latins–are apathetic and politically ineffective."[28] It is for this reason that traditionally political candidates in cities such as El Paso do not spend much time with Mexican Americans. "It's better to go to the shopping centers where the votes are than to mess around the pool halls of the South Side."[29]

Although it is possible that apathy resulting primarily from low socioeconomic status explains this level of participation, it is equally likely that such low levels of participation are a function of the political socialization which the Chicano has undergone. The net result of this process is either to alienate Mexican Americans and thus have them reject traditional forms of participation, or to convince them that their efforts will be meaningless, thus generating among Mexican Americans a profound sense of apathy. Since 1848 Anglo American institutions have taught Mexican Americans, explicitly and through example, that political decision making is the preserve of white males. School systems throughout the Southwest have deliberately humiliated the Mexican American and endeavored to insure that Chicano children internalize the notion that Anglos should rule.[30] Other institutions have reinforced this lesson through their dealings with Chicanos. As has been shown, political parties have done little to motivate participation. When Chicanos have become politically active they have been harassed and intimidated. When they protest to the courts, they find little relief. It is because of experiences such as these that Mexican Americans believe that public officials do not care about them.[31] In sum, it seems reasonable to hypothesize that Mexican Americans have been socialized into not participating. If so, then alienation and apathy resulting from political experiences more adequately explain the low levels of Mexican American voting than do socioeconomic factors.[32]

A third characteristic of Mexican American political participation is that the tactics used to gain access to the political system have varied to reflect changes in the socio-political environment.[33] Anglo American institutions proved impervious to Mexican American attempts to participate in them, and Mexican Americans were forced to develop parallel institutions to insure that needed social services were provided.[34] Thus, the League of United Latin American Citizens, the Mexican American Political Association, the Mexican American Legal Defense Fund, and La Raza Unida party all are manifestations of different strategies to protect the interests of the Mexican American community while simultaneously attempting to increase the voice of Mexican Americans in the political process and thus increase their share of the values allocated by society.

It appears, then, that the U.S. political process is structured so as to restrict the participation of Mexican Americans in American society. Although Mexican Americans have mobilized in support of the Democratic party, the Democratic party has not been supportive of Mexican American demands. Republican leaders, on the other hand, have been uninterested in the Mexican American people. Armando Rendon summarizes the manner in which these parties have treated Chicanos:

> ". . . [T]he Democrats have deceived and exploited the Chicano people as much as the Republicans, although the Democrats have relied on the Chicano vote as a sure thing, have divided Chicano political aspirations when they posed a threat, and have never rewarded adequately Chicano's allegiance with a share of the dividends of political success–recognition, inclusion in decision making, and patronage."[35]

This is why militant Chicano leaders refer to the two-party system as a two-headed snake. This is also the reason that rank and file Mexican Americans are no longer willing to support blindly any candidate sponsored by the Democratic party.[36]

If this analysis is correct and the system is structured to deny Mexican Americans access to decision-making arenas then to maintain this pattern of value allocations requires deliberate action by elite and rank and file Anglo Americans. Whether such actions exist can be measured through an analysis of voting patterns.

Given that Mexican Americans have nominal access, i.e., they are legally eligible to contest nominations and elections, to the formal political process, the party elites (Anglo Americans) cannot legally prevent Mexican Americans from becoming candidates for public office. Once Chicanos attain this status, elites may choose not to support them (as has often happened)[37] and they may actively campaign against them even when Chicano candidates have won the party's nomination. It is the rank and file voter, however, that determines the outcome of the election. Unless the rank and file voter decides to vote against Mexican American candidates and thus prohibit Mexican Americans from participating in political decision making (a function inherent in public office) the structures will be altered to include Mexican American office-holders. In other words, unless the Anglo American community votes primarily on the basis of the racial identification of candidates, a proportional number of Mexican American candidates will be elected to office.[38] Given the analysis presented here, however, it is hypothesized that the Anglo American population votes primarily on the basis of race.[39] In view of the fact that Mexican Americans have always devised tactics designed to counteract the prevailing style of Anglo Mexican behavior, it is also predicted that Mexican Americans also vote primarily on the basis of race so as to offset the effect of Anglo bloc voting.

II

The analysis examines ten elections contested by Mexican Americans in El Paso in 1972. The Democratic party exerts such control over Texas and El Paso politics that electoral competition exists only in Democratic primaries.[40] Thus, six of the elections analyzed here are primaries for state representatives and state senator. Two of these six are for representative and state senator runoffs that followed the primaries. Two school board elections are also analyzed. The final two elections analyzed are the general elections for governor and state treasurer. La Raza Unida challenged the Democratic party in these contests, and analyzing these elections provides additional insights into the patterns of Mexican American voting.

The hypothesis tested here is that Mexican American voters vote for Mexican American candidates, and conversely, non-Mexican American, i.e., Anglo voters, do not vote for Mexican American candidates. The hypotheses test voting patterns rather than other types of participation for two reasons. First, it is no longer acceptable to articulate frankly racist views. Thus, even had it been possible to conduct a survey of El Paso voters, it is unlikely that they would have voiced openly anti-Chicano attitudes.[41] Rather than be explicitly anti-Mexican American, Anglo American voters would most likely indicate that they support "the best man." If the hypotheses are valid, the behavioral manifestation of such an attitude will be to vote for Anglo candidates–i.e., the best man is always an Anglo.

The second reason for examining voting patterns is that although voting is but one of many types of political activities, in a democratic political system, voting is the most important activity in which citizens can engage for it is with votes that, in principle, citizens evaluate their leaders and public policies. Moreover, understanding voting patterns provides insights into other aspects of a community's socio-political character. Voting patterns reflect community life styles and levels of social and political integration—as is evidenced by the black community's repudiation of President Nixon in the 1972 election. Voting patterns indicate whether community cleavages are crosscutting or reinforcing.[42] Thus, if we understand the voting patterns of Anglo and Mexican Americans in El Paso we will also likely have a good insight into the socio-political milieu of the city and perhaps also of similar communities throughout the Southwest.

The dependent variable in the hypotheses, support for Mexican American candidates, is operationalized two ways. First, support is defined as the number of votes received by Mexican American candidates per precinct. For reasons explained later, the operationalization is then altered to the percent of the total votes cast received by Mexican American candidates per precinct.

The independent variables used are: voter ethnicity, income, education, and turnout. For reasons to be explained, ethnicity is operationalized in two ways: number of Mexican American voters per precinct and percent of Mexican American voters per precinct. Income and education data were taken from 1970 census tracts and ethnicity data were taken from 1971 El Paso voter lists. Turnout totals are from final published election results. Initially, the study included forty randomly selected precincts from a total of eighty precincts in El Paso. After the preliminary analysis [showed] significant support for the hypothesis, those precincts that had not participated in all the elections because of boundaries (as in the case of state representative elections) were dropped and the final analysis included thirty of the original forty precincts selected in the sample. The data were analyzed through the use of stepwise regression.

Data Analysis

[There is] the need to exercise caution in the analysis because of multicollinearity resulting from the high correlation of several pairs of independent variables. This is most obvious between the percent of Mexican American registered voters and median education ($r = -.941$). Other variables highly correlated are income and education, and percent Mexican American voters and income. Multicollinearity is not a problem in this analysis, however, because stepwise rather than multiple or partial correlation techniques are used to analyze the data.

[The data] reveals expected patterns of voting turnout. Mexican Americans turned out at an almost constant lower rate than non-Mexican Americans in each of the four types of elections studied here. The correlation coefficient between percent Mexican American voters and turnout varies from −0.452 to −0.435r.

The analysis indicates that the number of Mexican American voters in each precinct is the best predictor of the votes Mexican American candidates receive in each precinct. This variable alone explains from a third to eighty percent of the variation in votes received by Mexican American candidates. In school board elections, the number of registered Mexican American voters explains $.368R^2$ and $.423R^2$ of the votes cast for Chicano candidates. In Democratic primaries, the total explanatory power of this variable ranges from $.357R^2$ to $.85R^2$. The range of explanations in general election support for Raza Unida candidates is from $.40R^2$ to $.54R^2$. Moreover, the added explanatory power of income and education is slight in all of the elections analyzed.

Although the relationship of registered Chicano voters and votes received by Chicano candidates is statistically significant, a substantial amount of the variation in the number of votes received by Chicano candidates is left unexplained even after income and education are added to the analysis. A possible reason for this is the inverse relationship that exists between levels of Mexican American registration and turnout. As previously indicated, there is a small but negative correlation between turnout and total number of Chicano voters. In other words, because Mexican Americans turn out at lower levels than non-Mexican Americans, the number of registered Mexican American voters is at best a rough indicator of the number of votes received by Mexican American candidates. Therefore, as the number of Chicano voters increase, the votes cast for Chicano candidates also increase, but the rate of change between the two is not predictable and thus the total number of votes cast for Mexican American candidates is not predictable.

An alternative approach to predicting the support Mexican American voters give to Mexican American candidates is through analyzing the relationship between the percent of Mexican American voters in a precinct and the percent of the total vote cast received by Mexican American candidates. By standardizing the range of variation 0.00 to 1.00 in both the independent and dependent variables this approach controls for turnout. Rather than attempt to predict how many votes a Mexican American candidate receives as a function of how many Mexican American voters there are in a precinct, this approach attempts to predict what percentage of Mexican American voters of those who turn out supports Mexican American candidates, and as expected, this is a much more powerful predictor of the support given Chicano candidates.

In every election analyzed, the overwhelmingly best predictor of support for Chicano candidates is percent Mexican American voters per precinct. In the school board elections, the predictive power is .90R^2 and .91R^2 respectively. In the Democratic primaries the range of predictive power varied from .78R^2 to .96R^2. Although the explanatory power of this variable was far weaker in the case of Raza Unida candidates, percent Mexican American voters per precinct was the most important variable employed in the equation.

It is significant, moreover, that no Mexican American candidate who participated in a contested election and received the support of Mexican American voters became the Democratic nominee. In the two runoffs, the Chicano candidates were able to maintain their primary vote but were unable to win enough support from citizens who had voted for other candidates to triumph. In the runoff for state representative, the relationship between the Chicano candidate's primary vote and runoff vote is .98r. Given that Mexican American voters, measured in absolute numbers or in percentages by precinct, explain almost all of the vote received by the Mexican American candidate, the fact that a Chicano candidate's primary total is almost identical with his runoff total indicates that the candidate picked up almost no Anglo votes. In other words, in this election Anglo voters ranked all Anglo candidates as superior to Mexican American candidates.

Although this pattern characterized both runoffs, the senatorial runoff requires further analysis because the candidates in that election were both Spanish surnamed. Two Spanish surnamed and three non-Spanish surnamed candidates contested this primary. The two Spanish surnamed candidates received the most votes and they were the final contestants in the runoff.

Although the candidates had some characteristics in common, the differences between them were far more important. The similarities between the two were that both were Spanish surnamed and both had served as state representatives. The major difference between the two was that one campaigned as a Mexican American candidate while the other campaigned as a candidate for "all El Paso." Local newspapers carried stories and advertisements arguing that the Mexican American candidate would serve only "a special interest," i.e., the Mexican American people, and that because he had been active in attempting to impeach the incumbent governor and other state officials for their involvement in the Sharpstown scandal, this candidate would be ineffective as a senator.[43] The "candidate for all El Paso," on the other hand, was described as a man who would not be tied to one group. Moreover, because of his close ties with the business community, newspapers and campaign literature argued that he would be an effective senator.[44] Thus, by their own identification as well as by media description, one candidate was a Chicano while the other was not.

The results of the runoff differed significantly from the primary results. In the latter the Chicano candidate finished first in the field of five, and members of his campaign organization have stated that he felt confident he would also win the runoff. As in the runoff for the state representative, however, the Chicano candidate lost. Again, Anglo American voters found themselves unable to support the Mexican American candidate.

III

Discussion

Scholars have analyzed voting patterns of ethnic groups but these studies have been limited to immigrant ethnic groups in multi-ethnic communities.[45] This narrow focus minimizes the contribution such studies make to our understanding of the voting behavior of Chicanos because of the differences in relationships Chicanos and these ethnics have with Anglo American institutions. A more appropriate comparison can be made between black and Chicano voting patterns despite the significant historical and cultural differences that separate them.

The boundaries of American pluralism do not extend to include the black population.[46] Stokely Carmichael and Charles V. Hamilton in their analysis of American politics forcefully argue that "American pluralism quickly becomes a monolithic structure on issues of race."[47] Chuck Stone makes a similar argument in his analysis of black politics and supports his view by quoting an axiom of southern politics: "If you get the white folks on your side, you don't need the niggers."[48] The election of Mayor Stokes in Cleveland in 1967 provides evidence supporting these indictments and also serves to demonstrate the similarity between Chicano and black voting patterns.

Mayor Stokes won the Democratic primary in 1967 and should have been in a position to win an easy victory in the general election.[49] Not only did Democrats substantially outnumber Republicans but major unions and newspapers endorsed him. Nonetheless, Stokes barely won. In the primary he received 52.5 percent of the vote, and the decisive factor "was the size of the Negro turnout. While Negroes constituted only about 40 per cent of the voters, 73.4 per cent of them turned out, compared with only 58.4 per cent of the whites. Predominantly Negro wards cast 96.2 per cent of their votes for Stokes. . . ."[50] In the general election Stokes held the black vote but the pattern of white voting defied prediction. Approximately 90 percent of those Democrats who voted in the primary voted for Stokes' opponent, "many pulling a Republican lever for the first time in their life."[51]

Race was an important factor in this election, but voters refused to acknowledge that race was really an issue. Instead, voters attacked the race issue indirectly. Ethnic clubs rallied around phrases such as "protecting our way of life" and "false charges of police brutality." Such activities led analysts to conclude that race was the most important issue in the election.

> "An enormous amount of the white vote was, whether covert or overt, anti-Negro. It is hard to believe that Catholics, ethnic groups, and laborers who never voted for anyone but a Democrat should suddenly decide to evaluate candidates on their qualification and programs, and—in overwhelming numbers—decide that the Republican candidate was better qualified. The implication is that they were prejudiced. But to assume that such people perceive themselves as bigots is to oversimplify the nature of prejudice. And to call such people bigots is to make their responses even more rigid."[52]

Anglo voters in El Paso behaved as did their counterparts in Cleveland in the primary. Given the choice between a Mexican American candidate and an Anglo candidate, they voted for the latter. In the runoff when the choice was between two Spanish surnamed citizens—an unusual situation—Anglo voters supported the "best man," and the best man was the more "Americanized" of the two. Given that the Chicano candidate lost the [primary] election and could not contest the Republican nominee in the general [election], there are no solid empirical data on which to judge how the electorate would have voted. In view of the pattern described here and the history of Mexican American-Anglo American relations in El Paso and elsewhere in Texas and the Southwest, it is very likely that Anglo Democrats would have switched parties and voted for Republicans.[53]

This study, thus, suggests several conclusions. First, it appears that the political process does not offer Mexican Americans in El Paso a viable means for gaining representation in decision-making arenas. Anglo Americans do not support Mexican American candidates who identify with the Mexican American people, but they will vote for Spanish surnamed candidates who identify with "all El Paso," i.e., with the Anglo sectors. Such candidates serve to legitimize the Chamber of Commerce's platitudes about El Paso's bi-cultural heritage but they contribute little to solving the problems facing the Mexican American community.

A second conclusion suggested here is that it is extremely difficult for the Mexican American community to develop effective leaders. Those individuals whom the community trusts often are not acceptable to the Anglo majority.[54] Politically aspiring Chicanos, therefore, must recognize that if they maintain their ties with the community they will jeopardize their future. Conversely, they may attain high political positions but at the risk of being labeled Tio Tacos and being rejected by the Chicano community.

A third conclusion implicit here is that Mexican Americans are not taking advantage of their potential political power. Unlike the blacks in Cleveland, Mexican Americans did not turn out in sufficiently high numbers to counter the Anglo voter's majority. It is not certain that the Chicano candidates would have won had they done so, but there is no doubt that a high turnout of Mexican American voters would have greatly improved the probability of Chicano candidates winning these elections.

A fourth and final conclusion is that traditional generalizations describing ethnic voting behavior are not adequate to explain the voting patterns described here. Existing studies of ethnic political behavior focus on multi-ethnic, highly industrialized communities. Few southwestern cities are industrialized and even fewer are multi-ethnic in the sense that Boston or Chicago are. In such communities the ethnic groups compete among themselves and are able to form coalitions with established "Americans" so as to gain representation and share in the benefits inherent in holding office. In the Southwest, all such ethnic groups to the extent that they are represented join into an alliance against Mexican Americans in much the same manner that such groups form coalitions against blacks. Thus, theories of "racist voting" rather than "ethnic group voting" seem more appropriate for explaining the voting patterns identified in this study.

Overall, then, it seems that in El Paso Mexican Americans are indeed second-class citizens. By all indicators Mexican Americans in El Paso stand on the lowest rung of the community's social ladder. It would be incorrect to insist, however, that Mexican Americans in El Paso are a colonized people. Mexican Americans can and have won major local offices–from 1957-61 Raymond Telles served as mayor–and if they were able to mobilize their resources they would hold such offices much more frequently. This is *not* to say that there are not major systemic factors to overcome; it is to say that these factors are not insurmountable as would be institutions in a colonial system. Nonetheless, this study clearly indicates that the political process serves to keep the Mexican Americans "in their place" rather than to provide them a means for changing the system.

As indicated at the outset, it is impossible to generalize from this analysis of one year's voting patterns in El Paso to voting patterns in other southwestern cities. Given, however, that the historical relationships and general nature of Mexican American-Anglo American relations in El Paso are typical of southwestern cities, and that these are the sources of the polarization between Mexican Americans and Anglo Americans, it would seem reasonable to predict that similar patterns exist elsewhere. Hopefully, researchers will test these findings in other settings to determine their overall validity. By so doing we will not only add to our understanding of Mexican American political behavior but also to our understanding of the American political process.

NOTES

1. Miguel Montiel, "The Social Science Myth of the Mexican American Family," *El Grito* II, no. 4 (Summer 1970), 56-63; Octavio I. Romano–V.,

"The Anthropology and Sociology of the Mexican Americans: The Distortion of Mexican-American History," *El Grito* II, no. 1 (Fall 1968), 13-26; Romano, "The Historical and Intellectual Presence of Mexican-Americans," *El Grito* II, no. 2 (Winter 1969), 32-46; Nick Vaca, "The Mexican American in the Social Sciences, 1912-1970: Part 1: 1912-1935," *El Grito* III, no. 3 (Spring 1970), 3-24; Part 2, 1936-1970, *El Grito* IV, no. 1 (Fall 1970), 17-51.

2. Carlos Munoz, "Toward a Chicano Perspective of Political Analysis," *Aztlan*, Fall 1970, p. 18.

3. *Aztlan* and *El Grito* are the principal journals publishing these materials, but the increased attention given Chicanos is indicated in that an issue of the *Social Science Quarterly* is devoted to the study of Chicano socio-political behavior.

4. Leo Grebler, Joan W. Moore, Ralph C. Guzman, *The Mexican American People: The Nation's Second Largest Minority* (New York: Free Press, 1970) is the most comprehensive study of Mexican American people to date. The study suffers from several significant limitations, however.

5. This distinction is discussed in Rudolph O. de la Garza, Z. Anthony Kruszewski and Thomas Arciniega, eds., *Chicanos and Native Americans: The Territorial Minorities* (Englewood Cliffs: Spectrum Books, 1973).

6. Rodolfo Acuna, *Occupied America: The Chicano's Struggle for Liberation* (San Francisco: Canfield Press, 1972), for the history of this struggle.

7. Acuna, *op. cit.*, pp. 1-5; Joan Moore, "Colonialism: The Case of the Mexican American," *Social Problems* 17, no. 4, 463-471.

8. For arguments supporting the contemporary applicability of this view, compare the writings of Albert Memmi, *The Colonizer and the Colonized* (New York: Orion Press, 1965) with the findings of Thomas Carter, *Mexican Americans in School: A History of Educational Neglect* (Princeton: College Entrance Examination Board, 1970).

9. In Acuna, *op. cit.*, p. 255.

10. Herman Sillas, Jr., *Los Angeles Times*, November, 1972.

11. *Political Participation of Mexican Americans in California.* A report of the California State Advisory Committee to the United States Commission on Civil Rights, August 1971, p. 61.

12. Grebler, et. al., *op. cit.;* New Mexico is the only state with significant Mexican American representation in elected offices. Jose Angel Gutierrez, *El Politico* (El Paso: Mictla, 1972), p. 5, lists 736 Spanish surnamed officials in Texas. The total number of public officials in the state is not listed and thus it is impossible to determine the level of representation this indicates.

13. Carter, *op. cit.*, presents an excellent review of the literature making this argument. For empirical studies challenging these stereotypes see Grebler, et al., *op. cit.*, pp. 434-439, and William P. Kuvlesky, "Ambitions and Opportunities for Social Mobility and Their Consequences for Mexican Americans as Compared with Other Youth," in de la Garza, et al., *op. cit.*

14. Grebler, et al., *op. cit.*, p. 546.

15. David Easton, "An Approach to the Analysis of Political Systems," *World Politics*, IX (1957), 338-400, develops and discusses this definition.

16. Grebler, et. al., *op. cit.*, p. 546; Armando Rendon, *Chicano Manifesto* (New York: Collier Books, 1972), p. 273.

17. See Edgar Litt, *Ethnic Politics in America* (Glenview, Ill.: Scott, Foresman and Co., 1970), especially pp. 42-74.

18. Raymond E. Wolfinger, "The Development and Persistence of Ethnic Voting," in Lawrence H. Fuchs, *American Ethnic Politics* (New York: Harper and Row, 1968), pp. 192-193.

19. Rendon, *op. cit.,* p. 242.

20. *Ibid.,* p. 243.

21. Clifton McCleskey and Bruce Merrill, "The Political Behavior of Mexican Americans in Texas: A Preliminary Report," a paper delivered at the Southern Political Science Association, March 26-28, 1970, as quoted in Armando Gutierrez, "Institutional Completeness and La Raza Unida Party," in de la Garza, *op. cit.*

22. Matt S. Meier and Feliciano Rivera, *The Chicanos: A History of Mexican Americans* (New York: Hill and Wang, 1972), p. 247.

23. Rendon, *op. cit.,* p. 258.

24. Grebler, et. al., *op. cit.,* p. 546.

25. Rendon, *op. cit.,* p. 260.

26. Jack Anderson, *El Paso Times,* March 24, 1973, p. 4.

27. Grebler, et. al., *op. cit.,* p. 565.

28. Edward Banfield, *Big City Politics* (New York: Random House, 1965), p. 70.

29. *Ibid.,* p. 71.

30. Carter, *op. cit.,* describes how the school systems attempt to teach both Anglo and Mexican children their "respective places" in society.

31. Grebler, et. al., *op. cit.,* p. 567.

32. Herbert Hirsch, "Political Scientists and Other Camaradas: Academic Myth Making and Racial Stereotypes," in de la Garza, et al., *op. cit.,* discusses the socialization patterns of minorities in general and suggests that what is surprising is that there is such little apathy and/or alienation among Chicano, Black and poor whites. Also David Loye, *The Healing of a Nation* (New York: Delta, 1971), pp. 27-33.

33. Alfredo Cuellar, "Perspective on Politics," in Joan W. Moore with Alfredo Cuellar, *Mexican Americans* (Englewood Cliffs: Prentice Hall, 1970); Ellwyn R. Stoddard, "Significant Stages in Mexican American Organizational Development," summary materials from a presentation to a workshop on Southwest Ethnic Groups, The Cross-Cultural Southwest Ethnic Study Center, The University of Texas at El Paso, July 28, 1972.

34. A. Gutierrez, *op. cit.*

35. Rendon, op. cit., p. 263.

36. Acuna, *op. cit.,* p. 250; Rendon, *op. cit.,* p. 243.

37. Acuna, *op. cit.,* p. 247; J. A. Gutierrez, *op. cit.,* p. 19.

38. The alternative explanation is that Mexican Americans are never "the best man." Unless frankly racist arguments are accepted, this view is untenable.

39. Race as used here is national race. See Philip Mason, *Race Relations* (New York: Oxford, 1970), pp. 9-10. The significance of this is that not all individuals of Mexican ancestry are preceived by Anglo voters as Mexican

Americans. Moreover, those individuals acceptable to Anglo voters have often not been validated as leaders by the Mexican American people. See Section II.

40. Dan Nimmo and William E. Oden, *The Texas Political System* (Englewood Cliffs: Prentice Hall, 1971), pp. 55-57.

41. Jeffrey K. Hadden, Louis H. Masotti, and Victor Thiessen, "The Making of the Negro Mayors, 1967," *Transaction,* Jan.-Feb., 1968, pp. 21-30, discuss the complexity of identifying the American voter's racial attitudes.

42. Karl W. Deutsch, *Politics and Government: How People Decide Their Fate* (Boston: Houghton Mifflin, 1970).

43. *El Paso Times,* May 28, 1972.

44. *El Paso Times,* May 20, 1972; June 3, 1972.

45. Perhaps the most controversial studies in this area are Edward C. Banfield and James Q. Wilson, "Public Regardiness as a Values Premise in Voting Behavior," *American Political Science Review* 58 (Dec., 1964), 876-887; Raymond E. Wolfinger and John Osgood Field, "Political Ethos and the Structure of City Politics," *APSR* 60 (June, 1966), 306-326; Edward C. Banfield and James O. Wilson, "Political Ethos Revisited," *APSR* 65 (Dec., 1971), 1048-1062; Wolfinger, "The Persistence . . ."; For a useful collection of empirical studies see Brett W. Hawkins and Robert A. Lorinskas, *The Ethnic Factor in American Politics* (Columbus: Charles E. Merrill, 1970).

46. Michael Parenti, "American Pluralism: The View from the Bottom," *Journal of Politics* 32 (Aug., 1970) 501-530.

47. Stokely Carmichael and Charles V. Hamilton, *Black Power* (New York: Vintage Books, 1967), p. 7.

48. Chuck Stone, *Black Political Power in America* (New York: Delta, 1968), p. 51.

49. Hadden, et. al., *op. cit.,* pp. 21-30.

50. *Ibid.,* p. 24.

51. *Ibid.,* pp. 24-25.

52. *Ibid.,* p. 27.

53. Democrats in Arizona followed this pattern in voting against Raul Castro in the 1970 gubernatorial campaign.

54. Grebler, et. al., *op. cit.,* pp. 551-552 discuss the validation problem of Mexican American leaders. For an interesting exchange on this question see Rudolph O. de la Garza and John Womack, Jr., "An Exchange on 'The Chicanos,' " *The New York Review of Books* 20 (April 19, 1973), 41-42.

III. Nonconventional Politics

PLAYING AT ACCOMMODATION POLITICS, THE MEXICAN AMERICAN HAS MET very little success. The "old-style" politics does not seem to have enabled the Chicano to share in the rewards of pluralistic politics to the same extent that other ethnic groups have. Political achievements to this point in time, particularly before the "new-style" politics of the mid-1960s, have resulted in very little political power flowing to the Chicano community. Even in the case of a relatively successful state such as New Mexico where Chicanos occupy many political offices, the political, social, economic, and educational advances of the Chicano masses have been minimal, as is evidenced in the article on "Manitos and Chicanos in New Mexico Politics."

The fact that accommodation politics seems not to have sufficed for colored minorities in this day and age has led to the employment by these groups of "new-style" nonconventional type politics. These are politics which tend toward disruption or confrontation with the political power structure, politics whose tactics tend to upset defenders of the status quo. These include such activities as demonstrations, marches, boycotts, walkouts, sit-ins, etc.; tactics which have been used with substantial success by, for example, the Afro American, beginning with the civil rights activities of the mid-1950s and continuing through today.

Accommodation style politics does not seem to work for the Chicano for several reasons. One that cannot be overlooked is his color. Being a racial minority like the black, Asian American, or native American, he has been excluded for many decades from full participation in pluralist politics. This has led to his being estranged from the system. It has prevented him from developing the kinds of skills and resources necessary to more successfully participate in accommodation politics. Moreover, Chicanos are seeking new goals in their movement—not only a pragmatic accommodation through the rewarding of tangible benefits, but also the preservation of Chicano cultural values (*Chicanismo*). Most importantly, the system itself has changed. The social, economic, and political conditions of the 1970s are much different than those encountered by the earlier urbanized, mainly white, ethnic groups who have been able to achieve some level of success through the use of traditional politics. The classic urban political machine has largely disappeared; much of its political power has gone to Washington. Most of the preferred political positions are already occupied by old-line Anglos and by the newer white ethnics. Secondary preferment positions in the educational, economic, and social fields are already filled, leaving the current possessors of political office no room for movement. Thus the system is a great deal more rigid and closed to the Chicano than it has been to white ethnic minorities.

One way of viewing the different situation in which the Chicano has been placed compared to other ethnic minorities is the "colonial" analogy. Examining the Chicano's historical contact with the U.S. core culture, some political scientists hold that this analogy is the paradigm which best explains the position of the Chicano today. The model of *internal colonialism* is explained in the article by Professors Barrera, Muñoz, and Ornelas, who take issue with some previous studies and suggest that because the Chicano situation is much different than that of other groups in American society, Chicanos must employ different strategies to effect political change.

Following the two introductory articles, three types of nonconventional politics will be explored. First, we will look at some examples of the politics of Chicano separatism. Second, we will examine old- and new-style radical politics, often identified in the core culture's mind as *the* style of Chicano politics. And third, some views on the use of violence as a political resource will be presented.

19: MANITOS AND CHICANOS IN NEW MEXICO POLITICS

F. Chris Garcia

IN ANY DISCUSSION OF MEXICAN AMERICAN PARTICIPATION IN SYSTEM politics, the case of New Mexico is inevitably described as a "deviant" situation, the exception to many generalizations about Chicano politics in the Southwest.[1] Manitos[2] are usually described as participating in politics at a much higher level than persons of Mexican heritage in other states. The purpose of this essay is to elaborate in more detail the political status of Manitos in New Mexico and compare the situation in this state with that in other parts of Aztlan. We shall first briefly review the unique political history of the state, then survey the present socio-political status of its Spanish-speaking population, and finally examine the effects of the Chicano *movimiento* on Manitos in New Mexico politics.

THE HISTORICAL POLITICAL TRADITION

The "differences" in New Mexico are largely the result of its unique historical experience.[3] Exploration north from Mexico in the sixteenth century largely proceeded up the largest north-south river in the area, the Rio Grande, which runs down the center of the state. The first major Spanish-Mexican expedition to proceed a great distance inland was led by Coronado in the 1540s, and the earliest "permanent" settlement stemming from the exploration of the land at that time known as New Spain was established by the Onate expedition at the end of the century in what is now the Santa Fe-Espanola area. Santa Fe, the oldest capital city in the U.S., was founded in 1609. Thereafter, with the exception of the Pueblo Revolt period, the Rio

Reprinted from *Aztlan: Chicano Journal of the Social Sciences and Arts* 4, no. 2.

Grande Valley of New Mexico, particularly in the northern region, was the most populated of the Spanish-Mexican settled areas. Population branched out of the valley into the larger Rio Grande watershed area of north-central New Mexico. Because of the distance from what was two centuries later to become Mexico, the early Manitos were greatly isolated from the culture of the home base. Due to their isolation, the Manitos developed their own cultural styles which evolved from contact between the Spanish and Mestizo culture of the explorers and that of the indigenous dwellers of the area, primarily the (Pueblo) Indian. Parcels of land granted by the King of Spain provided for the development of a self-contained, pueblo-rural style of life which evolved into viable, thriving forms of social, economic, and political institutions. The residents developed valuable skills of political administration and organization necessary to provide for both their material and spiritual needs. Political mechanisms, including elected community councils, were established both for the allocation of water resources through an extensive irrigation system and for the self-government of land grants, including the determination of grazing rights. The Penitente Brotherhood, an indigenous religious and fraternal organization, provided additional political education.[4]

Crucial to understanding the unique situation of Manitos in New Mexico politics, then, are two facts stemming from the unique heritage of the area. (1) The Mexican-Spanish in New Mexico had less as well as briefer contact with Mexico and a much longer period of developing a distinctive Spanish-Mestizo-Pueblo Indian culture than did Chicanos in other parts of the Southwest. (2) Because of their relative isolation and consequent self-containment Manitos developed, by necessity, their own political (as well as social, religious, and economic) institutions, thus giving them invaluable experience in political affairs as well as providing them some organizational bases more resistant to extracultural influence.[5]

Most of what is now New Mexico became part of the United States as a consequence of the conquest by the United States in the Mexican War and legally through the Treaty of Guadalupe Hidalgo in 1848. At the time of the signing of the treaty, it is estimated that over 80 percent of the Spanish-speaking people in the Southwest resided in New Mexico.[6] Thus, when the United States government was imposed on this area, it was *super*imposed on an area with a well-developed political culture. Although substantial damage has been done to the Manito culture through its sometimes hostile encounter with the Anglo culture, the fact that a strong organizational base had been in existence for over two centuries has helped bolster the effort of individuals to retain their cultural and political heritage. Although contact with the Anglo-American core culture has vitiated many of the traditional facets of Spanish-American life, the political inheritance of the past continues to differentiate contemporary Chicano politics in New Mexico from those in other areas.

POLITICAL PARTICIPATION AND IDENTIFICATION

One of the distinguishing characteristics of Manito politics in New Mexico, *vis à vis* other states, is the high degree of mass political involvement. Politics is an integral part of the life of residents of northern New Mexico. Many families have been in electoral politics for generations and rare is the individual who is not aware of the current political situation in his locale. Unlike the general pattern of comparatively low level of voting found in many Mexican American areas, the Manito has participated to a degree at least equalling, if not surpassing that of the Anglo American in the same election.[8] Voter turnout is often as high as voter registration. Party identification as a whole usually parallels the national trends. Before the New Deal, Hispanos were mainly Republican-affiliated, but since then most are registered Democrats. This is not to say that they are captives of the Democratic party, because several Republicans have been elected from these areas into local and state offices.

Up to this point, our discussion has been somewhat misleading, because we have emphasized that area of New Mexico which is most distinctive.[9] Although north central New Mexico features the highest concentration of Spanish-speaking residents, they reside throughout the state. In the southern and particularly the southeastern portion of New Mexico, the situation is much more similar to that in other southwestern states, especially the bordering state of Texas. Most of the Mexican Americans in this part of the state are more recent immigrants, typically emigrating from Mexico after its independence from Spain and especially after the Mexican Revolution. As such, they entered an Anglo-dominated economic and political area much like the situation in Texas. The *Mexicanos* of these areas, subject to discriminatory treatment given minority groups, are accordingly less active in political affairs. Rather than being in a position of a stable, confident majority within which divisions along partisan lines occur, they are in a disadvantaged "minority" situation with a consequent alignment with the Democratic party.

Chicanos in the only metropolitan area of the state, Bernalillo County (Albuquerque), have found themselves in a rapidly transitional environment. Before World War II the Spanish-surnamed population residing in the original area of settlement, the Rio Grande valley, were a majority and were major forces in each party. However, with the great influx of Anglos in the last three decades, the Chicanos' situation has moved toward the role of the Democratic-affiliated minority group most influential in Democratic primaries. However, the voting level of Albuquerque Chicanos remains at traditionally high levels.

MANITOS IN DECISION-MAKING POSITIONS

Related to the distinctively high level of mass participation in electoral politics is the conparatively large number of positions of political authority occupied by New Mexico Hispanos. Political tradition dictates that one of the U.S. senators be of Spanish-Mexican heritage, and in addition the lieutenant governorship has developed into a Chicano spot. New Mexico, consequently, has the nation's only senator of Hispanic background, Joseph Montoya; its current lieutenant-governor is Roberto Mondragon. At the present time, one of New Mexico's two members of the U. S. House of Representatives is Manuel Lujan, a Republican representing the northern congressional district. Approximately one-third (32 percent) of the state legislature is of Spanish-Mexican descent—15 of 42 (36 percent) in the Senate and 21 of 70 (30 percent) in the House. This roughly equals the proportion of the Spanish heritage persons in the state population, estimated at between 30 and 40 percent.

At the local level, it has been noted that: "In New Mexico . . . Spanish Americans usually run their towns when they are numerous enough to do so; in Colorado, Texas, and Arizona they do not."[10] While this is not an entirely accurate description today, as a generality it still holds true. A recent analysis[11] reveals that in those areas where Manitos are generally over 50 percent of the population, the local governmental units are heavily occupied by Spanish-surname elected officials, contributing to a state-wide mean percentage of local officeholders quite proportionate to the state's percentage of Chicanos in the population. The average, however, obscures the great underrepresentation of significant proportions of Mexicanos in the non-Hispanic areas of the state.

IMPLICATIONS FOR THE CHICANO POLITICAL MOVIMIENTO

The discussion presented so far might lead one to believe that the current Chicano Movimiento would be largely irrelevant to the Spanish American in New Mexico, but such is definitely *not* the case. The reasons for this paradox can be understood upon closer examination of the apparently "satisfactory" political status of the Manito.

The existence of a large proportion of ethnic political representation might imply that the general population of that group enjoys commensurate social and economic advantages in terms of the customary socioeconomic indicators of education, income, occupation, and housing. A few statistics suffice to demonstrate that *La Raza* has not gained proportionate success in these areas. Median family income for Chicanos in the state is $6,057, compared to $8, 117 for Anglos; 29.4 percent of Mexican Americans have incomes below the poverty level, while only 16.4 percent of the Anglo population lives at that level. While Anglo Americans have attained 12.2 years of education, Mexicanos average almost three years less schooling, 9.7 years.[12] Moreover in the Hispanic counties, where most of the public officeholders are Spanish Americans, the poverty of the people is even greater.[13] It is apparent that the individual political and socioeconomic "success" of some Spanish Americans has not been reflected in a comparable elevation for the masses; the people remain in a subordinate socioeconomic position. The vertical mobility of some Spanish Americans has not brought a corresponding elevation in the body of the Chicano people. Thus a movement that, among other things, is aimed at improving the plight of *La Raza* as a whole has a considerable and constantly increasing appeal in the state of New Mexico.

It must not be forgotten that one of the earliest manifestations of *La Causa* was the effort of Reies Lopez Tijerina and the Alianza de Pueblos Libres to organize the poor in northern New Mexico into a concerted effort to secure justice for the residents of that area whose land had been unjustly taken from them.[14] While many New Mexicans, both Anglo and "Spanish," reacted in negative shock to some of his more notorious activities, today a great many Chicanos and a substantial number of Anglos lend sympathetic support to the objectives of the Alianza. Tijerina's activities plus the Huelga movement of Cesar Chavez have strengthened a sense of ethnic consciousness and solidarity and have sensitized the public to examine more closely the relationships between the Anglo and Mexican American citizens of the state.

A few years back, little or no notice was taken of Mexican holidays, for example. Today *el Cinco de Mayo* and Mexican Independence day are formally celebrated, and demands are made that educational administrators close the schools for their observance. Marches and mass demonstrations have been held in several of the cities and the UFWOC and Mexican flag are displayed prominently. Student groups such as UMAS (United Mexican American Students) at the University of New Mexico are actively pressing demands for greater cultural awareness and educational benefits at several universities and high schools throughout the state. In fact Chicano student pressure was largely responsible for the appointment of Dr. Francisco Angel to the presidency of New Mexico Highlands University. Self-defense organizations, such as the Black Berets (La Gorras Negras) in Albuquerque, have risen in reaction to perceived discriminatory treatment by the police.

In the past few years, local units of La Raza Unida party have been organized in several urban areas, mainly in those areas such as Albuquerque and southern New Mexico, where Chicanos have been influential only as a minority auxiliary of the Democratic party. Very recently, El Partido La Raza Unida de Nuevo Mejico has been certified as a political party at the state level.[15] Students of Manito politics have suggested that while, "in theory the organization of a third party based upon cultural affiliation has much to recommend it," it would be almost impossible to effectuate this because of the lack of economic independence of the Hispano, the intraethnic class distinctions and retaliation by Anglo Americans.[16] Deep-rooted party affiliations with the major parties are an additional obstacle. Yet, the spirit of the

Chicano movement based in the pride and determination of the working class, have overcome these hurdles. The unfortunate stereotyping of Manitos by Chicanos outside of New Mexico as unconcerned and uninvolved with *Chicanismo* and *La Causa* is certainly far from the mark. Because the development of the Chicano movement in New Mexico bears the stamp of the particular history of that state makes it no less significant, even though its manifestations and impact may vary from other sections of Aztlán.

In addition to these developments, which themselves are similar to those taking place wherever Chicanos are concentrated, some occurrences are more particular to the Manito situation. In many other regions, Chicanos are attempting to secure representation on governmental bodies, but in New Mexico the "quota" of such placements has already been attained in the northern area, although representation is still below proportionality in other parts of the state. In areas where Spanish-surnamed individuals occupy political offices, the strategy has been to either (1) persuade the individual officeholder to use his position to do more for the mass of Chicano people or (2) replace other officials (those considered irrevocably vendidos) with Chicanos more attuned to the needs and demands of *La Raza.* These efforts have indeed produced some negative reactions from persons, both Anglo and Spanish American, who are wary of any effort to change the status quo, in which they have secured a favorable niche. Some Spanish-heritage *politicos* still resent the term *Chicano* and prefer the euphemism *Spanish American*, for example. But this situation is changing rapidly. Senator Montoya for example, has incorporated the term Chicano as a referent, has been instrumental in efforts at organizing a national Chicano political caucus, and has been an outspoken critic of the depressed status of the Chicano. Other Spanish-heritage public officials have also come to identify themselves with Chicanos. Thus New Mexico Chicanos seeking political objectives similar to those being sought through Aztlán may have a potential advantage. Rather than working to replace Anglo officials with Chicanos, the strategy can be to overcome the reluctance of the Spanish American politician to identify himself with his own ethnic group.

One problem is that in many instances, the "power" of the Manito official is based not in the strength of his community but rather upon validation by those Anglos in actual control. Such is the case with many of the barrio leaders in the state's urban areas such as Albuquerque. Certain community representatives enjoy positions of prestige and authority primarily because of their role as a liaison between barrio residents and the Anglos running the local governmental institutions. It is true that these *politicos* are able to provide various intermediary and ombudsman services for their community. However, this role does not alter the basic inequality in the distribution of political power between the Chicano and Anglo communities, and as some Chicano activists have complained, the *patron* or *politico* role may only tend to perpetuate the imbalanced status quo. Although individual case problems may be temporarily resolved, because the *politico's* power is based more in the Anglo superstructure than in the barrio, collective socioeconomic advancement and redistribution of power may be retarded.

Even in instances where Manitos recognize and accept their cultural heritage and also owe their position to the Chicano community, problems still exist. In many of the northern *pueblos,* Chicanos' control of the political organization may be rather superficial successes, because the resources which could be allocated through politics are simply absent. Anglo control of the *economic* resources of these communities is a common feature. Many of the major businesses, such as banks, and much of the land is owned by the Anglo minority. While this form of separate spheres of influence, with the Chicanos dominating politics and the Anglos controlling the economic resources, allows for peaceful coexistence between the ethnic groups, it also means that not many mass material benefits are forthcoming to the Chicano community. Contributing to this is the poor economic condition of the state, which currently ranks forty-first in per capita income.[17] Many of the poor Chicano's living in the *pueblos* and barrios are thus dependent on federally-funded welfare programs for their survival.

Since traditional forms of local electoral politics seem to have reached their limits of achievement, new directions of Chicano politics are being evidenced. Political power is shallow if not rooted in economic foundations, and attempts are being made to raise the economic level of the people through alternative means. A multitude of efforts are being exerted in the field of education, which is one of the most direct routes to economic advancement. Demands for bilingual and bicultural programs, relevant to the Chicano student, are often heard. Educational institutions are pressured to employ Chicano administrators and faculty more representative of the population characteristics of the area in which they are situated. At the college level, in addition to the above needs, demands are heard for increased recruitment of Chicano students, more financial aid, and programs designed to increase their chances of obtaining a degree. At another level Chicanos are organizing to exert influence on the welfare bureaucracy. The "community participation" elements of OEO and Model Cities programs have provided the additional opportunities for gaining experience in bureaucratic politics and learning the rules of the political game. Nowadays, when decisions are made by the federal, state, or local agencies which directly affect the lives of the Chicano communities, it is almost always followed, if not preceded, by organized Chicano reaction.

Because many of these efforts are in the area of educational and administrative politics, Chicano participation more often than not takes the form of "direct action," i.e., marches, meetings with officials, petitions, and protest demonstrations rather than relying exclusively on those electoral forms of politics which seemed to have yielded very limited accomplishments even when played intensely and in the best "American" tradition. The pride and unity fostered by the Chicano movement has provided the socio-psychological foundations for these mass activities.

CONCLUSION

New Mexico Manitos are participating more and more in political activities similar to those of Chicanos throughout Aztlán. It is true that their distinctive political status, based on a unique historical experience, continues to characterize the Manito situation. A high degree of interest and participation in electoral politics has been and continues to be the norm; in addition, the comparatively large number of elected and appointed *Hispano* public officials has remained fairly constant. New political strategies cannot ignore these features.

Yet, while it is true that Manito politics are characteristically distinguishable in some ways from those in Texas or California, this is not to say that they are any less Chicano. To be successful the Chicano movement, while embodying many common goals, must adapt itself to the particular socio-historical circumstances of each region. California-style Chicano politics may not be wholly adaptable to the situation in New Mexico or Texas. Some common objectives, such as pride in one's cultural heritage, self-determination and equality of social, economic and political opportunity are found wherever the Chicano movement is occurring, but regional variations in political strategies and tactics should not be discouraged.

The politics of New Mexico Chicanos is benefiting from *El Movimiento* in that its reality has broken the enchanted spell which had seemed to prevent people from recognizing the depressed, subordinated status of the Manito masses in the "Land of Enchantment." As one observer has noted: "The Hispano people of northern New Mexico . . . have shown elephantine patience through over a hundred years of Anglo exploitation, abetted by assimilated Hispano local leaders. With the rise of effective protest by . . . Mexican Americans in equally desperate situations, it is doubtful that the frustrations of the Hispano people of the region will continue to be accepted as what life is or should be."[18]

The traditional political resourcefulness of the Manito, newly replenished and revitalized by the Chicano movement, will no doubt endure until the democratic tenets of equality, liberty, and justice *for all* become a reality.

NOTES

1. As, for example, by Y. Arturo Cabrera, *Emerging Faces: The Mexican Americans* (Dubuque, Iowa: William C. Brown, 1971), p. 32; Alfredo Cuellar,

"Perspective on Politics," in Joan Moore, *Mexican Americans* (Englewood Cliffs, N. J.: Prentice-Hall, 1970), p. 137; John Martinez, "Leadership and Politics," in *La Raza: The Forgotten Americans,* Julian Samora, ed., (Notre Dame, Ind.: University of Notre Dame Press, 1966), p. 47; and Joan Moore, *op. cit.* pp. 15, 20.

2. While many of the names used to describe those Americans of Mexican-Spanish ancestry, e.g., Chicano, Mexican American, Spanish American, Hispano, etc., will be used interchangeably in this report, the author is aware of the subtle connotations attached to each. However, playing the "name game" might detract from the substantive content of the article. The term *Manito* (shortened form of *Hermanito*) will be used to refer to those New Mexicans of Mexican-Spanish heritage, since the author is familiar with no instances of its being applied to other groups.

3. Nancie L. Gonzales, *The Spanish Americans of New Mexico: A Heritage of Pride,* (Albuquerque: University of New Mexico Press, 1969); Carey McWilliams, *North from Mexico: The Spanish-Speaking People of the United States* (New York: Greenwood Press, 1968).

4. Discussed at length by Jack E. Holmes, *Politics in New Mexico* (Albuquerque: University of New Mexico Press, 1967), pp. 29-38.

5. The importance of organizational bases for ethnic politics has been presented by Edgar Litt, *Ethnic Politics in America* (Glenview, Ill.: Scott-Foresman, 1970). For a discussion of the effect of ethnic organizations on rates of cultural integration see Raymond Breton, "Institutional Completeness of Ethnic Communities and the Personal Relations of Immigrants," *American Journal of Sociology* 70 (July-May, 1964-65), 193-205.

6. McWilliams, *op. cit.,* p. 52.

7. Clark S. Knowlton, "Changing Spanish American Villages of Northern New Mexico," *Journal of Mexican American Studies* 1, no. 1 (Fall 1970), 31-43.

8. Ernest B. Fincher has provided historical evidence of the higher level of voting participation by Hispanos in "Spanish-Americans as a Political Factor in New Mexico, 1912-1950," Ph. D. diss., New York University, 1950. See also Holmes, *op. cit.*

9. For an elaboration of the intrastate variations of political subcultures see F. Chris Garcia and Robert D. Wrinkle, "New Mexico: Urban Politics in a State of Varied Political Cultures," in *Politics in the Urban Southwest,* Robert Wrinkle, ed., (Division of Government Research, University of New Mexico, 1971); also Holmes, *op. cit.*

10. Garcia and Wrinkle, *op. cit.,* p. 20.

11. *Ibid.*

12. U. S. Bureau of the Census, Census of Population, 1970. *General Social and Economic Characteristics, Final Report PC (1)-C33, New Mexico.*

13. In the northern New Mexico county of Mora, 60.2 percent of the incomes of its Spanish-heritage families fall below the poverty level, and the median family income is $2,882, according to the 1970 census.

14. For accounts of the Alianza movement see Patricia Bell Blawis, *Tijerina and the Land Grants: Mexican Americans in Struggle for their Heritage,* New World Paperbacks (New York: International Publishers, 1971);

Richard M. Gardner, *Grito! Reies Tijerina and the New Mexico Land Grant War of 1967,* (Indianapolis: Bobbs-Merrill, 1970); Michael Jenkinson, *Tijerina–Land Grant Conflict in New Mexico,* (Albuquerque: Paisano Press, 1968); Clark S. Knowlton, "Tijerina, Hero of the Militants," *Journal of Mexican American Studies* 1, no. 2 (Winter 1971); Joseph Love, "La Raza: Mexican Americans in Rebellion," *Trans-Action,* February, 1969, pp. 35-41; Peter Nabokov, *Tijerina and the Courthouse Raid,* (Albuquerque: University of New Mexico Press, 1969); and Frances Swadesh, "The Alianza Movement: Catalyst for Social Change in New Mexico," *Proceedings of the 1968 Annual Spring Meeting of the American Ethnological Society,* Seattle, pp. 162-177.

15. *Albuquerque Journal,* July 28, 1972, p. 1.

16. Fincher, *op. cit.,* pp. 288-290.

17. U. S. Department of Commerce, *Survey of Current Business* 52, no. 4 (April, 1972), 20.

18. Thomas Maloney, "Factionalism and Futility: A Case Study of Political and Economic Reform in New Mexico," *Spanish-Speaking People in the United States, Proceedings of the 1968 Annual Spring Meeting of the American Ethnological Society.* (Seattle: University of Washington Press, 1968), p. 20.

20: THE BARRIO AS AN INTERNAL COLONY

Mario Barrera, Carlos Muñoz, and Charles Ornelas

MEXICAN AMERICANS HAVE OFTEN REFERRED TO THEMSELVES AS A FORgotten people, and to a large extent this has been true. Within the last few years, various dramatic activities connected with what is loosely referred to among Chicanos[1] as "The Movement" have led to a partial discovery of America's second largest minority by the media, politicians, academics, and government administrators. As in the case of Latin America after the Cuban Revolution, there is now being evidenced a sudden concern for the welfare of Chicanos and a desire to help them overcome their "underdeveloped" status. However, this latest Alliance for Progress venture on the domestic front is likely to produce the same striking non-results as its international counterpart, and if it does it will largely be due to the same sorts of causes. Chief among these will be a mistaken analysis, insufficient funding, a certain amount of self-serving by the earnest benefactors, and a determined unwillingness to see that the problems being treated have, in fact, been largely produced by those same benefactors.

What is needed at the present time is an analysis of the Chicano situation that avoids some of the more blatant distortions that have been perpetrated by writers viewing the Chicano reality through lenses colored by American society's dominant myths about ethnic relations. Our concern in this paper is to further such an analysis, focusing on the political dimension.

"The Barrio as an Internal Colony," by M. Barrera, C. Muñoz, and C. Ornelas in Harlan Hahn's (ed.) *Urban Affairs Annual Reviews,* Vol. 6 (1972), pp. 465-498, is reprinted by permission of the publisher, Sage Publications, Inc., Beverly Hills, Calif.

The authors would like to thank Carlos Cortés, Robert Blauner, Itsugi Igawa, and Marcelo Cavarozzi for their comments on an earlier draft of this paper.

One beginning point is the recognition that Chicanos are now predominantly an urban people. The popular stereotype of Mexican Americans as overwhelmingly rural continues to be perpetuated by television documentaries, and by the broad coverage given such rurally based movements as César Chávez's United Farm Workers in California and Reies Tijerina's Alianza in New Mexico. Yet the 1960 census shows almost eighty percent of the "Spanish-surname" population in the Southwest living in urban areas, a figure roughly comparable to that of the Anglo population (Grebler et al., 1970: 113). In the cities, most Mexican Americans continue to live in relatively well-defined areas, which are referred to as "barrios."

Although Chicanos are found in many areas of the Midwest and Pacific Northwest, they are concentrated in the five southwestern states, and this concentration increases their political significance. Mexican Americans outnumber all nonwhite groups combined in each of the southwestern states, and in 1960 constituted approximately twelve percent of the population in this area (Grebler et al., 1970: 105). The Chicano presence in such large, politically pivotal states as California and Texas should also be noted.

At the present time there do not exist a large number of studies that deal with Chicano politics in urban areas. . . . We summarize some of the dominant themes in this literature, and argue that these writings have been influenced by a latent model which we call the "assimilation/accommodation model." In analyzing Chicano politics, these writers dwell on what they perceive as weak leadership and lack of political organization, which they attribute to characteristics of Mexican American culture and social organization. They project solutions based on an analogy with European immigrants, calling for cultural assimilation and the politics of accommodation.

. . . We develop an alternative perspective. . . . Our view is that the barrio is best perceived as an internal colony, and that the problem of Chicano politics is essentially one of powerlessness. Powerlessness, in turn, is a condition produced and maintained by the dominant Anglo society through a number of mechanisms, some of which we have begun to identify. We consider the contemporary situation to be a form of internal neocolonialism, characterized by the predominance of relatively subtle and indirect mechanisms.

The concept of internal colonialism has been advanced by others to describe the position of Afro-Americans in the United States, and has also been applied by some Latin American scholars to situations in their countries. The general concept appears to apply to a number of cases, and is valuable in emphasizing the structual similarities and common historical origins of the positions of Third World peoples inside and outside the United States. However, it should not be used to obscure variations in individual cases. The situation of Chicanos is in many ways unique. . . .

To be colonized means to be affected in every aspect of one's life: political, economic, social, cultural, and psychological. In the present essay we have limited ourselves to discussing primarily the political aspect, not because we consider the other elements to be less important, but because of limitations of time and space. The economic aspect in particular needs to be much more thoroughly researched than it has been to this point. Hopefully it will be possible to put together a more complete picture of internal colonialism in the near future.

The development of an adequate model of the Chicano position is essential if realistic solutions to Chicano problems are to be forthcoming. In the concluding part of this essay we survey some aspects of the contemporary political scene and some of the strategies for change that have been adopted or tried out by various groups. While Chicano urban political groups vary in their analyses and their approaches, their actions can generally be seen as a response to some aspect of the Chicano's colonized status. . . .

THE ASSIMILATION/ACCOMMODATION MODEL

There are several themes and perspectives which recur in the studies which have just been summarized.* In this part, we shall indicate some of the most important ones and establish links among them in terms of what we will call the assimilation/accommodation model.

Lack of Representation

One observation on which all the authors agreed is that urban Chicanos are unrepresented or underrepresented politically. This nonrepresentation is expressed throughout the range of local offices, from mayor to councilman to grand jury to relatively minor administrative positions, and extends to party offices. This lack of representation is related to the Chicano's disadvantaged socio-economic position, and often condemns him to the role of victim of such public policies as urban renewal.

Weak Political Leadership and Organizations: Low Participation

Another common theme in these studies is a perceived lack of strong political leadership, weak or nonexistent political organizations, and generally

* [The summary is not reprinted here. The works referred to are: Ruth Tuck (1946), Sister F. J. Woods (1949), D'Antonio and Form (1965), Arthur Rubel (1966), Samora and Lamanna (1967), and Edward Banfield (1965). Consult reference list at the end of this article–Ed.]

low rates of participation. Several of the authors refer to factionalism among Chicanos and to a generalized feeling of suspicion toward the leadership. In most cases, the authors argue that it is these various elements which explain the lack of representation. In turn, these elements are explained in terms of two sets of factors, cultural and social-economic.

Cultural factors are given considerable weight by Woods, who refers to the Chicano's "individualism" as a barrier to collective action. This theme is frequently echoed in other studies of Mexican Americans. Sheldon (1966: 127) states that "Individualism is a major characteristic of Mexican culture . . . [whereas] Anglo-Americans have accepted the British tradition of working together to achieve a common goal and rallying round a common cause." As a consequence, "It is not surprising that Mexican-Americans have been unable to put to effective use the tool of the mass voice to promote the common good of their group."[2] Rubel . . . puts a great deal of weight on the Chicano's "personalism," which he sees as the antithesis of organized, instrumental group action. Banfield believes that Mexican Americans are held back by their fatalism.

Social-economic factors such as low levels of education and income are referred to by such authors as Banfield and D'Antonio and Form to explain the Chicano's political situation. Sheldon (1966:125) feels that the Chicano's heterogeneity is an important causal element. D'Antonio and Form also perceive a "low level of social integration."

While the existence of past and present discrimination is acknowledged by the authors (e.g., Rubel), and some even feel that this may have something to do with the Chicano's present position, only Ruth Tuck makes a point of stressing Anglo machinations as a major cause of the Mexican American's political nonrepresentation.

The Chicano as the Latest Urban Migrant

In striving to conceptualize the situation and prospects of the Mexican American community, social scientists have usually resorted to an analogy with European migrants to eastern U.S. cities. The idea here seems to be that just as various European immigrant groups have come from foreign countries to American cities, Chicanos have recently come to the cities either directly from Mexico, or by a two-step process involving initial settlement in a U.S. rural area. Thus the situation of the Chicanos now is essentially similar to the situation of the Irish or Italians at an earlier period. If Chicanos would pattern themselves on these other groups and learn from their experience, the argument goes, they can look forward to enjoying the same success those groups have gained.

The Assimilation/Accommodation Model

It is possible to view the Chicano-as-latest-urban-migrant theme as part of a broader conceptual framework, here referred to as the assimilation/accommodation model. It is our contention that this framework has functioned as a latent model for social scientists concerned with Chicanos and Chicano political patterns, affecting their perceptions and the way in which they have organized their observations. Consequently, it has also influenced their recommendations. The basic ingredients of this model are that:

(1) the situation of Chicanos is similar in most essential ways to that of European immigrants;
(2) the Chicano's disadvantaged political, economic, and social position is the result of factors inherent in Chicano culture and social organization; discrimination is mentioned as a secondary factor;
(3) through assimilating—that is, taking on the culture and ways of behaving of Anglo society—Chicanos will be able to achieve equal status with other groups in the United States;
(4) individual mobility through education is a central mechanism in this process;
(5) the process can be speeded up through organizing into pragmatic, instrumental political groups and engaging in bargaining behavior for marginal gains (the politics of accommodation).[3]

This would involve working through accepted channels and seeking change through such mechanisms as governmental programs aimed at education, employment, housing, and health. Essentially a liberal reformist position, it is compatible with the activist role assigned to the state since the Depression and the Roosevelt administration. Although the authors who have worked in this area are generally not political scientists, their political prescription fits well with the dominant pluralist model of American politics, and with the views of the policy process that derive support from the theoretical works of David Easton.[4]

A subcategory of this general model can also be identified, differing from the first slightly on point number five. This is Banfield's (1970: 257) point of view: "government cannot solve the problems of the cities and is likely to make them worse by trying. . . . [P]owerful accidental . . . forces are at work that tend to alleviate and even to eliminate the problems." The role of government is seen as essentially staying out of the way and not arousing false expectations by promising rapid change. Since Banfield shares the other assumptions of the assimilation/accommodation model, we might label his the "benign neglect" version, in order to differentiate it from the more widely held "administrative activism" variety.[5]

AN ALTERNATIVE VIEW: THE BARRIO AS INTERNAL COLONY

The basic tenets of the assimilation/accommodation model are widely held in American society, by scholars and general public alike. Perhaps the reason for its wide scholarly acceptance is precisely that is does fit well with the dominant myths and values of the wider society. In most cases, it appears to be accepted as a matter of course, without critical analysis or even acknowledgment that a particular point of view has been adopted. We hold that this perspective is mistaken. We propose an alternative means of thinking about the Chicano's urban experience: the barrio as internal colony. We believe that an internal colonial model is a more efficient means of singling out significant aspects of the Chicano's situation, more accurate in establishing cause-and-effect relationships, and more realistic in the kinds of solutions it suggests. It also serves better to organize information about Chicano politics, and thus "make sense" of it.

Adopting this point of view means accepting that the present disadvantaged situation of Chicanos is the result of oppression by the dominant Anglo society, and that this oppression is not confined to the past but continues today. Prejudice and discrimination are only one aspect of this oppression, although it may be the most widely recognized.

While the colonial status of a people is a generalized status, affecting all aspects of their existence, we will confine our discussion largely to the political dimension. In political terms, the situation of internal colonialism is manifested as a lack of control over the institutions of the barrio, and as a lack of influence over those broader political institutions that affect the barrio. In essence, then, being an internal colony means existing in a condition of *powerlessness.*[6] One result is that public and private institutions, in their dealings with Chicanos, are able to function in exploitive and oppressive ways, whether by ignorance or intent.

Before going on to describe the model in a more formal way, it is possible to indicate some of the implications of adopting this point of view. One is the rejection of the latest-urban-migrant theme. Rather than looking at Chicanos as a recently arrived group in the process of rapid assimilation into Anglo society, it must be recognized that in many cases Chicanos have existed in urban areas for a long period of time and that their disadvantaged position is actively maintained today through the workings of a set of mechanisms of domination. It is also true that many Mexican Americans have actively resisted assimilation in the interest of maintaining their historic culture and social organization.

Second, disadvantage is explainable not in terms of factors inherent in Chicano culture and social organization, but as a function of external causes.

Third, the analysis of Chicano politics in terms of weak leadership and organization is misleading. This line of reasoning is deficient in several respects: (1) It should be clear from looking at Mexico that there is nothing in the Mexican heritage that precludes effective leadership and strong political organizations from developing; (2) as Tirado (1970) has documented, there have in fact been many Mexican American community organizations that have played a political role, although often not considered political groups by outside observers because they also perform nonpolitical functions. In addition, many such organizations have been forced to adopt a low profile and conceal their political functions because of the threat of reprisal from the dominant society; and (3) the existence of overtly political organizations with a well-defined leadership varies considerably from locale to locale, as the studies reviewed earlier should make clear. One significant factor appears to be the degree of urbanization. An ongoing historical study (Cortés et al., forthcoming) shows considerable organizational variation among four Southern California cities. Much of the variation is not easily explainable and appears to be the product of complex factors and the specific historical development of the city. Unfortunately, such comparative studies are virtually nonexistent.

Finally, this perspective points to community control rather than individual mobility or the politics of accommodation as a solution to the colonized status of Chicanos.

THE INTERNAL COLONIAL MODEL

The concept of internal colonialism has been used by several American writers to refer to the ghetto or the barrio. Generally the term has been employed as an analogy with classic colonialism (Carmichael and Hamilton, 1967; Moore, 1970; Allen, 1970). The approach taken in this paper will be to define internal colonialism as a variety of the more general concept, colonialism, of which classic or "external" colonialism is another variety. We will also differentiate subcategories of internal colonialism.

Defining Characteristics

Colonialism is a complex phenomenon with many variations. No one disputes that colonialism in its modern usage refers to a relationship in which one group of people dominates and exploits another. Without going into great detail, we can adopt González-Casanova's statement (1969: 128) of colonialism as "a structure in which the relations of domination and exploitation are relations between heterogeneous and culturally different groups." The factor of race and culture is important, as González-Casanova points out, because it differentiates this exploitive relationship from one based on class, or on some other basis.

> The colonial structure and internal colonialism are distinguished from the class structure since colonialism is not only a relation of exploitation of the workers by the owners of raw materials or of production and their collaborators, but also a relation of domination and exploitation of a total population (with its distinct classes, proprietors, workers) by another population which also has distinct classes (proprietors and workers) [González-Casanova, 1969: 131-132].

The crucial distinguishing characteristic between internal and external colonialism does not appear to be so much the existence of separate territories corresponding to metropolis and colony, but the legal status of the colonized. According to our usage, a colony can be considered "internal" if the colonized population has the same formal legal status as any other group of citizens, and "external" if it is placed in a separate legal category. A group is thus internal if it is fully included in the legal-political system, and external if it is even partly excluded from equal participation in a formal sense. It may be that the term de facto colony better expresses this distinction, but the term internal is already in common use. At any rate, this definition would classify such groups as the native people of the Union of South Africa as an external colony, even though the dominant population does not have its center in an overseas metropolis. On the other hand, the Black and Chicano communities in the United States are internal colonies, since they occupy a status of formal equality, whatever the informal reality may be. The degree of formal inequality of the external colony may vary considerably, of course, so that some would resemble internal colonies more than would others.

The other important distinction to be made is that between interethnic relations that represent internal colonialism and those that are internal but noncolonial. It is precisely here that we differ from earlier writers, in that we consider Chicanos an internal colony, but not European immigrants. Robert Blauner (1969: 396) has specified four basic components that serve to distinguish the internal colonization complex:

> (1) *Forced entry.* The colonized group enters the dominant society through a forced, involuntary, process.
>
> (2) *Cultural impact.* The colonizing power carries out a policy which constrains, transforms, or destroys indigenous values, orientations, and ways of life.
>
> (3) *External administration.* Colonization involves a relationship by which members of the colonized group tend to be administered by representatives of the dominant power. There is an experience of being managed and manipulated by outsiders in terms of ethnic status.
>
> (4) *Racism.* Racism is a principle of social domination by which a group seen as inferior or different in terms of alleged biological characteristics is exploited, controlled, and oppressed socially and psychically by a superordinate group.

While Blauner's categories are useful in making the distinctions we wish to make, it is important to realize that the experience of each ethnic group in the United States has been unique in some respects. Some of his categories need to be qualified in order to fit the specific case of Chicanos.

In the first case—that of forced entry—the basic Chicano-Anglo relationship was formed in a context of conquest and subsequent take-over of the land. While it is true that a large number of Chicanos have come to the United States since that time, and may be said to have come "voluntarily," once in the country they found themselves in a situation that had been structured through violence. So while each individual may not have found himself involuntarily included in the system, the group as a whole did, and the structures and attitudes formed in the earlier period have continued in one form or another into the present.

In a more recent essay, Blauner (1972) has stressed the role of unfree labor as a factor differentiating the experience of Chicanos and other Third World peoples within the United States from the experience of European immigrants. This factor is closely related to the nature of entry into the society, and deserves more extensive treatment than we are able to give here.

Blauner's second point is also applicable, with qualification, to the Chicano experience. While it is not true that Mexican-derived culture and social organization were destroyed to the same extent as that of Blacks brought to this country in slavery, the dominant society has largely destroyed Chicano economic organization, severely limited political organization, and waged a constant attack on Chicano values and other cultural traits through the schools, the media, and other institutions.

Blauner's remarks about external administration are perfectly applicable to Chicanos, and constitute a central aspect of the internal colonial situation.

Racism, as Blauner uses it, clearly intended to include what has come to be called institutional as well as individual racism, and holds for Chicanos to a certain extent. However, it appears that in the case of Mexican Americans, cultural factors are at least as important as biological ones as a basis of discrimination, and probably more so, particularly in the urban areas. Racism should thus be considered a mixed biological/cultural category.

Combining and extending these various comments, then, we can specify what the status of internal colony means for Chicanos at two different levels. At the institutional or interpersonal level, internal colonialism means that Chicanos as a cultural/racial group exist in an exploited condition which is maintained by a number of mechanisms (to be spelled out below). This relationship is most clearly experienced as a lack of control over those institutions which affect their lives. These institutions are as a rule administered by outsiders, or at best, those who serve the outsiders' interests. This condition of powerlessness is manifested specifically in outside ownership of barrio business (Sturdivant, 1969), in Anglo domination of barrio schools, and in Chicano underrepresentation in every type of public institution. One result of this situation is that the Chicano community finds itself in a general condition of disadvantage: low incomes, poor housing, inadequate health care, low educational level, and so on. It also results in the community finding its culture and social organization under constant attack from a racist society.

At the individual level, the colonized individual finds that because he identifies himself with a particular culture, he is confronted with barriers that prevent him from achieving the economic, social, and political positions which would otherwise be accessible to him (for the economic aspect, see Schmidt, 1970). At the same time, he finds himself under psychological assault from those who are convinced of his inferiority and unworthiness.

For a Chicano, or at least for one sufficiently Caucasian in appearance, it would appear possible to escape his colonial status by completely taking on the culture of the Anglo majority, and renouncing his language, values, behavioral patterns, and self-identification. This would especially seem to be the case in the larger urban areas. While he would not achieve an equal status overnight, he would no longer be confronted with the same barriers. However, this would not produce a noncolonized Chicano, but a noncolonized non-Chicano. Thus the apparent semi-permeability of the colonial barrier for Chicanos is illusory, since there is no escape from the colonial status for an individual *as a Chicano.* If the Chicano community were to take this approach, the result would be cultural genocide. The choice presented to the Chicano community by Anglo society, then, is very clear-cut: colonialism or genocide.

The Political Dimensions of Internal Colonialism

Internal colonialism is manifested along many different dimensions: social, economic, political, psychological, cultural, and so on. Within each broad category we can identify further subdivisions. Among the political dimensions are the following.

Political Representation: Parties. While there appear to be no studies of Chicano representation within the major political parties, it is clear to those familiar with the political systems of the southwestern states that Chicanos have not been accorded many significant positions. Since Chicanos have been faithful to the Democratic party in their voting, one would expect to see many Chicanos in high Democratic party posts. Such is not the case. In California, for example, one rarely sees a Chicano name above the urban ward level.[7]

Political Representation: Governmental Bodies. Chicanos find themselves underrepresented at every level of government, from the national and state legislative bodies to county boards of supervisors, to city councils, boards of education, and grand juries (Grebler et al., 1970: 560ff, 222ff; U.S. Commission on Civil Rights, 1970, 1971). A typical situation was pointed up in a special report of the 1970 San Bernardino Grand Jury, based on a state Fair Employment Practices investigation. They refer to "gross inequities" in the hiring of Chicanos and other minorities in the various county administrative offices, and document it office by office. The investigators found that "The vast majority of those interviewed voiced no concern or knowledge of affirmative action, no need to make a concerted effort to increase the utilization of minorities, and no effort to disseminate this policy to employees" (California FEPC, 1970: 59). They also found on the part of numerous department heads attitudes that were either manifestly racist or very good substitutes (1970: 11).

The problem of nonrepresentation is even more acute than statistics show, since in many cases the representatives of the barrio are hand-picked by Anglos on the basis of acceptability to Anglos. It is also true that some Chicanos have collaborated with Anglos in every historical period. These Chicanos were often given some sort of official position, and thus are often cited to prove that Chicanos have "participated" in the system all along. But a close look will usually reveal that these representatives of the Chicano were in fact powerless subordinates of the dominant power structure. As Swadesh (1968: 165) has put it for New Mexico: "Hand-picked Hispanos served in the Legislature as junior partners to those who really held the reins. Their official task was to represent the overwhelming majority of the population, but in practice they helped keep this majority under control." Thus Chicano *interests* are even less represented than Chicano bodies. Again, this points to the centrality of the cultural factor. For a Chicano to self-consciously identify himself with the Chicano community, and with its culture and interests, is to virtually ensure that he will not be among even the token representatives chosen by outsiders.

Contact with Public Agencies. Chicano contact with public agencies is universally described in terms that can only be termed colonial. Easily the best-documented situation is that of the schools' treatment of Mexican Americans (for two recent discussions, see Carter, 1970; Castañeda et al., 1971). Among the many charges that have been listed and documented against the schools are suppression of the Spanish language, channeling Chicano children into vocational training and discouraging them from college-oriented courses, abuse of Anglo-biased testing instruments, underfunding of barrio schools, neglect of Chicano history and other academic areas, the instilling of a sense of cultural inferiority, and, in general, creating a climate that produces progressively worse performance with each passing year and results in a phenomenally high dropout rate.

While more scholarly attention has been given to education than any other area, the public agency does not exist that has not been subjected to harsh criticism by barrio representatives. The police have frequently been accused of brutality, harassment of political organization, and overzealous policing; at times they have been compared to an occupying army (U.S. Commission on Civil Rights, 1970; Morales, 1970). The courts have long been charged with discriminatory treatment (U.S. Commission on Civil Rights, 1970; Lemert and Rosberg, 1948).

The various welfare, housing, health, and antipoverty agencies operating in the cities are characterized as unable to communicate with their clients, as insensitive to the concerns of Chicanos, and as patronizing and paternalistic in their attitudes and practices (Grebler et al., 1970; Samora and Lamanna, 1967; Ornelas and González, 1971).

While the list could go on, the view from the barrio, which is to say the view of those with direct experience with these agencies, is generally clear. The kind of treatment meted out to Chicanos, of course, is a function of the overall lack of representation of Chicanos in the political system. The situation is compounded in the American political system by the way in which that system parcels out public responsibilities to private interest groups, and allows such groups to strongly influence or control public policy-making (for a detailed description and critique of this system, see Lowi, 1969). This is so because Chicanos have also been largely excluded from such groups as private real estate boards, which are incorporated officially or nonofficially into the policy-making activities of urban planning commissions, urban renewal agencies, and so on. Unfortunately, Chicanos have only begun to document the often subtle workings of the policy process as it affects Chicanos. For the time being, however, our concern is with the crude fact of external administration and its detrimental consequences for the barrio.

The Mechanisms of Political Domination

Central to an understanding of internal colonialism is a grasp of the mechanisms by which the colonial situation is maintained over time. While no definitive account is possible at this time, we can begin to list them and to advance some ideas as to their relative importance under various circumstances.

The most direct and obvious mechanisms are those involving force and outright repression. Instances range from the use of the Texas Rangers to repress Mexican American organizational efforts to the widespread Ku Klux Klan anti-Chicano terrorism of the 1920s, often with the complicity of the forces of law and order. Also included in this category would be the various forms of nonviolent reprisals that are taken against Chicanos who dare to break with established political patterns (for a recent case, see Hill, 1963; Grebler et al., 1970: 563).

A second set of mechanisms has the effect of disenfranchising Chicanos. Devices include poll taxes and literacy tests.

Outright exclusion of Chicanos from political parties and governmental bodies has already been discussed. The practice is often justified on the grounds that there are no "qualified" Chicanos available to fill the positions.

Gerrymandering is another mechanism that has found favor with those seeking to minimize Chicano political influence. Generally this consists of splitting Chicano voters into many districts, so that they do not form a sufficiently large group in any one district to elect their own representatives. The case of East Los Angeles is a prominent example (Grebler et al., 1970: 562).

A fifth mechanism involves changing the rules of the game when it becomes apparent that existing rules might lead to greater Chicano political strength. In El Paso, for instance, the political elite successfully carried out a campaign to make city elections nonpartisan after a Mexican American had won the Democratic primary election for mayor.

The mechanism of "divide and conquer" has been attested to by Pauline Kibbe (1964: 227): "When an ambitious and capable Latin American announces for office in opposition to an Anglo incumbent or candidate . . . Anglo politicians follow the tried-and-true formula of 'divide and conquer.' They immediately sponsor the candidacy of another Latin American, preferably a personal enemy of the man who has previously announced, and thereby split the Latin American vote and assure the election of the Anglo candidate." Ruth Tuck has already been cited in connection with Anglo attempts to create divisions among Chicanos.

When outright exclusion of Chicanos is not possible, the resort is likely to be tokenism. This involves minimal representation of Chicanos, with the representatives likely to be carefully selected so as to play the game. Tokenism includes not only "representative tokenism" but also "policy tokenism," in which minor but highly publicized policy concessions are made (Muñoz, 1971: 98-99).

The mechanism of cooptation has already been mentioned several times. By offering limited material and status benefits to those Mexican American individuals who are deemed acceptable on cultural grounds and who are willing to act as information sources and token showpieces, the Anglo elite in effect co-opts them into the structure of domination. Watson and Samora (1954) have carefully described the workings of this mechanism in one Colorado community, and have pointed out its detrimental consequences for the development of more effective Chicano political action.

Of all the mechanisms of domination, however, the racist mobilization of bias may be the most pervasive and the most subtle in its effects. Carlos Cortés (1971) has documented the way in which symbols are manipulated in the media and in the schools to perpetuate the myths of biological and cultural inferiority. In an earlier section of this paper we illustrated the defensiveness this produces in Chicanos, and the way in which this defensiveness prevents Chicanos from acting in the interests of their own community. Any Chicano in public office who self-consciously serves the needs of the Chicano community leaves himself open to charges of "reverse racism" and divisive parochialism. That such charges come from Anglos who have systematically excluded Chicanos for decades and who continue to serve only non-Chicano interests does not render their charges ineffective. To the extent that Chicanos have been manipulated into internalizing the prevailing biases, they are driven into a defensive posture and into seeking Anglo approval for their actions (see, e.g., the statements by Chicano politicians in a California city in Faragher, forthcoming . . .). This pattern of behavior is undoubtedly reinforced by the Chicano experience of having to function in institutions, such as the schools, dominated by non-Chicano authority figures from whom it is necessary to gain approval (Cortés, personal communication). Thus in this instance, as in many others, the various mechanisms of domination reinforce each other and multiply their effects.

Neocolonialism

The various mechanisms of domination that have been discussed vary considerably in their degree of subtlety or overtness. The mechanisms of force and repression are unmistakable and relatively uncomplicated; many of the others are more subtle, and thus more difficult to combat. There is a danger in focusing on the cruder measures and underrating the less direct, but often more effective, mechanisms. We are inclined to disagree with Blauner (1969: 404) when he states that "the police are the most crucial institution maintaining the colonized status of Black Americans." In most cases the police do not have to be used, because more sophisticated mechanisms have removed the threat, or, preferably, prevented a threat from arising.

What needs to be recognized is that the American political system has become increasingly sophisticated in its methods of exercising control, and that power holders prefer to use indirect methods wherever possible. In the case of the Chicano, the last one hundred twenty years have seen a change from a relatively direct system of exploitation aimed at depriving him of his land and establishing him in a subordinate status, to a more subtle system functioning to maintain him in that position. At this point it may be well to characterize this change by referring to the earlier situation as "classic" internal colonialism, and applying the term internal neocolonialism to the present-day situation. The basic distinction here is in the nature of the mechanisms of domination that are typical in each case. We do not mean to imply an either/or choice, of course. Thus force and the threat of force continue to play an important role in internal neocolonialism; but for the most part these direct measures tend to be held in reserve today, with the more indirect mechanisms being relied on for the day-to-day maintenance of the system.

Robert Allen (1970) has begun to sketch the outlines of such a model, which he calls domestic neocolonialism, for the case of Blacks in America. While he describes this as a shift toward "an indirect and subtle form of domination," he puts emphasis on the development of a Black bourgeoisie which would act on behalf of the Anglo elite and the status quo, in an American form of indirect rule. While this type of cooptation is undoubtedly important in the workings of a neocolonial form of domination, it should be kept in mind that other mechanisms also play an important role. One such mechanism which we emphasize is the mobilization of bias. It should also be noted that indirect rule is by no means restricted to neocolonial systems, but can be a feature of both classic "external" colonialism and classic internal colonialism, although playing a relatively less important role here.

If it is true that there has been a shift toward neocolonialism during the last century, it also appears to be the case that the process has been carried further in the more urbanized areas. It may be that the greater concentration of population and the greater social complexity of the city make indirect methods of domination more efficient. We could also hypothesize that it is in the more highly industrialized sectors of society that more sophisticated mechanisms of social control are developed, as in work relations, and that these carry over into the internal colonial relationship.

In addition, the shift over time can be explained in terms of the degree of stability of the relations of domination. In the early stages, a greater amount of force is needed to establish the initial relationship; once the situation is relatively stabilized, more indirect mechanisms are usually sufficient to preserve it, with force playing a secondary role. Of course, if the colonized population again begins to mount a strong challenge, we can expect the system to increasingly revert to the more openly repressive tactics typical of classic internal colonialism.

Assimilation and Cultural Defense

One theme that has been implicit up to this point is the authors' rejection of assimilation as a desirable goal for the Chicano community. The great bulk of the Chicano people have demonstrated through their tenacious cultural defense that they have little enthusiasm for assimilation, however much they may want to participate in the American prosperity that was built on their land and labor, and that of other Third World peoples. Our rejection of cultural assimilation is based on several grounds, among which are a belief in the value of the Chicano culture and a desire to see it develop according to its own internal logic; a distaste for cultural homogenization and a regard for human diversity; and a feeling that assimilation for most Chicanos would involve the trading of a genuine human culture for a bland, dehumanized, consumer-oriented, made-in-America mass culture. From this perspective, the assimilationist approach in America, intellectual or otherwise, is not only an expression of cultural imperialism but in effect an instrument of dehumanization.

THE CONTEMPORARY SITUATION AND PROSPECTS FOR DECOLONIZATION

An assessment of the contemporary scene must begin with an awareness that Chicano activists today are conscious of participating in what is generally referred to as "The Movement." While difficult to characterize in an unambiguous manner, the movement is marked by a self-conscious ethnic pride, a high rate of participation by youth, a developing Chicano nationalist ideology, and an attempt to achieve at least some degree of coordination among the various groups and regions involved. The idea of a Chicano movement is a product of the 1960s, and has continued to gain strength in the seventies. Preexisting political groups have become increasingly conscious of the movement, and some have identified themselves with it in various degrees.

Nevertheless, it is true that coordination is still highly imperfect, and the various political groups differ considerably in the problems which they identify, the manner in which they analyze them, and the tactics which they employ.

One broad category of approaches is fairly traditional, and is primarily aimed at public institutions. Falling within this category are pressure group tactics directed at administrative agencies and seeking to achieve greater attention to Chicano needs. Civil rights efforts fall under this broad heading. Generalized political groups such as MAPA (Mexican American Political Association) and PASSO (Political Association of Spanish Speaking Organizations) as well as more specialized groups such as AMAE (Association of Mexican American Educators) frequently employ such tactics. Actions aimed at the courts are initiated by such groups as the Mexican American Legal Defense and Educational Fund. Also within this general category should be included electoral strategies directed at increasing Chicano influence over elective offices. Traditionally Chicanos have been affiliated with the Democratic party. More recently there has been a tendency toward increased independence from the two major parties. Still, to the extent that this independence is aimed only at producing a kind of "swing vote" leverage for Chicanos, it should be included among this category of approaches.

There is another set of tactics that is directed more at the Chicano community itself, at least in the initial stages. This is generally more "activist" in nature. One such tactic might be termed "organizational," since it is aimed at building multipurpose organizations with a broad base. Such is the strategy currently being pursued by La Raza Unida in the California Inland Empire area (east of Los Angeles). There is also an attempt being launched throughout the Southwest to build an independent Chicano third party, an aspect of the movement which is rapidly gaining importance. This approach received its greatest impetus from the electoral victories of La Raza Unida Party in South Texas, and has since spread to Colorado and California. "Chicano Power" is its rallying cry. A third type of strategy in this general area has to do with the building of alternative institutions, such as schools and business enterprises. The Denver-based Crusade for Justice has made some interesting starts in this direction, as has the Los Angeles community known as TELACU. An effort to develop a joint Chicano and Indian university has begun in Davis, California, and a Chicano college was recently started in South Texas. Finally, there are a number of groups directing their efforts at communication and increasing Chicano cultural and political consciousness. Among these are the various movement-oriented newspapers and numerous Teatro groups which have followed the original Teatro Campesino formerly associated with the farmworkers' union.

A final set of approaches involve some form of direct action, ranging from peaceful boycotts and picketing to more disruptive sit-ins and demonstrations to force and violence. Such Chicano organizations as the Brown Berets and the Chicano Moratorium Committee have engaged generally in militant but nonviolent forms of direct action. Riots that have resulted from some demonstrations are blamed on the police by Chicano participants. More recently, however, a group identifying itself as the Chicano Liberation Front in Los Angeles has claimed credit for a number of bombings aimed at Anglo institutions.

It should be kept in mind, of course, that organizations often employ more than one kind of tactic, so that it is difficult to make one to one correlations. The most widespread Chicano student organization, MECHA, has used a number of different tactics in its efforts, as have other groups. It is also possible to think of approaches that have not been used extensively by urban Chicanos. There is, for example, no urban counterpart to César Chávez's Farmworkers Union, and there are few Chicano urban organizations that have actively sought long-term coalitions with non-Chicano groups.

At this point it is too early to tell which specific approaches are most likely to produce change in the situation of the Chicano. A variety of types of action is desirable, in that different appeals must be made to different sectors of the Chicano population in order to engage them in political action. It is also true that many of these activities are in essence "probes," designed to test reality in order to find out what works and what does not. Eventually these various activities may contribute to the development of a cohesive ideology which will be useful in clarifying the Chicano situation, specifying goals, and indicating future directions for the movement.

Nevertheless, it is possible now to begin to address the question of what constitutes a solution for Chicanos. To be considered an effective solution, a proposed change must contribute to decolonization–that is, it must enable Chicanos to gain greater control over their environment while maintaining their collective identity. This means, among other things, increasing the range of alternatives open to Chicanos and developing Chicano control over those institutions which most directly affect their lives. Those approaches which seek to incorporate Chicanos into Anglo institutions without making fundamental changes in those institutions will not contribute to decolonization, although they may allow individual Chicanos to increase their social mobility. Thus increasing the number of Chicanos in a school system that functions in such a way as to undermine Chicano culture does not contribute to decolonization. The same thing can be said of incorporating Chicanos into economic institutions that increase Chicanos' social and geographical mobility at the expense of their ties to the barrio.

In part this problem can be attacked through the creation of alternative institutions designed for and controlled by Chicanos. However, there is no way of constructing self-contained Chicano educational, economic, or political systems, so that successful decolonization will depend on producing far-reaching changes in the institutions of the larger society. Since it is doubtful that Chicanos can mobilize the necessary political strength to produce such adjustments on their own, there will eventually have to be coalitions and alliances formed with other groups interested in change. It may well be that a true decolonization for Third World peoples within the United States will require a radical transformation of the structures of this society.

NOTES

1. In the article we have employed the terms "Chicano" and "Mexican American" interchangeably, to refer to the population of Mexican extraction residing in the United States, whether citizens or not, and regardless of place of birth. "Anglo" is used to refer to the entire non-Chicano population, excluding Blacks and other racial minorities. The term "barrio" simply refers to the urban neighborhoods in which Chicanos are concentrated.

2. For general critiques of the tradition of attributing the Chicano's position to his culture, see Romano (1968), Vaca (1970), and Rocco (1970).

3. For a discussion of this concept and its limitations, see Litt (1970).

4. In this connection, see Easton (1965), and Schaefer and Rakoff (1970).

5. Ruth Tuck (1946) relates the man-in-the-street's version of benign neglect in the epilogue to her book, entitled "It Will All Work Out In Time."

6. Kenneth Clark has expressed this succinctly: "Ghettos are the consequence of the imposition of external power and the institutionalization of powerlessness. In this respect, they are in fact social, political, educational, and above all—economic colonies." (Clark, 1964).

7. Eduardo Pérez, Secretary of the California Democratic Party during the administration of Governor Edmund Brown, claims that he was appointed to his position only so that his name would appear on the party literature (Steiner, 1969: 191). Alex García, a California State Assemblyman, has testified that he was ignored by Democratic Party officials when he ran for office. After being elected, he was expected to endorse party positions and accept appointments without being consulted (written testimony to the Democratic Commission on Party Structure and Delegate Selection, June 21, 1969).

REFERENCES

Allen, R. (1970) Black Awakening in Capitalist America. Garden City, N.Y.: Doubleday Anchor.

Backrach, P. and M. Baratz (1970) Power and Poverty. New York: Oxford Univ. Press.

Banfield, E. (1970) The Unheavenly City. Boston: Little, Brown.

—— (1965) Big City Politics. New York: Random House.

Blauner, R. (1972) "Colonized and immigrant minorities," in R. Blauner (ed.) On Racial Oppression in America. New York: Harper & Row.

—— (1969) "Internal colonialism and ghetto revolt." Social Problems (Spring): 393-408.

California Fair Employment Practices Commission, FEPC (1970) Special Report of the San Bernardino County Grand Jury, based on an investigation of the county of San Bernardino.

California Roster of Federal, State, County and City Officials (1970).

Carmichael, S. and C. Hamilton (1967) Black Power. New York: Vintage.

Carter, T. (1970) Mexican Americans in School: A History of Educational Neglect. New York: College Entrance Examination Board.

Castaneda, A., M. Ramirez, C. Cortes and M. Barrera [eds.] (1971) Mexican Americans and Educational Change. Riverside: University of California.

Clark, K. (1964) Youth in the Ghetto. New York: Haryou Associates.

Cortes, C. et al. (forthcoming) The Bent Cross: A History of the Mexican American in the San Bernardino Valley.

—— (1971) "Revising the 'all-American soul course': a bicultural avenue to educational reform," pp. 314-340 in A. Castañeda et al. (eds.) Mexican Americans and Educational Change. Riverside: University of California.

D'Antonio, W. and W. Form (1965) Influentials in Two Border Cities [Notre Dame, Ind.]: Univ. of Notre Dame Press.

Easton, D. (1965) A Systems Analysis of Political Life. New York: John Wiley.

Faragher, J. (forthcoming) "Redlands," in C. Cortés et al. The Bent Cross: A History of the Mexican American in the San Bernardino Valley.

Gonzalez-Casanova, P. (1969) "Internal colonialism and national development," pp. 118-139 in I. L. Horowitz et al. (eds.) Latin American Radicalism. New York: Vintage.

Grebler, L., J. Moore, and R. Guzman (1970) The Mexican-American People. New York: Free Press.

Hill, G. (1963) "'Latinos' govern tense community." New York Times (September 21).

Kibbe, P. (1964) Guide to Mexican History. New York: International Publications Service.

Lemert, E., and J. Rosberg (1948) The Administration of Justice to Minority Groups in Los Angeles County. Berkeley: University of California Publications in Culture and Society, II, no. 1.

Litt, E. (1970) Ethnic Politics in America. Glenview, Ill.: Scott, Foresman.

Lowi, T. (1969) The End of Liberalism. New York: W. W. Norton.

McWilliams, C. (1968) North From Mexico. New York: Greenwood Press.

Moore, J. (1970) "Colonialism: the case of the Mexican Americans." Social Problems (Spring): 463-472.

Morales, A. (1970) "Police deployment theories and the Mexican American community." El Grito (Fall): 52-64.

Muñoz, C. (1971) "The politics of educational change in East Los Angeles," pp. 83-104 in A. Castañeda et al. (eds.) Mexican Americans and Educational Change. Riverside: University of California.

Ornelas, C. and M. Gonzalez (1971) The Chicano and Health Services in Santa Barbara. University of California, Santa Barbara: Chicano Political Communications Project, Report no. 3.

Rocco, R. (1970) "The Chicano in the social sciences: traditional concepts, myths, and images," Aztlán (Fall): 75-98.

Romano, O. (1968) "The anthropology and sociology of the Mexican American: the distortion of Mexican American history." El Grito (Fall): 13-26.

Rubel, A. (1966) Across the Tracks: Mexican-Americans in a Texas City. Austin: Univ. of Texas Press.

Samora, J. and R. Lamanna (1967) Mexican-Americans in a Midwest Metropolis: A Study of East Chicago. UCLA Mexican-American Project, Advance Report no. 8.

Schaefer, G. and S. Rakoff (1970) "Politics, policy and political science: theoretical alternatives." Politics and Society (November): 51-78.

Schmidt, F. (1970) Spanish Surnamed American Employment in the Southwest. Study prepared for the Colorado Civil Rights Commission.

Sheldon, P. (1966) "Community participation and the emerging middle class," pp. 125-158 in J. Samora (ed.) La Raza: Forgotten Americans. Notre Dame: Univ. of Notre Dame Press.

Steiner, S. (1969) La Raza. New York: Harper & Row.

Sturdivant, F. (1969) "Business and the Mexican-American community." California Management Rev. (Spring): 73-80.

Swadesh, F. (1968) "The Alianza movement: catalyst for social change in

New Mexico," pp. 162-177 in Amer. Ethnological Society proceedings of the 1968 Annual Spring Meeting.

Tirado, M. (1970) "Mexican American community political organization." Aztlán (Spring): 53-78.

Tuck, R. (1946) Not With The Fist: Mexican-Americans in a Southwest City. New York: Harcourt, Brace.

U.S. Commission on Civil Rights (1971) Participation of Mexican Americans in California Government. California Advisory Committee. (mimeo)

____ (1970) Mexican Americans and the Administration of Justice in the Southwest. Washington, D.C.: Government Printing Office.

Vaca, N. (1970) "The Mexican-American in the social sciences, 1912-1970." El Grito (part I, Spring: 3-24; part II, Fall: 17-51).

Watson, J. and J. Samora (1954) "Subordinate leadership in a bicultural community: an analysis," Amer. Soc. Rev. (August): 413-421.

Woods, Sister F. J. (1949) Mexican Ethnic Leadership in San Antonio, Texas. Washington, D.C.: Catholic University of America.

A. The Politics of Separatism

SOME CHICANOS HAVE GIVEN UP ON THE AMERICAN POLITICAL SYSTEM. They feel that the current situation in the United States is such that the use of the politics of accommodation or even radical politics which attempt to force an entry into the system is useless. It is felt that the only way to achieve the kinds of symbolic and cultural as well as material goals sought by the Chicano people is to develop their own countercultural institutions separate from those of the core culture United States society. Chicanos have established separate educational institutions such as colleges in Texas, California, and Colorado, in addition to precollegiate educational institutions in several southwestern states. Many other cultural institutions, such as schools of music, painting, and sculpture, have also been founded. Chicano community service agencies–for instance, health clinics owned and operated by the Chicano community–are scattered throughout the Southwest.

Separatism has found its primary political form in the establishment of La Raza Unida party. Although examined earlier in the discussion on preferment politics, in this selection Alberto Juárez, emphasizing the California experience, views LRUP as a "new form" of political organization. He distinguishes the aims of La Raza Unida from those of many third-party or splinter-group movements of the past and sees it as an integral part of the "youth revolt against the entirety of the political system."

The most exreme form of separatism, of course, involves demands for a separate political community. The term *Aztlán;* the ancient Aztec word for what is now the southwestern United States, is used symbolically to represent the political community of the Chicano movement. The concept of Aztlán sometimes embodies the idea of territorial separatism. Some Chicano activists feel that the lands taken away from the Mexican through conquest by the United States in the war with Mexico should be returned to the Mexican American people. Many more consider Aztlán as a cultural and spiritual community. One of the leading exponents of the concept of "cultural nationalism" and Aztlán in all its aspects is Rodolfo "Corky" Gonzáles, founder and leader of the Denver-based Crusade for Justice. His ideas and activities are presented in the article "The Poet in the Boxing Ring" by Stan Steiner.

In New Mexico a few years ago there was also a movement for territorial separatism when Reies Tijerina and his Alianza attempted to appropriate an area in northern New Mexico and establish some Chicano city-states on lands originally granted to La Raza. The new territory was to be renamed El Pueblo República de San Joaquín del Río Chama. Tijerina and the Alianza are discussed in the article by Professor Clark Knowlton.

21: THE EMERGENCE OF EL PARTIDO DE LA RAZA UNIDA: California's New Chicano Party

Alberto Juárez

THIS PAPER BRIEFLY EXAMINES THE RECENT EMERGENCE OF LA RAZA Unida Party in Los Angeles. It also considers the political climate and events that led to the development of this new party by young Chicano political activists throughout California and the Southwest. The paper also explores the feasibility and the required success factors involved in establishing such a party in light of the "Rise and Fall of Third Parties," in contemporary United States political history.[1] The purpose is analysis, not polemics.

In examining this nascent political effort, it is not the intent of this paper to argue the merits, for or against the development of the party, but rather to analyze those factors and events within the Chicano community which have given rise to the genesis and subsequent development of La Raza Unida as an independent Spanish-speaking political force. Until very recently, Chicano political history in the United States remained an unwritten chapter.[2] This paper is a contribution to Chicano political history.

POLITICAL CHARACTERISTICS OF THE CHICANO COMMUNITY IN LOS ANGELES AND CALIFORNIA

Chicano disenchantment with the existing political order in California primarily directed at the Democrats, stems from what Bert Corona describes as "a long history of political repression and exploitation . . . by the Democratic party in California."[3] Testifying recently before the California State

Reprinted from *Aztlan: Chicano Journal of the Social Sciences and Arts* 3, no. 2 (Fall 1972), pp. 177-203. By permission of the author.

Advisory Committee to the United States Commission on Civil Rights in Sacramento, Professor Corona stated:

> Both parties have been guilty of using the Spanish speaking and the Chicano vote for their imperative of control of the legislature. . . . they are cynical in their dealings with our needs and aspirations . . . Both parties ultimately have shown that they represent the big money interests.[4]

Other leading Chicano political figures in California, testified that few attempts have been made by the two majority parties to assist Chicano aspirants for political offices in the state or to name qualified Chicano candidates to important appointive offices in the state government. The most bitter remarks were those directed at former Speaker of the House Jess Unruh, who in 1965 played a key role in the reapportioning of the state's Assembly, Senatorial and Congressional districts. Chicanos believed this reapportionment gerrymandered the community "into political impotence."[5]

Testifying before the Committee on Reapportionment in October 1971, chaired by Assemblyman Henry Waxman, Professor Henry Pacheco and Dr. David López Lee presented the Committee with reports and detailed maps that showed that the Greater East Los Angeles Community, with a population of 600,000 persons, was sliced up into nine Assembly districts, seven State Senate districts and six Congressional districts. The districts were cut up in such a way that none of them had more than 35% Chicano voter registration. According to Professor Pacheco:

> The Assembly offer[s] a good example of gerrymandering practices. Using the legislature's own figures, five districts–the 40th, 45th, 48th, 50th, and 51st–dip into East Los Angeles to take 20-30 per cent registered Mexican American voters each, with four other districts–the 52nd, 53rd, 56th and 66th–dipping in for smaller amounts. The amounts are large enough to insure the reelection of Democratic incumbents but small enough to prevent Mexican American candidates from winning the districts.[6]

Professor Pacheco suggested that the county should provide the Chicano community with six Assembly seats, three State Senate seats and three U.S. Congressional seats. According to Pacheco, the increase in the number of districts can easily be justified by the numbers of Chicanos in the state's population and specifically that of the greater East Los Angeles area.

Chicano political experts contend that the under-representation in state government has been a direct result of gerrymandering. These claims were supported by the report of the California Advisory Committee to the U.S. Commission on Civil Rights in August of 1971, which documented and substantiated many of the charges made by Chicano witnesses at the January hearings.[7]

The report expresses the sentiment of the witnesses. It states that California's 3 million Spanish-speaking citizens have been discriminated against by reapportionment practices designed to protect incumbents. This fact was further substantiated by the testimony of Jess Unruh:

> In 1961, pursuant to a direct request, I think the principal thing that motivated legislature in reapportionment was after that all-important principle of protecting incumbents was to give to the then new Democratic president, John Kennedy, as big a working majority in the Congressional delegation of California as was possible. We did that. . . . In 1965, it was totally and completely for the protection of incumbents.[8]

Unruh was then asked if California's Democratic leadership would sacrifice an incumbent to satisfy Chicano reapportionment demands. Unruh responded:

> Certainly that would be better for the Mexican American population, but that just isn't going to happen. It just isn't going to happen.[9]

Following the testimony of Mr. Unruh, Henry Waxman was also questioned on the issue of Chicano representation. Committee Chairman Herman Sillas asked Assemblyman Waxman:

> Would you state your position on whether you would feel the consideration of increasing Mexican American representation outweighs the removal of an incumbent Democrat?
>
> *Mr. Waxman:* The only response I can give to that is that it is a speculative question and I would not venture to answer it at this time.
>
> *Chairman Sillas:* Is it your goal at this time to increase the representation of the Mexican American in the Assembly?
>
> *Mr. Waxman:* I don't think that is a very fair question to ask me, other than it has already been asked and answered a number of times in the testimony.[10]

In reference to the actual representation of the community in state and local government, the committee's report indicated two Mexican-American Assemblymen, Alex García and Peter Chacón of San Diego. The report also showed that there are no Spanish-surnamed state senators, and only one Congressman, Edward Roybal, 30th Congressional district in Los Angeles.[11]

Representation in the City and County of Los Angeles is far worse. According to the report Los Angeles has more than 1.1 million Chicanos, with half of these clustered in the Greater East Los Angeles area. In spite of these numbers no Chicanos are serving on the two key elective bodies: the 15 member Los Angeles City Council or the 5 member Los Angeles County Board of Supervisors. In 1969-70, efforts were undertaken by the Congress of Mexican American Unity and the Chicano Law Students Association, along with the help of Councilman Tom Bradley, to expand the City Council from

15 to 17 members. This measure failed when it was placed as a separate issue from the charter reform on the ballot of the 1970 city elections. The County Board of Supervisors rejected a similar request to expand their membership.[12]

On the subject of Chicano appointments to governmental positions, the report showed that only 1.98 per cent of California's appointed and elected officials were Chicano. The report cited the testimony of Dr. Francisco Bravo, an East Los Angeles physician, who has received more key political appointments than perhaps any other Mexican American in California history.[13]

> We have practically no appointments out of our 122 commissioners in the City of Los Angeles. Since we constitute somewhere around 20 to 30 per cent of the population, we should have 30 to 40 commissioners. In the time I served as commissioner–I was the first Mexican American commissioner in the city's history–Mayor Yorty came through with 19, but this has been reduced to about six or eight now. . . . In the critical boards, like the Board of Education, Welfare, Custodial Institutions, Athletic Commission, we should have two or more.[14]

Dr. Bravo stated that Governor Reagan had appointed 54 Chicanos to non-civil service jobs in the first four years in office, but said that: "we should have 500 to 1,000 in appointed positions." During the Brown administration only 30 Chicanos were appointed.

Chicanos fared no better in receiving judgeships. The U.S. Civil Rights Commission report showed that there are 1,179 superior, municipal and justice court judges and county constables in California, 21 of whom are Chicano. There are 3 Chicano Superior Court judges, all of whom are in Los Angeles County and 9 Chicano Municipal Court judges. There are no Chicano constables.

None of the top 40 state officials is a Chicano. None of the top 28 advisors on the governor's staff are Chicano. Out of 15,650 elected and appointed officials at municipal, county, state and federal levels in California, only 310–just 1.98 per cent are Chicano. Of the 4,032 positions in the executive branch of the State government including the boards, commissions and advisories, only 60–1.5 per cent–are filled by Chicanos. Of 10,907 city and county government officials in California only 241–2.2 per cent–are Chicanos. None of the 132 top state court positions–including seven supreme court justices, the judicial council, etc., are held by Chicanos.[15]

The committee report echoed the concerns of such key witnesses as Dr. Armando Morales, a staff psychologist at the UCLA Neuropsychiatric Institute. He stated that much of the civil strife and turmoil in East Los Angeles is a manifestation of the Chicano community's feelings of political powerlessness and inattention.

This inattention merely reflects a symptom of political powerlessness, as only political power elicits political interest. Related to this and intensifying the problem is the fact that Anglo-Saxon politicians are even less interested in the Mexican American poor.[16]

Dr. Morales complained of a "double standard" of government rule and of "selective democracy" in Los Angeles and stated further that:

Some people and some communities in Los Angeles enjoy the real advantages of democracy, but others such as the Mexican Americans in East Los Angeles do not. This is the primary reason why conflict exists between the police and Mexican Americans and the reason why these problems cannot be solved on the local level. Political self determination has to become a reality if one wishes to see a final end to the conflict between the Mexican American community and the police.[17]

In his closing remarks before the Advisory Committee, MAPA (Mexican American Political Association) President Abe Tapia stated tersely that "the two party system has failed the Mexican. We don't need it. We don't want it." Tapia stated that the Chicano community will now begin to work for political change outside of the existing two parties:

We are saying to our community that the La Raza Unida Party is the one that is going to fight them, no matter what. We are going to make it a reality in the state of California, such as it is in Texas, New Mexico, Arizona and Colorado.[18]

THE THIRD PARTY TRADITION IN THE U.S.

A third party advocating needed social, economic, and political reforms, designed to meet the needs of constituent elements within the U.S. political system, is hardly a novel idea. Without recounting the history of the 100-odd third party movements in U.S. political history, it can safely be asserted that the Chicano community shares with the rest of the electorate a historical if not traditional feeling of unrest with the existing bi-partisan system.[19] Without stretching the point, a cursory examination of U.S. political thought would reveal the early sanctions against majority domination at the expense of minority political and civil rights which James Madison argued for in *Federalist No. X* and incorporated into the Constitution.[20]

Although the cause and factors giving rise to third parties may be legion, leading political historians such as V. O. Key attribute the "principal episodes of third party activity . . . to serious economic discontent," most of which he found to be rooted in periods of agrarian and industrial "distress."[21] Of these "principal episodes," the most "spectacular" have been the farm labor movements of the Populist period, the Bull Moose Progressives and the later Progressives of Robert La Follette in 1924. "Measured by electoral strength," observes Key, "the populists and Progressives of La Follette were impressive as manifestations of economic discontent . . ." at the turn of the century and later during the economic depressions following the First World War.[22] The programs that these third party movements proposed were considered radical in their day. They brought about what Key considers to have been "realignments" that brought a "sharper contrast in the policy orientation of the major parties." Key further observes:

> The populists also had an influence that extended beyond the democratic acceptance of their doctrines. Their energetic agitations in support of their cause gave currency to ideas that eventually gained wide support and became law. They preached the doctrine of popular government and demanded the direct election of United States Senators, and direct primary nominating system, the initiative and referendum and woman suffrage. . . . La Follette's crisp platform was prophetic of the New Deal. It reiterated the old cry against monopoly and privilege. It proposed to guarantee labor the right to organize and bargain, and to abolish injunctions in labor disputes. . . . It urged immediate tariff reductions and ultimate public ownership of railroads and water power.[23]

Other political scientists such as William B. Hesseltine attribute the development of minor parties to the "inability of the major parties to create platforms reflecting the urgent priorities of discordant groups." Hesseltine considers this to be a result of mediocrity by the large parties:

> Because the two major parties have regularly tended toward mediocrity and conservatism, discordant groups have frequently attempted to erect parties to challenge the two major parties. . . . Often these third parties sent members to Congress, sometimes they influenced legislation, and occasionally they even educated the electorate.[24]

More recent students of ethnic politics such as Edgar Litt observe that the traditional "accommodation model" which has brought the disparate elements within the polity by the major parties has not worked for the non-white minorities as it did for the European immigrants during the 19th and early 20th century. Litt points out:

> Accommodation politics has been the most persistent type of American ethnic politics; indeed, it has become for many investigators the "natural" form of politics in general. This type of politics is a legacy from the efforts of white immigrant groups to wrest urban power from the Anglo-Saxons. . . . Classic accommodation politics has had some specific and limiting conditions that make it an unreliable guide to contemporary varieties of ethnic politics.[25]

The limiting conditions that Litt sees in accommodation politics contributes to what he describes as a "Slack system designed to produce selective change within a seemingly stable social order; the accommodation system is of limited value to either the ghetto Negro or the contemporary policy-maker seeking solutions for new ethnic politics." He states further:

> Party and ethnic communities are no longer sufficient instruments for determining and distributing such collective social goods as were part of the accommodation model. . . . Accommodation politics was highly repressive of cultural and psychological values, limited as it was to the hammering out of short term, pragmatic compromises. Separatist politics promises to provide individual and group reconstruction where accommodation politics had only a limited response.[26]

The importance of Litt's observations can be further substantiated by the current demands being made of the existing political apparatus by the various dispossessed ethnic and economic minorities, all of which are now searching for the "New Forms" that Hamilton and Carmichael outlined in their own work.[27] In California and the Southwest these "New Forms" are being exemplified in the organizing efforts of La Raza Unida Party.

The Chicano revolt is not merely an internal insurgency against the two-party system. This has often been the case with the splinter factions from the major parties, such as was seen with the Bull Moose Progressives of Theodore Roosevelt and the more contemporary American Progressive Party of Henry Wallace, the American Independent Party, and perhaps to a lesser degree the Peace and Freedom Party.[28] The Chicano third party movement is an external onslaught by the youthful leadership of the "movement" against the stranglehold that the Democratic party has had around the political self-determination of the Spanish-speaking electorate. This leadership is not composed of disenchanted political veterans nor active members of the party of their parents. Neither are the young Chicano political activists beholden to individuals or groups within the Democratic party who might impede their activity in organizing a political counter force. This is in contrast to many "old guard" Chicano elected officials and other veteran activists such as the rank and file Chicano trade union leaders (who must be regarded as a very important political force within working class Chicanos).[29]

The community's elder statesmen are essentially articulating the shortcomings of the Democrats in not ensuring Chicano political representation and a "fair share" of party patronage. The youthful leadership of the Chicano Movement is staging a broader attack on the inability of both parties and the whole political system to meet the most basic and fundamental needs of the Chicano people and the other exploited people making up the "Third World."[30] La Raza Unida is an autonomous, culturally distinct, yet analogous, integral part of a national political student and youth revolt against the entirety of the political system. These youthful concerns are thus reflected in the goals and objectives outlined in the platforms of La Raza Unida Party in California and Texas.

The populist, Progressives of La Follette and the Socialist Parties, white farmers, factory workers, and middle class elements challenged the political and economic power relationships in a period of economic upheaval. In contrast, the Chicano political efforts in the Southwest, especially in Texas, are to a greater degree analogous to those of the Southern Blacks, as seen by the early efforts of the Mississippi Freedom Party.[31] Both groups have remained in a "neocolonial" static condition, whereby they have been politically disenfranchised by the Democratic domination of Southern politics and economically dependent on the white-Anglo-American control of business, industry and agriculture. Thus, Chicanos who constitute the numerical majority of the twenty-six counties in the Rio Grande Valley of South Texas, remain in the same semi-feudal state as the Delta Blacks of Mississippi.[32] Both groups are either farm workers, sharecroppers or unskilled and semi-skilled workers employed by Anglo-owned agri-business concerns, or related food processing industries.[33] It was under these conditions that José Angel Gutiérrez and the students and youths of the MAYO groups emerged as the new political force in the Rio Grande Valley.

OBSERVATIONS ON LA RAZA UNIDA IN LOS ANGELES AND SOUTH TEXAS

. . . The election victories of La Raza Unida in Texas have swept into the barrios of the Southwest on a new wave of euphoric Chicano nationalism. Unlike its Texas counterpart, the party in California is loosely structured without the visible administrative controls or leadership. By and large the party organizational efforts have been dependent on the volunteer work being carried out by the youth and student groups on certain University and college campuses. Administrative control over these efforts have been relaxed to the degree that there are no clear, definitive lines of command–thus there appears to be a great deal of autonomy and lack of continuity in the platforms, objectives, and political philosophy among the party's advocates. The party structure in California is reflective of those organizations in the various regions of the state which are roughly in control of either the metropolitan areas of the North and South and thermal agricultural areas of Southern and Central California.[34] Consequently, outside of vague, all-encompassing remedies for the plethora of Chicano problems, which in each area take on a different emphasis–the party is still very much in the conceptual stages, and is kept alive by the statistical presence of formidable Chicano political power in California.

The recent candidacy of Raúl Ruiz, in the 48th Assembly District, which undoubtedly had an important effect on the Republican victory of Bill Brophy, significantly served to make the existence of the party known to the Chicano community throughout the state, principally in Los Angeles. In the absence of resources to finance a comprehensive public relations program and dependent on the leg work and word of mouth efforts of the youth and student organizers of the party, the resultant focus of the campaign on Raúl Ruiz became crucial to the organizing efforts of the party.

There are several other considerations of major importance which have a crucial bearing on the success of La Raza Unida Party in California as opposed to Texas. Chief among these considerations is that of the numbers of Chicanos in the population of California and that of Los Angeles in particular.

As noted in the South Texas counties, the Spanish-speaking constitute 70 to 85% of the total population, yet in the three key counties of Dimmit, La Salle and Zavala, which make up a surface area of 4,000 square miles, the total population numbers 600,000 persons. Out of the 2,250,000 Chicanos in Texas, the majority live in twenty-six counties, in which they constitute between 30 and 85% of the population and are concentrated in the South and in parts of West Texas.

In California, 2,980,000 Chicanos live throughout the state's 49 counties, one-third concentrated in Los Angeles. Chicanos constitute only 14.9% [sic] of Los Angeles County's population and are not the majority in any county. Admittedly, there are the vast concentration of Chicanos within certain areas of the state such as the greater East Los Angeles area, Fresno, San José and the parts of the San Joaquín, San Bernardino, Riverside and Imperial counties that make up the state's agricultural heartland. But in each of these instances Chicano communities have been divided into gerrymandered districts and thus are not afforded the ethnic homogeneity that is seen in South Texas, or even that of the Black community in Los Angeles, which, due to factors best explained in another treatment on the subject, have survived far better politically.

Another factor that would differentiate the conditions in California and Texas is the varying standard of living. In Texas, political platforms can readily be based on tangible economic problems accentuated by the stark feudal poverty of the area. In contrast is the "nickel and dime" affluence of the urban barrios in California which belies the impoverished conditions of Chicanos in the state. To illustrate the point, compare the statistical differences in the living conditions between Chicanos in Zavala County and those living in the greater East Los Angeles area. The median level of education among Chicanos in Zavala is 2.3 grades. In La Salle it is 1.5. The median family income in La Salle is $1,574 a year. In Zavala it is about $1,754. In East Los Angeles, the median income level is $5,000 and the median education level is 8.2 years. When ratios are considered involving doctors, health, housing, hunger, malnutrition, illiteracy and poverty, conditions are better in California than in Texas; yet these conditions are far worse for Chicanos in California than for the white Anglo groups.[35] Thus, it would appear that in spite of the lack of political representation among Chicanos in California, it often proves to be far more difficult to persuade a recent Texas emigre that the socio-economic conditions in California are such that they create the same urgency for aggressive political action as is being seen in Texas.

The poverty, the rural small town homogeneity, and the fact that South Texas is isolated from the diverse and unstable currents of change which sweep urban areas, have enabled the Chicanos to survive culturally, keeping alive language, traditions, customs and other lifestyles, in spite of the 13 generations of Chicano-Anglo conflict. Not so in California, where cultural fragmentation is a factor in community turmoil.

The homogeneity of the rural community's cultural, social, and political life has undoubtedly enhanced the successes of the organizing attempts of La Raza Unida in Texas, as has been the case with the United Farm Workers Organizing Committee in the San Joaquín Valley. Organizers for the Student Non-violent Coordinating Committee found this fact to be true in their efforts in Mississippi–away from the divisive factional infighting found in the cities.

In South Texas, the organizational leadership for the party, centered with the MAYO groups, created a catalytic effect which was aided by one basic philosophy which proved attractive to the Spanish-speaking citizens of that region. In California urban areas, the youth and student activist groups are not organizational catalysts, but more analogous to that of vanguards or "enlightened elites," who have come together from diverse political orientations and preferences.

In Los Angeles MEChA chapters are, to varying degrees of active participation, in general support of the Chicano party concept. The whys and wherefores for such a political alternative, however, become obscured in the milieu of political ideologies and philosophies espoused by the respective groups. Thus, one campus organization may be "heavy into the Marxist trip of the Maoist camp," while the more moderately inclined elements, such as the Catholic campuses, might be more readily identifiable with the posture of "Christian Democrats."

The relationships between such diverse groups are tenuously held together by the supporting commonality of pro-movement sentiment which provides a "live and let live" tolerance for one another. The continuation of this condition has probably been facilitated by the absence of any major party convention in which independent position papers and platforms must be stated. If and when the party is placed on the ballot, the next most important step will be for a general convention of party delegates to reach philosophical accord.

The generation gap, which La Raza Unida organizers in Texas were able to overcome, is clearly present in California. While the youth, as previously indicated, have been a very positive drawing force within the urban barrios, they have also created a negative backlash due to the uncompromising and often doctrinaire inflexibility of the attitudes of youthful leaders, who have in effect alienated former supporters.[36] This was, to a large degree, the situation that led to the demise of the Congress of Mexican American Unity, CMAU. As a consequence of this situation, coupled with the violent turmoils involving Chicano youth, community confidence in youthful leadership has been shaken. Yet, while the recent disorders may hamper their leadership role, the unrelenting position of the youthful idealist versus the pragmatic approach of veteran political activists, is a natural phenomenon not unique to this particular group or time. It is nevertheless, a formidable obstacle to organizational unity.

The young Chicano organizers have met an impressive amount of success in stimulating political interest among the elements of the so-called Chicano "hard core," which include the "vato locos," chronically unemployed, ex-convicts and welfare recipients and other elements of the disadvantaged, along with other elements of the "Movimiento."

The solidly entrenched Chicano Democrat must also be attracted. If his personalistic tendencies can be inspired by either charismatic candidates who appeal to his political and cultural sensitivities, or by a platform that will appeal to his Chicano consciousness, he may cross party lines to vote for the Chicano party or possibly even bolt the moderate posture of the community and its propensity to follow charismatic political figures, or be highly influenced by the tack taken by the few elected Chicano office holders. It would be of vital importance whether or not these individuals bolt the Democratic Party in favor of La Raza Unida. It should be noted that each of the secessionist and splinter parties in the past have had their initial successes due to the prominent leadership of major political figures such as La Follette's leadership of the Progressives, Strom Thurmond's leadership of the "Dixiecrats," and Henry Wallace's leadership of the American Progressive Party.

The reluctance of current Chicano elected officials to support the Party stems not only from philosophical positions which tie them to the liberal wing of the Democratic Party, but the more practical considerations such as the loss of financial and electoral support from the Democratic Party and liberal white elements that are not the determining elements in their respective districts. The Jewish liberal organizations, which must be credited for their support of the campaign efforts of numerous Chicano candidates, have been among the first to applaud the new levels of Chicano political activity and the first to fear the growing trend of Chicano nationalism and its ultimate development into a third party. Undoubtedly from the traditional liberal viewpoint these developments would be disruptive to the "consensus" approach to politics.

The ethnic political party presents a threat to the political tranquility of the system as seen by the liberals, and would thus disrupt the now traditional "Noblesse Oblige" relationship between ethnic minorities and the liberal white community. La Raza Unida Party is in effect being viewed as a "separatist nationalistic movement" that will disrupt the long established "cordial" relationships between the oppressor and the oppressed. . . . It should also be noted that many veteran Chicano political observers see another "episode" in which a field of Spanish-surnamed candidates are competing for the limited Spanish-speaking voters. In the aforementioned race for the 48th Assembly District in California, the four Chicano candidates were in effect competing for less than 30% of the electorate.

In the final election which saw Ruiz and Alatorre pitted against each other, regardless of the ideological and political differences, it was in the final analysis Chicano vs. Chicano, rather than the more politically informed viewpoint which saw it as La Raza Unida vs. The Democratic Candidate. What percentage of the 30% of the vote was garnered by each candidate is difficult to assess. An educated guess would place most of Raúl Ruiz's 7% of the total votes cast safely in the Chicano barrios of the district. Nevertheless, Ruiz's overall percentage and number of votes tallied in the primary and final election did not vary appreciably.

Since postwar political groups and factions within the Chicano community have sponsored candidates for local office, there has seldom if ever been a situation in which the community could unite behind one candidate. When it has, some political aspirant has entered either as a "ringer" hired by the Anglo opposition, or as an opposition candidate to his ethnic kinsmen.[37] The problem is not unique to Chicanos in California, as noted by James Wilson in his analysis of Black politics in Chicago.[38] But this problem of being able to capitalize on weak Chicano elements within the gerrymandered districts has led to a series of bitter and frustrating campaigns in which Chicanos have defeated themselves. Such was the case in the 1962 election to fill Roybal's vacancy in the City Council when 10 candidates ran for the office, seven of which were Spanish-surnamed. The most bitter race was that of Richard Calderón, who lost the newly apportioned Senate seat in 1966 by 301 votes to George Danielson. Two other Chicanos ran against Calderón. Again in 1970 Calderón was defeated by Danielson for the 29th congressional seat by 2,000 votes–2,000 votes captured by a Spanish-surnamed Democrat.

In those instances in which the community has been able to reach a consensus of opinion on selecting one standard bearer, the results have been mixed. A case in point is the now historic Congress of Mexican American Unity endorsing convention of February, 1968, at which time the presence of Chicano student power first made itself dramatically evident. Through the coalition of various youth organizations and the 10 Chapters of the United Mexican American Students, a Chicano union official, Jimmy Cruz, was selected as the candidate to fill the 40th Assembly seat of retiring Assemblyman Bill Elliott. In spite of the fact that he was the community endorsed candidate, he was still challenged by a host of other Chicanos–seven in number—of whom Alex Garcia was the eventual winner. Positive examples of community consensus are Edward Roybal, who has run unopposed by any other Chicano since his being elected to Congress, and Julian Nava, who has twice been elected to the Los Angeles Board of Education.

In light of what some persons regard as an almost pathological lack of unity among Chicanos, other Chicanos see an inherent independence in the Chicano character which is recognized in the Mexican maxim which states: "Cada cabeza es un mundo." Ralph Guzmán sees disunity as the most serious problem among the Mexican American people:

> The most serious problem of Mexican American leadership is its fragmentation and parochialism. After decades of organization activity, regional unity is still a distant goal. Although some of the ethnic associations have penetrated beyond their original base, usually Texas and California, each still has its main strength in the state in which it was formed . . . The difficulties posed by multiple bases of leadership have diminished the political effectiveness of many other minorities, but they appear to be especially acute among Mexican Americans.[39]

Laments on disunity, however, are not viable analyses. Overlooked is the fact that the Chicano community is politically diverse as it is diverse in other areas. More important factors in identifying causes for past disunity are the competitive and exploitive conditions maintained within the community by the colonial practice of "divide and conquer," and the active stimulation of fragmentation by institutions and politicians. Importantly, this is particularly acute in California, being a two party state as opposed to Texas, which is dominated by Dixie Democrats.

THE POTENTIAL EFFECT OF LA RAZA UNIDA ON CALIFORNIA POLITICS

Given the uncertainties of California partisan politics and keeping in mind the unsuccessful attempts to create effective third parties capable of challenging the two major parties, can La Raza Unida, as an ethnic party, effectively challenge the "system" in California, and thereby provide a viable political alternative for La Raza in California?

This question is today being asked throughout the state, not only by interested Chicanos who are vacillating between their current membership in either the Democratic or Republican party, but by general political observers. A number of California political figures were stunned by the upset victory of Republican Bill Brophy over the Democratic standard bearer Richard Alatorre in the November 16th, 1971, special election to fill the 48th Assembly seat vacated by Robert Roberti's election to the State Senate. The concern for the Democratic loss, in a district that has better than a 62% Democratic registration, not only stemmed from the added strength that the Republicans gained in the state assembly at a crucial moment when the state's reapportionment issue was to be settled, but from the impact which the unofficial* La Raza Unida party had in running Raúl Ruiz as an independent, on the final outcome of the election.[40]

Ruiz, a California State University, Northridge, Instructor, felt that the real winner in that election was not Brophy or the Republican party, but La Raza Unida which was able to pull "traditional Democratic Chicano voters away from him [Alatorre]."[41] Most political observers seemed to agree with Ruiz' assessment that he hurt Alatorre. In a *Los Angeles Times* interview following the election, Assembly Elections and Reapportionment Committee Chairman Henry A. Waxman (D-Los Angeles), was quoted as saying:

> The reason we lost was a cynical alliance of neo-segregationists in the Chicano community with the Republican party.[42]

The Democratic defeat was especially bitter for Waxman, who had long been at sword's points with Chicano political leaders over the creation of assembly districts in the Los Angeles area that would favor the 1.5 million Spanish-speaking residents in the County. Following the primary win of Richard Alatorre over a field of four other Democrats, of whom two were Chicanos, Waxman pointed to the Alatorre win as prima facie evidence that "safe" Chicano districts were not needed.[43] Meanwhile Republicans such as Caucus Chairman John Stull of San Diego County said:

> The election was a strong indication that Mexican Americans are no longer content to be taken for granted by the Democrats.[44]

La Raza Unida's role in the election was no doubt an important factor in the Brophy win in which he polled 16,346 votes, or 46% of the total. Alatorre received 14,759 votes, or 42%, while Ruiz polled 2,778, or 7%, and Blaine, the Peace and Freedom candidate, received 1,108 votes, or 3% of the total.[45] Thus, it would appear that if Ruiz' votes had gone to Alatorre, he would have had enough votes to slip past Brophy and keep the district in Democratic control. The greater concern is La Raza Unida's future role within the Chicano community. Although registration has been low in relation to the numbers of eligible voters, the Chicano vote has been regarded as decisive in past key elections. The most notable of these were Robert Kennedy's win in the 1968 Presidential primary in California, and the Los

*In order to be an "official" party in California, it must have, at least, registrants equalling 1% of the total number votes cast in the previous state gubernatorial election. La Raza Unida must get 66,340 registrants in order to be legal in California. eds.

Angeles Mayoralty race in 1969, which saw Sam Yorty carrying most of the Chicano vote in the City.[46]

The goal of the creation of a Spanish-speaking third party gives rise to consternation among both the major parties in the state, who nervously recall the narrow margin by which Richard Nixon defeated Hubert Humphrey in 1968. Nixon's victory, which received negligible support from the Chicano community, was seen by many political observers as having been primarily caused by the weakening of California's Democratic party. The Democrats had much of their strength sapped by the formation of the American Independent Party and the Peace and Freedom party. Former Democrats were found in the ranks of both of these minor parties. The right wing rhetoric of George Wallace attracted the labor "hard hat" elements which felt alienated by the "no-win" policy of the Democrats in Viet Nam and the liberal posture of the Democrats in the nation's domestic policies. Conversely, many of the Democrats' left of center youth and assorted liberals bolted the party over the U.S. presence in Viet Nam and formed the Peace and Freedom Party.[47]

The potential of La Raza Unida cannot help but haunt the Republican and Democratic leadership, who will have to contend with not only two other minor parties in the state but three.

In 1968, the Peace and Freedom Party, along with the American Independent Party, received a combined total of 500,000 votes–half a million votes that most experts feel might otherwise have carried the state for Hubert Humphrey.[48] The entry of La Raza as an organized bloc with the voting capacity that might outweigh the combined 1968 strength of both minor parties, gives rise to some provocative speculation as to the future of the state's traditional bipartisan balance of power, locally if not nationally.

Until recently Chicano voting strength was always a matter of conjecture. A recent study prepared by the League of United Latin American Citizens and the Mexican-American Bar Association of California, revealed that according to the Mexican American Population Commission's Official Census Report, the Chicano population in California is 2,980,000, which constitutes 14.9% of the state's 19,953,134 persons.[49] In Los Angeles County, Chicanos constitute one in every five persons, or 18.2% of the county's 7 million residents. This Census report further projects, based on recent population growth, that the Chicano population of Los Angeles County will be 21.1% by 1975.[50]

The number of potential eligible voters in 1972 is conservatively estimated to be 1,788,000. Assuming a 50% turnout, the number of Chicano voters would be 894,000, or 25 times greater than the difference between the Republican and Democratic presidential votes in the 1960 election; thus a shift of even 5% of the Chicano vote could affect the outcome.[51] In summary, the Partido de la Raza Unida could have an impact on any election in California since 14.9% of the population is Chicano. This impact, of course, will be enhanced by several factors: (1) the ability of the Partido to bring together the various factional groups within the Chicano community; (2) the ability of the Partido to attract and persuade the "older" Chicanos (who have been a stabilizing factor in the past); (3) the ability of the Partido to affect the strong Democratic ties of the unions (UAW; AFL-CIO; UFW) who are not as flamboyant as young student activists but serve as a quiet dominant political force in the Chicano community; and (4) the ability of the Partido to attract elected Chicanos to join the Partido.

NOTES

1. William B. Hesseltine, *The Rise and Fall of Third Parties* (Washington, D.C.: Public Affairs Press, 1948).

2. Outside of a few random comments or a footnote, the student of Chicano politics will find little in the way of secondary sources. One of the few authors to touch upon the Chicano, before 1965, is V. O. Key, *Southern Politics* (New York: Knopf, 1949). For a later treatment, see Leo Grebler, Joan Moore, Ralph Guzmán, *The Mexican American People* (New York: The Free Press, 1970).

3. Interview with Professor Corona, California State College, Los Angeles, June 1971.

4. California State Advisory Committee to U.S. Civil Rights Commission.

5. *Los Angeles Times,* "Letters to the Editor," Section II, October 1971.

6. Interview with Professor Henry Pacheco, Mexican American Studies Department, California State College, Los Angeles, November 2, 1971.

7. California State Advisory Committee to the U.S. Commission on Civil Rights.

8. Ibid., pg. 28.

9. Ibid., pg. 29.

10. Ibid., pp. 30–31.

11. Ibid., pg. 1.

12. Ibid., pg. 56.

13. Dr. Bravo has received appointments at the municipal, state and federal levels including Los Angeles City Police Commissioner and State Agricultural Commission. Although a life-long Democrat, he switched his much sought after support from Governor Brown in 1967 and supported Ronald Reagan, in protest of Democratic disinterest in Mexican American problems.

14. California State Advisory Committee, op. cit., pg. 45.

15. Ibid., pg. 46.

16. Ibid., pg. 59.

17. Ibid.

18. Ibid.

19. An in-depth account of U.S. third parties is given by Howard P. Nash in *Third Parties in American Politics,* (Washington, D.C.: Public Affairs Press, 1959), as well as the works of William B. Hesseltine, op. cit.

20. James Madison, "Tenth Federalist Paper."

21. V. O. Key, *Politics, Parties and Pressure Groups,* 5th ed., (New York: Thomas Y. Crowell, 1964), pp. 254–281.

22. Ibid., pg. 259.

23. Ibid., pg. 257.

24. Hesseltine, op. cit., pg. 55.

25. Edgar Litt, *Ethnic Politics in America,* (Scott, Foresman and Company, 1970), pg. 155.

26. Ibid., pp. 158–159.

27. See Stokeley Carmichael and Charles V. Hamilton, *Black Power: The Politics of Liberation in America,* (New York: Vintage Books, 1967), pp. 164–177.

28. See Nash, op. cit., pp. 241–314.

29. Interview with Professor Corona, op. cit.

30. Mario Compean and José Angel Gutiérrez, "La Raza Unida Party in Texas," a Merit Pamphlet (New York: Pathfinder Press, 1971), pg. 1.

31. See Carmichael and Hamilton, op. cit.

32. Ibid.

33. Compean and Gutiérrez, op. cit., pp. 14–17.

34. Grebler, Moore and Guzmán, op. cit., pp. 552–553.

35. Ibid., pg. 181.

36. It should be noted that the death knell of many of the other third parties was signalled by the uneasy coalitions between factions tenaciously clinging to doctrinaire positions. The most dramatic example can best be seen in the case of the American Socialist Party which achieved some limited success prior to World War I among Midwestern, German-American farmers, only to destroy itself over the ideological rifts caused by World War I.

37. Interview with Professor Corona, op. cit.

38. See James Wilson, *Negro Politics,* (New York: The Free Press).

39. Grebler, Moore and Guzmán, op. cit., pp. 554–555.

40. *Los Angeles Times,* November 18, 1971, pg. 1, Section II.

41. Ibid.

42. Ibid.

43. Ibid.

44. Ibid.

45. Ibid.

46. Interview with Maury Weiner, Deputy to Councilman Thomas Bradley, March 5, 1971, Los Angeles, California.

47. An account of the Chicano involvement in the campaign of John Kennedy in East Los Angeles is rendered by Louis Weschler and John Gallager, "Viva Kennedy," in *Cases in American National Government and Politics,* (Prentice Hall, 1966), pp. 51–62.

48. Frank H. Jones and John L. Harmer, "The 1968 Election in Califor-

nia," *The Western Political Science Quarterly,* (Vol. 22, No. 3, September 1969), pp. 468–480.

49. League of United Latin American Citizens and The Mexican-American Bar Association of California, *The Electoral College and The Mexican American: An Analysis of the Mexican American Impact on the 1972 Presidential Election,* (San Francisco, California, June 1971), pg. 5.

50. For example, California State Department of Education statistics show that as of October 1970, 23.7% of all kindergarten and first grade students in Los Angeles County were Spanish-surnamed.

51. Ibid., pg. 6.

22: THE POET IN THE BOXING RING

Stan Steiner

HE "LURKED LIKE A CAT FOR THE KILL." THE RITUAL LINGO OF THE BOXING ring described the fighting style of a young intellectual who read Lorca in the dressing room, and who fought seventy-five professional bouts and won sixty-five of them. He fought with the desperation of a kid from the barrios. The crowds savored the blood that dripped from his eyes, his lips, his bronzed face. "A crowd pleaser," one boxing buff recalls.

"Rodolfo is a gentle man," his wife says. "He is a poet." . . .

The Championship of the World was almost his. *Ring Magazine* hailed him as one of the five best boxers of his weight. He was rated the third ranking contender for the World Featherweight title by the National Boxing Association. When Gonzales was still in his teens he had won the National Amateur Championship and the International Championship as well. In the Lysoled corridors of the pugilistic kingdoms of the Mafia he was fingered as the coming "King of the Little Men." He was a "hungry fighter," the connoisseurs of flesh wrote in the sports pages. They did not know he was a poet.

He is a "poet of action" in the ring, the boxing writers wrote unwittingly. Lithe, his mind as quick as his body, he reacted like the reflex of a muscle. He was later to write of a young boxer, Manny, in one of his plays, "His movements are smooth, casual, and catlike." It may have been a self-portrait.

The Golden Boy of the boxing legend, he was to become the new voice of the Chicano movement. He was the idol of his generation, and he shared their frustrations. He was the embodiment of the confused barrio youth, the urban Chicanos.

He quit the ring. . . .

From *La Raza: The Mexican Americans* (New York: Harper & Row, 1969), pp. 378-392.

Where was he going? He did not know. "It's a long road back to yourself when the society has made you into someone else," he now says. "But I was determined to find my way, to rediscover my roots, to be the man I am, not the emasculated man that the Anglo society wanted me to be."

Rodolfo "Corky" Gonzales lived all the lives that "divide our hearts and emasculate our souls." In his young manhood he became an insurance salesman, a romantic poet, a big-city politician, a campesino in the fields, a soldier, a lumberjack, a playwright, the landlord in the ghetto, the leader of the Poor People's March on Washington, D.C., a high-ranking government official, a lone crusader, the father of eight children, the hero of the newspapers–and the villain, the All-American Boy, the victim of police riots, the descendant of the conquistadors, the "foreign Communist agitator," a political ward heeler, a successful businessman, and a revolutionary.

"The young Chicano is the most complex man in the country." He smiles, self-effacingly. "I guess that means me, too."

He was born in the barrios of Denver, a kid of the streets. Yet he grew up on the earth as well as the cement pavements, for his father was a Mexican emigrant, who worked as a campesino and coal miner in southern Colorado. As a boy he worked in the sugar-beet fields, beside his father, at the age of ten.

"Yes, I am a city man," he says. "But I did a lot of farm work. I have relatives in the villages in the San Luis Valley. Every spring and summer, as a boy, I worked in the fields. Every fall and winter I lived in the city slums."

Schools did not educate him. He learned of life in the fields and barrios. "The teachers taught me how to forget Spanish, to forget my heritage, to forget who I am," he says bitterly. "I went to four grade schools, three junior highs, and two high schools besides, because of our constant moving to the fields and back to the city." Even so, he graduated from high school at sixteen. He remembers working in a slaughterhouse at night and on weekends, so he could afford to go to school. He walked in so much blood that his shoes were always stained.

"I became a fighter because it was the fastest way to get out of the slaughterhouse. So I thought." He laughs. . . .

. . . A hero, Gonzales went into politics, opened a free boxing gymnasium for ghetto youth, was befriended by the mayor, became an after-dinner speaker on inspirational themes. "Like all boys growing up in this society, I identified success by wanting to be an important person loved by everyone."

He became a businessman. In one year he was owner of an automobile insurance agency and owner of a surety-bond business. Within three years, by 1963, he was General Agent for the Summit Fidelity and Surety Company of Colorado.

Once again he was too successful. He was the pride of the barrio. "Corky beat the Anglos with his fists, then he outsmarted them with his brains," a neighbor says. The fair-haired boy wherever he went, the "different" Mexican, he was beckoned with offers of political jobs. Los Voluntarios, a political action group, had been organized in Denver with Gonzales as chairman. "The sleeping giant was awakening."

The poet with scarred eyelids became a ward heeler. He was the first Chicano ever to be a district captain in the Denver Democratic Party at the age of twenty-nine. "Corky has charisma," says a City Hall hanger-on. "He zooms. That boy was a comer." In the presidential election of 1960 he was Colorado coordinator of the "Viva Kennedy" campaign, and his district had the highest Democratic vote in the city. He was rewarded for his victory. On a table in his old barrio office, beneath a flamboyant mural of the Statue of Liberty, her breast bared as she lay half-naked and raped by corruption, there was an array of bronzed and golden sports trophies, in the midst of which there was a photograph of the late President standing beside the ex-featherweight, and inscribed, "To Corky–John F. Kennedy."

In no time he was a one-man directory of poverty agencies. He was on the Steering Committee of the Anti-Poverty Program for the Southwest, on the National Board of Jobs for Progress (S.E.R., a major funding group for the barrios), on the Board of the Job Opportunity Center, President of the National Citizens Committee for Community Relations, and Chairman of the Board of Denver's War on Poverty.

Gonzales was rumored to be in line for state or even national office. The line was long. The Chicano was last in line. On the rising aspirations of the young and pugilistic barrio go-getter there was a political ceiling. And he was not yet poet enough to celebrate his frustrations. The poverty programs had disappointed him, much as party politics had disenchanted him. In the barrios the jobs were just as scarce, the poor just as poor. He attended conferences by the dozens, perhaps feeling the same as he imagined the delegates to the White House's Cabinet Committee hearings on Mexican American Affairs in El Paso, Texas, felt: "well-meaning, confused, irate, and insulted middle-class Chicanos who knew they were being had when they were asked to swallow and digest the same old soup and cracker disks fed by the politicians, with Johnson and Humphrey at the head of the line. Lacking was any positive direction or militant action. . . . What resulted was a lot of brave words, promises, motions–and no action."

Conferences and more conferences; how many times can he talk about poverty? The young man has heroic daydreams. . . .

On the bus going from Denver to El Paso to hear the President and his Cabinet, he envisions a mirage of revolution looming out of the gas-station desert towns: "We could have been a guerrilla force riding to keep a date with destiny, if only the time and place and emotions of the people were right." But there is soup and crackers awaiting them. . . .

"The politics of the Anglo emasculates the manhood of a man of La Raza.

It makes him impotent, a Tío Taco, an Uncle Tom. I was losing my cool," Gonzales says.

"I was used by the Democratic Party. I was used because I had a rapport with my people. Working in the two-party system I found out one thing, and I found it out very late. My people were exploited and men like I was are . . ." he falters, biting off the sentence. "But I was never bought. I could have accepted a number of payoffs from politicians and administrators. I never accepted them. Our people who get involved become political monsters." He pauses again and says, "Whores."

In his play, *A Cross for Maclovio,* the hero complains, "They're afraid, now they want to buy off our leadership. You stir up people, get them ready for a revolution, and the establishment comes running with a suitcase of pesos." . . .

The Golden Boy was ending his odyssey. When a Denver newspaper attacked him as "almost a thief," it was an insult to his dignity, a betrayal, he thought, of his "manhood." The poverty officials in Washington defended him, denying the accusations, but his friends in City Hall were strangely still. His scathing letter of resignation to the Democratic County Chairman, Dale R. Tooley, reverberated in the barrios of the Southwest:

> The individual who makes his way through the political muck of today's world, and more so the minority representatives, suffers from such an immense loss of soul and dignity that the end results are as rewarding as a heart attack, castration, or cancer! . . . You and your cohorts have been accomplices to the destruction of moral man in this society. I can only visualize your goal as complete emasculation of manhood, sterilization of human dignity, and that you not only consciously but purposely are creating a world of lackeys, political boot-lickers and prostitutes.

He resigned from the boards and councils of the War on Poverty one by one. He went "home again," he says. "Now I am closer back to home than I ever have been in that I am financially just as bad off as any Chicano," he says. . . .

The odyssey was ended. In an old red-brick building in the condemned barrio of downtown Denver, in 1965, the ex-almost-champion and past-president-of-everything founded *La Crusada Para la Justicia,* the Crusade for Justice. Gonzales declared this was "a movement born out of frustration and determination to secure equality with dignity."

In the politics of the Crusade for Justice there would be no wheeling and dealing. There would be no compromise with stereotypes. "To best serve our particular ethnic and cultural group our organization must be independent, and must not be dependent on the whims and demands of private agencies which are establishment-controlled and dominated. The services offered will not have the taint of paternalism, nor will the feeling of inferiority be felt when securing need, help and guidance."

In a few years, the Crusade was so influential that "the Anglos come to us for our help," Gonzales says. He tells how Archbishop James Casey of Denver came, uninvited, to the Easter "Mexican Dinner" they held. The Archbishop donned a tourist sombrero, told the guests, "Cherish your history, your culture, and preserve your wonderful language," and donated $100 to the Crusade's Building Fund.

The Crusade bought an old church in downtown Denver that resembled a miniature U.S. Treasury. In the colonnaded edifice there is "the most unique Mexican American center in the country," with a school of "Liberation Classes," a nursery, gymnasium, Mayan Ballroom, Chicano Art Gallery, Mexican shops, library, community dining room and community center, job "skill bank," legal aid service, Barrio Police Review Board, health and housing social workers, athletic leagues, a barrio newspaper [*El Gallo*], a bail bond service, a kitchen, and a "Revolutionary Theatre."

"No government money, no grants, no rich angels, no hypocrisy, no begging, no handouts" created El Centro Para La Justicia, boasts Gonzales. "We did it. We can do it. The Crusade is living proof of self-determination. The Crusade is not just an organization; it is the philosophy of nationalism with a human form.

"Nationalism exists in the Southwest, but until now it hasn't been formed into an image people can see. Until now it has been a dream. It has been my job to create a reality out of the dream, to create an ideology out of the longing. Everybody in the barrios is a nationalist, you see, whether he admits it to himself or not. It doesn't matter if he's middle-class, a *vendito* [*vendido*], a sellout, or what his politics may be. He'll come back home, to La Raza, to his heart, if we will build centers of nationalism for him."

In the Southwest, "nationalism is the key to our people liberating themselves," he says.

"Colorado belongs to our people, was named by our people, discovered by our people and worked by our people. We slave in the fields today to put food on your table. We don't preach violence. We preach self-respect and self-defense . . . to reclaim what is ours.

"I am a revolutionary," he says, "because creating life amid death is a revolutionary act. Just as building nationalism in an era of imperialism is a life-giving act. The barrios are beginning to awaken to their own strength. We are an awakening people, an emerging nation, a new breed."

Rodolfo "Corky" Gonzales feels that he has found himself among his people. He is a unique revolutionary in a time of ugliness and hatred in that he devotes his efforts to building his community. He is the happiest revolutionary in the country.

"Now I am my own man. I don't need to prove myself to the Anglos," he says.

"*Machismo* means manhood. To the Mexican man *machismo* means to have the manly traits of honor and dignity. To have courage to fight. To keep his word and protect his name. To run his house, to control his woman, and to direct his children. This is *machismo*," Gonzales says. "To be a man in your own eyes.

"If you are afraid of the Anglo he is like an animal. The human being is an animal; when you are afraid he attacks you, he punishes you, but if you are not afraid of him he respects you. The Anglo respects you only when you have power and respect yourself.

"We have been withdrawn. We have been quiet. And this has been mistaken for being afraid. We are not afraid. Look at the Congressional Medals of Honor our people have. It shows that when it comes to *machismo* there is no match for Là Raza. We have been withdrawn from this society to protect our culture, the values we have—not because we were cowards. Now we have to show them that we are strong. We have to use more forceful methods."

Gonzales is not talking of violence and nonviolence. The luxury of that choice he feels exists for those who have power to control and order their environment. It is meaningless in the barrio, as in the boxing arena, where violence is a normal act of everyday life that people are powerless to halt.

"Power is respected in this society," he says. "The black militants say the Negro needs black power to offset white power, and we need brown power to offset Anglo power.

"Are we endangering the economic system, the political system, by saying that? I think the system should be endangered. It is a system that is built upon racism and imperialism. That is why the low-income people and the minority people across the nation are rebelling. Unless the system changes, there will be more rebellions. Those who advocate change will save the country, not destroy it. Those who are resisting change are destroying the country.

"If there is no change by peaceful assembly, by demonstrations, by sitting down to discuss changes, then there will be frustration. Out of the frustration will come real violence, not riots. Unless everyone gets an equal share in this country, there won't be any country." . . .

On Palm Sunday, 1969, in the secular temple of La Crusada Para la Justicia the elated Rodolfo "Corky" Gonzales convened a national gathering of barrio youth. He called it, with a flourish, the Chicano Youth Liberation Conference. The young campesino activists, university graduate-school Chicanos, barrio gang members, *vados* [sic] *locos* from the streets, clever young government "Mexican Americans" incognito, and the wealthy children of the descendants of Spanish dons came to the temple-like building in downtown Denver to attend workshops in philosophy, self-defense, poetry, art, and identity. In all, more than 1,500 Chicanos come from as far away as Alaska, where no one thought there was any La Raza, and from Puerto Rico, and from all the states in between. They came from one hundred youth and student groups.

The conference of "music, poetry, *actos, embrazos,* tears, *gritos,* and the Chicano cheer: '*Raza, Raza, Raza, Raza,*' " went on for five days and nights. Afterward a youth wrote, "The building is just an ordinary building, but what counts is when you step through its doors. In this building we are not separated by the gringos. We are one."

" 'Conference' is a poor word to describe those five days," wrote Maria Varela, in *El Grito del Norte.* "It was in reality a fiesta: days of celebrating what sings in the blood of a people who, taught to believe they are ugly, discover the true beauty in their souls during years of occupation and intimidation. Coca-Cola, Doris Day, Breck Shampoo, the Playboy Bunny, the Arrow shirt man, the Marlboro heroes, are lies. 'We are beautiful'–this affirmation grew into a *grito,* a roar, among the people gathered in the auditorium of the Crusade's Center."

In the streets of Denver there were cries of youthful pain. The week before the Liberation Conference began some teen-agers walked out of the city's West Side High School to protest the insults of a teacher who had told his class, "Mexicans are dumb because they eat beans. If you eat Mexican food you'll become stupid like Mexicans." Students objected to his sense of humor and requested that the teacher be transferred. After a rally in the park the high school boys and girls tried to re-enter their school to present their demand to their principal. Two hundred and fifty policemen barred their way.

Soon there was "a riot." The ex-boxer hurried to the school. "Fearing the police were going to hurt the students I rushed forward to take a bull horn," Gonzales recalls. "I shouted to the young people to leave. The police were beating men, women, and children, indiscriminately." Gonzales' young daughter was one of those caught in the melee. "I heard my daughter Nita Jo scream. She was being mauled by a six-foot policeman." There were thirty-six Chicanos arrested.

Denver's barrios had never seen the kind of riots that had been desecrating ghettos in other cities. The people of the community walked to the school the following day to protest, in dismay as much as in anger. Some two thousand came, kids and parents, brown and black and white, teachers as well as students.

When the demonstration was over the police began to move in on those who lingered. There were curses hurled. In moments a battle erupted and dozens of police cars, riot police equipped with chemical Mace and a police helicopter, were ordered into the fray against the taunting teen-agers. "Some say it was a riot. It wasn't. It was more like guerrilla warfare," says one eyewitness. The helicopter dropped tear gas on the youths. "But the wind was blowing the wrong way and they [the police] ended up gassing their own men. This also happened with the Mace. The police were practically Macing their own faces," says another eyewitness.

George Seaton, the Denver Chief of Police, reported that twenty-five squad cars were damaged, "some extensively," and at least "seventeen police were assaulted, injured, and hospitalized." It was the worst street fighting in the modern history of the city.

"What took place after many people left was a battle between the West Side 'liberation forces' and the 'occupying army.' The West Side won," said Gonzales. He told the high school students, "You kids don't realize you have made history. We just talk about revolution, but you act it by facing the shotguns, billies, gas, and Mace. You are the real revolutionaries."

It was barely a year before that the Crusade for Justice leader had told me that he thought there would be no riots in the barrios. "The riots across the nation lead to the self-destruction of man. He acts like an animal," Gonzales had said. "I don't think it is in the Mexican temperament to riot, or to hurt your neighbor that way. Our way would be to pinpoint our enemy, where we wanted to attack him—not to riot."

Riots were "circuses," Gonzales had said then. He described the urban upheavals as the products of the "dehumanized cities," where life itself was riotous and people had no hope. "Why do blacks riot? Because they see no way out, because they feel trapped in the ghettos, because that is how mass society acts. I respect the suffering of the blacks. We have both suffered. We work together. But we work differently because we are a different people.

"Our culture is such that we don't like to march, to protest. We don't like to be conspicuous. We don't like to seem ridiculous in the public eye. That is *machismo.* That is a man's sense of self-respect. We are not nonviolent. But in the barrio self-determination means that every man, every people, every barrio has to be able to take care of themselves, with dignity.

"We are men of silent violence," Gonzales had said. "That, too, is *machismo*."

He voiced these thoughts in the summer of 1968, not in the spring of 1969. In the streets of the barrios of Denver something new had happened to the young Chicanos.

In the fiesta of the Chicano Youth Liberation Conference there emerged the "Spiritual Plan of Aztlán" that opened a new road for the odyssey of Rodolfo "Corky" Gonzales. The name of Aztlán had been that of the ancient nation of the Aztecs. Now the young Chicanos who had come from throughout the Southwest of the United States voted, almost unanimously, to revive the spirit of that defeated nation.

On the flowered and festooned platform the ex-boxer, former politician, and once-successful businessman, who had not so long ago sought so desperately to escape from the barrio, was the heroic host to the "Spiritual Plan of Aztlán":

In the spirit of a new people that is conscious not only of its proud historical heritage but also of the brutal "gringo" invasion of our territories, we, the Chicano inhabitants and civilizers of the northern land of Aztlán, whence came our forefathers, reclaiming the land of their birth and consecrating the determination of our people of the sun, declare that the call of our blood is our power, our responsibility, and our inevitable destiny.

We are free and sovereign to determine those tasks which are justly called for by our house, our land, the sweat of our brows, and our hearts. Aztlán belongs to those who plant the seeds, water the fields, and gather the crops, and not to the foreign Europeans. We do not recognize capricious frontiers on the Bronze Continent.

Brotherhood unites us, and love for our brothers makes us a people whose time has come and who struggles against the foreigner "*gabacho*" who exploits our riches and destroys our culture. With our heart in our hands and our hands in the soil, we declare the Independence of our Mestizo Nation. We are a bronze people with a bronze culture. Before the world, before all of North America, before all our brothers on the Bronze Continent, we are a nation, we are a union of free pueblos, we are Aztlán.

March 1969

Por La Raza Todo Fuera de la Raza Nada

23: GUERILLAS OF RIO ARRIBA: The New Mexican Land Wars

Clark Knowlton

FEAR HANGS LOW OVER THE GREEN MOUNTAINS OF IMPOVERISHED RIO Arriba County in northern New Mexico. Its tendrils swirl down the mountain sides into the irregular streets of the half-abandoned Spanish-American adobe villages. Local inhabitants tend strictly to their own affairs. Strangers are carefully observed and avoided. Guns and dogs are kept at the bedside. Fear penetrates the isolated ranch houses of the intruding Anglo-American ranchers who hire gunmen to protect their families and property. Fear chills the atmosphere around the ranger stations. Rangers avoid the isolated sections of the national forests. It is Alianza country. Fear glints from the badges of heavily armed state troopers and deputy sheriffs patrolling the roads and watching activities in the villages. The picturesque mountains are empty of hikers and campers.

Fear, although thicker today, has always haunted the hills and valleys of northern New Mexico. For almost 250 years, Spanish-American villagers and ranchers slowly moved northward against firm Indian resistance and without much government support. Unable to secure guns and ammunition until the coming of the Americans, Spanish-American frontiersmen adopted the lances, bows and arrows of their Indian opponents. The situation in many respects came to resemble that of the Scottish-English border of the seventeenth century. Apache, Navajo, Comanche and Spanish-American war parties regularly tithed one another's herds, crops and children. At the same time, an intensive trade in horses, slaves, hides, furs and other products was carried on.

Each village, socially and physically isolated by mountainous topography,

From *The Nation,* June 19, 1968. Reprinted by permission of the author and *The Nation.*

heavy winter snows, lack of roads, chronic Indian attacks and poverty, became a small, self-contained and slowly changing peasant world. The villagers, without schools or priests, had little contact for almost 300 years with other European groups. The distinctive peasant culture that evolved is somewhat different from the culture of other Spanish-speaking groups in the Southwest, and the reluctance of the village people to leave their villages except for short visits has always been recognized in New Mexico. The world outside was strange, alien and dangerous. Little sense of identity with any social unit larger than the village community has existed among these Spanish Americans until very recently. The concepts of ethnic solidarity, regionalism, or nationalism have had little meaning for them.

In 1847, the Spanish Americans were absorbed into the United States by military conquest and against their will. Although their property and civil rights were presumably protected by the Treaty of Guadalupe Hidalgo that ended the Mexican War, the Spanish Americans were treated as a conquered people by the incoming Anglos. Abandoned by both the American and Mexican governments, the rural, illiterate, Spanish-speaking village people, with little knowledge of American laws and customs, were left to the contemptuous mercy of the ruthless, dynamic, materialistic, individualistic frontier culture.

Ranchers with six-shooters drove them from their grazing lands. Businessmen entrapped them with credit and foreclosures. Anglo-American-controlled sheriffs seized their small farms and ranches for nonpayment of the hated land tax. State and federal agencies confiscated large areas of their lands without compensation. The Spanish Americans were caught in the web of unfamiliar political, economic and judicial systems. Stripped of their lands, they were reduced to the position of a rural proletariat. One authority estimates that the Spanish Americans from the 1880s to the 1930s lost more than 2 million acres of private lands and 1.7 million acres of communal lands to private holders, 1.8 million acres to the state government, and an even vaster but uncounted acreage to the federal government. The destruction of the Spanish-American rural village economy created a large depressed region marked by rates of disease, malnutrition, hunger, infant mortality, unemployment and welfare at least as high as similar rates among the Negroes of Mississippi.

Molded by their past experiences, the Spanish Americans are fearful and profoundly skeptical of the moral structure of the American political system. It is doubtful that many of them have ever understood its values or processes. And that is not surprising, since it is equally doubtful that these values or processes have ever been applied to northern New Mexico. To the local people, organized government is a conspiracy against the common welfare. Those individuals of Spanish-American origin who enter politics are dismissed as having sold out to the Anglo-Americans. Quite often the Spanish Americans are right.

Few state or federal political candidates ever visit the roadless Spanish-American settlements in the mountain canyons and valleys. Once every two years, political caravans tour the larger and more accessible villages. Alcohol, promises, money and oratory flow freely. Political manifestoes in debased Spanish (it is the one time that the Spanish language is even recognized in New Mexico) are widely distributed. Votes are bought and sold. The caravan departs in the morning, promises forgotten. For more than fifty years, Republican programs and Democratic programs have come in fanfare and departed in stealth, while social and economic conditions in northern New Mexico have continued to deteriorate.

The fires of discontent have always burned in the northern mountains. The anger flares up in an epidemic of fence cutting, barn and ranch-house burnings, and warnings to the Anglo-American ranchers and politicians to vacate Spanish-American lands. Cries for law and order bring out the troops and the National Guard. Numerous Spanish Americans are jailed, their protest organizations are repressed, their leaders are exiled, assassinated or imprisoned. The flames die down and the Anglo-Americans forget. However, the names and exploits of past Spanish-American leaders are kept alive in the stories and chronicles told and sung in the village bars. A new Spanish-American generation appears; new causes of protest arise; new protest organizations develop. The cycle starts all over again.

Anger, bitterness and resentment are blazing hot today. State officials armed with writs are traveling from village to village requiring that villagers prove their title to the irrigation water they use. Centuries-old Spanish-American customs of water use and ownership are being disregarded. The villagers are convinced that they are to lose their water as they lost their land. Spanish-American grazing rights in the national forests have been sharply reduced in the past two or three years. The small herds of beef cattle and sheep are thus forcibly reduced, since the village people have no other source of range. Anglo-American horses still graze freely in the forests. Hundreds of small farming and ranching families are faced with either emigrating to the urban slums or going on welfare.

The breaking point came suddenly in 1967. Thirteen fires were deliberately set that summer in the national forests. Anglo-American ranchers, schoolteachers, social workers and government employees reported growing hostility in the rural areas. Armed Spanish Americans were observed in the high mountains. Cars and pick-up trucks avoiding the police, whose presence is as heavy in northern New Mexico as is that of the civil guards in rural Spain, scurried from one village to another. Meetings took place in most of the villages. The local people bitterly denounced the closing of village schools, the lack of roads, malnutrition, loss of land and water, discrimination, erosion of grazing rights, and the failure of state or federal government agencies to pay attention to Spanish-American needs and aspirations. The Alianza Federal de Mercedes—the Federal Alliance of Land Grantees, now known as the Alliance of Free City States—is the largest, the fastest growing, the most vigorous, and the most important of a number of Spanish-American protest organizations. Formed around 1963, it was largely ignored by the Anglo-American community, and noticed only with ridicule by the press, which defined it as but one more of the many absurd organizations the Spanish Americans were always forming. Its meetings from 1963 to 1965 were attended largely by the rural poor, elderly Spanish Americans who still had hopes of recovering the lands taken from them.

In 1966, its membership began to spurt. Alianza organizers became active in most of the villages. Young people and veterans began to attend its meetings. Rural poor and urban poor flocked into its ranks. The message of the Alianza was simple and to the point: "You have been robbed of your lands, your water rights, your grazing rights, your language and your culture by the Anglo-Americans. No one is interested in helping you. Join us. Together, we will get the land back—preferably through the courts or Congress, but one way or another we will get it back." More and more Spanish Americans began to believe.

Reies López Tijerina, the tall, thin, nervous president of the Alianza, casts a growing shadow across New Mexico. A walking encyclopedia of land-grant history, he has traveled to Spain and to Mexico in search of data on the question. Constantly on the move from one village to another, he tirelessly repeats to receptive audiences the old stories of Spanish-American wrongs. Compelling and dynamic, he uses the common Spanish better than any other Spanish-American leader in New Mexico. To the despair of reporters and newscasters, he is capable of speaking for five or six hours at a time. He is now in jail, but he still dominates the scene.

The intensity of Tijerina's bitterness stems from his own history. He was born on September 21, 1926, into a poor rural migrant family in Falls City, Texas. His father, thrice widowed, raised ten children. The family moved in the migrant stream from the Lower Rio Grande Valley up to the Midwest and back through the Panhandle of Texas. Tijerina relates that he attended twenty different schools for a total of six months' education. He says that as a child he saw his family driven away from three farms at the point of an owner's gun, to avoid the payment of wages. His father had the tendons of one leg cut during a fight with Texas Rangers. Ranchers and rangers twice almost lynched his paternal grandfather in land conflicts around Laredo.

The New Testament changed the course of Tijerina's life. A Baptist minister left a copy with the family during a visit to a migrant labor camp in the Midwest. Tijerina read it through before falling asleep that night. In his sleep, he dreamed that he had been called to be a spiritual leader of his people. Leaving the harvest fields, he enrolled at an Assembly of God seminary in Ysleta, Texas. He was licensed as a minister and became an itinerant minister and missionary, working as a migrant and preaching in the fields and camps. To the despair of his wife, he thrice gave away everything he owned to needy migrants. He finally lost his license to preach when he told his audience that they had no right to give money to the church when their families were in need.

Leading a small congregation, he moved to Pima County, Arizona. The group worked together and managed to accumulate enough money to buy a piece of land. They built houses for their families and, by farming a little themselves and working for neighboring ranchers and farmers and in nearby towns, the small group eked out a living. At first, they got along well with their Anglo-American neighbors; then, it was announced that the site containing their land had been selected for the development of a retirement colony, and land values began to rise. Tijerina and his group refused to sell. Their refusal incensed the other owners and neighbors. Accusations of burglary, immorality, trespass and communist activities circulated in the county. Houses and other buildings were burned, and there were several violent encounters between Tijerina and the Anglo-Americans. In the end, Tijerina and a small group of families moved to Tierra Amarilla, New Mexico.

Tierra Amarilla, founded by Spanish-American pioneers who often rose against Spanish and Mexican governors, has always been a center of anti-American sentiment. The land grant on which the town and its neighbors stood was appropriated by prominent Anglo-American politicans in the last half of the nineteenth century. Their descendants sold the acreage to land and cattle companies. The directors of these companies have long been campaigning to clear the land of its Spanish-American inhabitants, many of whose ancestors were among the original settlers. The Spanish Americans organized small secret societies to cut the fences, burn the houses and barns, and snipe at the incoming ranchers. In typical Spanish-American manner, few lives were taken. The Spanish Americans abhor killing in cold blood.

Reies Tijerina and his little group of followers became embroiled in the land conflicts. It is rumored that he was active with one or more secret Spanish-American societies of night riders. In any case, enraged ranchers believed that he was and threatened to kill him. As a result, he moved to Albuquerque and there worked as a janitor in a Protestant church while organizing the Alianza Federal de Mercedes.

Like wrestlers in a game of catch as catch can, the Alianza and the Forest Service circled each other cautiously through 1966 and the early spring of 1967, with state and federal law-enforcement agencies acting as interested referees. The Alianza searched for a hold that would flip the Forest Service into a federal court suit to determine the validity of forest land titles. The Forest Service, aware of growing Spanish-American hostility toward its grazing policies and knowing that its titles were flawed, called for assistance from the referees.

Alianza leaders soon found a weak point in Forest Service defenses. A section of the Kit Carson National Forest containing the Echo Amphitheater public camp ground near Chama, New Mexico, was once part of a Spanish-American land grant. The titles of the villagers who had owned the land had never quite been quashed. The Alianza quietly called a series of meetings and told the local people that if they cooperated they might get some of their land back. A village organization was constituted with mayor, judge, council and sheriff.

Publicly advertised camp-ins were held at the camp ground. Reporters were in attendance. Forest signs were replaced with notices that the land once again belonged to the community of San Joaquín de Río Chama. Trespassers, including forest personnel, were warned to keep out. Several trees were cut to symbolize the change of ownership. Although a group of rangers and forest investigators watched the scene from a nearby ridge line, they did not come near the meetings. State police cars cruised in front of the camp ground, but did not enter. It looked as though the Alianza had won.

Then on the morning of October 22, 1966, when another camp-in was scheduled, the Forest Service acted. Two forest rangers and one forest investigator stationed themselves at the camp-ground entrance to require that all entering cars buy camping permits. A cluster of state police watched from the highway. A caravan of cars driven by Alianza members and sympathizers pulled up to the entrance. Asked to buy camping permits by the rangers, although no attempt had been made to sell them to people already on the ground, the drivers refused. The caravan started up again, and the rangers had to jump aside to avoid being run over. Hot words were exchanged. People left their cars and, joined by some already there, grabbed the rangers. There were cries in Spanish of "Lynch them," "Kill them" and "Now it is our turn." Reies Tijerina, his brother, and other Alianza leaders pushed their way into the crowd and took charge of the rangers. They led them to a table behind which sat the judge of the presumed village. The judge, a bizarre Anglo-American pretender to the Spanish throne, found them guilty of trespass and ordered them to leave the area. The rangers did so. The state police, in their role of referee, studied faces and noted license numbers.

After many months, federal attorneys in Albuquerque pressed charges. Further months of legal haggling ensued, during which the original charges were found defective, withdrawn, and replaced by new charges. The federal jury list for Albuquerque was challenged because it lacked Spanish Americans. The case was finally transferred from the friendly climate of northern

New Mexico to the frosty atmosphere of Anglo-American southern New Mexico. Although the Alianza leaders claimed that they had rescued the rangers from bodily harm a jury found them guilty in a Las Cruces courtroom of conspiracy to interfere with federal officials in the performance of their duty and of assault upon two forest rangers. A federal judge, who permitted considerable bullying of defense witnesses, sentenced the defendants to jail terms starting at six months and going up to two years for Reies Tijerina. The defendants were allowed bail. Round one, a very ambivalent victory, had gone to the Forst Service and the law-enforcement agencies.

Tensions over land, water, and grazing rights accelerated during 1966 and the early spring of 1967. The Alianza sponsored in Albuquerque a series of heavily attended meetings, where Anglo-American culture, the federal and state governments and the more conformist Spanish-American politicians were violently attacked. Representatives of militant Negro and Indian civil rights groups pledged support to the Alianza. Fraternal delegations attended from Spanish-speaking organizations throughout the Southwest. The meetings were widely reported, and New Mexico became charged with fear, excitement and unrest. Ranchers, newspapers and businessmen began to demand that the Alianza be stopped. A federal judge ordered the Alianza to turn over its membership lists. The demand was refused.

David Cargo, the governor of New Mexico, is a maverick Republican who won his office in part because the Spanish Americans had become disenchanted with the indifference of the Democratic Party to their demands and aspirations. He is married to a Spanish-American woman who had been a member of the Alianza. Cargo now began to visit many Spanish-American villages, accompanied by reporters. After listening quietly to the often bitterly stated problems and needs of the village populations, the governor brought these matters to the attention of the state. The first governor in more than twenty years to take the Spanish Americans seriously, he made systematic inroads into the weakening position of the Democratic Party in northern New Mexico.

To the great disgust of the state police and many Anglo-Americans, Cargo started to negotiate quietly with the Alianza. An agreement was worked out. An Alianza campground meeting scheduled for June 5, 1967, could take place. There would be no police interference as long as there was no violence, destruction of property or violation of the laws of the state. The Alianza went ahead with plans for the meeting, the inflammatory language of its advance proclamations cooling perceptibly.

The day before the meeting, Governor Cargo flew to Michigan to meet with Governor Romney and to attend a Republican fund-raising dinner. A few hours after his departure, two Democrats—Alfonso Sánchez, state district attorney, former Alianza lawyer, but long-time Alianza opponent, and Captain Joseph Black, state police chief—went on the air to announce that the meeting was banned. They denounced the leaders as radical agitators and con artists, the members as dupes; they threatened to arrest any member of the Alianza who came near the camp ground. Orders of arrest were issued for Reies Tijerina and other Alianza officials. Road blocks went up. The Alianza membership list was found in a car stopped on the road to the meeting. Shortly thereafter many people lost their jobs.

Reies López Tijerina and most of the important leaders of the Alianza eluded the police blockade. Furious and feeling that their agreement with the governor had been broken by the state, they decided to resort to violence. A raiding party was formed to attack the county courthouse at Tierra Amarilla, seize Alfonso Sánchez, and free arrested Alianza members.

District Judge Paul Scarborough was sitting on the morning of the raid; Sánchez sent an assistant to present the state's case. The judge dismissed the charges against the Alianza members on the ground that the evidence against them was inadequate; the defendants left the courtroom. A few minutes later, the armed raiding party entered the courthouse and forced everyone present to lie down on the floor. The Alianzistas searched for Alfonso Sánchez and for their missing members. Finding neither, they were at a loss. Two deputy sheriffs and a janitor were wounded; one of the deputies subsequently died. The raiders finally seized two hostages and fled toward the mountains, dodging their way through police blockades.

At the news of the raid, panic and confusion swept the state offices in Santa Fe. The northern mountains, so close to the state capital, suddenly became ominous. A mass Spanish-American uprising was rumored to be slaughtering the Anglo-American population in the north. Guerrilla bands, secretly trained and led by Cuban army officers, were said to be marching on Santa Fe. Other guerrilla forces were believed, in the hysteria, to be establishing bases in the remote mountain areas, and revolutionary urban cells of the Alianza to be planning to set fire to Santa Fe and Albuquerque.

The lieutenant governor called out the National Guard. Units equipped with artillery and tanks, and accompanied by heavily armed state police, sheriff posses and Apache tribal police, swept through the Spanish-American villages and manned road blocks on all approaches to the area. Though martial law had not been declared, they broke into homes without warrants, detained men, women and children in a sheep corral for many hours with no food and no water except that contained in a polluted sheep tank. Private property was confiscated and suspects were held. Every Spanish American was suspect. A large part of northern New Mexico was treated as though it were an enemy country in the process of occupation.

Early on the morning of January 3, the body of Eulogio Salazar, a resident of Tierra Amarilla and a major state witness to the Alianza raid on the courthouse there, was found on the road near his house. He had been beaten to death. The bail bonds for Reies Tijerina and the Alianza members accused of taking part in the court raid were immediately revoked, and the men were rounded up during the day. Their jailing sent another violent controversy swirling through the state. Police officers and a good part of the press believed automatically that the Alianza was guilty of Salazar's murder, while Alianza sympathizers claimed that the men were being tried without evidence in the court of public opinion. Throughout the week, the police searched for evidence to convict the Alianza, while the press, television and radio discussed the implications of the case. Finally District Judge Joe Angel, appalled by the publicity, signed a gag rule prohibiting any discussion of the murder by public officials.

The Alianza members jailed for the crime were brought before the state supreme court. Their lawyers argued that the bail revocation was "arbitrary, capricious, a naked exercise of judicial power without any rational basis in fact." Under questioning, District Attorney Sánchez said that the state had no direct proof that any Alianza member was involved in Salazar's murder. He therefore was unable to file charges against any of them, although he seemed convinced of their guilt. Captain Black stated: "Tijerina is bound to be tied into it somewhere." The supreme court on January 17 ordered that bond be reinstated for all the arrested Alianza members except Reies Tijerina and three others, holding that they, through their participation in the raid on the courthouse, had been involved in a capital crime.

The death of the deputy sheriff wounded in the courthouse raid remains unresolved. The district attorney and the head of the state police maintain that Reies Tijerina and the Alianza are responsible. Persistent rumors from the Spanish-American population of Tierra Amarilla blame a small group of Anglo-American militants, ranchers and small businessmen, who are believed to have done it to incriminate the Alianza. Other rumors spreading widely have it that the police also killed Salazar to remove a witness on the verge of changing his testimony.

Judge Angel on February 8, at the close of extensive hearings on the courthouse raid, ordered Reies Tijerina and ten Alianza members bound over for trial. Charges against them were reduced from first-degree kidnaping to false imprisonment. The judge ordered that all defendants be freed when bonds were made. Charges against nine defendants, including Tijerina's beautiful nineteen-year-old daughter Rose, were dismissed.

On April 28, Reies Tijerina spoke to the Mexican-American student convention sponsored by No Más, a student organization on the campus of the University of Texas at El Paso. The administration had barred Tijerina from speaking on campus, so the meeting was transferred to a local motel. Back in Albuquerque, Tijerina, along with twelve other Alianza members, was arrested once again by Alfonso Sánchez and Captain Black. Twenty-five counts of second-degree kidnaping and two counts of robbery and the carrying of concealed weapons were placed against the defendants by a hand-picked grand jury in Rio Arriba County. It should be noted that these charges of kidnaping had been thrown out by Judge Angel. Bail was set at $20,500 for each defendant.

These latest charges are but further steps in a long series of arrests and releases on bail designed to bankrupt the Alianza and its supporters and to keep Reies Tijerina and other Alianza leaders behind bars. Although the governor, the state legislature and the federal agencies have done nothing to diminish the tragic social-economic conditions in northern New Mexico that give rise to movements such as the Alianza, the state and federal law-enforcement agencies have adopted a repressive policy that will inevitably spark violence throughout the Southwest. Apparently, New Mexico must experience a serious outbreak of rural and urban terror before the authorities learn that repression and jailing are not the answer to Spanish-American problems. Reies Tijerina has become a martyr, a hero and the very symbol of the hopes and aspirations of militant young Mexican-American and Spanish-American groups from Los Angeles to San Antonio.

The massive violation of human and civil rights, the mistreatment of large numbers of rural Spanish Americans, many of whom had nothing to do with the Alianza, and the absolute refusal, thus far, of the Department of Justice and the Commission on Civil Rights to take any stand, have driven a wedge between the Spanish Americans of the north and the state and federal governments that will require years to overcome. Guerrilla warfare remains a distinct possibility. Groups more militant and deeper underground than the Alianza are being formed. The situation is not unlike that of Ireland just before the "Risings." A brooding calm now lies over the northern hills.

Editor's Note: Reies López Tijerina has since served over two years in federal prisons on three concurrent federal sentences and is on parole. His appeals to overturn two additional state convictions stemming from the Tierra Amarilla raid have been rejected by the New Mexico State Supreme Court. Tijerina now faces returning to jail unless pardoned by the Governor.

After his initial sentencing, Tijerina's wife and son were allegedly assaulted by police officers and several thousand dollars of Alianza money placed in the custody of local law enforcement officials has "disappeared."

The spirit of hope and protest raised by the activities of Tijerina and the Alianza lingers on, even though the potential immediate impact of the movement seems to have diminished.

B. Radicalism

IDEOLOGICAL, OR "OLD-STYLE," RADICALISM, PARTICULARLY MARXISM, has not historically attracted ethnic political movements.[1] Even racial minorities, largely excluded from the system, have not accepted the radical ideologue's analysis of the American system and his prescription for basic change. However, the continued exclusion of the Chicano and black, with the resulting frustration, have led to an increased questioning of the basic distribution of economic and political power in the United States. The alternative of democratic socialism is seriously considered as an option by some persons in the Chicano movement. In the first selection, Antonio Camejo, at the time of this interview a candidate for public office on the Socialist Workers party ticket in California, shares some of his thoughts on Chicano politics.

Camejo's is a more ideological viewpoint, but what has been termed "new-style" radicalism or "the politics of group passion" is emotional rather than ideological and is based on "a preference for action rather than cognition and polemics."[2] Such radical politics has been manifested in both violent and nonviolent mass protest. In his article describing the past Los Angeles "blow-outs" Louis Negrete includes some observations about the general efficacy of Chicanos' using mass protest as a political tactic. The largely successful nonviolent "Huelga" movement of César Chávez is examined and analyzed in the articles by Bob Fitch and Henry Weinstein.

In the interview "Tilting with the System," conducted before his major successes with the United Farm Workers Organizing Committee, Chávez explains why nonconventional tactics such as strikes and boycotts are necessary methods for people that are relatively powerless when engaged in traditional politics. He also stresses the importance of support by "outside parties" such as the general public and religious groups. The support of these and other allies, plus the personal character and dedication of Chávez and the other *Huelgistas,* led to the success and resultant optimism recounted by Henry Weinstein in mid-1970. As contracts expired in 1973 many of the hard-fought gains vanished as growers did not renew contracts with the UFW.

Chávez has pledged to renew the fight and has issued a call for continued boycotts.

NOTES

1. Edgar Litt, *Ethnic Politics in America* (Glenview, Illinois: Scott, Foresman and Co., 1970) pp. 92-101.

2. Litt, *Ethnic Politics*, pp. 101-102.

24: A NEW IDEOLOGY FOR THE CHICANO PARTY

Antonio Camejo

MY CONCEPTION OF AN INDEPENDENT CHICANO POLITICAL PARTY IS NOT that it has to be socialist or have a socialist program. It probably will develop a socialist program as the revolution approaches, but this will not be the case at the beginning. Socialists *will*, of course, be in the forefront of building the Chicano party, because this would represent a major break with the system and would be a giant step forward for the people. We would be active members of a Chicano party, and I, for example, would be proud to run as a candidate of such a party. But, there would also be large numbers of people in the party who have not yet been convinced of socialism, and who will only become convinced as a result of the struggle.

. . . Let me deal with some of these problems involved in building a party. First of all, an independent Chicano political party would not just run in elections. I think Roger Alvarado makes an extremely important point about elections. We cannot get into the bag of the Peace and Freedom Party which just brought a whole bunch of liberals and radicals together for the purpose of running in an election. The Peace and Freedom Party was an electoral coalition, nothing else. The day after the election, it fell apart. You never heard anything from them after that. And you're probably going to begin to hear from them again, because another election is coming up. They end up doing nothing except miseducating the people about what is really needed. I would be opposed to this type of formation.

An independent Chicano political party would not just take part in

From *La Raza! Why a Chicano Party?* (New York: Pathfinder Press, 1970), pp. 6-8. Reprinted by permission of Pathfinder Press.

Mr. Camejo's remarks were addressed to a symposium on Chicano liberation held at California State College, Hayward, November 13-14, 1969, sponsored by the college's La Raza organization.

elections, but it would also have to engage itself in the day-to-day struggle of our people. It would have to be a party which would lead such things as campus struggles, that could participate in helping to form the Chicano studies departments around the entire Southwest and the entire country wherever La Raza happens to be. It would be a political party that would participate in mass demonstrations over different issues in the community, in the schools, for housing, against the war. It would be the type of organization, for example, that would do the kind of things that the Crusade for Justice has been doing. It would do this as well as participate in electoral activity.

The point I am making about the Democratic and Republican parties is the following: that in my opinion it is a principle, a revolutionary principle, and in the tradition of Emiliano Zapata, you know, who said, "I will die a slave to principles, never to men," that you do not support those people who are oppressing you. Principles are important, and if you have incorrect principles, you cannot make a revolution.

It's a principle that you do not support those people who are oppressing you. That's a principle in my opinion. I refuse to support in any way the people who are responsible for my oppression. Now, in terms of elections, however, it would be incorrect for us to take the attitude that since we know that the electoral system in this country is a farce, since we know that the Republican and Democratic parties play a con game, since we know that you cannot make a revolution through elections, since we know that we are not going to take power in this country through elections, that therefore we don't participate in them. That would be a mistake.

The history of the revolutions throughout the world have shown that it is a tactical question whether you participate in elections, and how you participate in them. Lenin, for instance, in the Bolshevik Party, which made the first socialist revolution in the world, participated in elections. Fidel Castro ran in elections. The point is this, that even though we understand the whole question about electoral politics, the community does not. The majority of La Raza does not know the role that the Democratic Party plays, therefore it is our task to be able to reach them on this.

Elections are a tactic that can be used by revolutionaries to be able to reach the people, and to be able to organize the people. For instance, by running in elections you can get on television. It's incorrect to say that they won't let you on. An example of this is Paul Boutelle, who is a revolutionary Black nationalist and a socialist, who got on a half hour of national network time on the Joey Bishop show, where he got up there and rapped about how rotten this system is, how decadent it is, and why we have to have a socialist revolution.

How was he able to do this? Because there is a law which says you have to give candidates who are running for office equal time on radio and TV, and

Paul Boutelle was running on the Socialist Workers Party ticket. Sure they try to take this time away from us. They try to maneuver in every way they can. But, we fought back against them, we were right up there with our lawyers, and said, "Nothing doing, you've got Nixon up there, you've got Humphrey up there, we're going to talk for a half hour too." And they had to give it to us. We fought for it legally and we won that.

Now, we're going to do the same thing in the state of California with the election campaign coming up. We're running as revolutionary socialists in this campaign to reach thousands of people with our ideas and educate them about the needs of the people in this state. We are also running our campaign as an example of the type of thing that can be done if Brown people organize their own party. And we will be campaigning in favor of building a Chicano party. And if an independent Chicano party were formed in this state, we would be supporting it and building it. There is a tremendous potential for building such a party. We can do it. We can go in and talk to our people. We can win them over.

Let me say something about what we can do. It's true we are a minority, but the Democratic Party in the state of California can only win if the Chicanos vote for it. Think of that. We have the potential to wipe it off the face of the map as a political institution. And on a national scale, in alliance with Black people, we have the power to make it impossible for the Democratic Party to win another election in this country. Just think of what this means. We have the power to turn the political structure in this country upside down and inside out.

Now, what does that mean? Does that mean that the Republican Party would always run the country, and that we then would be worse off? The Democratic Party wins an election because it is supported by a coalition of the labor movement, Brown and Black people, and other Third World people, Native Americans, Asian Americans.

The labor movement which includes white racist workers–and they are racist–support the Democrat Party for two reasons: 1) they think the Democratic Party can produce on their demands and 2) they think the Democratic Party can win. However, if it can be proved that the Democratic Party cannot win another election, they would have to rethink their whole strategy. This is especially significant in terms of the radicalization in this country, where the Democratic Party is being exposed as the party of the Vietnam war, and where more and more people are beginning to see more clearly that the Democratic Party is not fulfilling their needs.

And you know, the American workers have been indoctrinated for 30 years that the Republican Party is their arch enemy. And it would be difficult for the ruling class in this country to turn around and say, "Now you've got to support the Republicans." The whole question of who the workers should support would be much more open to question and discussion. And those people within the labor movement who believe the workers should organize a labor party in their own interest, independent of the Republicans and Democrats, would get a much better hearing.

The point is that the formation of a Chicano party could help to change the whole political relationship of forces, and could help set an example for other people who want to fight oppression, for Black people, for people in the labor movement who are for organizing an independent political power.

At the same time we would be driving wedges into the majority population, breaking them up. You know how the ruling class maintains their position, how they divide and rule. Well, in a revolutionary struggle the smartest thing to do is to take your enemy and break him up, drive wedges into him, break off sections of the majority, and win alliances for yourself, and then your minority becomes larger and larger until it is no longer a minority but through alliances becomes a majority. That's the tactic that we can use in terms of building a political party.

If we don't take this step, if we don't use our political power, we will never get anything but crumbs. We will be guaranteed tokenism, and we will lose struggle after struggle. And let me end on Chavez. It's true that he would be able to talk to a lot of people, and tell the truth about the grape strike and tell about the oppression of LA RAZA. It's true that he would be able to do those things. But, that's not the key thing. He would be doing a disservice to the entire movement in this country because he would be miseducating people about the crying need to break with the Democratic Party. He would be miseducating people, and it's a lot harder to educate people after they've been miseducated about what is necessary.

It's like driving a stick shift for 30 years, and then trying to switch to an automatic. You end up having an accident because you keep pushing the clutch down, and there's no clutch there. That type of miseducation makes it harder to eventually form an independent Chicano party. It would make it harder for us to talk about a Chicano party if Chavez was at the same time campaigning and registering people in the Democratic Party. And the truth of the matter is that this has already been tried again and again and nothing has come from it.

Malcolm X made a very strong statement on this. He said, "Anyone who supports the Democratic Party after its record of oppression, and what it has done to our people, is not only a fool, but a traitor to his race."

25: CULTURE CLASH: The Utility of Mass Protest As a Political Response

Louis R. Negrete

THIS PAPER EXAMINES THE 1968 EAST LOS ANGELES STUDENT STRIKE AS A spontaneous mass protest by Chicano[1] students against the Los Angeles school board. It is the author's contention, unlike some of the points of view presented, that such mass protests by culturally different and powerless groups are effective political vehicles for needed change. This paper has obvious relevance for other minority communities.

COMMUNITY CONTROL

The phrase "community control" is often used in present day literature focusing on Chicano and urban problems. Seeman, Bishop & Grigsby (1970) define community control in a social psychological sense: community means attachment to a common identity, a common aim, a common fate, or any combination of these; and control is a sensed capacity to influence (i.e., social policy, political elections), a feeling of power. A more traditional definition of community control is as a political term, meaning control of a geographical area, usually a neighborhood (Sherrard & Murray, 1968). A neighborhood is defined by Kotler (1969) as a political settlement of a small territory and familiar association, whose absolute property is its capacity for deliberative democracy.

The barrios of El Sereno, Lincoln Heights, Boyle Heights, City Terrace and

From *The Journal of Comparative Cultures* I, no. 1 (Fall 1972), pp. 25-36. Reprinted with permission of the author.

The author is indebted to Professor Robert D. Kully, Speech Communications and Drama Department, California State University at Los Angeles, for helpful suggestions and comments.

East Los Angeles, having similar racial distribution and socioeconomic problems, meet the criteria of neighborhood as defined by Seeman, Sherrard, and Kotler. The area is heavily populated by Chicanos and constitutes the largest Chicano barrio in the nation. Los Angeles County has the largest concentration of Mexican Americans anywhere outside of Mexico and has almost as many Chicanos as the State of Texas. The Chicano barrio is characterized by high unemployment, high school dropout rate, inadequate housing and serious health problems associated with urban neighborhoods. The East Los Angeles section of the barrio is located in the county area outside the Los Angeles city limits while the remaining section of the barrio is located within the Los Angeles city limits. The Los Angeles school district covers both the county and city areas and includes Wilson, Lincoln, Roosevelt, and Garfield High Schools, which have predominantly Chicano student bodies.

Community control as used in this paper means the ability of Chicanos to influence directly public policy affecting them. In this study, the public policy refers to the policies and practices of the Los Angeles school system. A study of Chicano student mass protest is timely. Student activism during the 1960s on American campuses was more radical, more militant and involved more students than ever before. Student demonstrations against the war in Vietnam, the draft and university administrators became frequent throughout the nation. In his study of college student protest, Skolnick (1971) found that students protested and demonstrated out of anger and moral indignation over injustices in the system. Skolnick states the student case for mass protest as essentially based on contentions that mass confrontation and militancy arouse action, educate the public and young radicals, helps recruit non-student youth and middle-class militants, and that political "backlash" is usually exaggerated. Morales (1971) was unable to find a significant "white backlash" in the anglo community after two East Los Angeles riots, confirming the student contention on the latter point.

Lenski (1966) refers to the conflict between youth and adults as the most underrated, yet highly serious, class struggle in America today. Youth feel powerless in a world controlled by adults. Youth must abide by rules formulated by adults and which youth cannot change. Youth live in a world of their own made up almost entirely of other youth and which adults cannot understand. The hypocrisy of adult behavior is exposed by youth who in turn become more alienated from their elders. Youth are also at their physical best and freewheeling, not held back by marriage or other similar restraints. Thus the struggle between youth and adults may at times become revolutionary in tone and result in violence. Lenski foresees that although the character of the struggle may change from time to time, the struggle itself is destined to continue for some time. Perhaps the recent change in election laws permitting 18-year-olds to vote may tend to lessen their conflicts.

Pitt (1966) and McWilliams (1948) have made reference to mass protests by Chicanos in the early history of California and the Southwest. However, studies of contemporary Chicano mass protests are notable by their scarcity. Mass protest activities by Chicanos are generally assimilated and lost in studies of minority group protests, student power or urban problems. Ericksen (1968) viewed the 1968 East Los Angeles student strike as a case for bilingual education. Munoz (1971) studied the 1968 East Los Angeles mass protest by measuring the effectiveness of the Educational Issues Coordinating Committee (EICC) in negotiating with the Los Angeles school board on behalf of the striking students. Moore and Martinez (1971) studied the same activity in relation to the impact on the professionalism of Chicano teachers. Morales (1971) examined police-Chicano conflicts in East Los Angeles during the East Los Angeles Riots.

Ericksen omits consideration of community control. Bilingual education without community control would have limited impact on the sense of political powerlessness in the barrio. Barrio residents have long recognized that bilingual education without community control could be an empty gesture. Because Ericksen omits to consider this crucial issue, his writing is of limited value to the present analysis.

The approach used by Munoz assumes that the essence of Chicano mass protest can be captured by studying Chicano organizations. Little evidence is available to support that assumption. However, there is considerable evidence showing that the lower the socioeconomic status of a community, the less likely its members are to join and participate in voluntary organizations (Kornhauser, 1959). The selection of an inappropriate criteria to measure Chicano barrio actions will very likely lead to inaccurate conclusions. It may be possible for mass protest to begin and succeed even with the absence of an identifiable formal organization operating under Robert's Rules of Order. The use of the ad hoc committee which disbands after its goal is accomplished or a third party intervenes is increasing in the barrio. Chicanos in the barrio will follow a respected leader irrespective of the organizational flag, if any, he may be carrying. There are many leaders in the Chicano barrio. Some are publicly known, some are not, but each has his own sphere of influence, sometimes organized, sometimes with a loose following of supporters. To judge the effectiveness of Chicano mass protest by the degree to which Chicano organizations conform to accepted organizational theory is to miss the point. Munoz, for example, found EICC to be defective when measured against standard organizational criteria. Moore and Martinez gave the Association of Mexican American Educators (AMAE) a more favorable judgment. Such judgments, however, seem of limited value when studying mass protest in the barrio. They omit appreciation of the uniqueness of the Chicano movement which is often described as masses of people moving in the same general direction, sometimes with little or no formal organizational structure, and sometimes with no identifiable designated leader. Thus it appears that previous research reflects values which demand measurable formal organizational efficiency. That such a value is valid when studying Chicano mass protest in the barrio is yet to be established.

Additional research may be worthwhile to test the claim that a Chicano barrio without formal organizational structure has its advantages. Organizational leaders are easily identifiable and may be more easily co-opted or rendered ineffective by establishment groups. Leaders in what appears to be an unorganized, sometimes confusing, mass protest are not easily identifiable and may survive longer as effective agents of change.

THE BLOWOUTS OF EAST LOS ANGELES

Moral indignation over the inferior quality of education in their schools seems to have been a major factor in motivating Chicano students (in the nation's largest barrio) to mass protest. The high school student strike became known as the 1968 East Los Angeles Blowouts. Munoz described the school system as an essential part of the political system over which Chicanos felt powerless. Morales also found Chicanos in East Los Angeles politically powerless over public policy. This sense of powerlessness existing over curriculum, teachers, administrators and support services contributed to student frustration and anger.

A tremendous increase in communication among Chicanos in the barrio was spurred by Chicano community grassroot newspapers, most notably *La Raza.* The farm workers' strike in Delano had intensified Chicano pride. Reies Lopez Tijerina's revolutionary rhetoric and call to arms at Tierra Amarilla, New Mexico, was widely discussed by Chicano youth activists. Rodolfo Corky Gonzales had already begun the Crusade for Justice as part of the Chicano movement in Colorado. While establishment Chicano spokesmen were saying that Chicanos would not riot like the black rage that had exploded in Watts three years previously, Chicano youth were talking about revolution and liberation for the masses of Chicano people in the barrio.

Imbued with the rhetoric of the Chicano revolution, Chicano youth began to direct action to dramatize the high pushout rate in their high schools. In February, 1968, they drafted and distributed leaflets specifying their concerns and demands for a better, more relevant education. "Walk Out Now or Drop Out Tomorrow," became an oft-repeated slogan. The students were specific in their demands: the need of a reduction in class size, new schools with names consistent with community identity, Spanish-speaking counselors, more counselors, expanded library facilities, revitalization of the industrial arts program, roofed lunch areas, improvement of building facilities, removal of campus fences, unrestricted access to all buildings and restrooms during school hours, better janitorial services, abolition of current I.Q. testing, development of valid student testing techniques, improved teacher awareness of community problems, and the placement of proper emphasis on student violations (student leaflets). Although school officials knew that a student strike was a serious possibility (McCurdy, 1968a), they ignored the student demands.

On March 1, 1968, the National Advisory Commission on Civil Disorders had reported to the nation that "white racism" was responsible for city rioting and for the separation of the races in America (Burke, 1968). On that same day, several hundred Chicano students at Wilson High School in the El Sereno neighborhood moved to the center of the stage and raised the curtain on Chicano student mass protest in the United States.

Friday, March 1, 1968, began as usual at Wilson High School. But tension was explosive and anything could have ignited a student demonstration. An unenlightened principal gave the militant students an immediate, specific, dramatic reason to protest. The principal cancelled the play, "Barefoot in the Park," as being too dirty. A spontaneous protest began to develop against the principal's unilateral action. Word was quickly passed that a student walkout would occur at noon. A hundred students gathered at a school gate at the noon hour. At first, a handful of students walked out, followed by a few more cautious ones. Slowly, more students walked off the campus until hundreds of students were outside the school grounds. There was some excitement in the crowd. Fruit, eggs, books, and trash cans were thrown about. Everyone seemed to be leaving the campus until the police arrived. Most of the students then returned to the school, but several hundred refused to attend class and remained in the school yard. The police remained on duty at the school until the students left to go home (Student Leaflet, 1968).

The following day, the school superintendent was quoted in the *Los Angeles Times* (1968a) as saying that because of insufficient funds many children would continue to receive an inappropriate education. School system spokesmen persisted in viewing Chicano student demands as a financial problem rather than as a question of educational relevancy. Things were quiet on Monday but the word of what had happened at Wilson High School got around. The largest mass protest against the Los Angeles School system in its history was beginning to take shape. Then, on Tuesday, March 5, more than 2,000 students boycotted classes at Garfield High School. Two persons were arrested, but except for a broken window to a press car, the demonstration was a peaceful one. About 700 black students also boycotted classes at Jefferson High School that day to protest cafeteria conditions (*L.A. Times,* 1968b).

The following day, Wednesday, over 500 students refused to attend classes at Roosevelt High School, where a number of students were arrested after a student-police confrontation. At Garfield High School, over 300 students boycotted classes and two were arrested. Over 500 students walked out at Lincoln High School and marched to the office of the Los Angeles Board of

Education for a confrontation. On that same day, about 400 students continued to boycott classes at Jefferson High School. The students at Garfield High School returned to classes after the principal promised to meet with the students (*L.A. Times,* 1968a).

While Chicano students were being arrested for boycotting classes and demonstrating for community control, the lone Chicano member of the Los Angeles school board, Dr. Julian Nava, was in the State Capitol arguing against a legislative proposal to create a separate Chicano school board to operate Chicano schools. Nava, whose election to the school board was originally viewed as a victory for the Chicano community, argued that the proposal was segregationist and that he was strongly opposed to it (Fairbanks, 1968). Nava's position is not surprising. Chicano elected officials often function no differently than non-Chicano officials. Some are forced by political expediency to support the present method of electing the school board (seven members elected at large, serving part time). As a politician counting potential votes on election day, Nava may be compelled to oppose community control for Chicanos in the field of education. Under the status quo, only Chicanos acceptable to the general community can get elected to the Los Angeles School Board. Nava, who lives and works in a suburban, white, middle-income neighborhood, has that acceptability which he might risk by supporting Chicano demands for community control over the schools.

One alternative to the current method of electing the school board, recommended by the Los Angeles City Charter Revision Commission, would be to enlarge the Board of Education to consist of 11 members, each elected by a separate district, serving full time for a four-year term. Districts would be apportioned according to population every five years (Jaeger, 1969). Another more radical proposal is to establish a separate school board to operate the areas covered by the four Chicano high schools and a separate school board for the South-Central area of Los Angeles, where the black community is concentrated. Nava's defense of the current system of electing the school board can be understood when viewed as a necessity for his political survival, as well as an expression of his essentially moderate-to-conservative approach to educational problems affecting Chicanos.

On Thursday, the student strike continued with particularly intense student-police confrontations at Belmont and Garfield High Schools. Over 200 demonstrators attended a meeting of the school board that day to press their demands. The meeting was abruptly adjourned when a member of the Brown Berets attempted to address the audience. It had been a hectic day for school officials. Attempted arson and broken windows were reported at George Washington Carver Junior High School and the student strike had spread to Belmont High School where 10 persons were arrested (West & Larsen, 1968).

More than 1,000 students from Garfield, Roosevelt, Lincoln, and Wilson High Schools boycotted classes on Friday and attended a rally at Hazard

Park. Congressman Edward Roybal and other public officials also attended the rally. The students had by now spelled out in fuller detail some of their demands. A stronger emphasis for a curriculum relevant to their cultural heritage underscored all the demands (McCurdy, 1968b).

Meanwhile, at Belmont High School, 500 students boycotted classes and six more persons were arrested. Fourteen persons were arrested at George Washington Carver Junior High School and the teachers at Jefferson High School organized and staged a walkout of their own to protest student militancy and the student walkout (McCurdy, 1968b)!

The following Monday, the walkout continued with 3,500 students absent from classes at Wilson, Garfield, Roosevelt, and Lincoln High Schools. About 1,500 at Venice High School boycotted classes, Twelve students were arrested after a police-student confrontation there (McCurdy, 1968c). The student strike also spread to Grant High School in Van Nuys, where 200 students demonstrated against the school system (Burleigh, 1968).

Next day, the student-police confrontation continued at Venice High School where over 1,000 students boycotted classes and twelve were arrested. Over 800 students at Edison Junior High School also stayed away from classes that day (McCurdy, 1968d).

Concurrently, 25 Chicano parents staged a sit-in at the office of the District Attorney. They refused to leave until after the County Sheriff, Peter Pitchess, met with them and heard their complaints (McCurdy, 1968d).

The student strike meanwhile continued at the four Chicano high schools. At various times during the strike, this writer observed members of United Mexican American Students (UMAS), now Movimiento Estudiantil Chicano de Aztlan (MECHA), at California State University, Los Angeles, and some Brown Berets help striking students avoid arrest and in some instances avoid injury by placing themselves between the students and the police.

Paul Coates (1968), a featured columnist with the *Los Angeles Times,* blamed the Chicano community for its political powerlessness. He advised the "chicos" on strike to instead urge their parents to vote and to refer them to the League of Women Voters. Coates' simplistic faith in vote power ignored the reality of gerrymandered political districts designed to render the Chicano vote meaningless. Coates failed to recognize one of the major contributors to the sense of powerlessness in the barrio.

At a subsequent meeting of the school board, the student strike leaders announced that henceforth the student demands would be presented by the Educational Issues Coordinating Committee (EICC), a community group composed of a broad cross-section of Chicano activists. Eventually, the grand jury indicted 13 Chicanos associated with the blowouts on a conspiracy to disturb the peace charge and over 30 EICC members were arrested at a sit-in at the Board of Education in September, 1968. Disturbing the peace is a misdemeanor as an individual act. A charge of conspiracy to disturb the peace is a felony. This was to be the beginning of the use of the more serious conspiracy charge by law enforcement officials as a weapon against Chicano mass protest. The conspiracy charge also permits the power structure to label dissident community groups as criminal in attempts to discredit them.

AFTER THE BLOWOUTS

Some change has occurred since 1968, but not much. A bilingual education program has been slow and modest in starting. The token appointment of a few Chicano school administrators has shown some promise. The newly established Mexican American Education Commission as an advisory body to the school board is just beginning to prove its value to the community. Meanwhile, the pushout rate remains high and the overall quality of education in Chicano schools remains low (U.S. Commission on Civil Rights, 1971). The underlying causes of the 1968 student blowouts remain unresolved.

Chicano students and school officials realize that something must be done to improve education for Chicanos (Reich, 1968). One marvels at the very slow, sometimes repressive (*L.A. Times,* 1968c), process by which the school system responds to vital community needs.

An editorial in the *Los Angeles Times* (1968d) described the problem of unequal education of Chicanos as one due to lack of sufficient funds and implied that Chicanos should be patient until enough funds are available to educate them. This view was later reiterated by the school board in agreeing that 99 per cent of the student demands were sound but that the school district lacked the funds to implement them (McCurdy 1968e).

In his study of mass protests, Lipsky (1968) identified the technique of claiming relative impotence to do anything about a problem by establishment organizations as an effective response because it gives the impression that the establishment organizations appreciate the problem but are helpless to do anything about it. However, there should be no doubt that if the *Los Angeles Times* and the community generated sufficient pressure, the necessary funds could be found to give Chicanos a quality education. The school board has attempted to pass bond issues to finance school improvement projects, but the voters have rejected those attempts which would have increased the property tax.

Students, however, have shown that their patience is not eternal. They have discovered and made operational their own weapon against inferior education and an insensitive power structure. The students simply walk out. They learned how to bring together community militants and conservatives, including the "bato loco." The concept of "Chicano Power" has real meaning for Chicano youth. Shouts of "Viva La Raza," "Viva Zapata," and "Viva La Revolucion," communicate strong emotional and cultural appeals for community solidarity (Torgerson, 1968).

While there appears to be some consensus that the high pushout rate must be reduced (McCurdy, 1968f), nothing commensurate with the problem has been done. The future of education for Chicanos in Los Angeles seems bleak. It appears destined to recurrent student-police confrontations while alternatives to community control are rejected by the school board. Use of police power against Chicano youth in school has caused much resentment in the Chicano community. Two years after the 1968 walkouts, Chicano students at Roosevelt High School again boycotted classes for over a week, resulting in the arrest of 109 persons. Without consultation with the Mexican American Education Commission, school officials called the police to the school and another serious, intense police-student confrontation occurred. There were also demonstrations that week in support of the Roosevelt High School students at South Gate, Huntington Park, and Lincoln High Schools (Dreyfuss, 1970). When will it end? It will apparently end when Chicano students are provided an education which respects their culture and affords them a similarity of educational returns.

EFFECTIVENESS OF CHICANO MASS PROTEST

Munoz concludes in his analysis of the student strike that mass protest by powerless groups will not succeed. Paradoxically, Lipsky (1968), upon whose research Munoz based his theoretical framework, concluded his study by suggesting that mass protest activities may also be viewed as an organizing agent within a powerless community. (Lipsky cites Alinsky to support this observation.) Similarly, Haggstrom (1969) judges the success of a protest activity by whether power has increased among the powerless, even if radical organizational change has not occurred in the power structure.

The Chicano community, as Munoz found, considered the walkouts a success. The increase in community awareness is reflected, for example, in the emergence of direct action groups in the barrio such as the Chicano Moratorium Committee, Casa Carnalismo, Casa Venicidad, Casa Hermandad, and Barrio Defense Committee. The developing La Raza Unida Party as a political party for Chicanos, with sufficient popularity to prevent the election of a Democratic candidate in 1971 in a traditionally Democratic State Assembly district, is a significant organizing process for eventual community control. The serious threat of a boycott compelled the La Puente Board of Education, in a nearby community, to negotiate with the Organization of Mexican American Communities over Chicano demands for reform (Jones, 1972).

It should then be clear, that even a series of defeats or one major crushing blow can be advantageous to the Chicano movement for community control. As Haggstrom found, a major defeat may become a symbol around which the community can unite to continue its struggle. The violent removal of the National Chicano Moratorium Committee and its supporters from Salazar

Park by the Los Angeles County Sheriffs and the fatality of Chicano newsman Reuben Salazar during the East Los Angeles riot of August, 1970, aroused the Chicano community to new heights of militancy in the United States.

Many Chicanos understand that the movement for community control will be a long one. Spectacular, dramatic changes in the organizational structure by the establishment are not expected overnight. The view that mass protests do not succeed in producing structural change, in addition to being promulgated by Munoz, has been expressed by Los Angeles Superior Court Judge Leopoldo Sanchez and other Chicano activists (del Olmo, 1971). This view is just too limited in scope. It recognizes, but greatly minimizes, the organizing skills that take root after each protest and the enhanced community militancy which results. Unless Chicanos sustain their own militant movement with roots in the barrio, reflecting barrio aspirations for community control, the barrio will remain in the hands of liberal politicians who refuse to share their power.

Rosalio Munoz, past chairman of the Chicano Moratorium Committee, states the point clearly in his letter to the *Los Angeles Times* in January, 1971, which is cited in full by Morales (1971). Rosalio Munoz concludes his letter thusly:

> Rather than calling off our protests and return to a life of fear under police totalitarian aggression, we have to continue to protest for survival purposes. If Chicanos lose their right to protest in society because of police political violence, you likewise are losing your freedom in America. In this respect our insistence of the right to protest guarantees the right to *all* people in America to protest. If we allow police violence to intimidate us, it is really the broader society that is victimized.

Alinsky (1971) said that those who reject orderly revolution invite bloody revolution. Community control should not be feared by Los Angeles school officials. Alinsky describes fascism and dictatorship, with its correlates of apathy, hopelessness, frustration, futility and despair, as the poison which numbs a community denied control over institutions affecting their lives. The antidote is militant involvement, protest if necessary, characterized by concern, trust, accomplishment, satisfaction, and expectation.

Even in defeat, Chicanos may experience a sense of power against oppressive forces. Bloomberg and Rosenstock (1968) describe mass protest by the poor as a "sociotherapeutic" process by which individuals and groups may experience a sense of power against those institutions that have exploited them (c.f., Morris, 1972). So long as the Los Angeles power structure continues to permit an unresponsive system of inferior education for Chicanos, Chicano students may have little alternative but to organize mass protests against the school system, knowing that in all likelihood they face defeat, but with the hope and knowledge that each time it will become a little more difficult for the power structure to win.

NOTES

1. Chicanos in the United States have always had different symbolic self-designations. Depending on regional and personal political persuasions, descendants of Mexican immigrants have called themselves a wide range of names, including Spanish-speaking, Spanish surnames, Americans of Mexican descent, Mexicans and Mexican American, and simply, Americans. Today's Chicano youth has rejected the assimilationist melting pot theories of the past and insist on retaining their individual identity, cultural heritage and Spanish language. If they must compete with white and black America for the benefits of this society, they insist on doing so as Chicanos. Defining Chicano is like trying to define "soul." Chicano has come to mean honor, pride, and culture for increasingly greater numbers of individuals of Mexican descent. For purposes of this paper a Chicano is whoever calls himself a Chicano and whomever others call a Chicano.

REFERENCES

Alinsky, S. Reveille for radicals. In Gelb, J. & Palley, L. *The Politics of Social Change.* 1971.

Bloomberg, Jr., W. & Rosenstock, F.W. Who can activate the poor? In Bloomberg, Jr. W. & Schmandt, H.J., *Power, Poverty and Urban Policy.* Beverly Hills, Calif.: Sage Publications, 1968.

Burke, V. J. Panel warns of trend to 2 separate unequal societies. *Los Angeles Times,* March 1, 1968, p. 1.

Burleigh, I. 200 Grant High students tell grievances in leaflets. *Los Angeles Times,* March 12, 1968, pt. 2, p. 8.

Coates, P. The Mexican-American–Why they don't vote. *Los Angeles Times,* March 13, 1968. pt. 2, p. 6.

del Olmo, F. East L.A. leaders urge end to big rallies. *Los Angeles Times,* February 4, 1971.

Dreyfuss, J. Crowd jeers Roosevelt High administration supporters. *Los Angeles Times,* March 13, 1970, p. 3.

Ericksen, C.A. Uprising in the barrios. *American Education,* November, 1968.

Fairbanks, R. L.A. school officials and legislature clash. *Los Angeles Times,* March 7, 1968, p. 3.

Haggstrom, W.C. Can the poor transform the world. In Kramer, R.M. & Specht, H. *Readings in Community Organization Practice.* New Jersey: Prentice-Hall, 1969, p. 301.

Jaeger, H. School board changes proposed. *Los Angeles Times,* October 15, 1969.

Jones, G.L. School boycott called unlikely after meeting. *Los Angeles Times,* February 12, 1972.

Kornhauser, W. *The Politics of Mass Society.* Glencoe, Ill.: Free Press, 1959.

Kotler, M. *Neighborhood Government: The Local Foundations of Political Life.* New York: Bobbs-Merrill Co., 1969.

Lenski, G.E., *Power and Privilege, A Theory of Social Stratification.* New York: McGraw-Hill, 1966.

Lipsky, M. Protest as a political resource. *American Political Science Review,* 1968, *62,* 1144-1158.

Los Angeles Times

a. Crowther sees lean days for L.A. Schools. March 3, 1968, p. 11.
b. Classes boycotted by student groups at 2 high schools. March 6, 1968, p. 3.
c. Rafferty calls on state board to punish students in walkouts. March 15, 1968, p. 3.
d. School boycotts not the answer. March 15, 1968, pt. 2, p. 4.

McCurdy, J.

a. Student disorders erupt at 4 high schools; policeman hit. *Los Angeles Times,* March 7, 1968, p. 26.
b. 1000 walk out in school boycott. *Los Angeles Times,* March 9, 1968, pt. 3, p. 11.
c. School board yields to some student points in boycotts. *Los Angeles Times,* March 12, 1968, p. 1.
d. 1000 at Venice High clash with police; 8 seized. *Los Angeles Times,* March 17, 1968, p. 1.
e. Demands made by East Side high school students listed. *Los Angeles Times,* March 17, 1968, p. 1.
f. East Side dropout rate stressed in school unrest. *Los Angeles Times,* March 18, 1968, pt. 2, p. 6.

McWilliams, C. *North From Mexico.* Philadelphia: J.B. Lippincott, 1948.

Moore, J. & Martinez, A. The Grass Roots Challenge to Educational Professionalism in East Los Angeles. In Castaneda, A. & Ramirez III, M. *Mexican Americans and Educational Change.* Symposium at the University of California, Riverside, Mexican American Studies, 1971.

Morales, A. *Ando Sangrando! I Am Bleeding, A Study of Mexican-Police Conflict.* Los Angeles: Perspectiva Publications, 1971.

Morris, J. A. Rioting good for you, says psychiatrist. *Los Angeles Times,* February 10, 1972, p. 16.

Munoz, C. The Politics of Educational Change in East Los Angeles. In Castaneda, A. & Ramirez III, M. *Mexican Americans and Educational Change.* Symposium at the University of California, Riverside, Mexican American Studies, May, 1971, p. 83.

Pitt, L. *The Decline of the Californios.* Berkeley: University of California Press, 1966.

Reich, K. Principal walks narrow path in school walkout. *Los Angeles Times,* March 14, 1968, pt. 2, p. 6.

Seeman, M. Bishop, J.M. & Grigsby III, E. *Community and Control in a Metropolitan Setting.* University of California, Los Angeles, 1970.

Sherrard, T.D. & Murray, R.C. The Church and Neighborhood Community Organization. In Frieden, B.J. and Morris, R. *Urban Planning and Social Policy.* New York: Basic Books, 1968.

Skolnick, J. Student Protest. In Gelb, J. & Palley, M.L. *The Politics of Social Change.* New York: Holt, Rinehart & Winston, 1971.

Student Leaflet, Why should there be a student walkout. February, 1968.– Wilson Walkout, March 1, 1968.

Torgerson, D. Brown power unity seen behind school disorders. *Los Angeles Times,* March 17, 1968, sec. c., p. 1.

United States Commission on Civil Rights. *The Unfinished Education: Outcomes for Minorities in the Five Southwestern States.* Mexican American Educational Series, Report II, October, 1971.

West, R. & Larsen, D. Education Board halts meeting in climax to school orders. *Los Angeles Times,* March 8, 1968, p. 1.

26: TILTING WITH THE SYSTEM: An Interview with César Chávez

Bob Fitch

FITCH: The first question I'd like to ask is "Why boycott?"

CHAVEZ: You know, when you consider everything, we don't have any options. Most of the other things that would have been options depended entirely on the good will of the government and we know enough to know that they're not going to move. Especially, they're not going to move in a conflict situation like ours. Personally, the big reason was this: I thought the American public would respond affirmatively.

F: That's optimistic. Most of the predictions now about the American public are not optimistic.

C: They're not optimistic because they're clichés now—"the country's sick," and all those things. Really, we haven't tried to understand how institutions work. The common procedure is to insult your friends and to feel that they ought to drop everything they are doing and come in and help you. Theoretically that would be great. But if you're going to organize, and if you're going to be a realist, you know how much to expect and you're not going to be disappointed. You plan accordingly, along very realistic lines.

F: What's the realistic basis for optimism about a public response to the boycott?

C: Well, first of all, I contend that not only the American public but people in general throughout the world will respond to a cause that involves injustice. It's just natural to want to be with the underdog. In a boxing match, however popular the champion may be, if he begins to really get the other guy and beat him up bad, there is a natural tendency to go with the underdog. And in this struggle it's not a contest between two people or a team but a contest between a lot of people who are poor and others who are wealthy.

F: What happened to the other options? Such as legislation?

C: When you get into legislation you're playing with a borrowed bat. Once you get into legislation then it's the whole question of compromise. The only reason growers are seeking legislation now, after 35 years, is because they are under pressure. They want to use legislation to take away that new-found right the workers have found through the boycott.

F: What do you mean?

C: Legislation that's being proposed permits unions but takes the boycott right away from the workers, and doesn't permit them to strike during harvest time. Of course that's the only time we work. The proposal comes not out of a spirit of giving the workers civil rights, but as a gimmick to further restrict their rights.

F: Why can't you stop the importing of Mexican labor?

C: It's a long history of the government and the employers working together. Not the same program but different variations. In fact, it's part of the system. Even under the most liberal administrations we wouldn't get them to enforce border controls. The immigration service and the border patrol always worked on the assumption that it is not really illegal for these people to be here provided they are working, are being useful to the growers. The moment they stop being useful–either because they strike or because they don't work any more since the crops are finished–then of course it becomes very illegal and they are thrown out. It's a very corrupt system.

F: "Corrupt" implies collusion to break the law, which is a very heavy charge. Do you want to make that charge?

C: Sure, sure, except that I'm not saying that money crosses hands. What I'm saying is that the guy before me did it, the guy before him did it, so I can't change it. It's that kind of setup.

F: That takes any connotation of deliberate action away from the growers.

C: No, it's a deliberate attempt, it's very deliberate, most deliberate! What I'm trying to explain is that it is more sinister than if they were paying money. This way the immigration service people are as much servants as we are. They're not getting paid off. They do it because of the power that the industry represents. So it's worse than if they were actually being paid money.

F: What happened to the strike?

C: To strike in any rural setting in any state today–and I don't care what state it is, California, Texas, Florida, Arizona–you're fighting the growers in their own bailiwick. You're fighting them in their own setting, so they are able to bring the tremendous powers from the police and the courts and all the structures against you on the picket line to break it totally. For instance, with Giumarra we had a thousand people out, and we had 'em out for four days, and there wasn't a soul in the fields–50 people at most. At the end of the fourth or fifth day we were enjoined and we were permitted to have three people on either side of each entrance. Two days later people just went on through because the workers didn't know we were striking. The people who are being imported as strike breakers don't really know what's happening and sometimes don't care. The injunction is just a manifestation of the power they have. There isn't enough money or time or energy to be appealing all those things that they keep throwing at you. The boycott gets them out of the setting. They can't reach us in the boycott. The farther away from Delano, the more diffuse their power is.

F: Has the boycott worked?

C: We figure that we are cutting back the sales now by about 33 per cent. But all that means is that we are forcing them to cold-storage the grape. The grape hasn't been lost yet. And in order to be 33 per cent effective we would have to keep up the same kind of pressure or increase it in the coming weeks.

F: What is the main issue of the strike?

C: The central issue is the whole question of recognition. Do, or will, workers have the right to have a union and have it recognized by their employers?

F: How do the growers respond?

C: Mostly they say that workers don't want a union, that if workers wanted a union they would give them a union. Really what they're saying is that the only way they're going to recognize the workers is if the workers bring enough economic heat on. The employers are still at the point where industrial employers were 50 years ago. They say, "If you want a union come and get it." In other words, "Force me to give you a union."

F: And what evidence is there that the workers want a union?

C: Well, I think that the only kind of evidence we have that cannot be refuted is the experience we've had in eight different cases where they've given workers a right to vote on whether they want unions or not. They have overwhelmingly voted that they want a union.

F: So you're ready to put it to a vote?

C: Oh sure. See, when the employers say that we don't recognize the workers or that workers don't want a union, we say give the workers the right to make this self-determination by giving them the right to an election, with the understanding on our part that if the workers vote against the union we'll call the thing off. But if the workers vote for the union, then the employers are duty bound to bargain collectively and to sign a contract with the union.

F: Who supports you?

C: Number one, the public. They were given something to respond with. That's important. Then labor, for money and technical assistance–and from just being around them you learn a hell of a lot, you know. Not necessarily by asking but just by keeping your eyes open and seeing what's happening.

When it comes from a labor guy it means something, because they certainly have their experiences. And there are a lot of good guys in the labor movement generally. I defend them as much as I defend churches and other groups. It's funny how the guy who is so sensitive about making a general crack about blacks or browns thinks nothing about making a general crack at labor or the church or other groupings. I think the church brings the other kind of power. The moral power and the kind of assurance that what you're doing is really an important task. That fortifies you in your spirit. It legitimates the movement at least against the reckless attacks from the right.

F: What has the churches' Migrant Ministry done?

C: Well, in terms of any organized group it's the best by far. They were helping us from the first moment we came to Delano—way back, before the strike. In fact, the very first thing I did when I came to Delano was to meet with the Migrant Ministry up in the Sierras; they were having a retreat, and I spent three days with them. In C.S.O. [Community Service Organization] people used to kid me because I was very close to the Migrant Ministry. First of all, I've always been kind of—well, the word is not "religious," but "church-related." I dig it. And so whenever they had any meetings, when I could I would slip away and go to their meetings and be with them. It was relaxing. Besides being good people they were very committed and very strong. It was a joy to be there.

F: What do you want from the church?

C: It is very difficult to say what we want. The church should understand one thing that escapes many people. They are concerned to have people who are poor and dispossessed organize, but churchmen don't know the process of organization. A church group appropriates hundreds of thousands of dollars and after a few years doesn't have any results. They pull back and say, "Well, it can't be done." So many times the church makes the mistake of wanting to get something done, and not understanding that it takes a lifetime to do it. They throw in a lot of money initially to get things to change overnight, and nothing happens overnight. And it's not going to happen overnight. Then there's this general moralization, "It didn't work." They have to understand more about the workings of organizations in underprivileged groups, minority groups or farm workers. Now, in our case they need more of an understanding of how it works so that they can make wiser contributions, and make more long-term commitments.

F: The church isn't the organizer?

C: It can't be the organizer. It's got to be done by the people. But they've got to have the confidence in the people that it can be done.

F: Why are you an advocate of nonviolence?

C: Well, you see, it started before the union. The first day we took a vote to strike I asked for a nonviolent vote. I have been asked this question many times and I have really had to dig back and find out. I think it goes back to my family, particularly my mother. She's a very illiterate pacifist. She never learned how to read or write, never learned English, never went to school for a day. She has this natural childishness about how to live, and how to let people live. In the old days, at least when I was a kid–it was generally true in a lot of families, much less so now in my family–there were occasions when she would gather us around her and she would call it *consejo.* "Consejo" means to council, to advise, She didn't wait until it would happen–like: "You fight now? Well here it comes: I'm going to tell you how bad it is to fight." I remember that she would talk constantly about nonviolence–constantly. She used many *dichos.* "Dichos" are sayings, parables–for instance, things like "It takes two to fight; one guy can't fight by himself," or "Flies can't come into a closed mouth; keep your mouth shut."

F: So nonviolence was your nursery.

C: I would think so.

F: It's part of the family–in your blood, in your home, everything?

C: Yeah. And I've done a little tracing–not only my mother but both sides–and our people were very peaceful on both sides. We didn't have any generals or warriors. Very plain peons, so I think that's where it started. My Dad never fought. We never saw my Dad fight or drink or smoke–all the things that have a bad meaning. My parents weren't too young when they married. They were in their early 30s, so once they married they gave us children all their attention. They were with us all the time; she would never think of having a babysitter taking care of us. They enjoyed being with us. We weren't pampered either. They were strict.

F: I'm wondering if you had to do some reassessing of nonviolence in terms of some of the recent benedictions that violence has received.

C: No, no! You see, what is happening is that all or at least most of it is just theoretical violence.

F: There has been a lot of rationalizing of what is happening in the ghettos in terms of the riots. Some of it has been theological.

C: I don't buy it. How in hell can you get a theologian to accept that one or two or three lives are worth giving up for some material gain? It doesn't stop there, it's just the beginning. The real paradox here is that the people who advocate peace in Vietnam advocate violence in this country. Inconceivable; I don't understand it.

F: We've seen two movies on this trip through the eastern part of the country. One was *Midnight Cowboy,* the other was *The Battle of Britain. Midnight Cowboy* involves a rather gruesome murder in which a telephone is shoved down a man's throat. This seemed to be excused as an act of personal devotion to another man. *The Battle of Britain* involved a war to preserve a nation and its values. In both there was a high rationalization of the act. It seems to me that movies project violence as acceptable, more real, present, more of an experience, whereas nonviolence seems like an impossibility, unreal.

C: No! I think nonviolence is a very natural way of doing things, and violence is highly out of the ordinary.

F: That's an easy statement to make.

C: No, it's very true.

F: You said that nonviolence is more natural.

C: Sure. Remember, the moment you and I get together we're going to have to deal. Right? Or we're going to have to deal through violence, one or the other. If you and I talk here for 20 years no one is going to say much. But if we get into a big heated discussion and we stab each other, more people are going to know what happened here. It's not natural, you know. So what I'm saying is that a lot of good things happen. Who knows about all the contracts that we signed? With the exception of the three big battles, no one knows, because they weren't fights. Something was done without a struggle. It was nonviolent.

F: Does the United Farm Workers Organizing Committee want to be more than a union, a force for social reform?

C: I think that if the union loses the social force it has now it's going to become pretty meaningless. The most important thing is to provide an instrument with which workers, by their own actions and their own desires, can work themselves out of poverty.

F: It's an instrument or tool for poor people in this nation?

C: Yeah, for poor people. This is always the first order of business. But once that's attained and once they are well on their way to attaining the first contracts, to having the union recognized—along with that comes responsibility. If the workers keep that social consciousness and use it as an instrument, not only will they help themselves, but they will also help others less fortunate, and they will be a voice in society against those ills that are part of our life.

F: The C.I.O. started out with some of these aims. Why do you think you can succeed whereas that union wasn't able to?

C: Well, let's say we hope that it will be different; that remains to be seen.

F: What are you doing to make it happen?

C: We're making it uncomfortable on ourselves to be quiet. We're trying to build around ourselves a sort of in-group gadfly, if you please, that is going to keep us moving ahead on some of the social ills even though we have such a big job, an overwhelming job, in building the union. That job hasn't been done yet. We're just now beginning to do it.

27: NEW ROWS TO HOE

Henry Elliot Weinstein

DELANO, Calif.—Cesar Chavez is a 43-year-old Mexican-American who works for $5 a week plus room and board, less than he earned as a youth toiling in the grape and cotton fields of the Southwest. For that scant pay, he has been called everything from "saint" to "Communist" and has had to give up most of his family life with his wife and eight children, a plight he recognizes with much regret.

But his job has carried Cesar Chavez from a Don Quixote-like figure tilting at windmills to a labor hero on the verge of accomplishing the impossible in the annals of U.S. unionism: Organizing the nation's army of farm workers.

For nearly five years, his campaign has raised the wrath of table grape growers, his initial target, and rallied a coalition of Mexican-Americans, Filipinos, housewives, students and clergymen into a social action program that transcended the traditional union drive. Grape growers found themselves not only picketed in the fields but denounced from pulpits, and their products were boycotted throughout the nation. "Chavez is trying to destroy the grape industry and that means destroying the people he's trying to organize," claims John Giumarra, treasurer of the largest grape concern in California, the state that produces 90% of the U.S. crop. "Ultimately he wants to become czar of agriculture in the U.S."

However, on Wednesday Mr. Giumarra signed a contract with Mr. Chavez's United Farm Workers Organizing Committee (UFWOC). His capitulation signified that the five-year-old grape strike and boycott is about to end in a victory for the farm workers union.

A victory hardly seemed possible when Mr. Chavez took over a sputter-

From *The Wall Street Journal,* July 31, 1970, pp. 1, 15. Reprinted with permission of *The Wall Street Journal,*

ing strike in late 1965 in the vineyards around this arid town of 15,000, center of a $100 million-a-year grape industry. Until this spring, the UFWOC strike and subsequent boycott appeared headed to the scrap heap along with other agricultural union failures over the past decades. This spring, however, the boycott began to hit growers where it hurt them most, in the pocketbook.

The result: About 75% of the grape growers have signed contracts with UFWOC. The remaining 25% are expected to follow shortly. "It's dawned on everyone in agriculture that unionism has finally come to this industry and there's no sense pretending it will go away. The thing to do is come to the best possible terms," says John Giumarra Jr., counsel for Giumarra Vineyards Co. and son of the company treasurer.

UFWOC's recent success "is a historical development," remarks Don Vial, chairman of the Center for Research at the University of California's Institute of Industrial Relations in Berkeley. "We haven't seen anything the likes of this in agricultural collective bargaining."

FIGHT WITH TEAMSTERS

One reason for unions' past problems is that farm labor bargaining has been governed largely by the "law of the jungle," according to Mr. Chavez. When the Wagner Act in 1935 granted labor unions a "bill of rights" and formalized collective bargaining procedures for industry, agricultural workers were specifically excluded. So they have had to establish the right to bargain on their own without benefit of the orderly procedures provided for other industries under the law.

The success of UFWOC in the vineyards appears to have convinced some producers of other farm products that unionization of their workers is inevitable. On Tuesday, the Teamsters union announced it had signed contracts with growers in the Salinas area covering production of most of the nation's lettuce, about half of its celery, carrots and strawberries, and a sizable portion of dozens of other fruit and vegetable crops, including broccoli, cauliflower and potatoes.

Ironically, however, the Teamster announcement caused no joy among UFWOC leaders. UFWOC and the Teamsters have been battling furiously over the right to represent field hands in the Salinas Valley, known as the nation's "salad bowl."

SEN. MURPHY'S BILL

Some observers have speculated that the signings really were an attempt to head off the growth of UFWOC in the wake of the grape victory. Mr. Chavez referred to the Teamster agreements as "sweet-heart contracts."

The battle with the Teamsters may spur Congress to enact labor legislation for farm-workers. However, the only bill currently pending in Congress is given little chance of passage. Introduced by California Sen. George Murphy, a vociferous opponent of the grape boycott, the "Consumer Agricultural Food Protection Act of 1969" does provide for collective bargaining machinery. But the bill also would outlaw strikes at harvest time (the only effective time to strike, say farm workers) and product boycotts.

Buoyed by the victory in the grape struggle, Mr. Chavez appears calm about the battles that lie ahead. Petting "Boycott," the German shepherd that is his constant companion, Mr. Chavez says there is a simple reason for recent UFWOC successes: Hard work.

"Most of us in the movement get turned off by rhetoric. We're an action movement. We keep moving night and day," says Mr. Chavez. "I'd feel complimented if you called me a fanatic," he says. "The only ones who make things change are fanatics. If you're not a fanatic around here, you can't cut it."

"What's happened here is a miracle," says Dolores Huerta, 40, UFWOC vice president. "But it didn't come about by magic." One recent morning a reporter saw Mrs. Huerta at 4 a.m. as she was about to depart for a picket line. She had last been seen entering a midnight meeting with Mr. Chavez and Jerry Cohen, a union attorney. "Haven't you had any sleep?" the reporter asked. "No, why spoil the fun," replied Mrs. Huerta, who has a reputation as a "ferocious negotiator."

A SOCIAL MOVEMENT?

"There's still a long, long struggle," Mr. Chavez cautions. And he makes it clear that the emerging victory in the grape boycott is just the beginning. UFWOC is going after melon growers next, and other major commodities subsequently. Moreover, UFWOC recently signed a contract with Roberts Farms (total 46,000 acres) which not only grows grapes, but is also the world's largest producer of walnuts, almonds, persimmons and canned figs, thus giving the union a substantial wedge into production of those items. Coming in an era of social ferment where UFWOC activities have taken on all the trappings of a civil rights struggle, the potential for large scale farm unionism is now greater than ever.

Certainly for Mr. Chavez, organizing farm workers is not just a union battle; it is a broad social movement that he calls "*La Causa*," or "The Cause." In addition to its organizing and negotiating activities, the UFWOC runs a hiring hall (which it hopes will eventually phase out the middleman labor contractor in agriculture), a credit union (which will loan a member up to $500 at 1% interest, after he has made an initial investment of $5), a clinic, a cooperative gasoline station and a newspaper.

Sitting in the special rubber-backed rocking chair he uses because of back trouble, Mr. Chavez asserts that broad economic power is the key to uplifting the farm worker. He refers to the boycott as "our most effective nonviolent weapon."

(In his adherence to nonviolence, Mr. Chavez has sometimes been compared to the late Martin Luther King, a man with whom he corresponded but whom he never met. Even Mr. Chavez's bodyguards are unarmed. Some growers aren't convinced of Mr. Chavez's adherence to nonviolent principles, however; some violent attacks on nonstrikers and their cars occurred during the long grape workers dispute, though UFWOC has denied any responsibility for them.)

PLAID SHIRT, LEVIS

To his job as leader of "La Causa," Mr. Chavez brought deep religious conviction (a Roman Catholic, he takes communion every day) and a formal education that stopped at the seventh grade. In his plaid shirt, Levis and work boots, he still is indistinguishable in a crowd from the field hands themselves.

Bob Armington, 62, crew leader at the ranch of John J. Kovacevich in Arvin, about 50 miles south of Delano, says Mr. Chavez's ability to rally farm workers around him was not easily won. "We're very careful about who we look up to as leaders. We've been sold out in the past," says Mr. Armington as he uses a spectrometer to test grapes for sugar content on the first day of the harvest in sweltering 105-degree heat. He refers to Mr. Chavez as "a wonderful man." The reason? "He looks up to poor people."

The "real heroes of the struggle," in Mr. Chavez's view, have been the workers who have gone to urban areas to organize boycotts. Like Mr. Chavez, they are paid $5 a week, plus room and board. Their work is an endless series of meetings at churches, homes and schools, plus the organizing of picket lines and rallies and, of course, discussions with store managers and shoppers. "Waving flags, marches and demonstrations and other things are good and give publicity to the strike, but they are no substitute for convincing people, one by one, not to buy scab grapes," says Larry Itliong, national boycott coordinator and assistant director of UFWOC.

THEY DON'T UNDERSTAND

One problem at times has been UFWOC's need to control some of its sympathizers who have committed acts of vandalism at supermarkets. "Some people really believe they're helping us by destroying property," says Marcos Munoz, boycott coordinator for New England. "They don't understand how this destroys us."

William Kircher, director of organization for the AFL-CIO, says Mr. Chavez's development of "strong indigenous leadership" has been one of the keys to UFWOC success thus far. Every Friday night the union has a meeting conducted in English and Spanish at Filipino Hall in Delano, and Mr. Chavez attempts to get as many workers as possible to address the members so they will become accustomed to a leadership role.

Mr. Kircher also admires UFWOC's racially-integrated structure, almost a rarity in this era of separatist movements. At first the Filipinos, who constitute a sizable minority of farm laborers, were concerned about being "swallowed up" in the union because there are many more Mexican-Americans, says Mr. Itliong.

Mr. Itliong, 56, headed the AFL-CIO's Agricultural Workers Organizing Committee, which merged with Mr. Chavez's independent National Farm Workers Association to form UFWOC in 1966. Mr. Kircher says Mr. Chavez and Mr. Itliong are "without peer in understanding the need for one class of citizenship in the union structure, without regard to ethnic background."

THE CHURCH'S ROLE

Bob McMillen, the UFWOC's lobbyist at the California state legislature, says another facet of the union's strength has been Mr. Chavez's ability to build a coalition of supporters which runs the gamut from George Meany, president of the AFL-CIO, to student activists and Black Panthers. "That's no mean feat," he adds.

Perhaps even more crucial has been the role played by the Catholic Church. The Bishops Committee on Farm Labor has been instrumental in bringing UFWOC and the growers to the bargaining table–something that was once considered impossible. While the Bishops Committee has never formally endorsed the boycott, it has stated unequivocally that farm workers have the right to organize into a union and that they should be included under the National Labor Relations Act and national minimum wage and unemployment insurance programs.

Responding to criticism that the church has been overly zealous in pursuing these goals, Monsignor Roger Mahoney, secretary of the Bishops Committee, says: "Our participation in negotiations has usually been at the invitation of growers, not the union. So many people think the church has tried to push Chavez down on these companies–it's not the case."

Most of the contracts signed by UFWOC provide for a wage of $1.80 an hour, 15 cents above the current state minimum (and in contrast to $1.10 an hour before the strike began); this will be increased to $1.95 in 1971, $2.05 in 1972, and renegotiated thereafter. The contracts also call for incentive payments of 20 cents per box of grapes picked, 10 cents an hour for a health and welfare fund (named after the late Sen. Robert F. Kennedy, who was an ardent supporter of UFWOC and referred to Mr. Chavez as "one of the heroic figures of our time") and two cents a box for a special economic development fund (chiefly for housing elderly field hands who can work no longer).

A NEW BELL

In addition, jobs will be assigned through the union hiring hall. Formal grievance procedures will be instituted. Strikes will be prohibited during the three-year agreements. Every box of grapes shipped by the signatory company will bear the union label, a black Aztec eagle. And joint union-grower committees will regulate the use of dangerous pesticides, such as DDT and aldrin. Mr. Chavez is quite adamant on the pesticide question. "What's the use of getting your people a good contract if their health isn't protected?" he asks.

Near the end of a reporter's interview with Mr. Chavez, his secretary bursts into his office and says: "It's here. It's here. The bell."

Mr. Chavez walks outside to see "the farm workers" bell contributed by the Whitechapel Foundry in England, where the original Liberty Bell was cast, and driven across country in a panel truck contributed by the United Auto Workers, one of UFWOC's strongest supporters. At present, the bell is chained to prevent it from ringing, a symbol of the "slavery" of farm workers "to poverty and paternalism," Mr. Chavez explains.

The lock on the chain bears the UFWOC's black eagle and is not to be removed until all the grape growers have signed contracts with the union. "This bell is going to start ringing pretty soon," Mr. Chavez comments as he heads back to his office smiling.

C. Violence

THE LONG HISTORY OF OPPRESSION AND THE RESULTING SUBORDINATION imposed upon the Chicano has led to a great deal of frustration. This has sometimes resulted in the Chicano striking back at the core culture society. The last several years have witnessed several disturbances in the cities of the Southwest, most notably in Los Angeles. Professor Morales recounts the 1970 and '71 East Los Angeles Chicano-police riots. Antagonisms between the Chicano and the police have a long history. Police harassment and brutality have traditionally characterized Chicano-police relations and continue up to the present. Additionally, Chicanos have been denied equal access to legal remedies and are typically grossly underrepresented in the judicial and law enforcement agencies of the Southwest. These facts have been documented in a recent report by the U.S. Commission on Civil Rights entitled "Mexican Americans and the Administration of Justice in the Southwest."[1] Thus, it is more than a coincidence that many of the civil disturbances involving Chicanos have resulted from initially minor incidents between law enforcement officers and Chicanos.

One well-publicized incident in the state of New Mexico, again involving law enforcement agencies and Chicanos, was that of the raid on the Tierra Amarilla Courthouse in 1967 by Tijerina and his followers. In an earlier selection Professor Knowlton related this happening and its social and historical context in his piece on the New Mexico land wars. Violence, or perhaps more realistically speaking, reactive self-defense has been institutionalized to a certain extent in such organizations as the Brown Berets of California and the Black Berets of New Mexico. While primarily community self-help groups, these organizations also view themselves partly as self-defense organizations protecting the Chicano community from what are seen as core culture "occupation troups," the system's police forces. They do not hesitate to use violence as a tactic when violence is done to them. Note point twelve of the Black Beret platform presented here.

Have the civil disturbances and riots had any effect on the political system? What consequences are likely to ensue from these politics of passion? It is still unclear whether the black rebellions of the late 60s that occurred in Watts, Detroit, Newark, Cleveland, and many other cities have had, on balance, a beneficial or a harmful effect on the black community.[2] What is the situation for the Chicano? Can a close parallel be drawn between his situation and that of the blacks? Will psychic benefits, such as a heightened sense of personal and political efficacy and increased group consciousness plus a greater awareness and anxiety by the Anglo powers, outweigh the physical costs to the Chicano, including loss of property, injury, and perhaps greater repression and resistance? These are questions which can be completely answered only by history.

NOTES

1. United States Commission on Civil Rights, *Mexican Americans and the Administration of Justice in the Southwest,* March, 1970.

2. A thorough analysis of the Watts "riots" is contained in David O. Sears and John B. McConahay, *The Politics of Violence* (Boston: Houghton Mifflin, 1973). A general discussion of the advantages and disadvantages of radical tactics is found in S. J. Makielski, Jr., *Beleagured Minorities: Cultural Politics in America* (San Francisco: W. H. Freeman and Company, 1973).

28: THE 1970-71 EAST LOS ANGELES CHICANO–POLICE RIOTS

Armando Morales

WHAT WERE THE UNDERLYING CAUSES OF THE EAST LOS ANGELES JANUARY 1, August 29 and September 16, 1970 riots? A difficult, complex question indeed. Viewing the problems from a historical perspective one could say the conflict began when the Southwest Mexicans told the Anglos "Mi casa es su casa" (My home is your home) and the hospitable invitation was taken literally. The Anglo, a foreigner, conquered the native Mexican in his land and culture. But the Mexican, i.e. the Mexican American, really has not been conquered as evidenced by the existence and persistence of his culture in the United States, and the fact that he periodically asserts himself as a means of salvaging some of his dignity. Riots in this respect are a human, natural response for survival to a set of intolerable living conditions established by those in authority. The Mexican American, like the black man, merely conforms more often than not to the role of a conquered person. Perhaps some day a thorough, vigorous investigation will uncover what caused the East Los Angeles riots of 1970 and 1971.

Based upon the modest, documented information presented in this monograph, it is observed that in the East Los Angeles riots there are more similarities than differences in the prime, explosive mixture components that led to riots in 150 cities across the United States in 1967. Comparing the U.S. Riot Commission Report findings and basic causes of the riots with the East Los Angeles situation proved to be a frightening experience. All that had to be substituted was the word "Mexican American" for "Negro" and "barrio"

A longer version of this chapter appeared in *Ando Sangrando (I Am Bleeding): A Study of Mexican American-Police Conflict* by Armando Morales (La Puente, Calif.: Perspectiva Publications, P.O. Box 3563, 1972), pp. 91-122. It is being used with permission from the author and publisher.

for "ghetto" in order for the conditions to be identical. The following is from the U.S. Riot Commission (Kerner) Report:

> The record before this Commission reveals that the causes of recent racial disorders are imbedded in a massive tangle of issues and circumstances—social, economic, political, and psychological—which arise out of the historical pattern of Negro-white relations in America. . . . Of these, the most fundamental is the racial attitude and behavior of white Americans toward black Americans. Race prejudice has shaped our history decisively in the past; it now threatens to do so again. White racism is essentially responsible for the explosive mixture which has been accumulating in our cities since the end of World War II. . . .
>
> The ghettos too often mean men and women without jobs, families without men, and schools where children are processed instead of educated, until they return to the street—to crime, to narcotics, to dependency on welfare, and to bitterness and resentment against society in general and white society in particular. . . . A Climate that tends toward the approval and encouragement of violence as a form of protest, has been created by white terrorism directed against nonviolent protest, including instances of abuse and even murder of some civil rights workers in the South; by the open defiance of law and federal authority by state and local officials resisting desegregation; and by some protest groups engaging in civil disobedience who turn their backs on nonviolence, go beyond the Constitutionally protected rights of petition and free assembly, and resort to violence to attempt to compel alteration of laws and policies with which they disagree. This condition has been reinforced by a general erosion of respect for authority in American society and reduced effectiveness of social standards and community restraints on violence and crime. . . .
>
> Finally, many Negroes have come to believe that they are being exploited politically and economically by the white "power structure." Negroes, like people in poverty everywhere, in fact lack the channels of communication, influence and appeal that traditionally have been available to ethnic minorities within the city and which enabled them—unburdened by color—to scale the walls of the white ghettos in an earlier era. The frustrations of powerlessness have led some to the conviction that there is no effective alternative to violence as a means of expression and redress, as a way of "moving the system." More generally, the result is alienation and hostility toward the institutions of law and government and the white society which controls them. . . .
>
> These conditions have created a volatile mixture of attitudes and beliefs which need only a spark to ignite mass violence . . . all the major outbursts of recent years were precipitated by routine arrests of Negroes for minor offenses by white police. But the police are not merely the spark. In discharge of their obligation to maintain order and insure public safety in the disruptive conditions of ghetto life, they are inevitably involved in sharper and more frequent conflicts with ghetto residents than with residents of other areas. Thus, to many Negroes police have come to

symbolize white power, white racism and white repression. And the fact is that many police do reflect and express these white attitudes. The atmosphere of hostility and cynicism is reinforced by a widespread perception among Negroes of the existence of police brutality and corruption, and of a "double standard" of justice and protection—one for Negroes and one for whites.[1]

These, therefore, are the ingredients that are frequently found in communities that have rioted. These ingredients have been (and still are) present in the Mexican American East Los Angeles community for many years.* The Riot Commission's findings that channels of "communication, influence and appeal that traditionally have been available" to *other* ethnic minorites in the city which "enabled them—unburdened by color—to scale the walls of the white ghettos in an earlier era" does not hold true for American Indians and Mexican Americans. Even though the political, economic and education situation for blacks and Mexican Americans in Los Angeles is terrible compared to Anglo-Saxons, these conditions are even *more acute* for Mexican Americans than for blacks.

Accepting a preliminary, tentative observation (until that time when an official body makes a complete investigation of the 1970-71 East Los Angeles riots) that the East Los Angeles community possesses those explosive ingredients found in other riot cities, a rough sketch of the East Los Angeles riots will be presented. Preceding these discussions, however, some comments on the general theory of riots will assist in better understanding the East Los Angeles riots. The Los Angeles Zoot Suit and Detroit riots of 1943 could have been described as "communal" riots, i.e. one ethnic-racial group fighting a different ethnic-racial group for a contested area. The riots of the 1960's have been described mostly as "commodity" riots—the riots were an outburst against property and retail establishments, including looting.[2] The business establishments were mainly owned by outside white proprietors. The deaths and casualties resulted mainly from the force used against the Negro population by police and National Guard units. In describing the natural history of commodity-type riots, two considerations have to be kept in mind: One, the style of intervention by the law enforcement officers has deeply influenced the anatomy of race riots in the United States.[3] The response of the police at the outbreak of commodity riots in various communities was very different, ranging from highly effective and professional behavior to weak and irresponsible action that exacerbated rioting and prolonged tension. Thus, points out Morris Janowitz who had studied patterns of collective racial violence, "the stages of a riot are not pre-determined but reflect the pattern of intervention

*See Judge Schauer's controversial decision in Chapter IX, p. 132, against another minority group in Los Angeles attempting to reduce tension between the minority community and the police.

of law enforcement agencies."[4] The second consideration is that it is very difficult to assemble accurate documentation in order to describe the natural history of a riot—especially the behavior of rioters in a commodity riot. Janowitz further points out that from all sources, one conclusion emerges, namely the absence of organized conspiracy in commodity riots. The absence of organized conspiracy, however, does not mean the absence of a pattern of events.[5]

Research studies of some 75 riots in the 1965-67 period demonstrates a pattern of events in these outbursts. The difference from one outburst to another involved the extent to which each one proceeded through the various stages of increased and intensified collective behavior. Commenting on the various stages, Janowitz states:

> One is struck by the repeated reports of the carnival and happy-day spirit that pervades the early stages of a commodity riot. The new type of rioting is most likely to be set off by an incident involving the police in the ghetto where some actual or believed violation of accepted police practice has taken place. The very first phase is generally nasty and brutish: the police are stoned, crowds collect and tension mounts. The second stage is reached with the breaking of windows. Local social control breaks down and the population recognizes that a temporary opportunity for looting is available. The atmosphere changes quickly, and this is when positive enthusiasm is released. But all too briefly. If the crowds are not dispersed and order restored, the third stage of the riot is the transformation wrought by arson, firebombs, and sniper fire and the countermeasures taken by police and uniformed soldiers.[6]

The countermeasures employed by police deeply influence the course of rioting—even in some cases prolonging the period of reestablishing order. Too little response by law enforcement may escalate a riot as will an over-reaction by police. There were wide differences in response patterns to early manifestations of disorder by local police in the 1960's riots. For example, the police commissioner of Detroit followed a loose policy in the early phase of the Detroit rioting, assuming that local civilian Negro leadership would contain the disorder. He had previous experience in which this approach worked effectively. Knowledge of the community and its leaders coupled with confidence in the leadership would seem to play an important part in this approach.

On the other hand, New York City and Chicago police have an operational code to intervene with that amount of force judged to be appropriate for early stages of the confrontation. The objective was to prevent the spread of disorder. The police took special steps to prevent routine police performance from developing into incidents which might provoke tension. Janowitz states:

> If an incident became the focal point for tension and the collection of a crowd, the police responded early and in depth in order to prevent the

> second stage from actually expanding. Numerous police were sent to the scene or kept in reserve nearby. The police sought to operate by their sheer presence, not to provoke further counteraction. They sought to prevent the breaking of windows and the starting of looting that would set the stage for an escalated riot. If actual rioting threatened, one response was the early mobilization of local National Guard units and their ready reserve deployment in inner city garrisons. . . . Whereas the communal riot involved a confrontation between the white and the black community, the commodity riot, especially as it entered into the third and destructive phase, represents a confrontation between the black community and law enforcement officials of the larger society.[7]

If communal riots involve a confrontation between the black and white community, might not commodity riots of the 1960's actually represent a more sophisticated, advanced form of communal riots since most police are *white* and the targets for destruction are usually owned by *whites?"* It might also be theorized that while the "race riots" of the 1940's primarily involved white *citizen* aggression toward ethnic minorities that were making economic progress in the war years, i.e., a threat to established political-economic equilibrium, the white citizen attitude of the 1940's is now being expressed *through* and *by* the white police and, more important, *with the sanction of the dominant white society.* In this respect the writer would suggest that there is little difference between the communal and commodity riot as it involves ethnic minority groups. In this regard, Hugh Davis Graham and Ted Robert Gurr conclude that resistance to undesirable change has been a more common source of collective violence in America than "revolutions of rising expectations."[8] They maintain that most ethnic and religious violence in American history has been retaliatory violence by groups "farther up the socioeconomic ladder who felt threatened by the prospect of the 'new immigrant' and the Negro getting both 'too big' and 'too close.' "[9] They also state that aggressive vigilantism has been a recurrent response of middle and working-class Americans to perceived threats by outsiders or lesser classes to their status, security and cultural integrity. The Zoot-suit riots of the 1940's might be perceived in this manner. The armed forces "vigilantes" were envious of the Zoot suiter's freedom and threatened by his cultural style. The vigilante action was supported by a larger white community that was threatened by the Mexican American's progress in the war years.

Graham and Gurr assert that evidence from riots supports one basic principle: Force and violence can be successful techniques of social control and persuasion when they have extensive popular support. If they do not, they say, their advocacy and use are ultimately self-destructive, either as techniques of government or of opposition. They further remark:

> The historical and contemporary evidence of the United States suggest that popular support tends to sanction violence in support of the status

quo: the use of public violence to maintain public order, the use of private violence to maintain popular conceptions of social order when government cannot or will not. If these assertions are true – and not much evidence contradicts them – the prolonged use of force or violence to advance the interests of any segmental group may impede and quite possibly preclude reform.[10]

This observation appears questionable in light of the violent confrontation of demonstrators and police during the week of the Chicago Democratic National Convention of 1968. There appeared to be public support and a condoning of police violence against demonstrators by city officials and even though there was published criticism, the city's response was to ignore the police violence.[11] Although there was more public support for the police violence than not, demonstrators today assume credit for this having been an important turning point that resulted in greater Vietnam anti-war public support. It would appear important to analyze whether or not there was a loss of anti-war popular support to the Mexican American community following the August 29, 1970 riot.

A final factor to consider in the analysis of the East Los Angeles riots is the general response of the United States leadership to the riots reported in the Kerner Report. The Commission felt that the highest priorities for national action were funds and legislation to deal with the social and economic problems of the black ghetto. Instead of social legislation and funds to improve the social conditions that were a basic cause of the riots, numerous laws against riots and rioters and an increase in penalties was the approach taken.[12] This trend was also seen in the National Institute of Municipal Law Officers published report on riots which includes a bibliography of over fifty articles, journals and reports that appeared after the Detroit riots of 1967, dealing with riot *control.*[13] In other words, the approach taken was to *control* the symptom rather than treating the basic cause of the symptom. This attitude was expressed into law on June 19, 1968 (Public Law 90-351) by the 90th Congress and became known as the Omnibus Crime Control and Safe Streets Act of 1968. The sum of $50,000,000 was appropriated for projects to improve and strengthen law enforcement. Part C, Section 301b, 6, provided for:

The organization, education, and training of regular law enforcement officers, special law enforcement units, and law enforcement reserve units for the prevention, detection, and control of riots and other violent civil disorders, including the acquisition of riot control equipment.[14]

Perhaps confirming that the law enforcement *control* approach did not resolve ethnic problems in the cities, Urban America Inc. and the Urban Coalition, reporting on America's racial crisis one year after the Kerner Report, revealed that blacks and whites remained deeply divided in their perceptions and experiences of American society. In fact, blacks and whites were found to be a year closer to being two societies, increasingly separate and scarcely less equal. They stated that "Outright resistance to slum-ghetto needs and demands intensified during the same months."[15]

Following in the footsteps of the "hard-line" national trend and anticipating civil disorder in East Los Angeles, various city, county government and business leaders decided to build a $567,386 riot control center *in* East Los Angeles. Participating in the November 18, 1968 groundbreaking ceremonies were Roy Neshek, president of the Belvedere Rotary Club, John Espinosa, East Lost Angeles Realtor, Harry Rollett of the Southern California Edison Company, Sheriff Peter Pitchess, Art Chayra, president of the East Los Angeles Jay Cees, Robert Weber, industrialist, Manuel Veiga, Jr., of Veiga-Robison Mortuary, Supervisor Ernest E. Debs, Whittier Congressman Chet Holifield, Bell Gardens Mayor William R. Irvine, City of Commerce Mayor Maurice H. Quigley, County Engineer John A. Lambie, Assemblyman Jack Fenton, Assemblyman Walter Karabian and Judge Ben Vega. The East Los Angeles representatives were Espinosa, Veiga and Weber. The riot control center, named the "Special Enforcement Bureau," was financed by a joint-powers authority representing Los Angeles County, Bell Gardens (a predominantly middle class, Anglo-Saxon resident community) and the City of Commerce (a predominantly Anglo-Saxon business community). The Special Enforcement Bureau was erected to "provide facilities adequate for law enforcement reserve personnel used to back-up regular field deputies in emergencies throughout East Los Angeles (a predominantly Mexican American community) and portions of the southeast area (a predominantly black community) of the County."[16]

There were angry rumors in the Mexican American community that the Special Enforcement Bureau was designed to be used against them and that it housed two armored tanks. At a United Mexican American Students police-community meeting held at California State College on Saturday, August 2, 1969, Captain Tom W. Pinkston of the East Los Angeles Sheriff's station admitted to the writer that they "only had one" armored tank at the riot control center.

Applying this "control the symptom" approach as a solution to a very complex problem may create additional problems. For example, society in general begins to believe that this is *the* answer to urban unrest as they have not been exposed to other approaches. Secondly, it may have a psychologically provoking effect to the urban areas where these "control" measures are implemented by law enforcement. These measures may also have the effect of communicating an *expectation* to the ethnic minority community which is internalized–particularly by the militant element in the community–thereby fulfilling the expectation, i.e., a self fulfilling prophecy. Finally, this approach may unintentionally give sanction to an irresponsible element in the police agency to "act out" their anger and hostility toward the minority community, feeling secure that if they do provoke the community into violence, there quickly will be sufficient *control force* available to quell the disturbance. The Urban Coalition and Urban America, Inc., drew a similar conclusion regarding police irresponsibility when they stated:

> Incidents involving the police continued (after the riots) to threaten the civil peace in the slums and ghettos. There was some evidence of a hardening of police attitudes and a weakening of traditional civil controls over their activities.[17]

This feeling is also expressed in the following statement which appeared in the East Los Angeles community *Eastside Sun* newspaper on Thursday, December 3, 1970:

> Dear Editor,
>
> The Congress of Mexican American Unity, supported by the National Moratorium Committee and the Barrio Defense Committee, has issued an urgent appeal to the people of Southern California to rally in defense of the beleaguered Mexican community. According to the Moratorium leaders, the Los Angeles Police Department in East Los Angeles "is engaged in a deliberate campaign of terror—of force and violence against the Mexican youth in the community. Beatings, arrests, and roustings are daily occurrences."
>
> The young community leaders have compiled "a fact sheet of terror."
>
> Wed. night, Nov. 11 some 15 police cars were parked half a block from the Moratorium headquarters. "They did not raid the headquarters because we had several law students and a reporter present observing the activities."
>
> Fri. Nov. 13 at approximately 7:30 p.m., six members of the Special Operations Conspiracy Squad of the Police Dept. entered the headquarters of the Moratorium Committee without knocking and without a search warrant. When asked for a search warrant, they pulled out their service revolvers and their leader said, "These are all the search warrants we need." They then proceeded to bully and terrorize the people in the building.
>
> Sat. Nov. 14 at about 10:30 in the morning Ralph Flores was picked up as he was going to a drug store to purchase some medicine for his child. He was arrested, beaten, his life threatened, and then was released.
>
> Sat. Nov. 14, some 30 members of the Los Angeles Police Department again raided the Moratorium headquarters. They assaulted the people there, and as a result, three youths, Antonio Uranda, Juan Reyes and Roberto Flores required medical attention. They were subsequently charged with "felonious assault on a police officer." Three other young men, Ralph Ramirez, Sergio Robledo and Frank Martinez were charged with "interfering with a police officer."

Ralph Rodriguez, a young man crippled by spinal meningitis, was arrested on Wed., Nov. 18, questioned, "roughed up" and released.

Brown Beret Jesse Cevallos has been constantly harassed, his family threatened, and his own life is in danger.

It is the general feeling of some community leaders that the police department is deliberately attempting to foment rebellion as an excuse to enter the community on a "shoot-out basis." These community leaders, in a desperate attempt to forestall such action, are urgently appealing to the Anglo community throughout Southern California to come to the assistance of the Chicano people.

Your voice, your word, your support against a program of genocide by officials sworn to "law and order," is perhaps the only way to stop these growing assaults. We call upon all men and women of conscience to speak their mind now! End this organized terror campaign!

ESTEBAN TORRES,
ROSALIO MUNOZ,
REV. ANTONIO HERNANDEZ,
ANTONIO BERNAL,
RALPH RAMIREZ,
CELIA RODRIGUEZ,
MAURICIO TERRAZAS,
BERT CORONA,
HUMBERTO CAMACHO,
ABE TAPIA.[18]

The above signatures represent a very responsible element of the Mexican American community. Torres is chairman of the 300 organization Congress of Mexican American Unity, and Tapia is state chairman of the Mexican American Political Association.

To recapitulate, prior to examining the East Los Angeles riots, in analyzing the theory, history and experience of riots in America, the following circumstances seem to be present:

1. Social, economic, political and psychological oppression of the ethnic minority group.
2. White racism toward the ethnic minority group.
3. Ethnic minorities feel they are being politically and economically exploited by the white power structure.
4. Ethnic minorities lack influence and channels of communication.
5. Ethnic minorities are frustrated by a feeling of powerlessness.
6. There is alienation and hostility toward the institutions of law and government and the white society which controls them.
7. Major outbursts were precipitated by routine arrests of ethnic minorities by white police.

8. Police have come to symbolize white power, white racism and white repression to ethnic minorities.
9. There is a widespread perception among ethnic minorities of the existence of police brutality and corruption, and of a double standard of justice and protection—one for ethnic minorities and one for whites.
10. The riots of the 1960's have been mostly "commodity" riots.
11. Deaths and casualties resulted from the force used against ethnic minorities by police and National Guard units.
12. There is an absence of organized conspiracy by ethnic minorities in commodity riots.
13. A carnival and happy-day spirit pervades the early stages of a commodity riot.
14. The police are stoned, crowds collect and tension mounts in the first phase of the riot.
15. The second phase of the riot is characterized by loss of local social control, the breaking of windows and looting occurs.
16. The third stage is characterized by arson, firebombs, sniper fire and the countermeasures taken by police and uniformed soldiers.
17. Too little or an over-reaction by law enforcement may escalate a riot.
18. A flexible policy of minimum police intervention allowing the local civilian ethnic minority leadership to contain the disorder has been effective.
19. Another mode of intervention by police is to use that amount of force judged to be appropriate for the early stages of confrontation in order to prevent the spread of disorder.
20. The third phase of the riots represents a confrontation between the ethnic minority community and law enforcement officials of the larger society.
21. Most ethnic minority violence in American history has been retaliatory violence by groups farther up the socioeconomic ladder who felt threatened by the ethnic minority getting both "too big" and "too close."
22. Force and violence can be successful techniques of social control and persuasion when they have extensive popular support.
23. The prolonged use of force or violence to advance the interests of any segmental group may impede and quite possibly preclude reform.
24. Nationally, an approach to *control* riots rather than treating the basic causes of riots was adopted.
25. Incidents involving the police continued after the riots to threaten the civil peace in the ethnic minority community. There was some evidence of a hardening of police attitudes and a weakening of traditional controls over their activities.

The above twenty-five items will serve as a framework for a preliminary analysis of the three 1970 East Los Angeles riots. The data will be taken from three sources: newspapers, the California State Advisory Committee Report to the United States Commission on Civil Rights, and a few in-depth interviews of witnesses.

THE JANUARY 1, 1970 EAST LOS ANGELES RIOT:

There was very little information available regarding this riot. The *Los Angeles Times* carried a very brief article on the incident on page three of the paper. The article reported that on January 1, 1970, about one hundred persons smashed windows and looted stores after New Year celebrations by a crowd of 5,000. It was labeled a major disturbance by police as it took law enforcement officers more than two hours to disperse the crowds. Damage occurred as forty two storefront windows were shattered and some stores were looted along the mile long Whittier Boulevard business district. Sheriff deputies arrested eleven persons on charges of looting and resisting arrest.[19] The businesses are primarily owned by non-Spanish surnamed whites who do not live in the Mexican American community. Much more information is required to make an adequate analysis of the January 1, 1970 riot.

THE AUGUST 29, 1970 EAST LOS ANGELES RIOT:

Approximately 15,000 to 20,000 persons—mostly Mexican American—were in East Los Angeles on August 29 to attend a well-publicized National Chicano Moratorium March. The event was organized by Rosalio Munoz, former UCLA student body president, and supported in near unanimity by Mexican American organizations throughout the Southwest.

The Moratorium was to protest America's involvement in the war in Southeast Asia and, simultaneously, to decry the high percentage of Mexican American battle casualties, both wounded and killed in action. Moratorium leaders urged young Mexican Americans to resist military service abroad in favor of fighting for social justice at home. The Moratorium Committee had kept the police fully informed of its intentions and program. It provided monitors to accompany the marchers and maintain order.

The Los Angeles County Sheriffs were to clear the parade route and to direct traffic as necessary at cross streets. The Sheriffs, being concerned by the influx of young Mexican American militants from all over the Southwest for the event and by reports of possible trouble from revolutionaries and other subversive groups, also made additional preparations to meet any situations which might develop.[20] No public announcement of any dangers from revolutionaries seeking a confrontation was made, and many of those who attended the event brought their entire families.

The marchers gathered in East Los Angeles' Belvedere Park and followed a scheduled parade route down East Third Street, Beverly Boulevard, Atlantic Boulevard, and Whittier Boulevard where it ended at Laguna Park. According to sheriffs' reports, the marchers had traveled only five blocks when some deputies became targets for rocks and bottles. It was there, according to Sheriff Peter Pitchess, that marchers took over the entire width of the street, violating their parade permit which limited them to only one-half of it.

At 2:34 p.m., a liquor store at 3812 Whittier Boulevard was looted and windows were broken and a second store was looted at 3:25 p.m. according to the sheriff. Officers with riot guns were already stationed at street-corner barricades. It was at 3:10 p.m. that the sheriffs had decided to declare the situation "critical" and move in to disperse all crowds in the area. They used tear gas freely.

At the peak of the turmoil, a dozen fires burned out of control along Whittier Boulevard, and about 500 police and sheriff's deputies were involved. Sheriff Pitchess reported that 40 officers were injured in the melee and that 25 radio cars were damaged. A main battleground was Laguna Park, at the end of the parade route, where marchers had settled on the grass to listen to music and hear a series of speakers.[21]

Following a disturbance at the edge of the park, the sheriffs moved in with tear gas to disperse the entire crowd. It is this action and resultant incidents which have drawn most of the complaints from the community. Community members charge that the sheriffs over-reacted and, in breaking up a peaceful assembly, turned on the panic and hostility. Citizens have complained by the dozens of unwarranted brutal treatment by the deputies. An exact toll of injured civilians is not yet known, but arrests during and following the confrontation exceeded 400.[22]

The above information was based upon the California State Advisory Committee's evaluation of information gathered by its members and by members of the United States Commission on Civil Rights Western Regional Field Office and the Commission's Office of General Counsel. The following witness account was taken from *La Raza,* a local East Los Angeles barrio newspaper:

> The marchers proceeded peacefully down Atlantic Blvd., watched by curious people on the sidewalks who have not fully grasped what "Chicano Power" means. While marching on Whittier Blvd. near Eastern Ave., the marchers were hit with bottles from the overpass. The overpass is part of the Long Beach Freeway that runs parallel to Eastern Ave., North and South. Some of the marchers were cut.
>
> The march proceeded West on Whittier Blvd. It was a hot summer day and some of the marchers fainted along the way, but they were quickly taken care of by medical crews that were assigned to station wagons.
>
> Two blocks before Laguna Park, a scuffle occured between Sheriff's

SOME COMPARISONS OF USE OF DEADLY FORCE BY POLICE IN WHITE AND CHICANO CITIZEN CONFRONTATIONS

Occasion	*Protestors*	*Property Damage*	*Police Injured*	*Police Hospitalized*	*Police Shot*	*Citizens Injured*	*Citizens Hospitalized*	*Citizens Shot by Police*	*Citizens Killed by Police*
June, 1967 Century Plaza anti-war protest	15,000 white, middle class protestors	?	4	0	0	178	4	No shots fired	0
August, 1968 Democratic Natl. Convention, Chicago	10,000 to 15,000 white protestors	$1,000,000	192	49	0	425	101	No shots fired	0
May, 1971 Washington, D.C. anti-war protest.	12,000 white protestors arrested, most released.	?	34	?	0	?	?	No shots fired	0
January 31, 1971 ELA Chicano police brutality protest, 10,000 people.	500 to 700 Chicano protestors on Whittier Boulevard.	$200,000	1	0	0	35+	?	35+	1

The FBI riot-control manual states: "The basic rule, when applying force, is to use only the minimum force necessary to effectively control the situation. Unwarranted application of force will incite the mob to further violence, as well as kindle seeds of resentment for police, that, in turn, could cause a riot to recur."* Riots again visited East Los Angeles on August 8, 1971, August 22, 1971 and September 16, 1971. This resulted in a total of eight riots during the 1970–71 twenty-one month period, making East Los Angeles the most crisis-ridden community in America today. The President's Task Force Report, *The Police* (p. 145), revealed that poor police-community relations had been a contributing factor to the disturbances and riots which afflicted the cities in the mid 1960's. This also appears to be the case in East Los Angeles.

**Report of The National Advisory Commission on Civil Disorders,* United States Government Printing Office, Washington, D.C., March 1, 1968, p. 176. For more details about the above protests, see "Day of Protest, Night of Violence: The Century City Peace March," A Report of the American Civil Liberties Union of Southern California, Sawyer Press, July, 1967; and *Rights in Conflict: The Walker Report to the National Commission on the Causes and Prevention of Violence* (New York: Bantam Books, 1968). The "Kent State" incident ($126,000 riot damage) in which thirteen persons were shot–of whom four died–was not included in the above comparison as it involved a confrontation with the National Guard rather than a police agency. There is no doubt that a great deal of deadly force has also been used against blacks, but they were not included in the above table as the intention was to contrast Chicano and "white" experiences as they are engaged in conflict with law enforcement agencies.

deputies and the marchers. No one seems to know how or why it started, but it was quickly quieted by the monitors.

It took almost one hour for all the marchers to file into Laguna Park, rest their tired aching feet, and find a place on the lawn. Many families began to open up their picnic baskets and have a late lunch. Others were searching for refreshments to cool off.

This is where the trouble started. Many Chicanos went to a liquor store to buy sodas and beer. The owner of the liquor was swamped with business. He attempted to close his doors in order to deal with the customers inside. In fact, he succeeded in doing so.

The sheriff's station in East L.A. (where in the past two years six Chicanos have "supposedly" committed suicide) claims to have received a call from the owner asking for their assistance in calming the people coming into the store (the store owner denies calling the sheriff's station). The sheriffs responded to the call by sending more units into the area. Next they moved in numerous police units across the street from Laguna Park. Obviously, this drew the attention of some of the people in the park, especially since there were about 40–50 sheriff deputies standing behind their cars. Th e deputies then formed a parallel formation and with their billy-clubs started advancing. No warnings about illegal assemblies or such. At that time, the Chicano Moratorium security personnel came in to keep peace and they would have been able to do so if the sheriff's deputies had gone back to their cars, but instead of retreating, they attacked not only the monitors, but the people who were peacefully hearing the speakers. They indiscriminately fired tear gas capsules into unaware crowds of Chicanos who were sitting on the grass. Shoes, purses and lost children on the field stood as symbols of the inhumanity expressed by the deputies.

As chaos ensued, children were lost from their parents, fathers who came to the front to defend their children were beaten, bloodied and arrested! Chicanos and Chicanas everywhere were crying in amazement over what they were seeing.

Men were kicked, struck in the chest and stomach and brutally beaten over the head. They were then dragged unconsciously to awaiting police cars. Our people rallied time after time and pushed the perros back with stones and fists but sticks, stones and fists cannot stand against guns, clubs, and tear gas missiles. After an hour or two of fighting, the Metropolitan Police from Los Angeles City reinforced the sheriffs. The Metro Police are trained to deal with demonstrations. They hit first and ask questions later.

Men, women and children were indiscriminately tear-gassed. The fighting spread into the side street and spilled onto Whittier Blvd. A few police cars were set on fire but Chicanos paid dearly for it. The fighting spilled over onto Whittier Blvd. Store windows were broken and buildings set afire. The following night Wilmington erupted along Avalon Ave. Results: The same as in East Los Angeles, destruction in the business areas and numerous arrests.

That same night, four policemen were shot in the Chicano area, the Casa Blanca district of Riverside.

> Now that most of the turmoil has stopped, many people are walking around as if in shock, with questioning expressions on their faces. The most interesting questions come from the Anglo community. Why did it happen? Why?
>
> That question has been asked in numerous black ghettoes throughout the nation. Puerto Ricans have heard it in New York, and New Jersey and now that same question is being asked again in our Chicano communities. Why did it happen?[23]

. . .

Dr. James S. Koopman, a physician at the UCLA school of medicine's department of pediatrics, was a participant in the Moratorium march along with his wife. He commented:

> Everyone was assembled peacefully at Laguna Park. My wife and I sat on the grass amongst diverse people. Immediately around us were little children playing with a puppy, an older woman with a cane, a pregnant woman with a small baby and a family eating hamburgers and French fries. The program began and after two speeches a Puerto Rican rhythm group was providing entertainment. The first sign of any disturbance I saw was when some people in the distance began to stand up. The loudspeaker calmly assured us that nothing was happening and that we should sit down. Seconds later I saw a row of gold helmets marching across the park, forcing everyone toward the high fences. The exit was too small for everyone to leave quickly. I, along with everyone else, panicked. The terrible tragedies of human stampedes in the soccer stadiums of Peru and Argentina were uppermost in my mind.[24]

Sheriff's deputies responded to a "burglary in progress" call at the Green Mill liquor store (owner Morris Maroko denied making the call) and deputies responded with red lights flashing. A sheriff's spokesman said that the two units that arrived were met with "overwhelming resistance and more units responded." One of the second wave of sheriff's units responding was a unit from the Special Enforcement Bureau, the specially trained anti-riot detail. Special Enforcement deputy Ray Baytos, 26, and his partner left their vehicle and were on the northwest section of the park at Whittier and Alma (the liquor store is a block away from Laguna park and cannot be seen from the park) when the two were assaulted by a group of people. Baytos was beaten with a large board, kicked, struck, his helmet taken and his revolver stripped from him, according to the Sheriff's Department. Then, two shots were fired at him from his own gun, both missing deputy Baytos. The incident was observed by other deputies and a radio call of extreme urgency went out for help. The participants were unaware of the Baytos incident. "The first sign of any disturbance I saw was when some people in the distance began to stand up," said Dr. Koopman.[25]

Attorney Toby Rothschild claims that the red lights and sirens of the oncoming deputies caused a crowd to gather at the northwest edge of the park. Parade monitors attempted to move the group back to the park and away from the deputies on Whittier Boulevard, Rothschild said. Rothschild further stated:

> Most of them were turned and going back and the debris [being thrown] had stopped. Then there were sirens, and eight or ten [Sheriff's] cars and a bus arrived. The sirens attracted the entire group back. There was very little that could be done to stop people from either side from doing things. I did not hear any order to disperse.[26]

The Sheriff's Department claimed, however, that dispersal orders were given from several loud-speakers on patrol cars surrounding the park. Sheriff Pitchess said that the decision to clear the park came after "a very thorough assessment of the situation."[27] The events flowed swiftly and the deputies formed their line. Skirmishes broke out and then died down. A line of parade monitors linked arms between the deputies advancing from the north and body of demonstrators on the south. The bombardment from missiles reached an intense level and then died off. Many thought the rally would be allowed to continue. The monitors shouted "Get out of here, leave us alone," at the deputies.[28] This was followed by a long lull as monitors and deputies looked at each other across a narrow no-man's-land. Javier Gonzalo maintains that "After that interval, somebody flipped a finger or words were interchanged and then it really got nasty."[29] As startled demonstrators fled in panic, some in the crowd decided to fight the deputies. According to the *Los Angeles Times,* it was 2:50 p.m. when the Green Mill liquor store was crowded with customers and 3:25 p.m. when the first reports of looting reached the Sheriff's Department. At 3:36 p.m. a fire station at Eastern and Verona was under attack and the riot was under way.[30] The Mexican American-police confrontation at the park occurred at approximately 3:00 p.m.–*before* the riot began. Most minority group-police confrontations in other riots occurred *after* the riots were underway.

THE SEPTEMBER 16, 1970 EAST LOS ANGELES RIOT:

For almost thirty years, the Mexican American community in Los Angeles has honored the anniversary of the Mexican Independence by having a parade. Because of the August 29, 1970 disturbance, there was much discussion about whether to hold the 16th of September parade. It was cancelled but a week before the 16th, it was decided after consultation with the Sheriff's Department, the Mexican consul general and the sponsors to hold the parade with the help of the monitors.[31] The sponsors wanted to take the crowd to East Los Angeles College Stadium for speeches and an opportunity to give vent to emotions there, instead of in the streets. A representative of Sheriff Pitchess told the Board of Trustees of the Los Angeles Community Colleges–the group that had the authority to make the decision–that the sheriff "had no objection to the use of the stadium, and it might have advantages."[32] But the conservative majority of the board voted 4 to 3 against allowing the Mexican American groups to use the college stadium. Esteban Torres, executive director of the Congress of Mexican American Unity, who sought the permit, then said his group would seek a Superior Court order to force the board to allow holding a rally at the school. Torres felt that it would have been disastrous to end the parade at Belvedere Park rather than the college stadium because: "There are no real facilities there for speakers. Our biggest concern is the security of the area. I understand there is a sheriff's substation in the park."[33] On Wednesday, September 16, the College Board of Trustees' decision was upheld when Superior Court Judge Richard Schauer* denied a restraining order that would have allowed the parade participants the use of the college stadium.[34]

At 5:15 p.m., the parade began. The following is a newspaper account of the parade preceding the disturbances:

> A Marine Corps color guard carrying the flags of the United States and Mexico stepped out smartly. Behind them were carloads of politicians and public officials, a traditional part of Independence Day parades. Then charros–Mexican cowboys–on spirited horses, and pretty girls on decorated floats. Interspersed were organizational groups, but many appeared militant in nature. The first carried the banner of the National Chicano Moratorium Committee, the organization which staged the parade and rally that turned into violence Aug. 29. Originally numbering about 200, their ranks swelled as the parade proceeded along First to Gage Avenue, then north to Brooklyn Avenue and eastward toward the [Belvedere] park. Spectators dashed from the sidewalks to join the line and shout the chants of "Chicano Power," and "Raza si, guerra no" (people yes, war no). In front of them marched a somber line of green-sashed members of the Congress of Mexican American Unity, which had earlier distributed hundreds of lapel buttons stating "Non-Violence Sept. 16."[35]

The first deviation from the original plan of the parade, according to the *Los Angeles Times,* came when the marchers bypassed Belevedere Park, the intended end of the route, and continued to the college. There had been some general movement to disperse once the marchers reached the stadium parking lot and monitors and deputies alike appeared relieved. By that time, several hundred of the unofficially estimated 150,000 persons who had lined the

*See Leonard Pitt. *The Decline of the Californios.* (Los Angeles: University of California Press, 1966), p. 160. In his "Race war in Los Angeles" chapter, Pitt states: "Plainly, by 1854 the Spanish-speaking of Los Angeles felt oppressed by a double standard of justice such as some of them had previously experienced in the gold mines. One sees here in embryo resentments about 'Anglo justice' similar to those that have incited Mexican Americans in more recent times."

parade route began to join the more militant elements among the marchers. The first sign of violence came at 7:10 p.m., a few minutes before the parade officially ended. The last marching group, predominantly teen-agers and militant youths, reportedly began throwing rocks and eggs at reserve deputies who were riding motorcycles, policing the end of the event. The deputies sought shelter behind parked cars. A second call was received moments later when Monterey Park police said they were facing a hostile, rock-throwing mob at the corner of Floral Ave. and Collegian Way, near the college campus. Shortly afterward, windshields of three sheriff's patrol cars were smashed, a truck and a Los Angeles Department of Parks and Recreation Trailer were reported afire at Belvedere Park, and rocks shattered windows at the Constitution Savings and Loan Co., 1200 W. Riggin Street. Other shops were smashed and looted at the Atlantic Square Shopping Center, a liquor store and an electrical supply store were looted, and Monterey Park police asked Los Angeles police for aid. Instead, they were reinforced by the Sheriff's Department. Deputies reported that attempts to burn the college administration building were unsuccessful, but the sound of smashing glass and shots continued for several hours.[36] More than 100 persons were injured and three persons–one a sheriff's deputy–were shot. At least 68 persons were arrested. In all, 64 peace officers were injured, 45 sheriff's deputies and 19 Monterey Park officers. Sheriff Pitchess said that bullets fired from the crowd wounded two civilians and a deputy. Pitchess said his officers fired no shots. Chief Holladay of the Monterey Park Police said his officers fired no shots. Two attorneys acting as observers who asked not to be identified, told the *Los Angeles Times* that they didn't see how monitor Raymond Hernandez could have been shot by deputy sheriffs. One of the attorneys said he didn't see the deputies fire at all. The other said the deputies did fire in the direction of flashes and says there were either firecrackers or shots from the direction of the park–a block to the east of the intersection of Brooklyn and Mednik Avenues. Victim Raymond Hernandez, however, disagreed with the testimony of the attorney observers. Hernandez stated:

> It had just gotten dark and we were moving the crowd back, pushing them back. All of a sudden to my right side I heard four shots. I turned around and saw deputies aiming their rifles straight ahead–not into the air, but straight ahead, down, in my direction. I said "Don't shoot! Don't shoot!' But they fired again and I got hit. They were firing like a firing squad.[37]

Hernandez said he was facing the deputies when he was shot and saw them fire their weapons.[38] Serious allegations against the Sheriff's Department such as these make an impartial investigation of the disturbance mandatory.

An in-depth witness report was given to the writer by Luis Oropeza, currently a graduate student at the University of Southern California School of Social Work. Oropeza was a parade monitor. . . .

Here is my account of the events as I witnessed them on September 16, 1970, in East Los Angeles. I arrived at Rowan and Brooklyn at about 5:30 p.m. to catch the tail end of the parade. The streets were lined with people who seemed in a festive mood. Many of the people were women and children. The sheriffs and LAPD were manning the parade. The sheriffs seemed to outnumber the LAPD however many LAPD were without guns, there were many previously plain cars that appeared to have been marked with "to protect and serve" emblems just for this occasion. Another noticeable fact was that the sheriffs were not standing at intersections as on August 29 (the moratorium march), but were standing on the sidewalk behind the crowd watching the parade.

As we marched to Belvedere Park, many marchers began to turn into the park, others ahead of me were turning around and returning to the park area. However, several hundred were continuing toward Atlantic Boulevard. As we passed the street which leads to the ELA Stadium, I saw about two-hundred people on this street and I heard shouts to this crowd telling them to turn around. The group that had been carrying a picture of Ruben Salazar marched up the ELA College steps and placed the picture on the roof connecting the admissions building and student center. The crowd was very excited and I had very definite fears about the possibility of the beginning of a riot.

After the picture had been placed on the roof, the crowd moved quickly toward Atlantic Boulevard and within a minute or two, someone threw a rock through Constitutional Savings Bank. The violence grew quickly and without my realizing it, as I was making efforts to help control the violence, a line of the Monterey Park Police was forming across Atlantic Boulevard. There were approximately two or three hundred Chicanos confronting the police with a fairly steady flow of rocks and bottles. However, out of these hundred, only about fifteen or twenty were actually coming forward sporadically to throw something.

I went back to the police line and spoke with a Monterey Park Officer with double bars on his lapels who seemed to be in charge. I asked him not to move in and to send a car to contact our security people so they could come to the "front line." He refused and told me to speak to the sheriffs of whom there were now a few. I could not see anyone in charge but the sheriff I approached said they could not help, that they had been called to assist and the Monterey Park Police were in charge. I re-approached the officer in charge who seemed to be making some effort to contact our people, however I now feel I misinterpreted his behavior since we never received any kind of major help from the Belvedere Park area. The main difficulty in controlling the crowd was the fact that those few of us who were trying for some reason were not maintaining a strong line. Also the few throwing things would dash out then dash into the crowd to hide.

I approached the police several times trying to reassure them we could control and move back the crowd, asking them to be patient, warning of escalation if they moved in. I was told I had a few minutes several times, but whether or not the police were actually allowing extra time or were adhering to a previously agreed to schedule or time limit, I'm still not sure. I heard two comments made by different officers. A sheriff apparently in charge turned to the officers behind him and said (in reference to the hail of rocks) "Alright, just keep cool." I heard another officer say angrily "we're going to kick some Chicano ass." By this time the sheriffs had completely taken over the riot control. Suddenly, without any warning or command to disperse, tear gas was fired into the crowd and the police moved forward. The confrontation lines moved back to directly in front of East L.A. College, where a small fire was started. I started to help put out the fire when I felt a club in my back and heard an officer tell me angrily to move out. I remarked impatiently that I had done nothing. Suddenly he said, "I saw you throw a rock, [turning to another officer] didn't you see him throw a rock?"

The officer responded, "Yeah, I saw him." I was put into a car hurriedly without being handcuffed. A few minutes later two younger Chicanos were put in the car with me. I then heard an officer outside the car say in reference to me "What's he doing in there, he's not even handcuffed." The response, from another officer, "I don't know, someone just threw him in there." The second officer got into the car next to me and I commented that the police had been "sorta" cool. He said that it was pretty hard to keep your cool. Although the other two were handcuffed I remained free all the way to the sheriff's station. On the way, one of the officers warned us not to fool around, and pointing the handle of a metal flashlight at us said that we should remember that in the car, "there are no witnesses." . . .

A PRELIMINARY ANALYSIS OF THE ELA RIOTS

In the following preliminary analysis of the East Los Angeles riots of 1970, there are certain problems in the data that prohibit one from reaching definite conclusions because of outright contradictions in many of the witness statements–monitor Hernandez stating that he saw the deputies shoot him and Sheriff Pitchess denying that his deputies fired–that would require intensive legal investigations to get at the true facts. Rather than dealing with specific, minute facts, the writer has presented some information regarding the East Los Angeles riots in order to place them in a conceptual framework based on prior riot experience as seen in the United States. In this way one can better understand the underlying dynamics of riots and be in better position to predict and more important, hopefully *prevent* future collective violence that involves Mexican Americans and the police. The following Riot Analysis Framework represents an abbreviated version of the twenty-five circumstances and conditions (mentioned earlier in this chapter) found in the riots of the 1960's.

RIOT ANALYSIS FRAMEWORK

Circumstance-Condition Found in 1960's Riots		*ELA 1-1-70 Riot*	*ELA 8-29-70 Riot*	*ELA 9-16-70 Riot*
1. Socio-economic, political and psychological oppression	yes	yes	yes	yes
2. Evidence of Racism	yes	yes	yes	yes
3. Feeling of Exploitation	yes	yes	yes	yes
4. Lack Influence and Communication Means	yes	yes	yes	yes
5. Feeling of Powerlessness	yes	yes	yes	yes
6. Hostility Toward Law and Government	yes	yes	yes	yes
7. Outburst precipitated by Routine Arrest	yes	no	in part	no
8. Police Symbolized White Power	yes	yes	yes	yes
9. Perception of Police Brutality and Double Standard of Justice	yes	yes	yes	yes
10. a. Commodity Riot	yes	yes	yes	no
b. Communal Riot	no	no	in part	yes
11. a. Deaths resulted from police force	yes	no deaths	yes (2)	no deaths
b. Injuries resulted from police force	yes	?	yes	yes
c. Police injuries	yes	?	yes	yes
12. Absence of Organized Conspiracy	yes	yes	yes	yes

RIOT ANALYSIS FRAMEWORK

Circumstance-Condition Found in 1960's Riots		*ELA 1-1-70 Riot*	*ELA 8-29-70 Riot*	*ELA 9-16-70 Riot*
13. Carnival Spirit Prior to Riot	yes	yes	yes	yes
14. 1st Phase: police stoned, crowds collect, tension mounts	yes	no	yes	yes
15. 2nd Phase: breaking of windows and looting	yes	yes	yes	yes
16. 3rd Phase:				
a. Arson, Firebombs	yes	no	yes	yes
b. Police countermeasures	yes	no	yes	yes
17. Police Escalate Riot by:				
a. Too little Reaction	yes	?	no	no
b. Over-reaction	yes	no	yes	no
18. Local Citizens Allowed to Handle Disorder; Minimum Police Intervention Approach	yes	no	no	yes
19. Preventive Appropriate Police Force Approach	yes	?	no	yes
20. 3rd Phase of Riot A Minority Group - Police Confrontation	yes	?	all three phases yes	yes
21. Retaliatory Violence for Minority Getting "Too Big."*	?	?	?	?
22. Force and Violence Can Be Successful Social Control Techniques.*	?	?	?	?

RIOT ANALYSIS FRAMEWORK

Circumstance-Condition Found in 1960's Riots		*ELA 1-1-70 Riot*	*ELA 8-29-70 Riot*	*ELA 9-16-70 Riot*
23. Minority Group use of Violence May Preclude Reform* (Backlash)	yes	no	no	?
24. Control of Riots Rather than Treating Basic Cause of Riots was Adopted	yes	yes	yes	yes
25. Evidence of A Hardening Police Attitude Toward Minority Group and Weakening of Controls Over Police Behavior	yes	yes	yes	yes
TOTAL: "Yes"	27	14	22	22
"No"	1	9	4	5
"?"	2	7	2	3
"In Part"	0	0	2	0

*Items 21, 22 and 23 represent theoretical propositions or hypothetical statements rather than circumstances, conditions or behavior observed in the U. S. 1960's Riots.

DISCUSSION

From the above information, it is seen that the three ELA riot circumstances were very similar to those situations found in the U.S. riots in the 1960's. The core ingredients for riots as seen in the first nine items were practically identical. However, not much can be concluded regarding the natural history of the 1-1-70 ELA riot because of the lack of information. The little information that is available, however, indicates that the 1-1-70 riot fits the pattern of a commodity riot in that it took place in a business district and the outburst was primarily directed at retail establishments–not the police. Although the 8-29 riot could be labeled a commodity riot because of the burning of business establishments on Whittier Boulevard, it still had some elements that would support it being labeled a *communal* riot due to three factors: (1) there was a severe Mexican American-Anglo Saxon (police) physical confrontation at the park *before* the riots; (2) there was a battle over the park, i.e., a "turf," and (3) it all occurred *in* the Mexican American community. The statement "Get out of here, leave us alone," shouted by the monitors (in-group) defined the social situation thereby placing the police in the "out-group" category. The subsequent commodity-type behavior could be seen as *displaced anger* provoked by the Sheriff's deputies. In this context, James P. Comer in explaining the dynamics of black and white violence states:

> A black student was ordered off the lawn at his predominantly white college campus by a white policeman. To be a man–a black man–he had to hit the policeman, a symbol of oppression. But it was a "minor incident" and to avoid difficulty he had to hold back. In fury, rage and confusion he smashed his arm through a plateglass window a few minutes later. Such feeling occasionally results in a loss of control after "trigger incidents" (reflecting white superiority and black helplessness) with attendant burning of property. With a breakdown in personal control, blacks, employed and unemployed, loot and plunder the "symbolic enemy." Such reactions on the part of oppressed groups have been reported throughout human history."[39]

Within the above context, it would seem that the Sheriff's Department, by moving in on the unsuspecting audience, panicked and "triggered" the crowd into fight and flight action. The physical power and the tear gas of the deputies apparently overwhelmed the crowd (reflecting Anglo-Saxon superiority and Mexican American helplessness) to the degree that they displaced their anger onto Whittier Boulevard.

The September 16th disturbance appeared to be even more of a communal riot than the August 29th incident. Evidence to support this observation is seen in the fact that most of the violence was directed at the police. The result was that a very large number of police were injured. Furthermore, it appears that the Sheriff's Department initially cooperated with the sponsoring agencies by allowing them to use Mexican American citizen monitors to police the parade. While the 1-1-70 incident appeared to be a spontaneous commodity riot explosion, and the 8-29 disturbance a *displaced anger* response to an over-reaction by the Sheriff's Department, the 9-16 disorder appeared to reflect retaliatory behavior by militant youth toward the police for their aggressive actions against Mexican Americans on August 29.

There is no evidence to support, or not support, that a white "backlash" occurred following the 1-1-70 disturbance. In fact, not too many citizens are even aware that the incident occurred. While there is evidence to show that a white backlash occurred following the riots of the 1960's, this did not appear to happen following the 8-29-70 ELA riot. In fact, there appeared to have developed greater cohesion in the Mexican American community and a general support from the broader white community. This undoubtedly was a reason for the impressive public turnout for the September 16th parade.

Item twenty-five concerns abrasive police practices that occurred *after the riots* threatening "the civil peace in the slums and ghettos," and a "hardening of police attitudes and a weakening of traditional civil controls over their activities."[40] This is very much dangerously so in the Mexican American East Los Angeles community. Might this not be a form of "white backlash?" If it does not stop, it is because the dominant society *wishes that it not stop!*

Still another tragic episode, the Los Angeles community witnessed a fourth riot involving Chicanos and the police as on January 9, 1971, the Los Angeles Police Department disbursed a crowd of about 1,000 Chicano Moratorium demonstrators at the department's Parker Center headquarters. The Chicanos were protesting the brutality of the police in their transactions with barrio residents in the Chicano community. Forty-two persons (some injured) were arrested in the clash which was followed by a brief spree of window breaking in the downtown Los Angeles shopping area.[41] LAPD Chief Edward Davis blamed "swimming pool Communists" and Brown Berets "sophisticated in Bolshevik tactics" for the disturbance. Viewing the Chicano demonstration as child-like and hence applying a paternalistic solution to the problem, Chief Davis warned Mexican American parents that "they're [Communists] using the young Mexican Americans as prison fodder. And I suggest that the parents put a stop to it."[42] As a means of attempting to clarify the viewpoint of the Chicano Moratorium Committee which scheduled another demonstration for January 31, 1971, the following letter was submitted to the *Los Angeles Times* for publication:

Dear Editor,

We, of the Chicano Moratorium Committee are writing to you in response to your plea for some social facts to understand the strained situation between Chicanos and the police. The current conflict between Chicanos and the police is a political confrontation that historically has its roots in the mid 1800's when another police government body–the U.S. Army–forcibly took the land away from the Mexicans in this area. Subsequent brutal acts by border patrol and immigration law enforcement officers frequently leading to reciprocal violent defensive reactions by Mexicans made the situation more acute. The deportation of 312,000 persons of Spanish-surname–many American citizens–by Immigration law enforcement officials during the Great Depression for political-economic reasons, further strained and intensified the anger of people of Mexican descent toward the law and law enforcement.

Denying the Mexican American population in Los Angeles protection from rioting vigilante servicemen during the 1943 "Zoot Suit" riots, raised further doubts in Mexican Americans as to who it actually was that the police were there to "protect and serve." Labeling the riots "Zoot Suit" only served to reveal the racist motivations of the press by applying a historically permanent label that implied "the Mexicans did it," thereby simultaneously protecting the servicemen from public ridicule. The Sheriff's Department Captain Ayers' "biological basis" racist report to the county grand jury during this period—that people of Mexican descent were biologically prone to criminal behavior—further intensified public racist attitudes toward Mexican Americans which also had the effect of permitting more aggressive police behavior toward a "biologically crime prone" population. The report was commended as an "intelligent statement" by LAPD Chief Horral. Subsequently in 1960, Chief Parker revealed his racist attitudes toward Mexican Americans (and absorbed by LAPD) when he said that Mexican Americans were like "wild Indians from the mountains of Mexico," and that genes had to be considered when discussing the "Mexican problem." Today police have changed the label to "Communists" to discredit legitimate Chicano grievances and elicit public support for police initiated violence.

It has been a Chicano experience that when he has attempted to peacefully protest against the educational institutions that produce an excessively high Chicano student drop-out rate; the wealthy Catholic Church that has milked the Chicano of his meager financial resources with no reciprocal benefits; and the U.S. invovlement in the Vietnam war which has resulted in a severe overrepresentation of Chicano deaths—in effect depriving the Chicano community of its future youth resource—these efforts have always been met with police initiated political violence. In this respect the police have been given and have adopted, a sentry role to protect and serve these institutions that are gradually, socially and psychologically, destroying a class of people with a rich, proud heritage and tradition. Chicanos, by day and night, are reminded of their low status in society by a sentry helicopter that was not a "called-for" service by the Chicano community. The Chicano lives in a totalitarian-like atmosphere within a broader Los Angeles community that is comfortably (with the exception of the black community) functioning as a democracy. Being a population group numbering close to a million people in this area, we have no city or county elected Mexican American political representative to assist us with our problems. Our behavior can only be seen as a normal response to an abnormal condition created by those in political power.

The police brutality that occurs ten to twenty times a month in East Los Angeles again communicates to us our worth to the broader society that does not seem to care. We have not received federal protection against this abuse since the law was initially enacted in 1872. We desperately wish to be a part of this society but your powerful sentry repeatedly sends us away bleeding. We are now directly protesting against the sentry. But it is not only the day to day police brutality that we have experienced for numerous decades that gravely concerns us, but rather a far more severe problem that our society isn't even aware of, and that is that the police are increasingly becoming a more powerful, political force in our increasingly less, free democratic society. The recent Skolnick Report to the National Commission on the Causes and Prevention of Violence warned that "the ranks of law enforcement have become an ultraconservative social force which shrilly protests positive change." The Report also concluded that the increasing police militancy is hostile to the aspirations of dissident groups in society and that the police view protesters as a danger to our American political system. Although this is a national report, the situation is identical in Los Angeles as confirmed not only by our experience, but by the recent UCLA Report of the 5-5-70 student-police confrontation which stated that "police attack was discriminatory, focusing on minority group members and long hairs."

Rather than calling off our protests and return to a life of fear under police totalitarian aggression, we have to continue to protest for survival purposes. If Chicanos lose their right to protest in society because of police political violence, you likewise are losing your freedom in America. In this respect our insistence of the right to protest guarantees the right of *all* people in America to protest. If we allow police violence to intimidate us, it is really the broader society that is victimized!

Sincerely,

Rosalio Munoz,
Chicano Moratorium Committee [43]

And on January 31, 1971 there was another riot which resulted in $200,000 worth of damage of business on Whittier Boulevard in East Los Angeles, eleven Sheriff's deputies injured, thirty-five Mexican Americans wounded by police rifles and guns, and one killed by police gunfire.

KABC-TV Channel 7's General Manager, John J. McMahon, presented the following "Moratorium Aftermath" editorial:

> This weekend, a wave of senseless, pointless violence in East Los Angeles left damages totalling over $200,000 in its wake.
>
> It was a largely teen-aged response to the Chicano Moratorium rally attended by an estimated 4,000 Mexican-Americans on Sunday.
>
> Police and Moratorium leaders—Rosalio Munoz in particular—deserve credit for the fact there were no outbreaks at the Belvedere Park rally or during the three-day march preceding it. Both factions promised to exert every effort to avoid violence. Those promises were kept.
>
> It was afterward it happened. About a thousand angry youth, perhaps inflamed by rally speeches, certainly frustrated by the ghetto conditions in which they live, turned to meaningless destruction and violence. They first attacked the Sheriff's station on 3rd Street, then stores on Whittier Boulevard.
>
> Sheriff's officers still did not appear in force until after firemen attempting to put out blazes were met by a hail of rocks.
>
> The Moratorium was to protest alleged police brutality in the Mexican-American community. But there can be little question about the validity of Sheriff Peter Pitchess' statement that: "They can't say we provoked them this time."
>
> Moratorium leaders are already claiming police over-reaction. The final

facts are tragic. A young man is dead, 35 others wounded, a number of community businesses destroyed—and no positive purpose has been served.

There's no question that there was over-reaction—but it was initiated by young Chicanos who ignored pleas by Rosalio Munoz that they disperse peacefully after the rally ended.

The Mexican-American community is a vitally-important part of our Southern California society. But such immature displays by a minority of the citizens there are major obstacles in keeping it from gaining the position of respect it deserves.

The above Editorial was telecast at prime time a total of four times, on February 1 and 2, 1971. The response to McMahon's editorial by Armando Morales, representing "*Trabajadores de la Raza*," an East Los Angeles social work organization, is as follows:

Mr. McMahon's editorial labeled the recent East Los Angeles incident a wave of "senseless, pointless violence." The violence *had* a sense of direction and a point to make. The violence was directed at black and white cars, white business and the police. This was an effort of an active minority announcing their unwillingness to continue accepting indignity and frustration without fighting back. Their point was that they were communicating their desperation through violent acts since no other channels of communication were open to them.

The focus of Mr. McMahon's editorial was on Chicano violence and ignored other expressions of violence. Violence is a destructive force that injures persons. When social institutions begin to injure persons, it becomes *institutional violence,* as expressed through a Los Angeles political system that does not permit one Mexican American city or county elected representative; a school system with a 50% drop-out rate; inhumane welfare and Medi-Cal cutbacks; a severe overrepresentation of Mexican American Vietnam casualties; innumerable acts of police brutality; and a strict law enforcement shooting policy that allows for "ricochetting bullets" that wounded thirty-five Mexican Americans. These are the necessary ingredients that result in overt violence.

The Moratorium demonstrations unintentionally led to the uplifting of a scab that revealed a deep, unhealed wound in the Mexican American community caused by years of societal neglect and current institutional violence. The broader community does not want to be reminded of this neglect as expressed by the Mayor who, critical of the Sheriff's Department "low profile" strategy, promises an even higher profile police retaliation if this symptom expresses itself again. This type of leadership will only serve to escalate the violence and it is in *this* respect that it becomes a "senseless, pointless" exercise. The violence in the streets will end when society no longer permits the day to day institutional violence. Let us, together, be against *all forms* of violence.

NOTES

1. *Report of the National Advisory Commission on Civil Disorders.* (New York: Bantam Books, 1968), p. 206.

2. Hugh Davis Graham and Ted Robert Gurr. *Violence in America: Historical and Comparative Perspectives.* (New York: Bantam Books, 1969), p. 420.

3. *Ibid.,* p. 418.

4. *Ibid.,* p. 419.

5. *Ibid.*

6. *Ibid.,* p. 420.

7. *Ibid.,* p. 421.

8. *Ibid.,* p. 805.

9. *Ibid.*

10. *Ibid.,* pp. 813-14.

11. Daniel Walker. *Rights In Conflict.* (New York: Signet Books, 1968), p. 3.

12. Richard A. Chikota and Michael C. Moran. *Riot in the Cities.* (Rutherford: Fairleigh Dickinson University Press, 1970), p. 107.

13. *Ibid.*

14. Public Law 90-351, 90th Congress, H.R. 5037, June 19, 1968, Omnibus Crime Control and Safe Streets Act of 1968, Part C, Section 301, p. 2-3.

15. Urban America, Inc., and The Urban Coalition. *One Year Later.* (New York: Frederick A. Praeger, publishers, 1969), p. 115.

16. *Belvedere Citizen,* Thursday, November 21, 1968, p. 1.

17. *One Year Later,* p. 115.

18. *Eastside Sun.* Thursday, December 3, 1970, p. 1.

19. *Los Angeles Times,* Part I, Friday, January 2, 1970, p. 3.

20. "Police-Community Relations in East Los Angeles, California," A Report of the California State Advisory Committee to the United States Commission on Civil Rights, October, 1970, p. 14.

21. *Ibid.,* p. 15.

22. *Ibid.,* p. 16.

23. *La Raza,* El Barrio Communications Project, P.O. Box 31004, Los Angeles, p. 2.

24. *Los Angeles Times,* Wednesday, September 16, 1970, Part I, p. 25.

25. *Ibid.*

26. *Ibid.*

27. *Ibid.*

28. *Ibid.*

29. *Ibid.*

30. *Ibid.*

31. *Los Angeles Times,* Thursday, September 17, 1970, Part I, p. 26.

32. *Los Angeles Times,* Wednesday, September 16, 1970, Part I, p. 3.

33. *Ibid.*

34. *Los Angeles Times,* Thursday, September 17, 1970, Part I, p. 3.

35. *Los Angeles Herald-Examiner,* Thursday, September 17, 1970, p. A-6.

36. *Los Angeles Times,* Thursday, September 17, 1970, Part I, p. 3.

37. *Los Angeles Times,* Friday, September 18, 1970, Part I, p. 30.

38. *Ibid.*

39. James P. Comer. *Violence in America,* p. 460-61.

40. *One Year Later,* p. 114.

41. *Los Angeles Times,* Wednesday, January 27, 1971, Part I, p. 19.

42. *Los Angeles Times,* Friday, January 15, 1971, Part I, p. 1.

43. The letter in its original form was obtained from Mr. Munoz. The *edited* version of the letter was published by the *Los Angeles Times* on Saturday, January 23, 1971, Part II, p. 4. The editor, Anthony Day, edited out comments about Chief Horral, Chief Parker, Chief Davis, and practically all of paragraph four. This form of editing does not allow the general reader to have sufficient information upon which to make a more intelligent evaluation of the police-Chicano conflict. Although perhaps not intended, the effect is one of eliciting more support for the police which then might tend to escalate the conflict.

29: BLACK BERET ORGANIZATION

WE, THE MEMBERS OF THE BLACK BERETS OF ALBUQUERQUE, AZTLAN being aware of the injustices, discriminatory, and oppressive actions against La Raza, hereby pledge to commit our lives to the *Service, Education, and Defense* of La Santa Raza.

In order to combat injustices, racial discrimination and oppression we have set up a defense against the repressive agencies which carry out these established practices against the Chicano and all Third World peoples. To have an effective defense against these practices we must observe at all times the federal, state, local, and other agencies which are the main contributors to the repressive conditions which exist among La Raza and all other Third World peoples.

To serve the people means not only to correct the injustices, but to provide, wherever necessary, the necessities for a complete humane society. Whatever these necessities might be, a Black Beret will do everything within his power to provide them. We realize that to save our people we must be motivated, not only by the hatred for the marrano racista, but by the great emotions and feelings of love that we have for our Raza and the Third World peoples.

We have come to the conclusion that we cannot solve the total problems by ourselves so one of our most important tasks is to make our people aware. This is education. In order to completely educate the people we must not only concentrate on the problems and the causes, but we must instill in our people pride in our culture and heritage and love for that which is ours.

THEREFORE THE BLACK BERET'S DUTY IS TO SERVE, EDUCATE, AND DEFEND.

BBO 12 POINT PROGRAM & PLATFORM

1. WE WANT SELF-DETERMINATION AND LIBERATION FOR ALL THE CHICANOS IN THE U.S.A.

Before the Amerikkkans came into being we were here in the Southwest. When they came we taught them how to survive in the Southwest. Yet they have cheated, killed us, and exploited us. Now the time has come to stop all this. We demand control over our own destinies and the power to be placed in the hands of the Chicano people in order to make *Aztlan* a reality and to insure our future existence. *Que Viva Aztlan Libre!*

2. WE WANT SELF-DETERMINATION FOR ALL LATINOS AND THIRD WORLD PEOPLES.

We will not be free until our Puerto Rican, Black, Indian, and Asian brothers in the U.S.A. are also free from the oppressive and colonial rule of this system. We are not free until our brothers in Latin America, Africa, and Asia are liberated. Our struggles are basically the same. We must unite to end discrimination, injustices and to rise out of poverty. *No Chicano Is Free Until All Oppressed People Are Free!*

3. WE WANT COMMUNITY CONTROL OF OUR INSTITUTIONS AND LAND.

We want control of our communities by our people and programs to quarantee that all institutions serve the needs of our people. People's control of Police, Health Services, Churches, Schools, Housing, Transportation and Welfare are needed. We want an end to attacks on our Land by urban renewal, highway destruction, universities and corporations, *La Tierra Es de la Gente!*

4. WE WANT A TRUE EDUCATION OF OUR MESTIZO CULTURE AND SPANISH LANGUAGE.

We want an end to the cultural genocide perpetuated by the Amerikkkan educational system against Chicanos. We must be taught about our ancestors truthfully. Pancho Villa and Zapata were Revolutionaries, not bandits. Spanish is our language and must be taught as so. Our culture, a revolutionary Culture is the only true teaching. *Viva Nuestra Cultura Mestiza!*

5. WE WANT FREEDOM FOR ALL POLITICAL PRISONERS.

All Chicanos must be freed since they have been tried by racist courts and not by their own people. We want all freedom fighters released from jail. *Free Tijerina Ahora!*

6. WE OPPOSE THE AMERIKKKAN MILITARY AND ITS UNJUST WARS OF OPPRESSION.

We want the U.S.A. out of Vietnam and *Latin America* and the oppressed communities of the U.S.A. *Chicanos* should not serve in the Amerikkkan armed services, since they are denied the right to live with dignity and pride here in the U.S.A. *U.S.A. out of Vietnam, Latin America, & Aztlan!*

7. WE WANT EQUALITY FOR WOMEN. MACHISMO MUST BE REVOLUTIONARY . . . NOT OPPRESSIVE.

Under this system our women have been oppressed both by the system and our men. The doctrine of Machismo has been used by our men to take out their frustrations on their wives, sisters, mothers, and children. We must support our women in their struggle for economic and social equality and recognize that our women are equals within our struggle for Liberation. *Forward Hermanas in the Struggle!*

8. WE WANT AN IMMEDIATE END TO POLICE HARASSMENT, BRUTALITY, AND MURDER OF LA RAZA.

For years the colonizing army in our barrios, the police, have been beating, killing, and imprisoning our RAZA. The police must stop now and not tomorrow. They must realize they they can jail us, beat us, and kill us, but they will never stop our determination to be free. We demand Community Control of the Police. *End Police Brutality Now!!!*

9. WE WANT FOR OUR PEOPLE TO HAVE THE BASIC NECESSITIES TO EXIST.

We want for our people to be given the things necessary for existence, such as decent housing, clothing, food, transportation and medical services. Luxuries are privileges that must be paid for, but a man has the basic rights to have a roof over his head, to have food and clothes for him and his family, to good health, and transportation wherever he has to go. We *Demand* that the people receive all this from the Amerikkkan government as is their *Right. Hasta la Victoria Siempre!*

10. WE WANT FULL EMPLOYMENT FOR OUR PEOPLE.

We believe that the federal government is responsible and obligated to give everyman employment and a guaranteed income. We believe that if the white Amerikkkan businessman will not give full employment, then the means of production should be taken from the businessman and placed in the community so that the people in the community can organize and employ all of its people and give a high standard of living. *No More Unemployment.*

11. WE OPPOSE CAPITALISM AND ALLIANCES MADE BY OUR TREACHEROUS POLITICOS.

We oppose the politicos which oppress our people and give us empty promises before elections. We oppose the poverty pimps which keep our people down through useless and stagnated programs, social workers which keep our barrios divided and brothers fighting each other for crumbs. These people keep us from achieving our freedom. We demand that the people be given control of their barrios through political and economic power. *Venceremos!*

12. WE BELIEVE ARMED SELF-DEFENSE AND ARMED STRUGGLE ARE THE ONLY MEANS TO LIBERATION.

We are against violence, the violence of illiteracy, the violence of hungry children, the violence of diseased old people, and the violence of poverty and profit. We have gone to the courts to protest racism and discrimination, we have voted for the politicos who have given us empty promises, we have demonstrated peacefully for what we believe in only to be met with more violence, injustices and discrimination. We have to arm ourselves now to protect ourselves and the people from the oppression perpetuated by the businessmen, government, and police. When a government oppresses our people, we have the right to abolish it and create a new one. *El Chicano Ha Despertado! Cuidate Chota!*

IV. Retrospect and Prospects

IN THIS SECTION, THE POSITION OF THE CHICANO IN THE AMERICAN political system will be reviewed and some insights into his future status will also be attempted. Professor Cuéllar, having earlier traced the historical political development of Chicanos, provides hints as to the future directions the Chicano political movement will take. Professor Ralph Guzmán asks the questions: Will Chicanos continue to be forced to engage in the politics of passion? Must they riot, espouse the politics of violence, in order to have their voices heard and heeded by the core culture political system?

One of the successes of Chicano politics and perhaps a model for future Chicano political development has been La Raza Unida party in Texas, most vividly in Crystal City. Much of the story of Crystal City was told by Antonio Camejo in article 16 of this collection. In order to include some later developments of the story we have chosen excerpts from a book on Crystal City by John Shockley. But also, and more importantly, Mr. Shockley provides an excellent overview and analysis of the Crystal City situation from both Anglo and Chicano perspectives. He examines those conditions and events which made possible the great success of La Raza Unida in this one town of South Texas and assesses the prospects for the future. He feels that, although the Crystal City experience is a unique case not likely to be duplicated in other areas of the Southwest, it can serve as a special example of what can be more generally achieved through Chicano politics, for example, the development of indigenous leadership and community organization. As such it is an important source of pride and stimulus toward a heightened political consciousness. Finally, he poses some fundamental questions of identity which must be faced by the movement.

There is no way of accurately predicting what the future of Chicano politics will bring. Chicanos have come a long way in the last several years. Their progress will continue. A movement has begun which will not and cannot be halted. Many questions cannot yet be answered. What shape will the movement take? How will the American society react to it? What effects will *La Causa* have on the Chicano people and on the larger American system? Whatever the answers, the Chicano people are determined to obtain for themselves the place due them in the American political system.

30: PERSPECTIVE ON POLITICS: Part II

Alfredo Cuéllar

HOW MUCH HAS THIS [LARGELY POLITICAL] STUDENT MANIFESTATION of the *Chicano* movement affected the larger Mexican community? At this writing the ideological reverberations have been considerable, particularly among the young people of college age and including also those in the secondary schools. We must not forget that the Mexican American population is very young. Some counterparts of *Chicano* college militancy have appeared throughout the Southwest in high schools as, for example, among students in Denver, Los Angeles, San Francisco, and many smaller cities.

The demands have often been modest, in most instances no more than for increased counselling services for Mexican American students and other changes in the methods and content of instruction. In some Texas cities and in Denver, Colorado, the student militants further demanded the end of punishment for using Spanish on the school grounds. In most cases the school boards have acceded to this particular demand. But the reaction of the Anglo community has often been fierce. In Los Angeles a school "walk-out" by Mexican American students in 1968 resulted in the arrest of 13 alleged leaders for criminal conspiracy. In Denver a sharp reaction by the police resulted in the injury of 17 persons and the arrest of 40. In other areas in the Southwest there have been similar, if less publicized, responses to *Chicano* militancy.

Neither the Anglo reaction nor the rapid spread of *chicanismo* should be taken to mean that a full-blown social movement is in progress among Mexican Americans. In many areas, on the contrary, established Mexican

American leaders have dissociated themselves from the *Chicanos.* For instance, a school walkout by Mexican students in Kingsville, Texas brought an angry denunciation from a Mexican American Congressman from Texas and other community leaders. At the same time, the *Chicano* movement poses a very difficult dilemma for most older Mexican Americans. They sympathize with the goals of *chicanismo,* yet they fear that the radical means used to pursue these ends will undermine their own hard-earned social and economic gains. The Anglo community expects a denunciation of what it considers to be irresponsible acts of these young people. But for the older leaders to oppose the *Chicano* protest might be a slow form of personal political suicide as well as acting to exacerbate divisiveness in the Mexican American community.

In California, *Chicano* student groups have grown rapidly; they have acquired the power to pass on Mexican American faculty appointments in many high schools and colleges. Typically such faculty members are avidly sought to assist with the new ethnic studies programs and centers. Ultimately, though, *Chicano* students are faced by responsibility to the community. These students are aware that the popularity of *chicanismo* among Mexican American students means a major opportunity for the development of an entire new generation of young professionals to carry these ideas back to the Mexican American community.

Beyond the universities there have been other sources of support, some of them quite substantial. Grants and direct organizing assistance have come from American Protestant denominations, notably the National Council of Churches. In 1968 a substantial ($630,000) grant from the Ford Foundation to the Southwest Council of La Raza (headquarters in Phoenix) helped the organization of a number of militant *Chicano* groups. The Southwest Council of La Raza considers itself permanent and accepts money for "*barrio* development" from not only the Ford Foundation but churches, labor groups, and other interested organizations. Both the announced ideals of the council and its membership assure commitment to the ideals of *chicanismo.*

The *Chicano* movement began as a protest. Only later did its dynamics carry it toward an increasing cultural nationalism. The first steps toward social change did not go beyond demands for equality of opportunity for Mexican Americans, which are still being made (by the less militant in the movement). Until recently no Mexican American had tried to define the problems of the community in any terms except those of assimilation. It is precisely these ideas of assimilation and social "adjustment" that the *Chicano* militant rejects. As a new alternative, *chicanismo* represents a conception of an autonomous and self-determining social life for Mexican Americans.

It is interesting that it was not until the 1960s that the *Chicano* leaders emerged to question some of the oldest and most fundamental assumptions of Mexicans in American society. This protest probably would not have been possible in a period of general social calm and stability. That the *Chicano* protest emerged when it did is perhaps due in large part to the emergence of other social groups that also began to question basic notions about American society. But if these other groups feel a sense of alienation in American society, the *Chicano's* alienation is doubly acute. It is not only from American society that he feels alienated; he also feels left out of the mainstream of Mexican history and, simultaneously, he feels a sense of guilt for having "deserted" the homeland. It is this sense of being in two cultures yet belonging to neither (*ni aquí ni allá*) that is the source of his most profound alienation and now, anger. It is against this background that the *Chicano* is attempting with a deep sense of urgency to reconstruct his history, his culture, his sense of identity.

In practical terms the result is increasing radicalization, with which comes a new set of problems. Cultural nationalism has emerged, bringing with it questions that must be answered if the *Chicano* movement is to become a potent force for all Mexican Americans in their diverse circumstances throughout the Southwest and other parts of the United States.

31: MEXICAN AMERICANS IN THE URBAN AREA: Will They Riot?

Ralph Guzmán

MAGIC WAS THE MEANS BY WHICH PRIMITIVE MAN MADE THE WORLD meaningful to himself. Modern America is on the verge of resorting to magic because the ideas and information available to it no longer explain the reality of its own life. Part of this phenomenon reflects an attempt to explain urban complexities with agrarian symbolism and value systems.

The real revolution in our time is not only the upsurge of the Negro toward dignity; it is not merely the rebellion of children against their parents; it is not just the erosion of eternal verities; it is not even the fantastic rate of technological development and redevelopment. The real revolution of our times is all of these, in juxtaposition to one another, and more.

One of the sad features of our modern society is that those who gained the most from this age of affluence have never asked: "Who lost?" In a sense, most of the facets of this age of unlimited expectations, this age where nothing seems impossible, is that the revolutions of our generation seem to be separate and apart from one another. But, the distance between the middle-class American who complains about his teen age children and says: "We don't speak the same language" is about the same as that of the Mexican American parent who regrets that his child refuses to learn Spanish. The distance is more apparent than real.

The arid phrases, normally used to describe the transformation of American life in the last decade, obscure rather than reveal the remarkable impact this revolution has had on individual lives and destinies. To say that this revolution has technological aspects does not explain to a 45-year-old man with family responsibilities that he is too old to learn a new trade and too

Reprinted with permission of the author.

young to vegetate for the rest of his life. Technological unemployment reveals nothing of the despair of an illiterate adolescent when he finds that he is economically irrelevant—or in short that he can't get a job. The words generational gap fail to convey the dilemma of a man who has sacrificed everything to give his children security only to find they reject it.

Fundamental anti-intellectualism in American society has over-shadowed the fact that in the arts, the sciences and the humanities, every tradition has been toppled and supplanted. The fight between college and town is a reflection between different views of the universe. In California the insistence that the university conform to the taxpayer's idea of a university stands in direct contrast to the idea that a university should be a place for the search of truth, however outlandish and antagonistic to the interests of the taxpayer.

Our society has still not assimilated the full implications of the change of the role of the government from that of the necessary evil to that of a force for positive good. This leaves liberals with visions of omnipotence and conservatives with nightmares of disaster. Neither view, of course, accords with reality. Governmental activism cannot resolve all problems; for these are problems that are rightfully beyond the reach of governmental purview. Neither is governmental intervention an automatic evil; for there are some problems that only government can reach.

Even as the churches have up-dated their rituals and theology, America is long overdue in renovating its supply of ideas. Symbols and values relevant to an agrarian past must be re-cast for our urban present. Notions of community solidarity; I-thou relationships; salvation through work; the Horatio Alger myth must be discarded. We must recognize and cope with the solitude; the privacy; the mobility and the restlessness of the city. For the city is not just a network of freeways. It is not just the decisions of the zoning commission. It is not merely a marble and concrete mechanism. It is a totally new way of life; an organism of immense complexity. It teems not with millions of cogs and wheels but with millions of people.

And for those millions of people the revolution of our time has been dangerously encapsulated in the equation; Negro equals riot equals revolution. For above all, minorities in these United States have been affected adversely by the onslaught of this new age of affluence. Both its victims and its prisoners; they have been the forgotten losers in the game of material acquisition. In the miles and miles and acres and acres of housing developments, few minority members are found. In the myriad expansion of services and luxuries, few minority people benefit. In the explosion of information and learning that circles the earth our ethnic minorities remain a mystery. They have been the most conspicuous of those who have not shared in this era of plenty. But along with the majority they have shared the loss of those psychic comforts associated with a simpler society. For, if the sense of rootlessness afflicts the Negro, it also afflicts the inhabitants of split-level ranch houses. If the loss of identity causes anxiety for the Mexican American he shares that problem with the bulk of American youth. If the break-up of the family exacerbates the problem of the poor let it be known that homes for the aged are not filled with the elderly of the poor and of the minorities.

This community of concern, that faces all Americans, has been strangely twisted into the problem peculiar to the racial and ethnic minorities of our country. Nowhere is the lack of intelligent comprehension of what this nation is, more evident than in the utter lack of knowledge shared by the majority and the minority about each other. Because of this simplistic equation, the search for concepts and solutions has been the province of a thin strata of the American establishment.

No one can say that the problems of the poor have not been researched, studied, examined, handled, committee-ed, anachronimed, and sloganed. There is hardly a letter of the alphabet that has not been used to form an abbreviation for an agency. Government has created OEO, CAP, EDA, MDTA, and HEW. All of these are part of the vast arsenal that comprise the invested personnel and resources in job training programs designed to diminish poverty. Church groups have been conspicuous in the attempt to enliven the conscience of the country about conditions related to poverty and race. In the 1930s the Rockefeller Foundation could deny a grant to aid the Mexican American poor on the grounds of insufficient data about these people. Today, it and other foundations eagerly encourage innovative programs to alleviate poverty and prejudice. But, let there be no mistake, this activity, this flood of concern engages but a minute percentage of the total population. This empathy is restricted to the elite of the American establishment. Between the vast majority and growing minority there exists a gulf of understanding, of information and knowledge that will never be bridged by the jargon of the elite.

Let there be no mistake. Programs designed to help the poor and the deprived have been the product of the top layer of American society. These programs have been created by them, administered by them, supported by them and, in some instances, even thwarted by them. They have been a meager response to the threat of violence. Their existence is predicated upon that threat. Consequently, they have no roots beyond this threat of social disruption. Therefore, the vast majority of the American people have absolutely no involvement intellectually or emotionally in any program designed to aid minorities that is not based on force and the restoration of the old order. This antipathy, on the part of the overwhelming majority, can be directly laid to blame at the doorstep of American leadership. For if one of the functions of leadership is to educate; to help make understandable the events of a nation's life, our leadership is largely talking to itself.

Perhaps this is most evident in the employment of a special new language devised by the elite and debased in popular usage. A term such as "hard-core unemployed" means to the elite an individual who lacks the necessary skills to perform minimum tasks in a highly developed technology. It also includes assumptions about value orientations and environmental disabilities. To the poor it means they can't get a job. Surprisingly enough, they knew this before someone told them they were "hard-core unemployed." But, to most Americans hard-core unemployment means: "too lazy to work." Another term that indicates myopia of the elite is "culturally deprived." One suspects that 97 percent of the entire population of the world would fall into that category. It is a term with meaning only to those who assumed that they have culture. Lumped together, as beyond the pale, are both those with a different culture and those without season tickets to the opera. The net result has been to increase the ignorance of various sectors of American society about each other. In a way the elite have ministered to the poor in a fashion not alike preachers riding circuit in the past. By day they travel to the ghettos of despair and at dusk they return to the security of their suburban retreats. They have become the buffer between the miserably poor and the misunderstanding many.

For the poor the application of terms to their economic circumstances does not increase their ability to escape. For if the poor really knew the causes and remedies for their poverty they would surely choose them of their own accord. Instead, however, they become cases, objects and problems. They themselves are called upon to play a passive part in their own rescue. The traditional values of the poor: suspicion, hostility, mistrust, doubt, hopelessness–all of these are re-enforced by the paternalism of the elite and the contempt of the majority.

The fact that so many of the poor are also ethnic and racial minorities has consequences for both the elite and the white middle classes. For the elite the reigning paternalism is increased by the fear of the mob. Thus what started out as a response to a single aspect of violence has become a defensive maneuver designed to maintain the urban peace; to preserve law and order; to keep the people quiet. For the white middle classes contempt has mingled with fear producing a tension level unparalleled in recent history. For the white middle classes are scared. They expect violence and their only substantive response, thus far, is repression. This misunderstanding of the revolution of our time; by all participants; by the elite; by the poor and by the white middle classes; has produced an atmosphere of terror and anxiety that certainly does not augur well for the future of our democracy. In the effort to repress violence the poor will never miss traditional civil liberties; for they have never had them. And it is increasingly clear that the white middle class will gladly trade traditional liberty for false security. Moreover, this dangerous equation: Negro equals riot equals revolution, has left many groups of people, who are part of this revolution, with neither the benefits of those efforts that have been made nor the goodwill of the society. The Indian and the Mexican American are the preeminent examples of the lost children of the urban revolution.

Right now no one knows exactly how many Mexican Americans there are in the Southwest. Estimates range between six and seven million. We do know that the median age of this group is 19.5 years; that the average family size exceeds that of the white majority and the Negro minority. However, modern statistics cannot reveal the context in which this group has developed. To the people of the Southwest the region itself is a closed book. Movies and television have projected an image of the Southwest in which numerous Nietzchean supermen constantly ride off into the sunset, clutching their saddles, after another sortie against savage Indians and/or villainous Mexicans. We Americans are a strangely historic people. By this I mean that the actual history of the Southwest; the history of violence and exploitation; the lessons of the conqueror and the conquered; the harsh combat of all against an inhospitable land–all these are forgotten, if they were ever known.

Conflict and guile guided the development of this area. Law was the weapon of the strong against the weak. And few people confused law with justice. In their role as conquered, Mexican Americans became prisoners of a popular stereotype of a triumphant and rampant mythology. They became a sideshow; a humorous diversion in the struggle of the victor against nature. Considered as foreigners they were excused their ethnic eccentricities. As peasants they were not supposed to be too bright. As idol-worshippers they were an American brand of basically inferior heathens. Even today the legend persists in the minds of many southwesterners, and practically all who are not from the Southwest. Despite the popular stereotype, however, the Mexican American has felt the urban revolution of our time–no less than his Anglo counterparts.

Technological developments have reduced his employability. First, the increased emphasis on formal language and social skills has erected a formidable barrier to upward occupational mobility. Second, the concommitant decrease in the need for unskilled labor has created a surplus of Spanish surnamed unemployed. Thirdly, mechanization in the agricultural sector has augmented the surplus and the exodus to the urban ghettos. Thus, while fewer jobs are available to the Mexican American in the cities hundreds of thousands stream toward the large metropolitan centers in search of non-existent, unskilled jobs.

With more than a four hundred year history in the Southwest–more than European immigrants, only recently, in the last 25 years, has the majority of the Mexican American people become a part of the urban reality of this region. Long a rural people, this minority is today 87 percent urban.

Many now live in these cities armed with inadequate attitudes and social skills of an agrarian past. Desperately, against tremendous odds, many seek to maintain crumbling idylls that have no roots in the urban reality. Such is the impact of the social forces within the city. Nor have ethnic intellectuals been much help. First, because their numbers are limited. Second, because many are ideologues who look to the restoration of a lost grandeur while obsessively denying the presence of ragged poor. Every day the irrelevance of the latter becomes more apparent. For the Mexican American population of the Southwest is not foreign and archaic but overwhelmingly American by birth, young and grossly disadvantaged.

Moreover, the generational problem in the majority society is more than matched among Mexican Americans. If the old ideologues have little to say to their peers they have nothing to say to the young. Young Mexican Americans are living the urban revolution thus the values of the parent generation and the visions of the offsprings are as sharply contrasted within this minority group as they are in the larger society. The neglect of the young by both the old ideologues and the larger society has left them disillusioned, bitter and deeply resentful. While some may seek an artificial identity with the Che Guevarra and Negro militancy, others withdrew into an anguished apathy. Still others, the majority of the young, await viable direction for their destiny. The majority of them ignore their parents and await for one of their own to articulate grievances and direct social energy.

We cannot expect the young to remain polite and powerless. We cannot expect them to continue saying thank you for nothing. Social disorder is a function of the young. They question contracts established before their birth. And they challenge forces applied to maintain these contracts. The whole litany of inherited problems will never again be accepted as part of the natural order of things.

Still many Mexican American leaders bring up these problems in the same strident tones of their Negro opposites. They call for caution and patience; for thought and logic, and for ethnic unity built upon deference to age. All this is rejected by the young, particularly those who stand in envy of the Black Power movement. For most of the young want to escalate the drive for social change.

The question: "Will the Mexican American riot?" is probably irrelevant. Answering the affirmative or the negative sheds no light on the problems of this minority or this nation. Regretfully, present programs, conceived merely as a response to a threat of social disruption, whether continued or expanded, probably will not prevent violence in the streets. For, given the rapidity and intensity of the revolution convulsing our country, the question is not *whether they will riot or when they will riot.* For all of us the question is: "Will riots become a permanent and enduring part of our national existence? Will riots become the only means to affectuate meaningful social change? Or, because of intelligent and reasoned application of resources will urban anarchy pass away into a footnote to history?"

Finally, there is one group that is not well-known. It has not been well-studied, but we do know that it has a propensity for violence exceeding that of either the Negro or the Mexican American. It too, has been equally a victim of revolutionary developments in our history. Any total response to the urban revolution of our times must include programs to assuage the fears of the white, middle-class American who has not yet rioted in full force. For it is this sector of our society whose history of hysterical outburst portends tragic consequences for the future of this country. We would be unwise and unrealistic: all of us Americans, minorities and non-minorities, if we ignore the white, middle class. After all, most members of this strata of our society have rarely displayed either the rural patience of the Negro or the agrarian politeness of the Mexican American.

32: CHICANO CONTROL AND THE FUTURE

John Staples Shockley

ALL THE CHANGES AND DEVELOPMENTS IN CRYSTAL CITY HAD THEIR impact on the elections in the spring of 1971, after La Raza Unida's first year in office. The campaign for the school-board and city-council elections quickly shaped up to be as heated as the campaign in 1970, and on both the city council and the school board, control was at stake.

On election day there was no violence and the voting went smoothly. With La Raza Unida in control of the voting machinery, there appeared to be no attempt to impede the voting process. Ironically, Gutiérrez spent most of the day on duty in the army reserves. Close to 3,000 people voted, which was far more than had ever voted in a presidential election and around 400 votes more than had voted in the 1970 election. With this even greater turnout, La Raza Unida candidates were swept into office with an increased margin. Three days later, La Raza Unida candidates won the city-council positions in another record turnout. They also increased their margin of victory, winning nearly two-to-one over the all-Mexican, Anglo-supported slate. As a further indication of the intense mobilization and polarization in the community, the three independent candidates drew hardly any votes at all.

After a year in office, La Raza Unida thus solidified its control. It now had total control of the city council, and a five-to-two majority on the school board. This meant that for both the city and the schools, control would remain in their hands for at least two more years. More so now than ever, what had traditionally been considered an apathetic, powerless Mexican community was being transformed into an organized, mobilized majority fully in control of the political institutions of the city. Faced with the clear possibility of changes in the structure of the community and the schools, and then given the opportunity to pass judgment on these changes, Crystal City's Mexican community had turned out in phenomenal numbers to register approval.

The strengthening of La Raza Unida's control after a year in office was in marked contrast with the Cornejo years ["First Revolt," 1963-1965]. Mexicans had been able to run the community without the aid of the local Anglos and without the degree of chaos and confusion that had followed the Cornejo victory. The election thus seemed to vindicate those Mexicans who had argued against the idea that a coalition with the Anglos was the only way Mexicans could improve their condition in the town.

For the same reason the election results were a bitter blow to the Anglos, in several ways more painful than the preceding year's disaster. After the school strike, many Anglos had realized that Gutiérrez and his radical band had been strengthened, but they consoled themselves with the belief that once the "Gutierristas" gained control, the resulting incompetence would be so obvious that a successful reaction would set in similar to the reaction against Cornejo in 1965. Through trying to remain relatively quiet and by allowing the "Gutierristas" to "dig their own grave," the Anglos had generally hoped that racial polarization in the town would subside and "responsible" Mexicans would rise up and (with Anglo help) throw out the irresponsible radicals.[1]

With the turmoil in the city and schools during the year of La Raza Unida rule, as evidenced by numerous court suits and investigations and by the rebuke from the Texas Classroom Teachers Association, most Anglos in the community had remained guardedly optimistic that La Raza Unida could be thrown out of office. The Anglos were also encouraged by the response to the firing of the twenty-three Anglo teachers, which seemed to further unite all those people opposed to La Raza Unida.

Their hopes for a return to moderate rule were thus rudely shattered by the election results, and it was extremely hard for them to understand what had happened. Said one of the Anglos, "After all the turmoil in the school, obvious to even the densest of minds, you would think a fair number of voters would have been switched during the year. . . ."

Most Anglos in the community just could not believe that the changes being made in the schools and city were changes which the majority of citizens in the community urgently wanted. It was impossible for most Anglos to believe that, when contrasted with the decades of Anglo rule, the citizens preferred the new leadership and the changes. The Anglos appear instead to have persisted in believing only those things which would not radically overthrow their own belief structures. Thus they tended to believe that the Mexicans had been bought or had been intimidated, which was something they knew from their own experience was a way to win an election. To explain the phenomenal voter turnouts, one Anglo commented that La Raza Unida had "high-school students racing along the streets knocking on doors and persuading the occupants to go to the polls in transportation provided while studying a marked ballot." This was an accurate observation, as La Raza Unida did indeed have a very comprehensive network for getting people to the polls. But from this fact this same Anglo concluded, "They simply overwhelm the people, many of whom might not have the least interest in voting until pressured into it." Another cried, "They had them hypnotized!"

It was indeed ironic for Anglos to claim that Raza Unida was voting people who might have had no interest in voting, particularly after CASAA had so magnificently developed their own absentee-voting system for sick, elderly, and dependent Mexicans. *La Verdad,* the Spanish newspaper for Crystal City which was begun by Gutiérrez, commented on the Anglo feelings after the election:

> It is not possible to dispute the results of the elections, which were honest and open. La Raza Unida has obtained political control of this city through the democratic process of free elections, and this is what hurts the gringo like a kick in the –, that the system which he has proudly presented as the best in the world has been used with success to destroy his tyranny.
>
> And if they fear what Chicano control means, it is because they have guilty consciences over the injustices which they have perpetrated on Chicanos for so many years.[2]

La Verdad also noted that "it seems that the gringos are incapable of losing political control without losing at the same time all sense of fair play and decency. . . . We know of at least six cases in which Chicanos who have supported La Raza Unida have had their salaries cut, have been demoted, or have been fired."

Whatever the reasons for their crushing defeat, Crystal City Anglos now had to face the fact that La Raza Unida would be in control of the city and the schools for at least two more years. This led them to some painful and difficult choices, as they realized that "the reputation of the town as an undesirable place to live [will keep] out those with enough energy and ambition to benefit the community." There was also an increased sense of isolation and bitterness among Anglos, and a resentment over the role federal programs were playing in the new government. It seemed as if their own government were abandoning them through providing support and jobs to the opposition. But many Anglos also continued to believe–much as United States policy makers seem to have believed about the Viet Cong–that the Mexicans couldn't go on like this forever, that they were bound in the end to be conquered by the superior might and intellectual skills of the Anglos, and that this was so because of the Mexican's inherent incapacity to rule without Anglo guidance. Said one Anglo in the wake of the defeat, "The city is bound to be on the brink of a crisis, if not complete collapse."[3] The city simply *had* to be in this condition after a year of "irresponsible" Mexican rule.

Conditions in the town thus produced continued polarization, with Anglos increasingly aware that their methods of regaining control were not working, and with the Mexicans more and more successful in establishing Crystal City as a beachhead and model for Chicano power in the Southwest.

Following the spring elections of 1971, most Anglos withdrew their children from the Crystal City schools and sent them to nearby communities or to a newly established private school, "open to all races and religious groups" and "free of politics and harassment by La Raza."[4] By the fall of 1971 less than twenty Anglos remained in the public-school system.

The city was stymied in its attempt to annex and tax the huge Del Monte Corporation. At first it seemed likely that the city would win at least a partial victory, because of the 1970 agreement between the lame-duck city council and Del Monte over not annexing the plant involved what to Raza Unida was a clear conflict of interest. The city attorney and a city councilman at the time of the agreement were both being salaried by Del Monte. But after three years of legal appeals, a federal jury ruled that the city did not have the right to annex and tax the corporation.[5] Thus it seemed likely that the huge Del Monte corporation would continue to pay no city taxes, at least until the seven-year contract expires in 1977.

The city and school elections of the spring of 1972 were less heated than the previous races, as control of either unit was not at stake because of staggered terms. La Raza Unida, however, won by the greatest margins yet, electing all its candidates by over two-to-one margins. The previous autumn the party had made the decision to run candidates statewide, and thus much of their political effort was spent developing the party elsewhere.[6] In September, 1972, the party hosted its first national convention. Delegates from around the state and from over a dozen other states met in El Paso, organized the party structurally, and formed a *Congreso de Aztlán* to serve as the party's main body. José Angel Gutiérrez served as the party's temporary chairman, and was later elected director of the *Congreso.* In organizing and leading such a national movement, Gutiérrez was clearly hoping to expand the impact and size of the party far beyond Crystal City and the Winter Garden area.

Although Raza Unida candidates ran in other states in the November elections, the party was most successful in Texas, where Ramsey Muñiz, the party's candidate for governor, drew more than six percent of the votes cast (over 200,000) and very nearly caused the Republican candidate, Henry Grover, to be elected.[7] The other statewide Raza Unida candidates, however, did considerably worse.[8] Altogether La Raza Unida had forty-nine candidates running in the state, with most seeking county office. Seven were successful: two in La Salle County (Cotulla), and five in Zavala County. In fact, in Zavala

County the party was finally able to crack the Anglo domination of the county, in one of the toughest and most bitter battles to date.[9] Unlike the 1970 county elections, where the party had been unable to get on the ballot, in 1972 Raza Unida narrowly elected Rey Pérez county attorney, defeating long-time Anglo leader R. A. Taylor. And Sheriff C. L. Sweeten was at last beaten, falling to José Serna by a larger margin.

The county elections represented an expansion of Raza Unida strength, but the party still did not have control of the county. That could not come before 1974, when County Judge Irl Taylor and two other commissioners would be up for reelection. The closeness of the vote surprised many in the party who had hoped Raza Unida would win bigger victories. The fact that Anglos controlled the election machinery, and that there was perhaps growing resentment among some Chicanos over the role of Ciudadanos Unidos and the party leadership, together seem to have accounted for the close outcome.

Expansion of La Raza Unida's base beyond Crystal City was slow and tedious, as even gaining a foothold in the county required enormous mobilization.

The spring 1973 school-board elections became another torrid affair. Significantly, all the incumbents on the city council and school board, including Gutiérrez, chose not to seek reelection. Their stated reason was to allow others in the community a chance to serve, and thus avoid the habit, so prevalent among South Texas Anglos, of staying in office for decades. The results showed that La Raza Unida had lost considerable ground since the 1972 election, although they again emerged victorious.[10] Rudy Palomo, an old friend of Gutiérrez, was elected the new school-board president, and Ventura Gonzales became the new mayor.

A series of disparate, yet related, events underscored the power of the Chicanos and La Raza Unida in Crystal City. In the fall of 1971 the local Catholic priest, who had been critical of La Raza Unida, was replaced by one far more in sympathy with "la causa." In January, 1972, a "huelga" occurred when one of the local packing sheds lowered wages from $1.60 to $1.30 an hour.[11] Many people from the community and schools (including the new Catholic priest) journeyed to the fields to picket, and the strike ended successfully when the owner agreed to restore wages. Another important event occurred in 1972 when President Luis Echevarría of Mexico gave Crystal City a bust of Benito Juárez, which was dedicated with much fanfare. Next to Juárez were inscribed the words, "El respeto al derecho ageno es la paz."[12]

Episodes such as these—involving both great symbolism and clear evidence of political power—emphasized the transition that had occurred in the town.[13] The city was changing from the "Spinach Capital of the World" to the "Chicano Capital."

AN ASSESSMENT OF THE ANGLO FAILURE

All these changes and developments emphasized again that the Anglos had, temporarily if not permanently, completely lost control of the politics of the town. The polarization of the races in Crystal City and the strength of the reactive cultural nationalism in the Mexican community had bewildered nearly all the Anglos in the town.[14] Like colonizers, most Crystal City Anglos had grown up assuming that their culture was superior and had taken for granted their right to rule. And like colonizers, they ended up being amazed that the numerically dominant "natives" should question the superiority of Anglo rule. But in defense of the Crystal City Anglo it is important to realize that what they had assumed and tried to implement in Crystal City, particularly concerning making rewards to the Mexican population dependent upon acculturation, was in many ways the essence of what the dominant groups in American society seem to have done for centuries.

Although there were several important differences between the Crystal City Anglo and the American Anglo-Saxon, perhaps the greatest is simply that the American Anglo-Saxon won whereas the Crystal City Anglo failed. It should not be forgotten that, as Sheldon Wolin has commented, history has been written by the victors; thus what the Anglo-Saxon in America has done—in teaching everyone to speak English and to give up his native language, in integrating and acculturating to a large extent the various white ethnic groups which came to America—is either accepted as *fait accompli* or commended as an example of nation-building for others to emulate.[15] But the failure of the Anglos in Crystal City has made it easy for them to be condemned for trying to do many of the things which seem to constitute much of the essence of the American system.

In truth, the differences between the Crystal City Anglo and the American Anglo-Saxon were probably not so great as the differences in the population with which each had to work. The size and tenacity of the local Mexican population made them different from the millions of European immigrants who voluntarily left their countries to come to the New World. One might argue that the Anglos of Crystal City set up more barriers for the Mexican population than did Anglos elsewhere in the country, but many Mexicans also did not want to be "Anglicized," and they were buttressed in their cultural orientations by having Mexico just across the river and by viewing this area of Texas as being historically their own.

It is also clear that before either of the revolts [1963, 1969] in Crystal City occurred, the Mexican population had been making some improvement, both in absolute terms and in relation to the Anglo minority. How much this improvement occurred because of or in spite of the Anglos is a matter of dispute, but the improvement should not be forgotten. This obvious betterment has meant that Anglos have been all the more bewildered by the polarization that has occurred in the community. To them there had been obvious signs of improvement in race relations in the community and of an increase in Anglo tolerance toward Mexicans, at least toward those who were becoming more like the Anglos. Yet in their view, their own increasing tolerance was met by increasing intolerance in the Mexican community.

Their ultimate failure led them to much soul-searching and bitterness, and in this process it became clear that many local Anglos either did not understand some of the basic tenets of democracy, or that if they did, they rejected the concept. Said one Anglo matron, "Something is wrong with the government when we allow them to overthrow the government."[16] She seemed unable to recognize the distinction between personnel in office and the offices themselves, and that being able to "overthrow" the personnel in office is one of the essential features of democracy. But after the many years of rule by Anglos in Crystal City, this confusion was perhaps understandable.

There was thus among the Anglo community of Crystal City tremendous alienation from their own system of government, both local and national. Those who didn't understand what democracy involved tended to think the whole Raza Unida movement was antidemocratic. Those who did understand what democracy involved tended to *be* antidemocratic. Many social scientists have argued that the masses don't understand what democracy involves and that in important ways they are antidemocratic.[17] In Crystal City, however, many of the Anglos seemed to be fundamentally antidemocratic because of the experiences they had endured and because they had always been a privileged minority.

Although hindsight does reveal that the Anglos committed some glaring blunders, it does not show that their errors were foolish ones, obviously destined to fail. We have argued from the beginning that much of the reason for the explosive situation in Crystal City lay more in the history of the community than in what any one Anglo or group of Anglos did at the time of the revolts. The history of settlement of the community—the economic base in agriculture and its concomitant land use—led to a heavy preponderance of poor Mexican Americans in the community. This economic base (more specifically the seasonal nature of agriculture in the area) produced migrant workers who could be more easily mobilized for radical politics than permanent residents of the community.* And the introduction of outside capital

*The reasons for this seem to relate to what S. M. Lipset and William Kornhauser have observed in the socioeconomic basis for radical politics.[18] The isolation and geographic mobility of migrant farm workers means that they have few ties to the existing order. Thus once organized, they tend to be radical. Their suffering from recurrent unemployment and underemployment may have further radicalized them, as Maurice Zeitlin found in the case of Cuban workers in similar situations.[19]

and management through the Del Monte plant (and especially its decision to allow unionization of its packing plant) changed the balance of resources between the Anglos and Mexicans in the community. The combined set of factors produced a community in South Texas which was more nearly unique than general.

Both revolts occurred at times which were difficult to predict. That is, in neither instance did it appear that the Anglos could have had clear and incontrovertible evidence that a successful revolt was about to occur. The Anglos could not have been prepared for the unprecedented Teamster and PASO involvement in community politics, and in the spring and summer of 1969 it was not obvious that denying the students their demands was playing into the hands of the radicals. By negating the concessions and by issuing a strong statement on what would happen if any further attempts at agitation were to occur in the schools, the board thought it was handling the situation in the best possible way. It seems to have been a very reasonable gamble to try to crush the incipient organization through intransigence. This had worked before, as for example when some of the protests over the poverty program had ended in failure, when high-school students had protested over discrimination in the high school in the late fifties, and even when Diana Palacios and her supporters had protested the discriminatory nature of cheerleader selection the year before. And this intransigence has continued to work in many other places in South Texas.

The logic behind this intransigence has been explained clearly by Michael Parenti in his examination of the successful defeat of an attempt to build a community organization in Newark, New Jersey. In noting that the incipient ghetto community organization was defeated even on the most reasonable of demands, such as on the demand for a traffic light at a corner where several people had been injured, Parenti concluded that the political officials' "unwillingness to make tangible allocations is due less to any consideration of immediate political expenditure than to their concern that present protests are but a prelude to more challenging and more costly demands."[21] He noted that a victory even on some things as reasonable as a traffic light "might have strengthened precisely the kind of oppositional activity that Newark officials wanted to discourage."[22] Instead he noted that the ghetto residents' defeat reinforced the status quo by leading them to conclude once again that there was no use trying to better their condition since they saw no opportunity for effective protest.

The decision by the school board to nullify the superintendent's April,

---

Migrant workers can be contrasted with those Mexican Americans who are tied to a particular piece of land which their *jefe* or *patrón* would own. Tenants and sharecroppers would be far more susceptible to control, as indeed those in the outlying parts of Zavala County were. Ozzie Simmons has noted this distinction in South Texas, as did Eric Wolf more generally.[20]

1969, agreement with the students was without doubt prefaced in large part on the hope that through sternness the students and their supporters would return to apathy. The board also feared that by giving in on these points, authorities would merely be whetting the appetites of the students. Only with the return of Gutiérrez and his conscious attempt to lay the foundations of a community organization did the balance of power between the two groups appear to shift. Thus even with these explosive preconditions in Crystal City, it seems likely that the Anglos could have maintained power had it not been for extremely sophisticated and astute leadership within the Chicano community.

"CONTAINMENT" OF CRYSTAL CITY

The example of Uvalde, Texas, a community only forty miles north of Crystal City, proved a few months later that intransigence in the face of organized opposition can in different circumstances be an extremely successful tactic against the Chicano movement. In the aftermath of the Chicano victory in Crystal City, euphoria set in over much of South Texas, with Chicanos elsewhere wanting to duplicate the feats of "Cristal." Thus when the Uvalde school board refused to renew the contract of a Mexican-American teacher who had run for office, students launched a boycott. While organizing around the firing of this Mexican-American teacher, the Chicano students demanded many of the things the students in Crystal City had wanted. Although the Chicano community of Uvalde united to extent never before known in the town, and although several hundred students participated in a school strike which lasted longer than the Crystal City strike, their protest ended in disaster. The board refused to give in, and all the striking students were flunked.[23]

There were several important differences between the two strikes. Crystal City's occurred at a tactically stronger time of the year, near the Christmas holidays rather than near the end of the school year. Second, and at least as important, the Chicano community in Uvalde constituted slightly less than one-half of the voting population of the town. Thus Chicanos alone could not take control of the community, even though in the school system they constituted slightly over sixty percent. Also, the Uvalde community apparently did not undergo the preparation in terms of community organization and parent-student cohesion which the Crystal City Chicano community had received.[24] This latter point, however, may have been less important than the second point, which was that the Anglo community knew they could continue to rule indefinitely so long as they remained united; they did not, in other words, need any Mexican support in order to stay in office.

The Anglo victory in Uvalde was not without certain consequences, however. Racial polarization in the community increased and Chicanos became more and more resentful because they were not able to crack the system. Because of the strike activity, the federal government also became involved. In September of 1970 the Department of Health, Education, and Welfare issued a report which was strongly in sympathy with the Mexican-American community's demands.[25] But the board continued to refuse to negotiate with the students or with the parents, and conditions remained at a deadlock, with the Anglos on top and the Mexicans on the bottom. At the first school-board election following the strike, one of the leaders of the Mexican-American movement ran for the board. She was beaten nearly ten to one in a turnout which saw very few Mexicans go to the polls. The Mexican community apparently realized they were a minority (albeit one constituting over forty percent of the voters of the community), and knew that her race was doomed to failure. Her defeat, however, allowed Anglos to claim that the protest movement had been crushed and that their own intransigence had proved to be the wisest policy in discrediting the Mexican leadership which had arisen during the school crisis.

THE UNIQUENESS OF CRYSTAL CITY

The foregoing thus indicates that it does not seem inevitable that La Raza Unida or militant Chicanos will take over South Texas. On the contrary, the results so far seem to indicate that the success story of Crystal City, in both 1963 and 1969, was dependent upon characteristics which have not been at all common in South Texas: a homogeneous (and largely migrant) Mexican-American community lacking "upper-class Spanish" leaders; an Anglo community accustomed to running the town almost completely on their own; a history of settlement which led to a heavy numerical preponderance of Mexican Americans over Anglos; the presence of an international union; and lastly the development of extremely intelligent, politically-astute Mexican leadership. All these characteristics which were involved in one or both of the Crystal City revolts do not seem to be present in great quantities across South Texas. Where many of the characteristics are present—as in the towns of Carrizo Springs and Cotulla and in the new towns of the Valley—it seems that the lack of any one of them, such as the presence of politically-astute leadership, can frustrate the entire movement.

As we noted earlier, in most areas of South Texas, including the large cities of San Antonio, El Paso, and Corpus Christi, Mexican Americans do not constitute even a slight majority of the voting population. And in those areas, such as Brownsville and Rio Grande City, where Mexican Americans do constitute an overwhelming numerical majority, we have noted that, rather than a homogeneous Mexican-American community, there have tended to be a few old, established Mexican families who have played important parts in governing. In these communities Anglos have been accustomed to ruling in concert with upper-class Mexicans rather than ruling completely on their own.

We also noted the scarcity of unions in South Texas and the rather dismal prospect for unionization in South Texas. This further reinforces the uniqueness of Crystal City. The most serious attempt at unionization was the attempt by the United Farm Workers to organize workers in the Rio Grande Valley in 1967–1968.[26] This ended in failure when Mexico permitted strikebreakers to cross over to work the fields and when the Texas Rangers and local law officials had most of the strike leadership put in jail.[27]

Only in the development of politically astute leadership would the future for South Texas Mexican Americans seem to augur well. With the gradual educational upgrading of the Mexican-American population, Chicanos are becoming increasingly self-confident and knowledgeable and are developing tactics of community organization. Concerning this important characteristic of the second Crystal City revolt, then, it seems that this necessary but not sufficient condition for the revolt will spread to other communities in South Texas.

Even on this condition, however, the development of political leadership would not occur without a serious effort and much opposition. The Raza Unida mayor of Cotulla, for example, found himself unemployed and unable to find work after his election, even though he was qualified to be a teacher.[28] The basic problem facing those who wish to expand the Chicano movement in South Texas was noted by Albert Peña, the former Bexar County Commissioner (representing the West Side of San Antonio), who of all big-city Mexican-American leaders in Texas sympathized most with the Raza Unida movement. Peña remarked, "It is so difficult for leadership to stay in these small towns" even if they are local, indigenous leaders, because they cannot find jobs. Referring to Anglo tactics, he commented "They cut off your leadership."[29] Given this political, social, and economic situation of tremendous inequality between Anglo and Mexican American, the need for outside funds to support and protect community organizers while they are in the field would thus appear absolutely essential. For even in Crystal City (which has had a base far more favorable to organization than most other communities), the Teamsters Union and PASO, and later the outside support given to Gutiérrez and his organization, all seemed to be critical for starting in motion the process of organization and for preventing it from being derailed by the greater resources and greater skills of the Anglos.

There is a further problem facing the development of leadership among the Mexican-American people of South Texas. The younger, better-educated, and more radical leadership that are likely to spearhead the Chicano movement are separated from the mass of Mexican Americans by their education and by their greater affluence, much as the colonial intellectuals were separated from their native populations.[30] The gap between the leadership and the masses is essential for any other successes in South Texas because the history of the first revolt in Crystal City indicates that leadership truly *of* the people, truly representative of the Mexican-American population of South Texas, simply cannot survive in the economic, social, and political structures of South Texas. Yet as a corollary, for the movement to win more successes ways must be devised to bridge the gulf between the leadership and the masses. Otherwise, it seems the masses will retreat into apathy or despair, or will be resentful of the "success" of the leadership. And the leadership can always be tempted by inducements the Anglos are able to offer.[31]

As examples of surrounding communities seem to indicate, even in areas where Chicanos are numerically dominant the movement can be deflected either through the lack of mass participation and mass mobilization or through cooptation of the leadership. And in areas where Chicanos form a significant portion of the population, but less than half of the voting population, the movement could fail even as it mobilizes and politicizes the Chicano community. It seems, then, that a sharp distinction should be made between the development of Chicano consciousness and their assumption of political and economic power. It is possible that the Chicano community in most of Texas could become radicalized, embittered, and basically excluded from the political process as a consistently losing minority. Since the Chicano is a minority in nearly all of Texas and the Southwest, his radicalization would not occur without reactions from the dominant Anglos. It is also quite possible that the rhetoric of some in the Chicano community, particularly the use of the word "gringo" and the goal of at least partial separatism, would mean that Anglo communities might react with increasing distrust of Mexican Americans. Already some Anglo politicians in South Texas seem to be trying to forge Anglos into a countermonolith by citing the example of the takeover in Crystal City.[32] Those Mexican Americans who are elected to office with Anglo support might be forced to abandon basic desires and goals of many in the Mexican-American community or risk political extinction.[33]

While retrenchment could be the basic direction Anglos will choose to follow, it is also possible that the radicalism of the young leadership in Mexican-American barrios across South Texas would cause officials to work to defuse the situation by acting on some of the demands, coopting some of the leadership, or trying to create their own kind of moderate Mexican leadership. It is possible that in this manner gradual amelioration of the tremendous economic, social, and political disparity between Mexican Americans and Anglos would take place. That is, the radicals might increase the parameters of politics and might in this way broaden the area within which politicians, businessmen, educators, and others would all be willing to act. But the example of Crystal City from 1965 to 1969 should remind us of the danger of losing perspective on the degree and importance of changes that have occurred, as indeed should the radicalization of the Black movement in America at the very time when many whites preferred to think that civil-rights questions had been settled.

It is of course possible that something less than a complete Chicano revolt of the sort that Crystal City has known might be possible in circumstances where conditions were not quite so favorable. That is, a coalition of Mexicans and Blacks, or of Mexicans, Blacks, Labor, and Anglo liberals might be possible which would constitute a revolt capable of implementing a number of similar changes. In Karnes City, Texas, for example, a coalition of Mexicans and Blacks has organized to protest discrimination against both groups in the school system.

A revolt which represents a broader-based coalition thus might be possible in a number of communities. Such a revolt would incorporate the Chicano community but would not be composed solely of them.

Whatever does happen in the future concerning Chicano politics, it does seem that an important distinction should be made between the development of political awareness and the assumption of power. That Mexican Americans will increasingly desire change and will in the process move toward greater interest and activity in political, social, and economic spheres seems very likely. But that they will also move toward greater power, or greater control over their own destiny does not necessarily follow. Crystal City has been an exception, and in the end it is likely to remain an exception.

THE FUTURE OF CRYSTAL CITY

As for the town of Crystal City iiself, it seems likely that La Raza Unida will continue to dominate the politics of the community. With the exodus of Anglos, the opposition was further depleted in their resources to fight Raza Unida, and the Mexican community was increasing its already overwhelming numerical dominance in the town. Only loss of contact with the masses or a split in leadership similar to that which occurred under Juan Cornejo would appear capable of bringing in a regime more in sympathy with Anglo and business interests in the town. There clearly have been tensions along these lines, as the desertion by Mike Pérez and the firing and resignation of two police chiefs indicated. But so far the movement has stayed united enough to keep political control, and its activities have been enough in line with the majority of the town's thinking to keep winning elections. Although Gutiérrez's term of office on the school board was over in 1973, and he decided to resign from the board and instead oversee the Carnegie Institute grant to train Chicano administrators, it is not clear what effect this will have on the unity and style of the movement.

At any rate, it seems clear that how long the community migrants and uneducated masses will continue to allow themselves to be led by outside educators and local boys who in making good have removed themselves somewhat from the plight of the migrants will depend to a great extent upon the sensitivity of the leaders to the continued sufferings of the migrants and on the degree to which they will be able to upgrade the still extremely impoverished and disadvantaged community. A leader as brilliant as Gutiérrez, who continued to spend part of his summers traveling north with the migrants to found and teach in migrant schools, might be able to hold together such a coalition indefinitely. And the development of Ciudadanos Unidos, which under the present leadership had allowed the Mexican community a say in the development of programs and ideas for the community, was another essential bridge between the leaders and the masses.

Yet the demands on the time of the leadership, particularly on José Angel Gutiérrez meant that important decisions concerning priorities had to be made. From the beginning of his involvement in Crystal City, Gutiérrez accepted speaking tours around the nation. The growth in the Chicano movement also meant an increase in conferences, which Gutiérrez often attended or keynoted. Gutiérrez also began teaching courses on the history and politics of Mexican Americans, and expressed a desire to finish his doctorate in political science at the University of Texas. And of course journalists and researchers were constantly after him for interviews. All this meant that his time in Crystal City itself was limited, and some Mexican Americans complained of this. They argued that Gutiérrez and the leadership should have been spending more time helping and encouraging the people of Crystal City.

One who was a supporter of La Raza Unida added that the leadership should be putting more emphasis on teaching the Mexicans responsibility and competition, and should spend less time teaching them bitterness. Others argued that more time should be spent teaching illiterates, although this is a taxing and heavily time-consuming job. And there was some local resentment at the number of outside leaders and teachers. Said one Mexican, "Students can't look up to [outside leaders] because they don't know them. They should build indigenous leaders. Students feel deflated when they see people passed over that have tried."

Gutiérrez was no doubt aware of these problems, and through Ciudadanos Unidos the regime showed a willingness to work not just to win elections but to change things after being in office. Yet the demands on the leadership were enormous, and if anything, they seemed to increase as the mass of poor Mexican Americans responded to the rhetoric of fundamental change. Adding to all these difficulties, however, was the clear fact that many Mexican Americans of the community, although as of now a distinct minority, disapproved of the "gringo-baiting" and "chicanismo" ideology and tactics of the Raza Unida leadership. These Mexican Americans, often better-off and more established than the majority, will continue to oppose La Raza Unida, and their long-term impact on the movement is uncertain but cannot be ignored.

The importance of Anglo machinations in preventing the Raza Unida leadership from disintegrating should also not be forgotten. But policy decisions on how far to press the Anglos, how many teachers to fire, which court suits to bring, which issues to press, and how to balance their limited resources between statewide and national work and fund raising versus help to the local Mexican Americans continue to strain the movement, as it would strain any movement which was committed to so many changes. As long as the Anglos remain actively involved in trying to overthrow La Raza Unida, there will probably be much less chance for division of the Mexican community in Crystal City, since bitter polarization has already been accomplished. But should the Anglos ever simply give up and/or leave in great numbers, then the strains within the Mexican-American community would most likely become greater. Questions over who should do the leading and how far the movement should go would then assume even greater importance as the need to unite in the face of hostility abated. And how La Raza Unida will change as a result of years in power is the subject of intense speculation. Will it gradually "come to terms with its environment," or will it continue to try to change drastically the opportunities and resources of Chicanos in the area?

At the same time, with the opportunities for migrants drying up rapidly, and with the community having already lost population between 1960 and 1970, it is apparent that the future of the community rests upon more than the community's willingness to try new approaches to bring in industry and to upgrade the skills and education of the community. The future also depends, as we noted earlier, upon decisions Anglos will make regarding the community. They are the ones who hold the capital. There is little doubt, for example, that a decision by Del Monte to leave the community would be devastating. Both the Raza Unida leadership and the Del Monte management itself are aware of this fact.[34] Yet the community is not dependent only upon Anglo business. Important national developments have aided the Chicano activists, particularly the increase in federal funds. A corollary of this, however, is that a drying up of these funds would devastate the community. These programs have not only poured money into the community; they have also been an important source of income for the leadership.

In the years since the Cornejo failure other changes in national attitudes and policies toward Mexican Americans and the poor have also occurred. Foundations and churches are more aware of problems of poverty and discrimination, and they are willing to help out in Crystal City in both public and confidential ways. These changes made the leadership less vulnerable to local economic intimidation than was the leadership in 1963, but these national organizations were at times concerned about the militancy, the direction, and the rhetoric of the leadership.[35] At any rate, the need for funding of programs and for technical expertise in developing and manning the numerous programs which would have to be launched in Crystal City if the migrants are to be upgraded and the community developed will no doubt continue to grow. To what extent the community can find resources to meet these needs remains unclear.

CONCLUSION

We see then that any assessment of the success of La Raza Unida in Crystal City, or its applicability to the rest of South Texas and the Southwest, must be qualified. In comparison with the first Chicano takeover in 1963, the current regime showed important differences. Their goals were clearer and more unified. Their leadership was more confident and experienced. The community now had more resources available to it because of the greater political consciousness of the local Mexican community. La Raza Unida had produced a political situation where the community's Anglos, long accustomed to governing, were now locked out of the local government. And in their victory over the Anglos, they also discredited Mexican Americans who had worked closely with or identified with the local Anglos.[36]

This was a situation unprecedented elsewhere in South Texas. But even in their victory over Anglos, and more conservative Mexican Americans, tremendous tasks still faced the new regime. How to attract and keep outside help while not slighting or overlooking indigenous leadership and manpower would continue to require careful balancing and sensitivity. Second-level leadership in the Chicano community remained weak, although it was improving in experience. The egalitarian spirit of the revolution and the common struggle in the Chicano community had as by-products introduced women and young people into the leadership councils of the movement. Tapping both these resources already strengthened the leadership, but steering a steady course between the twin pitfalls of ideological purity at the expense of the desires of the indigenous population, or coming to terms with the many forces that opposed them in a manner that deflated the people, would continue to be difficult. Federal programs and national foundations were helpful, but they carried with them serious constraints in being designed much more for incremental change than radical innovation. And the threatened Nixon Administration cutbacks again emphasized the precariousness of the Crystal City economy.

Owing to these and to further institutional constraints which have been placed upon protest organizations, such as the need for funds, the need to attract and then hold together divergent interests within their coalition, and the difficulty of overcoming biases found in the setup of political institutions they sought to control, La Raza Unida was thwarted in important ways even as it won astounding victories. Perhaps in gaining control of the county they would be able to acquire considerably greater revenues through taxing the large Anglo landholders, but until this happened they would continue very much in need of outside funds.

And finally, it should also be remembered that in Crystal City there were peculiarly auspicious circumstances for revolt. Thus, to say that the Raza Unida revolt was achieving unqualified victories or that its successes in Crystal City could be duplicated elsewhere would be both naive and adventuristic. In communities such as the old border towns, where Mexican Americans have always had an important role in governance even as their substantive policies have been oppressive, race and class lines do not clearly merge. It is thus difficult to see how the Crystal City strategy could work without important changes. In communities where a majority of the population is Anglo, not only must the strategy be modified in important ways, but the impact of the rhetoric of Crystal City militants might easily damage those Chicanos who must work in coalitions, either with Blacks or with labor and liberal Anglos.

Also, even though the goals of La Raza Unida have been far more carefully constructed than were those of Los Cinco Mexicanos, the regime will eventually be faced either through success or through failure with deciding upon what the whole policy of self-determination for the Chicano community really means. Just how to relate to Anglo cultural domination, whether and how to blend with it or fight it or isolate themselves from it, are questions which remain unresolved. How much the Chicano movement should be one of separate cultural nationalism, and how much it should be one which would eventually prepare Chicanos for integration with Anglos as equals, remains unclear. How this basic question is answered will have important consequences upon the relationship of Mexican Americans to Mexico itself. Gutiérrez has said, for example, that "the Rio Grande never has separated us and never will."[37] But if this is true, does it follow that an upgrading of the Mexicans of the United States can only occur as Mexico itself develops? As long as there is an inexhaustible supply of cheap labor just across the border, eager to enter the United States to find work, how much can Mexican-American communities uplift themselves as they are constantly influenced by and replenished by Mexicans from Mexico? How can the problems facing Mexican Americans be disassociated from problems facing Mexicans on the other side of the border? How this question is answered will depend in great part upon the attitudes of Mexican Americans and Mexicans of Mexico themselves. These questions of identity are not unique to Chicanos of Crystal City, or of the Southwest. They involve fundamental questions of identity facing all cultural minorities and all disadvantaged peoples. In fact they involve all human beings, who must in the end decide as individuals what their identity and what their goals should be.

But in facing these problems and difficulties, which at times may seem overwhelming, the Chicano community can call upon the very resources which have been opened up by their struggle in Crystal City: the confidence, the pride, the experience, and the feeling of community. Their successes have brought a feeling of control over their own destiny that is simply not measured in terms of dollars spent, legal suits filed, or theoretical and practical problems which must be resolved. The stereotype of a fatalistic Juan Tortilla, a loyal servant happiest when he is stooped in the fields picking spinach for the Anglo, has been shattered for both Anglos and Chicanos alike. As the Chicano community goes about trying to overcome the enormous problems they must face, this faith in themselves may be their most valuable possession. It will mean that the choice will be theirs to a greater extent than it ever has been before.

NOTES

1. From interviews with several Anglos in Crystal City.
2. *La Verdad,* May 6, 1971, p. 3 (these and other translations are by the author).
3. From an interview with a Crystal City Anglo who had already left the community.
4. *The Zavala County Sentinel,* July 1 and June 17, 1971. The community school has continued to grow, and as of the spring of 1973 it numbered around 100 students, approximately half of whom were Mexican Americans.
5. *The Zavala County Sentinel,* April 12, 1973, p. 1.
6. The party met in San Antonio, elected state executive committee officers (who were mainly from the earlier MAYO chapter), and adopted a platform. Gutiérrez was elected convention chairman by acclamation. He was, however, one of those reluctant to make the move to statewide races, fearing that the party might be spread too thin. (See *The Zavala County Sentinel,* November 4, 1971, p. 1.)
7. Zavala County was one of three counties in the state carried by Muñiz. Far fewer people voted in the presidential election, with Nixon narrowly edging out McGovern in the county.
8. They averaged between one and two percent of the vote. Interestingly, even Ramsey Muñiz did considerably less well than Henry González had done in his Democratic primary race for governor in 1958. At that time González polled over a quarter of a million votes, which was over twenty percent of the votes cast.
9. An article on this election, written by John Fry and very much in sympathy with La Raza Unida, has appeared in *Christianity and Crisis,* November 27, 1973, pp. 253-257. Luz Gutiérrez, the wife of José Angel Gutiérrez, and several others were arrested on election day while trying to serve as poll-watchers. The whole day was quite tense.
10. The margins of victory were very similar to La Raza Unida's victories in 1971; however, considering that many Anglos had left the community in

order to place their children in other school systems, the results represented a drop in Raza Unida support among the Mexican Americans of the community greater than the vote totals themselves indicated.

11. Warren Wagner, the owner, argued that the quality of spinach was poorer because of a freeze. He lowered wages because he could not get as much as previously for the spinach. (See *La Verdad,* January 24, and February 2, 1972.)

12. This translates roughly as "Respect for the Rights of Others Is True Peave."

13. Even the town's name began to be affected. It was increasingly referred to as "Cristal."

14. Although I am generalizing about the Anglo community, it should be repeated that were perhaps as many as ten local Anglos who supported La Raza Unida out of a total Anglo population of nearly 2,000.

15. This point is made by Sheldon Wolin, "Political Theory as a Vocation," *The American Political Science Review,* 63, no. 4 (December, 1969), pp. 1062-82.

16. For this quotation I am grateful to Mike Miller.

17. The best-known study of this sort is that by Samuel Stouffer, *Communism, Conformity, and Civil Liberties* (Garden City, NY.: Doubleday, 1955); a penetrating answer to this mode of thought occurs in Michael Rogin, *The Intellectuals and McCarthy* (Cambridge, Mass.: M.I.T. Press, 1967).

18. See Lipset, *Political Man,* Garden City, N.Y.: Doubleday and Company, 1960; Kornhauser, *The Politics of Mass Society.* Glencoe, Ill.: The Free Press, 1959.

19. See Zeitlin, *Revolutionary Politics and the Cuban Working Class,* Princeton: Princeton University Press, 1967.

20. See Simmons, "Anglo-Americans and Mexican-Americans in South Texas," Ph.D. dissertation, Harvard University, 1952, p. 287; and Wolf, *Peasant Wars of the Twentieth Century,* New York: Harper and Row, 1969.

21. Michael Parenti, "Power and Pluralism: A View from the Bottom," *Journal of Politics,* August 1970, p. 521.

22. Ibid.

23. For this information I am grateful to Josué Cruz. For more on the Uvalde school strike, see the San Antonio newspapers for this period, and *Newsweek,* "Side by Side—And a World Apart—In Uvalde, Texas," June 29, 1970, p. 24.

24. It should be emphasized that I did no personal interviewing in Uvalde and that my knowledge of what occurred in the town during the strike is therefore very limited.

25. This report was temporarily made public by Senator Walter Mondale; upon writing for a copy of the HEW report I was told by Mrs. Dorothy Stuck of the Dallas office that their report was considered confidential because negotiations were still going on with the Uvalde district.

26. The long, bitter strike at Farah in El Paso seems likely to equal the struggle of the farm-workers strike in the Valley. At this writing, however, it is not clear how the strike will be resolved.

27. For more on the farm-workers strike in the Valley, see Ben H. Procter, "The Modern Texas Rangers: A Law Enforcement Dilemma in the Rio Grande Valley," in *The Mexican Americans: An Awakening Minority,* ed. Manuel Servin (Beverly Hills, California: Glenco Press, 1970), pp. 212-27, and *The Texas Observer* for the period from 1967 to 1968.

28. See, for example, William Greider of *The Washington Post* staff, "Cotulla Mayor Raps Town, Schools," reprinted in *The San Antonio Express,* August 20, 1970, p. 18-A.

29. From an interview with Albert Peña (San Antonio, November, 1970).

30. For more on the transformation of intellectuals in colonial states, see Edward Shils, "The Intellectuals in the Political Development of the New States," *Political Change in Underdeveloped Countries,* ed. John Kautsky, (New York: John Wiley, 1962), pp. 195-234.

31. This phenomenon of needing to have the most educated and acculturated members of the Mexican community—those who understood the system best—become the backbone of the leadership, has produced a number of ironies. One of the greatest is that the leadership of the Raza Unida movement has itself been far more acculturated, educated, and "Anglicized" than many of the Mexicans who have been supporters of the Anglos. It has also produced the irony of many Chicanos arguing for their "rights" as American rather than Mexican citizens. For a definite segment of the Mexican-American population, their view of themselves as Americans seems itself to have been a radicalizing influence. In noting this, one Raza Unida leader has commented that the Mexican Americans of the border communities are often more conservative in part because they still compare themselves with Mexicans of Mexico. This comparison, he has argued, leads them to feel gratified that they are "better off" than the Mexicans on the other side of the river than to feel angry that they are not as well off as the Anglos.

32. See, for example, *The Houston Chronicle,* March 21, 1971, Sec. 4, p. 1.

33. But it should not be forgotten that a significant number of Mexican Americans do not identify with the Chicano movement, its goals, or its tactics.

34. In an attempt to prevent the possibility of Del Monte leaving the community, one Raza Unida leader indicated that steps had been made to launch a nationwide boycott of Del Monte products should Del Monte leave the community.

35. Leroy Aarons, in his *Washington Post* article "The Chicanos Want In," has maintained that Gutiérrez was forced to tone down his rhetoric because of the reaction from various national foundations.

36. It should not be forgotten that some of La Raza Unida's most bitter struggles were with other Mexican Americans. This became all the more true as the years passed and Anglos realized that their own political opposition could be counterproductive. Ted Muñoz, a prominent Mexican American who had fought and run against La Raza Unida, was quoted as saying of La Raza Unida, "They've actually increased discrimination here. They not only dis-

criminate against Anglos, but they have turned Mexicans against each other. They attack those of us who don't agree with them and pressure our friends into turning against us." (*The Los Angeles Times,* September 3, 1972.)

37. From a speech by José Angel Gutiérrez at the University of Wisconsin (Madison, Wisconsin, May 1971), attended by the author.

CONTRIBUTORS

MARIO BARRERA is an Assistant Professor at the University of California, San Diego.

ANTONIO CAMEJO is a former instructor in the Chicano Studies Department at Merritt College, Oakland, California and has been a Socialist Workers Party candidate for public office in California.

TONY CASTRO is now a staff reporter and political and urban affairs feature writer for the *Houston Post*.

CESAR E. CHAVEZ is the leader of the United Farm Workers, AFL-CIO.

JOHN C. COMER is an Assistant Professor of Political Science at the University of Nebraska, Lincoln.

ALFREDO CUELLAR is an Assistant Professor of Political Science at Pitzer College in Claremont, California.

RUDOLPH O. DE LA GARZA is an Assistant Professor of Political Science, Colorado College, Colorado Springs.

BOB FITCH is a United Church of Christ clergyman who works as a photo-journalist.

DONALD M. FREEMAN is the Chairman of the Department of Political Science, Onega College, University of West Florida.

F. CHRIS GARCIA is Associate Professor of Political Science at the University of New Mexico.

LEO GREBLER is a Professor Emeritus in the Graduate School of Management at the University of California, Los Angeles.

ARMANDO GUITERREZ is an Assistant Professor in the Department of Political Science at the University of Texas at Austin.

JOSE ANGEL GUTIERREZ is a founder of the Mexican American Youth Organization and *La Raza Unida* party.

RALPH C. GUZMAN is an Associate Professor of Politics and Community Studies at the University of California, Santa Cruz.

HERBERT HIRSCH is an Associate Professor of Political Science at the University of Texas at Austin.

ALBERTO JUAREZ is in the Political Science Department at California State University, Dominguez Hills.

CLARK S. KNOWLTON is a Professor of Sociology at the University of Utah.

MICHAEL S. KRAMER is a consultant to the Institute of American Research.

MARK R. LEVY is an Associate National Affairs Editor of *Newsweek* magazine.

CLIFTON MCCLESKEY is the Director of the Institute of Government at the University of Virginia.

BRUCE MERRILL is an Assistant Professor of Political Science at Arizona State University.

JOSEPH M. MONTOYA is the senior United States Senator from the state of New Mexico.

JOAN MOORE is a Professor of Sociology at the University of Southern California.

ARMANDO MORALES is Adjunct Associate Professor in the Department of Psychiatry at the University of California at Los Angeles.

CARLOS MUÑOZ is an Assistant Professor of Political Science and Comparative Cultures at the University of California, Irvine.

LOUIS R. NEGRETE is an Assistant Professor in the Chicano Studies Department at California State University, Los Angeles.

CHARLES ORNELAS is an Assistant Professor of Political Science at the University of California, Santa Barbara.

GEORGE RIVERA, Jr., is an Assistant Professor in the Department of Sociology at the University of Colorado.

JULIAN SAMORA is a Professor of Sociology and Anthropology at the University of Notre Dame.

JOHN S. SHOCKLEY is an Assistant Professor of Political Science at Western Illinois University.

PEGGY SIMPSON writes for the Associated Press.

STAN STEINER is a professional writer currently residing in Sante Fe, New Mexico.

MICHAEL STEINMAN is an Assistant Professor of Political Science at the University of Nebraska, Lincoln.

MIGUEL DAVID TIRADO is an Assistant Professor of Political Science at Sonoma State College in California.

JAMES B. WATSON is Professor of Anthropology at the University of Washington, Seattle.

HENRY E. WEINSTEIN is a staff reporter of the *Wall Street Journal.*

SUSAN WELCH is an Assistant Professor of Political Science at the University of Nebraska, Lincoln.